Knowledge Mapping and Management

Don White, Ph.D.
University of Lincoln, UK

IRM Press
Publisher of innovative scholarly and professional
information technology titles in the cyberage

Hershey • London • Melbourne • Singapore • Beijing

Acquisitions Editor:	Mehdi Khosrow-Pour
Managing Editor:	Jan Travers
Assistant Managing Editor:	Amanda Appicello
Copy Editor:	Amanda Appicello
Cover Design:	Tedi Wingard
Printed at:	Integrated Book Technology

Published in the United States of America by
    IRM Press
    1331 E. Chocolate Avenue
    Hershey PA 17033-1117
    Tel: 717-533-8845
    Fax: 717-533-8661
    E-mail: cust@idea-group.com
    Web site: http://www.irm-press.com

and in the United Kingdom by
    IRM Press
    3 Henrietta Street
    Covent Garden
    London WC2E 8LU
    Tel: 44 20 7240 0856
    Fax: 44 20 7379 3313
    Web site: http://www.eurospan.co.uk

Library of Congress Cataloguing-in-Publication Data

Knowledge mapping and management / [edited by] Don White.
     p. cm.
  A collection of 30 papers written by White and an international group of scholars.
  Includes bibliographical references and index.
   ISBN 1-931777-17-9 (paper)
   1. Knowledge management. I. White, Don, 1957-

HD30.2 .K6393 2002
658.4'038--dc21   2002017345

eISBN: 1-931777-34-9

British Cataloguing-in-Publication Data
A Cataloguing-in-Publication record for this book is available from the British Library.

Other New Releases from IRM Press

Knowledge Mapping and Management

Table of Contents

Foreword

The emerging concept of Knowledge Management (KM) has achieved increasing prominence over the last ten years. As with many new and emergent concepts, it has provoked debate amongst both academics and practitioners about its status, provenance and validity. Is it really a new concept or just a repackaging of existing truths? Is it the latest fad of a business and organisational consulting profession that is ever hungry for new conceptual products to add to their repertoire? Is it merely a new name for an already extant issue–the re-branding of an approach? In this respect it shares much with previous so-called new approaches to the problems of organizations and attempts to solve them. Is KM the panacea for the new century as TQM was for the 1980's and BPR was for the 1990's?

Perhaps only history can judge the efficacy of these various approaches. Whatever the case, Knowledge Management has developed into an important area of interest that has generated much debate and activity amongst the information profession. In this brief discussion, the nature and origins of the concept and its importance to organizations will be discussed.

It is clearly a topic that has aroused and stimulated a great deal of interest in companies and the business world in general. It has become a much discussed issue in the general management press and among a diverse practitioner community. This has stemmed from the recognition of a genuine problem and opportunity within business based on the harnessing and utilisation of the organizational knowledge base for effectiveness.

"To a growing number of companies, KM is more than just buzz-words or a sales pitch, it is an approach to adding or creating value by more actively leveraging the know-how, experience and judgement residing within and, in many cases, outside an organization." (Ruggles, 1998: 82)

Business, therefore, recognises it as a genuine practical issue that has a "bottom-line" contribution to make. But it is also clear that organizations have found the concept difficult to capture or turn into reality despite much effort and considerable investment. (Birkinshaw, 2001). It has certainly captured academic interest in recent years and generated a growing literature. For example, Swan et al. (2000a) reported both an explosion in the number of journal articles produced between 1995 and 1998 and a greater number of literature search requests for the topic in that period. This indicates that the issue is, currently, on a wave of interest and intellectual endeavour in both academic institutions and organizations.

THE NATURE OF THE CONCEPT

What is Knowledge Management? It does seem to be a hard term to define and many authors have abandoned attempts to closely define it, preferring to fallback on a broad definition which encompasses "… any processes and practices concerned with the creation, acquisition, capture, sharing and use of knowledge skills or expertise." (Swann et al., 2000b)

Knowledge Management cannot yet be defined as a science or a discipline. It may more usefully, at this stage of its development, be regarded as a multi-disciplinary problem, which is informed by a number of core theoretical areas. These include data and information management and techniques, artificial intelligence, organizational theory and behaviour, sociology of knowledge and knowledge representation, and business economics and strategy.

Knowledge and Knowledge Management are complex and multi-faceted issues closely entwined in ongoing debates about the nature of organizations and the role of technologies in modern post-industrial economies. They have become central to attempts to understand what drives innovation and competitive advantage by replacing the exploitation of physical and material resources with the exploitation of intellectual capital as the key engine of business success.

"KM is the process of capturing a company's collective expertise wherever it resides and distributing it to wherever it can help produce the biggest payoffs." (Blake, 1998:2)

Such expertise, or "knowledge resources" are defined as "core competencies" (Prahalad and Hamell, 1990) or "routines" (Nelson and Winter, 1982) "capabilities" (Collis, 1991) and "core skills" (Klein et al, 1991). These are seen as "…. the well-spring of future product development …. the roots of competitiveness, and individual products and services are the fruit." (Prahalad and Hamell, 1990: 202).

In terms of how KM harnesses these resources, "KM is equated to data mining, digging and drilling …. its aim is to 'mine' the tacit knowledge, skills and expertise of people" (Gardner, 1998: 24). Furthermore, the idea behind KM is to collect and make accessible workers' knowledge "…. via a searchable application" (Cole-Gromolski, 1997: 6). Information technology is, therefore, a key enabler to KM: "KM is primarily IS/IT driven" (Scarborough et al, 1999: 27).

Typically in the KM literature the dimensions of knowledge types are classified along two axes: subjective/objective and tacit/explicit (Nonaka and Takeuchi, 1995). Explicit knowledge is held to be that which can be captured and expressed in formal systematic language and is, by definition, codifiable. Tacit knowledge resides in people and social processes within an organization and is therefore less easy to capture and codify. It is a cultural concept in organizational terms. The relationship between tacit and explicit knowledge has not been satisfactorily explained and most of the KM literature still seems more comfortable with describing tools and techniques for knowledge capture and distribution. This is problematic as the technological focus on knowledge handling may ignore the critical human and social aspects through which actual success is derived. This issue, therefore, is the subject of a brief critique of KM, which is included here.

KNOWLEDGE MANAGEMENT: A CRITIQUE

The key criticism of much of the KM literature is the emphasis on technology-based approaches to harnessing and transferring the knowledge resource of organizations. Recent surveys of the literature have highlighted the "..overwhelming emphasis on IT and major gaps in the treatment of people" (Swan et al., 2000b). Knowledge occurs within the context of the social processes of organizational life. It is therefore essential that Knowledge Management and its relationship to decision-making and organizational or business success is understood within a human and social framework.

There is a concern that the current emphasis on technological-based representations of knowledge does not adequately reflect the richness of this issue. It presents too limited a view of the problem. It assumes that knowledge can be fully and accurately transferred among groups in organisations in an objective and unproblematic way. This ignores the less concrete aspects of knowledge and information which are influenced by both people and the context of organizational activity.

"(KM) depends on tapping the *tacit* and often highly *subjective* insights, intuitions, and hunches of individual employees and making those insights available for testing and use by the company as a whole" (Nonaka and Takeuchi, 1995: 24).

In this way KM is involved in attempts to capture and represent some kind of organizational reality, which can help make sense of what we are doing in everyday activities. This brief critique will, therefore, begin by exploring KM's underlying paradigm, and will then consider the validity of its relationship to the kind of knowledge underpinning human expertise.

As indicated in the above description of the processes involved in KM, it is characterised by a scientific approach to knowledge and knowledge transfer.

Reality is perceived to be an immutable phenomenon; areas may, therefore, be fragmented without loss of emergent properties. This paradigm asserts that the world can be exhaustively analysed in terms of determinate data or atomic facts. The assumption that all knowledge can be faithfully represented in codes, and shared amongst individuals is a natural consequence of these beliefs. Thus, this "techno-cratic intervention" (Scarborough et al, 1999: 50) can successfully divorce knowl-edge from its organisational context, and *all* that is relevant to intelligent behaviour can be formalised in a structured description.

In summary, the kinds of rationalist assumptions about knowledge creation and use, which characterise KM, are inadequate. Knowledge and meaning cannot be transferred as easily as data. The current approach adopted by KM is, therefore, too simplistic, limited in scope and somewhat naïve. It is suggested that a broader approach to, and definition of, "knowledge" is not only possible in this context, but an essential pre-requisite to attempts to harness and exploit it. It is also suggested that KM must have a social dimension if it is to realise its potential. If it is to avoid being consigned to the ranks of yet another "management fad," it must recognise and address the issues raised by the fact that knowledge is socially-located and constructed and cannot successfully be detached from the social context within which it is created and operates.

SUMMARY

Clearly, Knowledge Management has become an important area of both aca-demic debate and practical application in the management of organizations. It has been recognised as an issue that is critical to the innovative and competitive development of organizations for the new century. Knowledge Management is best understood as a complex concept influenced by a set of multiple disciplines and subjects. It is concerned with the processes of how knowledge in organizations is best captured, described and disseminated to users and managers in order to maximise the effectiveness and competitive advantage. Reviews of the literature have suggested that the area is predominated by concerns with techniques and tools for handling knowledge. There is a view that this is leading the area of Knowledge Management into technocratic paradigm, which ignores the very real human and social processes that lie at the heart of knowledge as both a concept and a practical issue. The relationship to people management will dictate how successful Knowl-edge Management is as an engine for organizational and business innovation and growth. Clearly there are tremendous potential advantages for technology-based solutions to improve the effectiveness of knowledge handling. But there is a need to reaffirm Knowledge Management as a socio-technical issue by linking it to the established concepts of organizational learning and development.

The collection of papers in this book represents some of the latest academic and practical research from a wide field of international contributors. It is a complex issue, which may require many approaches. We trust that the material presented here will stimulate more thinking about this area and serve to broaden the already growing base of interest from the information and management community.

REFERENCES

Birkinshaw, J. (2001). Why is Knowledge Management so difficult? *Business Strategy Review*, 12(1): 11-18.

Blake, P. (1998). The Knowledge Management expansion, *Information Today*, 15(1): 12-13.

Checkland, P. (1981). *Systems Thinking, Systems Practice*, Chichester: John Wiley & Sons.

Cole-Gromolski, B. (1997). Users loathe to share their know-how, *Computerworld*, 31(46): 6.

Collis, D. (1991). A resource-based analysis of global competition; the case of the bearings industry, *Strategic Management Journal*, Summer Special Issue, 12: pp. 49-68

Gardner, D. (1998). Knowledge that won't fit the database -people, *Infoworld*, 20(14).

Klein J.A., Edge, G.M., and Kass, T. (1991). Skill-based competition, *Journal of General Management*, 16(4) Summer, pp. 1-15.

Nonaka and Takeuchi, I. (1995). The knowledge-creating company, In *Harvard Business Review on Knowledge Management*, Boston: Harvard Business School Press.

Prahalad, C.K., and Hamel, G. (1990). The core competencies of the corporation, *Harvard Business Review*, May - June, pp. 79-91

Ruggles R (1998). The state of the notion: Knowledge Management in practice, *California Management Review*, 40(3): 80-89.

Scarborough, H., Swan, J., and Preston, J. (1999). *Knowledge Management: A Literature Review*, London: The Institute of Personnel and Development.

Swann et al. (2000a). Knowledge Management – When will people management enter the debate? *Proceedings of the 33rd Hawaii International Conference on Systems Sciences.*

Swann et al. (2000b). Limits of IT-driven Knowledge Management initiatives for interactive innovation processes: Towards a community-based approach. *Proceedings of the 33rd Hawaii International Conference on Systems Sciences.*

Don White
University of Lincoln, United Kingdom

Preface

Knowledge Management is fast becoming a hot topic of discussion and research. The capture, use, production and storage of knowledge is an issue of paramount importance for businesses, universities, public and private organizations. Because this is such an important topic, it is essential for researchers, academicians and managers to stay up-to-date on the current practices and techniques relating to knowledge mapping and management issues. The chapters in this book report on the latest efforts to improve and use knowledge management techniques. The authors offer may definitions of knowledge and offer concrete suggestions for organizations on how to better capture and use knowledge. The chapters also address the questions of who uses knowledge, how it can be better shared and how knowledge is currently being managed and how the management efforts can be improved.

Chapter 1 entitled, "Is Knowledge Management Really an Oxymoron? Unraveling the Role of Organizational Controls in Knowledge Management" by Yogesh Malhotra of @Brint.com (USA) fills the critical void of incomplete and incorrect interpretations of organizational controls by developing a better theoretical and conceptual understanding of organizational controls and their pragmatic implications. The chapter also proposes an organic model of organizational controls for design of knowledge management systems that can effectively enable the creation of new knowledge, the renewal of existing knowledge and knowledge sharing.

Chapter 2 entitled, "Strategically-Focused Enterprise Knowledge Management" by Robert Mockler of St. John's University and Dorothy Dologite of City University of New York (USA) describes the characteristics and types of strategically-focused knowledge management systems and the key conditions affecting their development and success. The discussion, based around company examples, focuses on various strategic management uses of these systems. The chapter describes a knowledge management process designed to increase profitability and competitive advantage in the marketplace.

Chapter 3 entitled, "Knowledge Mapping: An Essential Part of Knowledge Management" by Jay Liebowitz of the University of Maryland Baltimore County (USA) discusses the role of knowledge mapping for improving knowledge management projects and the specific tool Wisdom Builder to aid in the creation of knowledge maps. The chapter concludes that the basic purpose of knowledge management is to capture and express expertise so that it can be used by others and that meticulous planning with higher level of IT inputs is one mechanism of reducing costs and making the knowledge management systems more efficient.

Chapter 4 entitled, "Knowledge Management System: A Case Study of RDCIS Laboratories" by R.K. Jha, K.K. Mallik and R.N. Mukherjee of Steel Authority of India, Ltd., discusses knowledge management systems and associated database capabilities, test methods, references and expertise of individuals in the Research and Development Centre for Iron and Steel (RDCIS) through existing widespread LAN on windows systems. The authors note significant improvement in effective utilization of equipment potential through systematic approaches of knowledge sharing.

Chapter 5 entitled, "Three Problems of Organizational Memory Information Systems Development" by Fons Wijnhoven and Kees van Slooten of the University of Twente (The Netherlands) discusses organizational memory information systems (OMIS) objectives and presents a conceptual OMIS model. The authors indicate that an OMIS needs clear role definitions of its stakeholders, an organization change scenario and a non-linear systems procurement scenario. Consequently, the OMIS development discussed has to cope with high levels of complexity, diversity and organizational and IT developments.

Chapter 6 entitled, "An Empirical Study of Knowledge and Organizations" by Andrew Doswell and Vivien Reid of Glasgow Caledonian University (UK) investigates perceptions about the handling of knowledge in organizations. The findings presented are based on replies to a non-random postal survey. The findings confirm both ideas from the current literature and from specific studies. Additionally, the authors report new information which shows support for the ideas of professional groups holding onto knowledge and for the existence of ambivalence towards the emphasis placed on the role of information technology in conducting knowledge mapping.

Chapter 7 entitled, "Facilitating Sensemaking in Knowledge Integration within Geographically Dispersed Cross-Functional Teams by Thekla Rura-Polley, Ellen Baker and Igor Hawryszkiewycz of the University of Technology (Australia) looks at knowledge management within geographically dispersed cross-functional teams. In particular, it describes an electronic knowledge management system, LiveNet, which combines support for rational innovation processes with collaborative support mechanism. The collaborative support mechanisms extend previously available group support systems by incorporating sense-making tools.

Chapter 8 entitled, "Evaluating Organizational Patterns for Supporting Business Knowledge Management" by Danny Brash of Stockholm University (Sweden), Nikos Prekas of the University of Manchester Institute of Science and Technology (U.K.), Georges Grosz and Farida Semmak of the University of Paris (France) applies a pattern framework adopted from software development in a project for managing business knowledge. The pattern development process includes the evaluation of the suitability of candidate patterns. The authors also present criteria for considering and measuring suitability of the knowledge for reuse.

Chapter 9 entitled, "ERP-Based Knowledge Transfer" by Zoonky Lee and Jinyoul Lee of the University of Nebraska-Lincoln (USA) and Tim Sieber, Lincoln, Nebraska (USA) investigates how organizational specific requirements and technology constraints inherent in software packages interact in this knowledge transfer process. The results are based on in-depth interviews, process analysis and documentation analysis. This chapter provides a new angle to adopting ERP in an organization and provides organizations with a better understanding of competitive advantage based on process knowledge.

Chapter 10 entitled, "Knowledge Management in U.S. Federal Government Organizations: Can it Work?" by J. Judah Buchwalter of the University of Maryland, Baltimore (USA) addresses government initiatives used to entice organizations into creating the culture needed for knowledge management. The authors propose a way to effect changes in the culture by implementing a specific social initiative that has proven successful in other organizations. The combination of the two proposed initiatives is expected to create a culture which allows knowledge management to flourish—even in the infamous governmental organizations.

Chapter 11 entitled, "A Conceptual Model of Collaborative Information Seeking" by Ric Jentzsch and Paul Prekop of the University of Canberra (Australia) examines collaborative information seeking and suggests a conceptual model for collaborative information seeking. The chapter relates this model to current information technology initiatives such as computer supported collaborative work, knowledge management and electronic commerce.

Chapter 12 entitled, "Information Manager/Librarian to Knowledge Manager: Change of Role" by K. Nageswara Rao and K.H. Babu of Defence Research and Development Laboratory (India) discusses the broad classification of knowledge and the mechanisms of its transmission and transformation. The authors discuss the human element in knowledge management systems for the benefit of information managers and librarians.

Chapter 13 entitled, "Social and Cultural Barriers for Knowledge Databases in Professional Service Firms" by Georg Disterer of the University of Applied Sciences (Germany) analyzes the discrepancy between the expectations and actual benefits of knowledge databases construed and maintained by the massive use of IT. This chapter analyzes the differences between professionals collecting paper documents manually and databases constructed. The chapter looks at the existing social barriers to creating knowledge databases.

Chapter 14 entitled, "Web-Based Knowledge Management" by Ruidong Zhang of the University of Wisconsin-Eau Claire (USA) looks at the current Web-based knowledge management as a medium to support the collective nature of knowledge management. The chapter concludes that the potential of Web technology based on knowledge management has just started to be realized. The chapter discusses four models that provide insights on leveled knowledge management, what should be contained in higher levels of knowledge management systems and how these support systems can be technically implemented.

Chapter 15 entitled, "The Innovation Link Between Organization Knowledge and Customer Knowledge" by Helen Mitchell of UNITEC Institute of Technology (New Zealand) presents the results of a survey, and concludes that a database provides good opportunities for analysis, and identifies a need for organizations to identify why they gather and hold information on the database. The chapter also suggests that the idea of analyzing the information from a perspective of gaining knowledge about how and where the organization will grow rather than simply storing the information will bring greater rewards.

Chapter 16 entitled, "Implementing Knowledge Management: Issues for Managers" by Charles Snyder of Auburn University and Larry Wilson of LearnerFirst, Inc. (USA) presents definitions of KM and raises important issues for managers to consider. The chapter discusses categories of knowledge and their relevance for managers. The authors provide the elements that every organization should consider in assessing their readiness for knowledge management and present the components of knowledge harvesting and reasons that knowledge management efforts fail.

Chapter 17 entitled, "Knowledge Sharing Across Organizational Boundaries with Application to Distributed Engineering Processes" by Gerd Frick, Eric Sax and Klaus Muller-Glaser of Forschungszentrum Informatik (Germany) discusses collaborative engineering processes with more than one company and the need for knowledge sharing across organizational boundaries. The chapter discusses this problem in general within the background of the real-world application domain of the automotive industry. The authors present a solution concept called virtual project database and explain deficits in the status quo of information technology.

Chapter 18 entitled, "Organizational Learning by 'Segmented Networks': Breeding Variations and Similarities Together–What is Optimum?" by Bishwajit Choudhary of Bankenes BetalingsSentral (Norway) develops specific factors that conceptualize an optimum distance in teams and later extends the factors to argue of a novel organizational form, i.e., the segmented network. The paper concludes by looking at the implications from past research, which indicates that segmented networks will be manageable, but leading such a team would demand greater managerial competence at result orientation.

Chapter 19 entitled, "Client/Server and the Knowledge Directory: A Natural Relationship" by Stuart Galup and Ronald Dattero of Florida Atlantic University (USA) discusses a client/server architecture that employs the knowledge directory to support the development and ongoing maintenance knowledge management systems. The chapter concludes that three-tier client/server architecture provides a seamless integration of the variety of technologies required for a knowledge management system.

Chapter 20 entitled, "An Informational Perspective Towards Knowledge Work: Implications for Knowledge Management Systems" by Brian Detlor of McMaster University (Canada) presents an informational orientation towards knowledge work and draws implications of such a perspective on the functionality offered by knowledge management technologies. The chapter then presents discussion on the nature of organizational knowledge and its strong association with information. The authors present a discussion of knowledge work and draws implications based on this perspective.

Chapter 21 entitled, "Argumentation and Knowledge-Sharing" by Mike Metcalfe and Samantha Grant of the University of South Australia discusses the conceptual basis for social-technical systems aimed at assisting geographically separate companies to use the Internet to achieve the economic benefits of clustering. The first section of the chapter looks at evidence for structured talk, which includes the role of argumentation systems on research, problem solving, communication and decision-making. The authors argue further that rural regions have the core competencies needed to cluster but not the interaction.

Chapter 22 entitled, "Supporting Knowledge Creation: Combining Place, Community and Process" by I.T. Hawryszkiewycz of the University of Technology (Australia) identifies three major components of knowledge sharing and creation within enterprises as a combination of place, community and process. The way these are combined will depend on the particular goal and enterprise structure. The chapter then claims that computer support systems must provide user driven methods to easily integrate these components to fit in with organizational culture and knowledge goal. The authors then present ways to create the optimal environment.

Chapter 23 entitled, "A Study of Knowledge Benefits Gained From Projects: The Electric Utility Industry Y2K Project Experience" by Murray Jennex of San Diego State University and the University of Phoenix, San Diego and Joseph Weiss of the Electric Power Research Institute (USA) reports on a survey of utility Y2K projects on knowledge generation, perceived knowledge benefits and methods used to capture knowledge benefits. The results of the survey were mixed. While project personnel were strong in their belief that there were knowledge benefits and could identify several, they were much less positive in their identification of methods for capturing knowledge-lending doubt to the amount of organizational learning that was achieved.

Chapter 24 entitled, "Designing Organizational Memory for Knowledge Management Support in Collaborative Learning" by Kam Hou VAT of the University of Macau investigates the design of organizational memory targeted for knowledge management support tailored for collaboration among academic staff and students in a university environment. Specifically, the chapter describes the author's knowledge management initiatives to support organizational learning and depicts new ideas on knowledge items regarding their meta-modeling, indexing and ontological aspects.

Chapter 25 entitled, "Getting over 'Knowledge is Power': Incentive Systems for Knowledge Management in Business Consulting Companies" by Harald F.O. VonKortzfleisch of the University of Kassel and the University of Cologne (Germany) and Ines Mergel of the University of St. Gallen (Switzerland) looks closely at the importance of incentive systems for knowledge management in the business consulting industry. The authors investigate 10 leading German business consulting companies. Their results indicate that information systems do play an important part in the knowledge driven industry, but currently incentives do not focus on the issues of knowledge sharing. The chapter concludes that in order to implement a more efficient knowledge management systems among consultants, incentives need to be developed.

Chapter 26 entitled, "The Information Laws" by Andrew Targowski of the Western Michigan University (USA) discusses the concept of macro-information ecology. This concept is just emerging along with the development of Information Wave practice. The author indicates that researchers should turn their attention into the application of the information laws discussed in this chapter. By so doing, the further discoveries and corrections in application in the analysis and design of values and tools of the Information Wave and civilization will receive great benefit.

Chapter 27 entitled "Supporting Organizational Knowledge Management with Agents" by Prashant Pai, L.L. Miller, Vasant Honavar, Johnny Wong and Sree Nilakanta of Iowa State University (USA) focuses on making vast amount of unstructured text more useful to committees. The chapter discusses the design and implementation of an agent environment and looks at the desire of businesses to enhance the business process and take advantage of the explosion of data available to all organizations.

Chapter 28 entitled, "Knowledge Management and Virtual Communities" by W. Jansen, and H.P.M. Jägers of the Royal Netherlands Military Academy and G. C. A. Steenbakkers of Ordina Management Consulting (The Netherlands) attempts to illuminate the relationship between knowledge management and virtual communities. The paper presents a model, which comprises four types of knowledge management. One of the central themes is the suggestion that knowledge management is not an unequivocal concept, but rather knowledge management will different in focus and content depending on the environment of the organization.

Chapter 29 entitled, "A Research Model for Knowledge Management" by Pamila Dembla of the University of Memphis and En Mao of the University of Wisconsin-Milwaukee (USA) suggests a research model for knowledge management. The authors discuss the various components of knowledge management in detain to explain the process of knowledge management. They then present two case studies and analyze the process of knowledge management in the two organizations based upon their research model.

Chapter 30 entitled, "'Knowledge Management': A Telling Oxymoron?" by D.A. White and Y.M. Sutton of the University of Lincolnshire and Humberside (U.K.) seeks to develop a critique of knowledge management with a view supporting more informed theory and practice in the area. The critique is based upon recent empirical research, and the methods of this research are the subject of the chapter. The authors indicate that the current approach to knowledge management is simplistic and by broadening the approach businesses maybe better able to exploit and use knowledge management techniques.

Whether or not knowledge management is an oxymoron, how knowledge can be best captured, used and stored by organizations and how knowledge can be best shared are just some of the topics addressed in this timely book. The information contained herein is useful to academics as they attempt to understand the theory of knowledge management and mapping, to researchers as they attempt to evaluate the efficacy of knowledge management systems, and to businessmen and practitioners as they strive to implement the most current, best practices in knowledge management and mapping. This book will prove to be useful to all those associated with this most timely and emerging field.

IRM Press
October 2001

Chapter 1

Is Knowledge Management Really an Oxymoron? Unraveling the Role of Organizational Controls in Knowledge Management

Yogesh Malhotra, Ph.D.
@Brint.com L.L.C., USA

Many current implementations of organizational knowledge management, although based on the most advanced information technologies, are hobbled by the pervading organizational controls. Such information systems related organizational controls could spell the success or failure of organizational management initiatives despite application of latest groupware and collaboration software. Often, such failures of knowledge management systems implementations arise from incorrect understanding and misapplication of the notion of "controls." Hence, it is critical to develop a better understanding of information systems related organizational controls so that they can facilitate the success of knowledge management systems implementations. This chapter fills the critical void of incomplete and often incorrect interpretations of organizational controls by developing a better theoretical and conceptual understanding of organizational controls and their pragmatic implications. The chapter also proposes an organic model of organizational controls for design of knowledge management systems that can effectively enable creation of new knowledge, renewal of existing knowledge and knowledge sharing.

Previously Published in *Challenges of Information Technology Management in the 21st Century* edited by Mehdi Khosrow-Pour, Copyright © 2000, Idea Group Publishing.

INTRODUCTION

Despite advanced information systems that support "rich" information exchange and collaboration within the members of groups or organizations, many current implementations of knowledge management systems have shown limited success. Often the problems may not be with the design of such knowledge management systems, but their appropriation and effective utilization by the members of the organizations. The key argument of this article is that information systems, when applied to knowledge management, are limited in their success by the pervading organizational controls. Often the notion of *knowledge management* is confused with the notion of *controlling the members' knowledge sharing behavior*. A review of the literature on organizational controls suggests that this may be a dangerous and fallacious premise that may hobble the success of knowledge management systems implementations. In fact, a better understanding of organizational controls would suggest that *to manage* is not *to control*. In other words, success of knowledge management systems could often result from propagating and nurturing the autonomy and self-control of organization members instead of exerting external influences to modify or manipulate their knowledge creating and knowledge sharing behavior. More importantly, in most cases, despite good design of information technology based architecture of knowledge management systems, attempting to modify or manipulate creating and knowledge sharing behavior may have result in the failure of knowledge management systems.

Section 2 provides a literature review about the concept of "organizational controls." Section 3 discusses the limitations inherent in the mainstream model of knowledge management. Discussion in this section also expounds how inadequate understanding and application of organizational controls may often lead to failure of knowledge management implementations. Section 4 proposes and illustrates an organic model of organizational controls that is better suited to creation of new knowledge, renewal of existing knowledge and sharing of knowledge between the organizational members. Based on the preceding discussion, section 5 underscores that "knowledge management" is as much of an oxymoron as any other related notions such as information systems management, human resource management, business management and so forth.

LITERATURE REVIEW ON ORGANIZATIONAL CONTROLS

Despite lack of a commonly accepted framework or typology of organizational controls (Merchant and Simon, 1986; Green & Welsh, 1988; Simons, 1990), invariably, most authors (cf., Eisenhardt, 1989; Flamholtz et al., 1985; Henderson & Lee, 1992; Kirsch, 1996; Lawler, 1976; Orlikowski, 1991b; Tannenbaum,

1962) have interpreted control in terms of the *influence* exerted on the subordinates to seek their *compliance* with organizational goals. Most such interpretations have used the thermostat analogy of the control system (cf., Anthony, 1988; Grant & Higgins, 1991; Lawler & Rhode, 1976). In most such "thermostat" models, performance level of the subordinate is measured and compared with a *pre-set* standard and the subordinate acts on the feedback received from the superior to decrease the variance between the measured performance and the pre-defined standard. It has been assumed that the controller seeks compliance by exerting control, say in terms of pre-specified performance criteria, and the desired organizational outcomes are achieved through compliance of the controllee. In addition, it has also been assumed that organizational outcomes resulting from the enforcement of compliance are generally favorable to the organizational well-being.

In most existing research and practice on knowledge management, such manipulation of behavior and actions of organizational actors is treated in the context of utilization, processing, creation, dissemination and sharing of knowledge. Increasing awareness about the tacit or intrinsic knowledge of organization members (cf, Davenport and Prusak, 1997; *CIO Enterprise,* 1999; Malhotra, 1997, 1999e) has resulted in the premise that knowledge cannot be managed, i.e.,"knowledge management is an oxymoron" (cf, *Information Week,* 1999; *Computerworld,* 1998; *Wall Street Journal,* 1998; Sveiby, 1998). In addition, operational measures often recommended for facilitating knowledge management have included bonuses and incentives (cf, Davenport and Prusak, 1997) or other means of modifying or manipulating knowledge sharing behavior. The dominant model of knowledge management based on *control by compliance* assumes that such operational measures would have a positive influence on knowledge creation and knowledge sharing behavior. However, a deeper understanding of organizational controls developed in this article suggests otherwise.

CONTROLS THAT CONSTRAIN KNOWLEDGE MANAGEMENT

Several conceptualizations of organizational control have assumed alteration of the controllee's behavior (regulation) to be a direct consequence of the communication (feedback) from the controller. However, Giddens' (1984) notion of agency, known as the *dialectic of control*, recognizes that: "All forms of dependence offer some resources whereby those who are subordinate can influence the activities of their superiors." In other words, assumption of the passive and compliant knowledge workers is inaccurate given that the controllee can "choose to do otherwise" (Giddens, 1979, 1984; Orlikowski, 1991a), despite attempts to manipulate or control one's knowledge sharing behavior. Manz et al. (1987, p. 5) recognize controllee's choice between compliance and non-compliance in that observation that: "Persons may exercise self-control even when they choose to acquiesce to external demands, as acquiescence still implies choice." The active role of controllee in choosing between compliance and non-compliance has also received empirical support from more recent field studies conducted by Malhotra and Kirsch (1996) and Malhotra (1999a, 1999b).

It is a different matter that in the "world of re-everything" (Arthur, 1996), passive compliance to the status quo may be detrimental to the competitive health of the organization. Traditionally, organizational controls have been "built, *a priori*, on the principal of closure" (Landau & Stout, 1979, p. 150) to seek compliance to, and convergence of, the organizational decision-making processes (Flamholtz et al., 1985). The fundamental assumption underlying such controls is that goals have been pre-decided, *recipes* for achieving those goals have been pre-decided and translated into procedural guidelines that need to be *followed* by the employees. Such organizational control systems were designed to reinforce stability and maintain the status quo. However, the cycle of doing "more of the same" tends to result in locked-in behavior patterns that eventually sacrifice organizational performance at the altar of the organizational "death spiral" (Nadler & Shaw, 1995, p. 12-13). Hence, although knowledge management systems based on compliance may *ensure* conformity by enforcing task definition, measurement and control, yet they may *inhibit* creativity and initiative (Bartlett & Ghoshal, 1995). Emphasis on the obedience of rules at the cost of correction of errors (Landau & Stout, 1979) constrains creation of *new* knowledge and renewal of existing knowledge.

The problem is compounded by incorrect assumptions about human knowledge underlying the currently popular notion of knowledge management systems that are supposedly expected to "find useful knowledge, bottle it, and pass it around" (Hildebrand, 1995; Stewart & Kaufman, 1995). Such representations often assume away the *proactive* role that knowledge workers need to play in the success of such systems (Newcombe, 1999). Knowledge needs to be understood as the *potential for action* that doesn't only depend upon the stored information but also on the individual interacting with it.

The dominant conception of IS-based organizational knowledge systems is constrained by the very nature of the knowledge creation processes: it ignores the dynamic and continuously evolving nature of knowledge; it ignores the tacit and explicit dimensions of knowledge creation; it ignores the subjective, interpretative and meaning making bases of knowledge construction; it ignores the constructive nature of knowledge creation; and it ignores the social interactive basis of knowledge creation (Malhotra in press). The model of organizational control embedded in such systems is also overwhelmed by the intense information flows required for (Bartlett & Ghoshal, 1995):

a) keeping the centralized knowledge base and its custodians (managers) *continuously* current with the *discontinuously changing* external environment,

b) continually updating the employees on the latest changes in their outputs (goals) and changes in procedures to achieve those outputs.

Under conditions of ambiguity, of loose coupling, and of uncertainty that characterizes the new business environment, measurement of knowledge worker's performance with reliability and with precision is not possible. A control system based on such measurements is likely to systematically reward a narrow range of maladaptive behavior, leading ultimately to organizational decline. The new business environments require new models of knowledge management and related organizational controls conducive to sustainable competitive advantage in the face of radical and unpredictable change (Malhotra, 1998b, 1998c, 1999c). The knowledge management model enabled by self-control is discussed in the next section as one such model.

CONTROLS THAT ENABLE KNOWLEDGE MANAGEMENT

Organizations in dynamically changing environments need to behave experimentally. Since they will come across few lasting optima, they ought to gear themselves to impermanency and plan as if their decisions were temporary and probably imperfect solutions to changing problems. Accordingly, knowledge management systems need to encourage experimentation and be easy to re-arrange and adapt with changing business environment. Such dynamically adaptive knowledge management processes and systems need to be driven by self-evaluation and self-design (Hedberg et al., 1976).

 Successful implementation of knowledge management systems is driven by the simultaneously processes of ongoing learning and unlearning that have been characterized elsewhere as *loose-tight systems* as illustrated in Figure 1. Such systems are *loose* in the sense that they allow for continuous re-examination of the assumptions underlying best practices and reinterpretation of this information. Such systems are *tight* in the sense that they also allow for efficiencies based on propagation and dissemination of the best practices. Such *loose-tight knowledge management systems* (Malhotra, 1998a, 1999d) would need to provide not only for identification and dissemination of best practices, but also for continuous re-examination of such practices. Specifically, they would need to also include a simultaneous process that continuously examines the best practices for their currency given the changing assumptions about the business environment. Such systems

Figure 1: Loose Tight Knowledge Management Systems

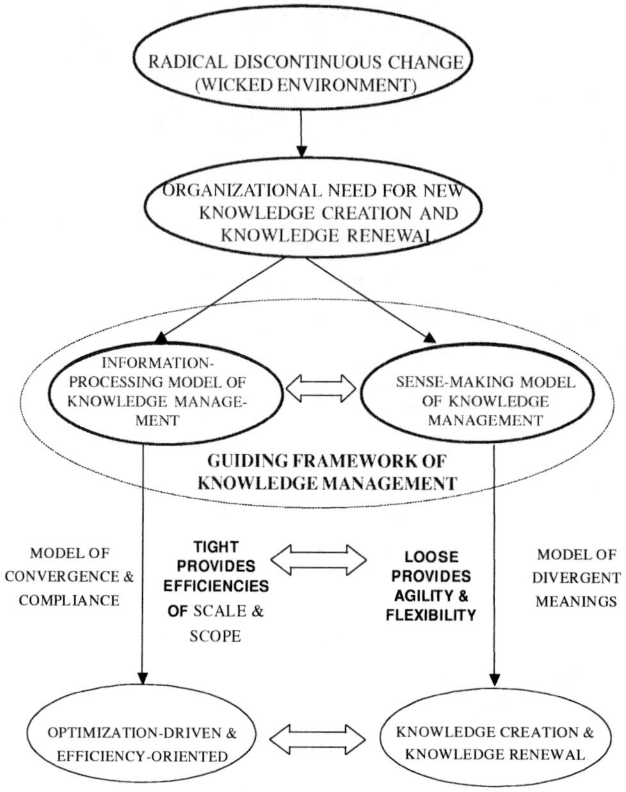

would need to contain *both* learning and unlearning processes. These simultaneous processes are needed for assuring the efficiency-oriented optimization based on the current best practices while ensuring that such practices are continuously re-examined for their currency.

The proposed organizational control model "actually exploits benefits hidden within properties that designers have generally regarded as liabilities" (Hedberg & Jonsson, 1978, p. 45). This observation seems important given that unclear objectives and ambiguous work roles have been suggested by some management scholars (cf, Burns and Stalker, 1961) as *desirable* properties of organismic organizations for thriving in dynamic environments. Design of knowledge management systems thus needs to take into consideration ambiguity, inconsistency, multiple perspectives, and impermanency of existing information. Such systems need to be designed along the principles of *semi-confusing information systems* (Hedberg and Jonsson, 1978) that facilitate exploitation of previous experiences and detected causalities, but ensure that experience of past doesn't hinder ongoing adaptation for the discontinuous future.

Figure 2: Success Factors for Knowledge Management: Contrasting Stable and "Wicked" Environments

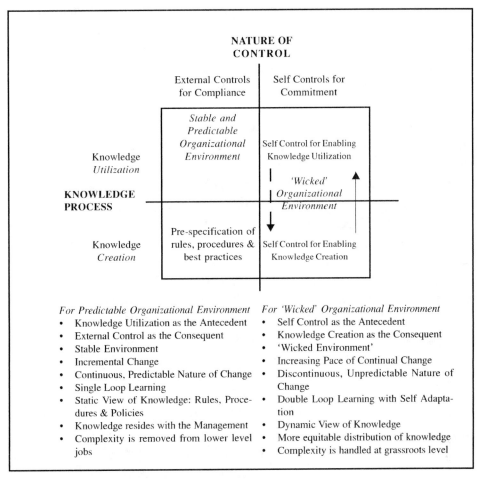

For Predictable Organizational Environment
- Knowledge Utilization as the Antecedent
- External Control as the Consequent
- Stable Environment
- Incremental Change
- Continuous, Predictable Nature of Change
- Single Loop Learning
- Static View of Knowledge: Rules, Procedures & Policies
- Knowledge resides with the Management
- Complexity is removed from lower level jobs

For 'Wicked' Organizational Environment
- Self Control as the Antecedent
- Knowledge Creation as the Consequent
- 'Wicked Environment'
- Increasing Pace of Continual Change
- Discontinuous, Unpredictable Nature of Change
- Double Loop Learning with Self Adaptation
- Dynamic View of Knowledge
- More equitable distribution of knowledge
- Complexity is handled at grassroots level

As illustrated in Figure 2, the proposed model of organizational control recognizes self-control as the driver of human actors' behavior and actions across all organizational decision and task processes and acknowledges that control over employees is ultimately self-imposed. Instead of emphasizing unquestioning adherence to pre-specified goals or procedures, it encourages the use of intuition through "playfulness" (Cooper et al., 1981, p. 179). The model of knowledge management through self-control also facilitates error detection and error correction (Stout, 1980, p. 90) instead of compliance with pre-specified rules and procedures. Instead of emphasizing "best practices," it encourages development of a large repertoire of responses to suggest not only alternative (complementary and contradictory) solutions, but also different approaches for executing those solutions. In the emerging business world (Wheatley, 1994, p. 151): "solutions...are a temporary event, specific to a context, developed through the relationship of persons and circumstances." The proposed model is based on the premise that (Landau & Stout, 1979, p. 152): "solutions to problems cannot be commanded...[they] must be discovered: found on the basis of imagination, analysis, experiment, and criticism."

These observations illustrated in the schematic highlight the contrast between the traditional organizational environment characterized by predictability and emphasis on "forecasts" and the emergent "wicked" environment characterized by unpredictability and emphasis on "anticipation of surprise." As the world economies transition from the traditional model of "workers" to the new model of autonomous "free agents" and "knowledge intrapreneurs" (Malhotra 1998a), the distinctions made in this article achieve greater significance. In the emergent organizations, managers will need to nurture self-leadership and self-regulation as emphasis shifts from utilization of "canned knowledge" to continual creation of new knowledge and renewal of existing knowledge. Previous models of "canned knowledge" resident in organizational intranets and best practice databases will be increasingly vulnerable as their underlying premises need to be questioned on a daily basis by those making decisions and taking actions in the field. The key challenge for managers in the forthcoming turbulent environments will be to cultivate commitment to the organizational visions. As it becomes increasingly difficult to specify long-term goals and objectives, such commitment would facilitate real-time strategizing in accord with the organizational vision and its implementation in the field. Knowledge workers would need to take autonomous roles of self-leadership and self-regulation as they would be best positioned to take into consideration the dynamic changes in the business environment. Compliance will loose its effectiveness as the managerial tool of control as managers removed from the field have lesser and lesser knowledge needed for enforcing such compliance. In absence of more and more incomplete knowledge of the situation at hand, forcing compliance may not even be the last resort. Managers would need to facilitate confidence of knowledge workers in acting on incomplete information, trusting their own judgments and taking decisive actions for capturing increasingly shorter windows of opportunity. In the new world of business, the *control over employees will be ultimately self-imposed*, and that managerial controls would need to seek proactive self-control (Malhotra and Kirsch, 1996; Hopwood, 1974; Manz et al., 1987). Argyris (1990) has referred to the transition from traditional external control mechanisms to the paradigm of self-control as "the current revolution in management theory."

CONCLUSION

This article was motivated by increasing recognition of critical relevance of "organizational controls" in successful knowledge management implementation. A review of existing research and practice of knowledge management suggests that such controls are often incorrectly understood and applied. Specifically, it was observed that the concept of "management" has been interested in very narrow terms of *control by compliance* which may not be very effective for facilitating knowledge utilization, new knowledge creation, knowledge dissemination and knowledge sharing by knowledge actors. Better understanding of "management" in terms of "self-control" seems pertinent for remedying this fallacy that could have dire implications for new business environments. The framework of knowledge management based on self-controls discussed in this chapter advances the model of commitment based knowledge management that is more conducive for effective knowledge performance in the new business environments.

This chapter has attempted to address the critical issue of organizational controls as they are relevant to the success of knowledge management systems in new business environments. However, many important questions need to be addressed for actualization of such systems. Some such questions include: How to design and implement "loose tight" knowledge management systems proposed in this article? How can knowledge management systems design and implementation enable self-regulation and self-control of users without sacrificing performance? How to design and implement systems that can better integrate the organismic model of knowledge management needed for new organizational environments? It is anticipated that the theoretical and conceptual contributions made by this paper would facilitate design of more robust knowledge management systems that can withstand the impact of radical and discontinuous changes in the business environment.

REFERENCES

Anthony, R.N. (1988). *The Management Control Function*, Boston, MA: Harvard Business School Press.

Argyris, C. (1990). *Integrating the Individual and the Organization*, Transaction, New Brunswick, NJ.

Arthur, W. B. (1996). Increasing Returns and the New World of Business. *Harvard Business Review,* July-August, 74(4), pp. 100-109.

Bartlett, C.A. & Ghoshal, S. (1995). Changing the Role of the Top Management: Beyond Systems to People, *Harvard Business Review*, May-June, pp. 132-142.

Burns, T. and Stalker, G. M. (1961). *The Management of Innovation*, London: Tavistock.

CIO Enterprise (1999). Does KM=IT? written by Carol Hildebrand. Sep. 15. Online version accessible at: http://www.cio.com/archive/enterprise/091599_ic.html .

Computerworld (1998). Knowledge management: Some "there" there, written by John Gantz, October 12.

Cooper, D.J., Hayes, D., and Wolf, F. (1981). Accounting in Organized Anarchies: Understanding and Designing Accounting Systems in Ambiguous Situations, *Accounting, Organizations and Society*, 6(3), pp. 175-191.

Davenport, T.H. & Prusak, L. (1989). *Working Knowledge: How Organizations Manage What They Know*, Boston, MA: Harvard Business School Press.

Eisenhardt, K.M. (1989). Agency Theory: An Assessment and Review, *Academy of Management Review*, 14(1), pp. 57-74.

Flamholtz, E.G., Das, T.K. & Tsui, A.S. (1985). Toward an Integrative Framework of Organizational Control, *Accounting, Organizations and Society*, 10(1), pp. 35-50.

Giddens, A. (1984). *The Constitution of Society: Outline of the Theory of Structuration*. Berkeley: University of California Press.

Giddens, A. (1979). *Central Problems in Social Theory: Action, Structure and Contradiction in Social Analysis*, Berkeley, CA: University of California Press.

Grant, R.A. & Higgins, C.A. (1991). The Impact of Computerized Performance Monitoring on Service Work: Testing a Causal Model, *Information Systems Research*, 2(2), pp. 116-142.

Green, S.G. and Welsh, M.A. (1988). Cybernetics and Dependence: Reframing the Control Concept, *Academy of Management Review*, 13(2), pp. 287-301.

Hedberg, B. (1981). How Organizations Learn and Unlearn. In P. Nystrom and W. Starbuck (Eds.), *Handbook of Organizational Design*, New York: Oxford University Press, pp. 1-27.

Hedberg, B. & Jonsson, S. (1978). Designing Semi-Confusing Information Systems for Organizations in Changing Environments, *Accounting, Organizations and Society*, 3(1), pp. 47-74.

Hedberg, B., Nystrom, P.C. & Starbuck, W.H. (1976). Camping on Seesaws: Prescriptions for a Self-Designing Organization, *Administrative Science Quarterly*, 21, pp. 41-65.

Henderson, J.C. & Lee, S. (1992). Managing I/S Design Teams: A Control Theories Perspective, *Management Science*, 38(6), pp. 757-777.

Hildebrand, C. (1995). Information Mapping: Guiding Principles, *CIO*, 8(18), July, pp. 60-64.

Hopwood, A. (1974). *Accounting and Human Behavior*, London, UK: Prentice-Hall.

InformationWeek (1999). Stay In Touch With Information, written by John Eckhouse, April 5th.

Kirsch, L.J. (1996). The Management of Complex Tasks in Organizations: Controlling the Systems Development Process, *Organization Science*, (7:1), pp. 1-21.

Landau, M. & Stout, Jr., R. (1979). To Manage is Not to Control: Or the Folly of Type II Errors, *Public Administration Review*, March/April, pp. 148-156.

Lawler, E. E. (1976). Control Systems in Organizations. In M.D. Dunnette (Ed.), *Handbook of Industrial and Organizational Psychology*, Rand-McNally College Publishing, Chicago, IL, pp. 1247-1291.

Lawler, E., E., & Rhode, J.G. (1976). *Information and Controls in Organizations*, Goodyear, Santa Monica, CA.

Malhotra, Y. From Information Management to Knowledge Management: Beyond the "Hi-Tech Hidebound" Systems. In K. Srikantaiah and M.E.D. Koenig (Eds.), *Knowledge Management for the Information Professional*, Information Today, Inc., Medford, NJ, [in press].

Malhotra, Y. (1997). Knowledge Management in Inquiring Organizations. In the *Proceedings of 3rd Americas Conference on Information Systems (Philosophy of Information Systems Mini-track), Indianapolis, IN*, August 15-17. Accessible online at: http://www.brint.com/km/km.htm .

Malhotra, Y. (1998a). Toward a Knowledge Ecology for Organizational White-Waters, Invited Keynote Presentation for the *Knowledge Ecology Fair 98: Beyond Knowledge Management*, Feb. 2 - 27, accessible online at: http://www.brint.com/papers/ecology.htm.

Malhotra, Y. (1998b). Deciphering the Knowledge Management Hype, *Journal for Quality & Participation*, July/August, pp. 58-60.

Malhotra, Y. (1998c). Role of Social Influence, Self Determination and Quality of Use. In Information Technology Acceptance *and Utilization: A Theoretical Framework and Empirical Field Study*, Ph.D. thesis, July, Katz Graduate School of Business, University of Pittsburgh, 225 pages.

Malhotra, Y. (1999a). Bringing the Adopter Back Into the Adoption Process: A Personal Construction Framework of Information Technology Adoption, *Journal of High Technology Management Research*, 10(1), Spring.

Malhotra, Y. (1999b). Extending the Technology Acceptance Model to Account for Social Influence: Theoretical Bases and Empirical Validation. In the *Proceedings of the Hawaii International Conference on System Sciences* (HICSS 32) (Adoption and Diffusion of Collaborative Systems and Technology Minitrack), Maui, HI, January 5-8.

Malhotra, Y. (1999c). High-Tech Hidebound Cultures Disable Knowledge Management. In *Knowledge Management* (UK), February.

Malhotra, Y. (1999d). Knowledge Management for Organizational White Waters: An Ecological Framework. In *Knowledge Management* (UK), March.

Malhotra, Y. (1999e). What is Really Knowledge Management?: Crossing the Chasm of Hype. In @Brint.com web site, Sep. 15. [Letter to editor in response to Inc. Technology #3, Sep. 15, 1999, special issue on Knowledge Management]. Accessible online at: http://www.brint.com/advisor/a092099.htm.

Malhotra, Y. & Kirsch, L. (1996). Personal Construct Analysis of Self-Control in IS Adoption: Empirical Evidence from Comparative Case Studies of IS Users & IS Champions. In the *Proceedings of the First INFORMS Conference on Information Systems and Technology (Organizational Adoption & Learning Track)*, Washington D.C., May 5-8, pp. 105-114.

Manz, C.C., Mossholder, K. W. & Luthans, F. (1987). An Integrated Perspective of Self-Control in Organizations, 19(1), *Administration & Society*, May, pp. 3-24.

Manz, C.C. & Sims, H.P. (1989). *SuperLeadership: Leading Others to Lead Themselves*, Berkeley, CA: Prentice-Hall.

Manz, C.C. & Sims, H.P. (1987). Leading Workers to Lead Themselves: The External Leadership of Self-Managing Work Teams, *Administrative Science Quarterly*, 32, pp. 106-128.

Manz, C.C. & Sims, H.P., Jr. (1980). Self-Management as a Substitute for Leadership: A Social Learning Theory Perspective, *Academy of Management Review*, 5(3), pp. 361-367.

Merchant, K.A. and Simons, R. (1986). Research and Control in Complex Organizations: An Overview, *Journal of Accounting Literature*, 5, 183-201.

Nadler, D.A. & Shaw, R.B. (1995). Change Leadership: Core Competency for the Twenty-First Century. In D.A. Nadler, R.B. Shaw & A.E. Walton (Eds.), *Discontinuous Change: Leading Organizational Transformation*, San Francisco, CA: Jossey-Bass.

Newcombe, T. (1999). Knowledge Management: New Wisdom or Passing Fad? *Government Technology*, June. Accessible online at: http://govt-tech.govtech.net:80/gtmag/1999/june/magastory/feature.shtm .

Orlikowski, W.J. (1991a). Information Technology and Structuring of Organizations, *Information Systems Research*, 2(2), pp. 143-169.

Orlikowski, W. J. (1991b). Integrated Information Environment or Matrix of Control?: The Contradictory Implications of Information Technology, *Accounting, Management and Information Technology*, 1(1), pp. 9-42.

Ouchi, W.G. (1979). A Conceptual Framework for the Design of Organizational Control Mechanisms, *Management Science*, 25 (9), p. 833-848.

Simons, R. (1990). The Role of Management Control Systems in Creating Competitive Advantage: New Perspectives, *Accounting, Organizations and Society*, (15:1,2), pp. 127-148.

Stewart, T.A. & Kaufman, D.C. (1995). Getting Real About Brainpower, *Fortune*, December 11.

Stout, R., Jr. (1980). *Management or Control?:The Organizational Challenge*, Bloomington, IN: Indiana University Press.

Sveiby, K.E. (1998). Intellectual Capital and Knowledge Management, Online document at Sveiby Knowledge Management (http://www.sveiby.com.au/).

Tannenbaum, R. (1962). Control in organizations. *Administration Science Quarterly*, 7, 236-257.

Wall Street Journal (1998). The End of Knowledge Management, in Tom Petzinger's column: 'The Front Lines,' B1, January 9.

Wheatley, M.J. (1994). *Leadership and the New Science*, San Francisco, CA: Berett-Koehler.

Chapter 2

Strategically-Focused Enterprise Knowledge Management

Robert J. Mockler
St. John's University, USA

Dorothy G. Dologite
City University of New York, USA

This chapter describes the characteristics and types of strategically focused knowledge management systems and the key conditions affecting their development and success. The discussion, which is based around company examples, focuses on various strategic management uses of these systems. The knowledge management process is designed to increase profitability and competitive advantage in the marketplace.

INTRODUCTION

Narrowly defined, knowledge refers to practical skills or expertise gained from actual experience, as shown in Figure 1. In practice, however, knowledge management generally refers to the process of identifying and generating, systematically gathering, organizing and providing access to, and putting to use anything and everything which might be useful to *know* when *performing* some specified business activity. The knowledge management process is designed to increase profitability and competitive advantage in the marketplace.

Previously Published in *Managing Information Technology in a Global Economy* edited by Mehdi Khosrow-Pour, Copyright © 2001, Idea Group Publishing.

Figure 1: Basic Definition

> **Knowledge**: includes data and information (organized data which is relevant and purposeful), and knowing how to apply and use that information and data. The term "ledge" means to put to work or apply. The word knowledge, therefore, means knowing how to put to work what we know, and so in popular usage can in certain situations encompass information and data.
>
> The following is a composite of various definitions found in Webster's dictionary and in writings on the subject by a variety of commentators. As seen from these definitions or descriptions of the connotations of the terms, it is useful to distinguish rigidly among many of the concepts only in selective clearly circumscribed situations.
>
> **Data**: something given or admitted as a fact on which an inference may be based. Simple observations of the world, which are often quantified, and easily structured, captured on machines, and transferred. The number of "baby boomers" born in a given year is data.
>
> **Information**: knowledge derived from reading, observation or instruction, at times consisting of unorganized or unrelated facts or data. Data endowed with relevance and purpose, for example, a firm's balance sheet and income statement.
>
> **Knowledge**: familiarity gained by actual experience, practical skill, or expertise. The act, or state, of understanding. Valuable information arising from reflection, synthesis, and other cognitive activities of the human mind. It is often, but not always, hard to structure, difficult to capture on machines, sometimes tacit, and hard to transfer.
>
> **Intelligence**: information, news, and advice. Brain power or cognitive skills. IBM uses the term "Business Intelligence Systems" to describe their mixed integrated knowledge systems.
>
> **Technology**: applied science, systematically organized knowledge.

Part of the difficulty in defining "knowledge" arises from the fact that "inform" and "know" refer to just about anything, which makes it difficult to foist a strict definition of "knowledge" onto the average reader.

As seen from Figure 1, which includes both commentators' and *Webster's Dictionary's* (2000) definitions of relevant terms, since the knowledge management process involves keeping informed about and getting to know anything useful to doing a business task, the process can encompass data, information, and knowledge. Further, the knowledge management process can involve employing any useful and practical means of communication and storage, manual or electronic. Useful manual means might include: service manuals; professional publications; personal correspondence and conversations; special studies and reports; client correspondence and summaries; competitor role playing; sales force feedback; current news; supplier feedback; and the like. Useful computer-based electronic technologies might include: e-mail; hierarchical, network, and relational databases and data warehouses; group decision support systems; Lotus Notes; intranets and internet web sites; browsers and search engines; expert and knowledge-based systems; and the like.

Because of the wide range of concepts and activities involved, the term knowledge management can more easily be understood by examples. Figure 2 outlines the knowledge management system (KMS) at a large consulting firm (Engoron, 1998). The strategic focus is the individual consultant who needs access to data, information, and knowledge in order to do his/her job. Since consulting is its business, the system is strategic. The system provides this access in large part electronically.

Figure 2: The Knowledge Management System at a Major Consulting Firm

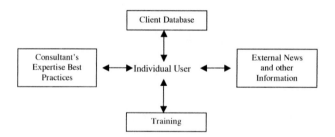

At the top of Figure 2 is a large computer database of information about clients, covering past assignments, consultants who worked on the assigned projects, outcomes, organized data on the company involved, and contacts who can provide further information. On the right, there is a system incorporating expert knowledge-based systems which scans news media and library resources daily and daily directs relevant intelligence material to different consultants (Newing, 1999). On the left is a database of consultants' expertise or knowledge including that acquired from experience during past assignments. This includes written summaries of what was learned from the assignments, videos in which consultants describe the highlights of their experiences or general knowledge, and contingent best practices guidelines in different areas (such as strategic alliances, all marketing and production areas, human resources management, and the like). At the bottom, there is available a bank of online training programs, which a consultant can make use of (privately) to sharpen skills needed to improve job performance.

On any given day that a consultant receives a new assignment, he/she could immediately review current relevant information in the media (intelligence) about the client and project area, gather information quickly about the client and past assignments involving the client, review the related knowledge expertise of other consultants, and brush up on needed skills. It is not hard to envision the enormous amount of preparation time the firm's composite knowledge management system saves and the speed with which a consultant is able to be ready to start an assignment – often a very critical factor when the assignment involves an emergency. At the same time, the consultant would make use of any relevant personal knowledge sources. The system is a good example of using a knowledge system to strategically manage resources – that is of a strategic management knowledge system.

Not all knowledge management systems are that complex or that *multidimensional* in scope. Some are narrowly *focused* on single activities. For example, Xerox in 1996 developed Eureka, an intranet communication system linked with a traditional corporate *computer database* that helps service representatives share repair tips, that is, knowledge. To date, more than 500 tips have been entered by Xerox technicians, and this practical knowledge is available to all via their laptops. For employees scattered around the world who travel often, the ability to share such know how means they don't have to miss out on the kind of knowledge typically exchanged at the watercooler (Hickens, 1999).

A number of key characteristics of knowledge management can be identified from company experiences. These can apply to strategic and operational knowledge systems. First, the *types of knowledge management systems vary* considerably depending on the company situation requirements, a *contingency perspective*. Second, *knowledge generation* involves identifying knowledge relevant to strategic business activities, as well as its source and the way it is used or exploited. Third, *structuring* refers to designing knowledge management systems to capture and deliver the knowledge generated; such structures can range from simple ones involving individual business process areas, as at Xerox, to multidimensional complex enterprise-wide ones, as at the consulting firm. Their content can involve any company activity/business process or combination of them. Fourth, *diffusing* or communicating any type of relevant data, information, or knowledge involves transferring and absorbing knowledge to put it to work. In the company experiences studied, the main means of diffusion was electronic and audio/video tools. Knowledge is also very often continually transferred and absorbed informally through personal interaction.

The success of KMS is highly dependent on the *strategic fit* of structure and content with strategic requirements or critical success factors in the situation. The success of knowledge management also depends on the participation of *people sharing their knowledge* expertise with others, which in turn can depend on the way the system is designed, implemented, and managed *(the operational fit)*, as well as on the degree to which a firm has a "learning" *organization culture* (Lucier and Torsilieri, 1997). Nurturing this sharing culture requires active leadership by a knowledge management champion, since very often people are reluctant to share their expertise (Manchester, 1999b). Like the structure, content, strategic and operational fit, design, implementation, organization, participation, management, and use or exploitation, the *enabling tools or technologies* used are contingent on the requirements of the situation. The following sections cover these basic knowledge management areas.

THE MAJOR TYPES OF KNOWLEDGE MANAGEMENT SYSTEMS

The following discussion describes a range or systems now in use by business. Many of the systems described in this paper were originally computer information systems to which were added knowledge expertise which complemented the information and data communicated. As use of the Internet expanded and intranets within companies were developed, many new knowledge expertise exchange systems were established. As seen in the above and following discussions, many knowledge systems are therefore *mixed,* that is, *integrated with traditional information and decision support systems*, as at the consulting firm, while many such as Xerox's focus specifically on expertise knowledge storage and transfer and so can be designated *focused* knowledge management systems. Expert knowledge based systems generally are *pure* knowledge systems (Mockler, 1992, 1996; Mockler and Dologite, 1992).

The Ford Motor Company case provides an example of how at a large firm the company-wide strategic knowledge systems are closely linked to and dependent on computer information systems (Austin, 1997, 1999). Ford is a multinational company with hundreds of locations in every major country. As part of an integration program in the early 1990s, computer information systems at Ford were standardized across the company, which enabled installation of an external Internet network – Extranet – with appropriate Web sites linking Ford with its suppliers and with its customers. Most of these were used initially for communication of information on available models, prices and availability of supplies, and other information (that is, targeted organized data). It also enabled development of an internal company Intranet system which also focused mainly on information conveyance initially.

The system also, however, served as a basis upon which to develop broader more strategic knowledge systems. For example, in the design area, as auto design and development facilities were more closely coordinated worldwide, knowledge about solving design problems and inconsistencies could now be resolved using the Intranet, a knowledge exchange process based on experiential expertise. Knowledge about lessons learned from experience in other business process areas, such as manufacturing, could also now be exchanged, since a worldwide system with Web sites was in place. Ford in early 1999, was exploring adding even more knowledge dimensions to their existing information systems structure.

Complex strategic knowledge management systems can also focus on critical business activity areas. For example, strategic alliances are extremely important to multinational companies today (Mockler, 1999; Sparks, 1999). They involve, however, complex human and business processes whose management requires in-depth expertise gained from experience. Capturing this developing knowledge base is a knowledge management activity. As a company undertakes alliances and begins learning from successes and failures, leaders in alliance management within a company emerge. These leaders, who are essentially gurus with experience and knowledge gained from experience, are the firm's initial imbedded alliance expertise capability. This initial experiential expert knowledge base in successful firms is extended in several ways. First, formal processes and procedures and a staff capable of managing alliance processes are developed. This is the initial knowledge depository for future use. The steps taken to collect, store, and disseminate this knowledge and to train people in order to further institutionalize alliance capabilities vary at different firms (Harbison and Pekar, 1997a, 1997b, 1997c; Pekar and Harbison, 1998).

Hewlett-Packard (H-P), for example, found that general seminars for managers on alliances were not enough. Managers needed H-P specific information on the best practices guidelines developed from H-P alliance experiences. A database of case histories, tools kits, checklists, and best practices was, therefore, developed and incorporated into training seminars. This database material was supplemented with studies of the best practices of other companies (Harbison and Pekar, 1997a, 1997b, 1997c).

In general, such a knowledge database would include a specific company's experiences with each of its alliance partners in each of the applicable best practices guidelines areas, areas which are outlined in alliance guidebooks (Mockler, 1999). These areas include strategic planning, negotiation, alliance structures and contracts, operational planning and management, and control. Companies, such as Ford, IBM, and Dun & Bradstreet, are in various stages of creating such company-specific database repositories; most often these are mixed systems – using computers and other approaches, as for example at H-P. The alliance knowledge databases include information on alliance partners, market reactions to alliance moves, and press releases related to company alliance. Several companies, such as Booz-Allen & Hamilton and Xerox, have created Web sites to disseminate alliance knowledge bases, Web sites which are accessible from laptop computers by consultants or service personnel at clients' offices (Harbison and Pekar, 1997a, 1997b, 1997c).

As part of their strategic knowledge management systems, dissemination of this knowledge is usually supplemented through seminars and workshops. BellSouth, for example, has offered a two-day alliance workshop for 150 senior managers, a major means of developing personal information networks to encourage ongoing knowledge dissemination. H-P has conducted 50 two-day seminars on alliances for its top 1000 executives prior to 1999 (Harbison and Pekar, 1997a, 1997b, 1997c).

CONCLUSION

These strategic alliance experiences are included here to illustrate the extent to which knowledge management, while using computer technology, goes well beyond it. First, supplemental knowledge dissemination approaches, such as seminars and workshops, are used where appropriate. Second, these supplemental approaches are used to communicate information on the field experiences which led to the knowledge developed, and so in this way help the users to acquire the knowledge in a more systematic, in depth, meaningful way. Third, knowledge repositories can include audio/video material and documents such as manuals. It is an example of the way in which knowledge systems, though related to and reliant on computer information systems, are more than computer information systems and build the intellectual capital of a firm in a way computer information systems by themselves cannot. these experiences also show that the concept "knowledge management" as used in general encompasses all useful forms of knowledge, information, and data.

As also seen in these experiences, for any type of strategic knowledge management effort to work, corporate culture must be favorable to the transfer of knowledge, that is, there must be a learning environment (Manchester,1999a). This culture involves both the willingness of experts to reveal their expertise (and take the time to do that) as well as the willingness of people to listen to and absorb the expertise, which also takes time and a personality receptive to change (Glasser, 1999).

REFERENCES

Austin, R. D. (1999). *Ford Motor Company: Supply Chain Strategy*, Study, Boston, MA: Harvard Business School.

Austin, R. D., and Coteleer, M. (1997). *Ford Motor Company: Maximizing the Business Value of Web Technologies,* Case Study, Boston, MA: Harvard Business School.

Engoron, F. (1998). Organization Effectiveness and Development, Global Leader, PricewaterhouseCoopers, New York: New York University (Center for Research on Information Systems), October 28.

Glasser, P. (1998/1999). The Knowledge Factor, *CIO*, December 15/January 1, pp. 108-118.

Harbison, J.R., and Pekar, P. (1997a, 1997b, 1997c). *A Practical Guide to Alliances: Leapfrogging The Learning Curve* (1997A), *Cross-border Alliance in the Age of Collaboration* (1997B), and *Institutionalizing Alliance Skills: Secrets of Repeatable Success* (1997C), New York: Booz-Allen & Hamilton.

Hickens, M. (1999). *Management Review*, September, pp. 40-45.

Lucier, C. E., and Torsilieri, J. D. (1997). Why Knowledge Programs Fail: A CEO's Guide to Managing Learning, *Strategy & Business, Fourth Quarter* (Issue 9), pp. 64-79.

Manchester, P. (1999a). A Marriage of Culture and Technology, *Financial Times*, Knowledge Management Survey Section, November 10, p. 1.

Manchester, P. (1999b). Fundamental Dilemma Over Ownership of Knowledge, *Financial Times*, Knowledge Management Survey Section, November 10, p. 5.

Mockler, R. J.(1992). *Developing Knowledge-Based Systems Using an Expert System: A Guidebook for General Business Managers and Computer Information Technicians (includes 19 Sample Prototype Systems and a Development Shell)*, Upper Saddle River, NJ: Prentice-Hall/Macmillan. This text has been revised and translated into Chinese and was published in Beijing, China, in July 1998 by the China Railway Publishing Corporation.

Mockler, R. J. (1996). Artificial Intelligence Models and Applications, 5,000-word state-of-the-art entry, *International Encyclopedia of Business and Management*, volume 1, pp. 250-260, London: Routledge Publishers, International Thompson Business Press, August.

Mockler, R. J. (1999). *Multinational Strategic Alliances*, New York and Chichester, UK: John Wiley & Sons.

Mockler, R. J., and Dologite D. G. (1992). *Expert Systems: Am Introduction to Knowledge-Based Systems*, Upper Saddle River, NJ: Prentice-Hall/Macmillan.

Newing, R. (1999). A Fundamental Pillar of Knowledge—and of Wisdom, *Financial Times*, Knowledge Management Survey Section, November 10, p. 2.

Pekar, P., and Harbison, J. R. (1998). Implementing Alliances and Acquisitions, *The 1998 Strategic Alliances Conference*, New York: The Conference Board, April 30/May 1.

Sparks, D. (1999). Special Report: Partners, *Business Week,* October 25, pp. 106-134.

Webster's Dictionary [Online]. (2000). *WWWebster Dictionary*, *http://www.m-w.com/cgi-bin/dictionary.* Merriam-Webster, Inc. Accessed January 20.

Chapter 3

Knowledge Mapping: An Essential Part of Knowledge Management

Jay Liebowitz
University of Maryland-Baltimore County, Maryland

Knowledge management is one of the fastest emerging fields in industry today. Unfortunately, however, most of the knowledge management endeavors do not seem to have rigorous and comprehensive knowledge management methodologies, tools, and techniques. One technique that can greatly aid the knowledge management field can be borrowed from the concept mapping community, namely the use of knowledge maps. This chapter will discuss the role of knowledge mapping for improving knowledge management projects, and the specific use of a tool called WisdomBuilder to aid in the creation of the knowledge maps.

INTRODUCTION

Knowledge management is one of the emerging trends that is striving to give organizations a sustainable competitive edge. Knowledge management is the process of creating value from an organization's intangible assets. Specifically, it deals with how best to capture, secure, distribute, coordinate, retrieve, store, and manage knowledge assets so that the organization can best leverage its knowledge (and associated intellectual capital assets) internally and externally (Liebowitz, 1999, 2000; Liebowitz and Beckman, 1998).

Many organizations are applying knowledge management methods and practices. General Electric Company has GENet, a corporate intranet at GE, which

Previously Published in *Challenges of Information Technology Management in the 21st Century* edited by Mehdi Khosrow-Pour, Copyright © 2000, Idea Group Publishing.

provides the best and worst practices throughout GE. Hewlett Packard captures and leverages HP product knowledge for the Computer Products Organization dealer channel. The system became known as HP Network News (Lotus Notes-based). Reuters established an international case base which serves as a knowledge repository for their offices worldwide. The Reuter Global Case Base Project is one of the first projects to focus on building a knowledge base from expertise existing in many areas around the world. Knowledge is then distributed to multiple Reuter sites worldwide that need and want this knowledge. Skandia feels its knowledge management (KM) efforts reduced the startup time for opening a corporate office in Mexico from 7 years to 6 months. Steelcase cites an upswing in patent applications and a threefold increase in productivity due to their KM efforts. Canadian Imperial Bank of Commerce (CIBC) established a Leadership Centre to provide the organization with systematic practices for the generation and renewal of tacit knowledge and intellectual capital. CIBC is measuring the flow of knowledge from people (new ideas generated and implemented) to structures (new products introduced) to customers (% of income from new revenue streams). The list continues of how organizations are now trying to practice knowledge management and be competitive in the marketplace.

An important element of knowledge management is knowledge reuse and the development of corporate memories. Knowledge reuse provides for the capture and reapplication of knowledge artifacts (episodes in memory, stories, relationships, experiences, rules of thumb, and other forms of knowledge acquired by individuals or groups). It relies as much on the use of negative experiences, flawed reasoning, or wrong answers as on correct results. Much of the knowledge reuse is predicated on the construction of knowledge repositories or corporate memories. Some guidelines that have been suggested are: It should be easy for individual workers to access the knowledge in the corporate memory to facilitate individual learning from a combination of sources; it should be easy for workers to determine which co-workers could have the knowledge needed for a particular activity; it should be easy for workers to decide which of the co-workers would be interested in a lesson learned; it should be easy (and rewarding) for a worker to submit a lesson learned to the corporate memory; there should be well-defined criteria for deciding if something is a lesson learned, how it should be formulated, and where it should be stored; there should be mechanisms for keeping the corporate memory consistent; the corporate memory should have a facility to distribute a newly asserted piece of knowledge to workers who need that knowledge.

In order to help create these knowledge repositories and corporate memories, a "knowledge mapping" should be conducted. According to Wiig (1993), knowledge mapping:

- is used to develop conceptual maps as hierarchies or nets;
- may support knowledge scripting and profiling, basic knowledge analysis, etc.;
- provides highly developed procedures to elicit and document conceptual maps from knowledge workers, particularly experts and masters;
- analysis is based on interactive work session/interviews and self-elicitations;
- may rely upon critical knowledge function analysis to identify areas of interest; and
- is a broad knowledge acquisition methodology.

At Monsanto Company, a leading manufacturing and engineering international firm, they have developed a Knowledge Management Architecture (KMA). It includes a learning map that identifies questions answered and resulting decisions made, an information map that specifies the kind of information that users need, and a knowledge map that explains what users do with specific information (conversion of information to insight or knowledge).

KNOWLEDGE MAPPING

According to Jan Lanzing (1997) at the University of Twente, concept mapping is a technique for representing knowledge in graphs. Knowledge graphs are networks of concepts. Networks consist of nodes (points/vertices) and links (arcs/ edges). Nodes represent concepts and links represent the relations between concepts. Lanzing (1997) further explains that concepts and sometimes links are labeled. Links can be non-, uni-, or bi-directional. Concepts and links may be categorized, they can be simply associative, specified, or divided in categories such as causal and temporal relations. Recent research by McDonald and Stevenson (1999) has showed that navigation was best with a spatial map, whereas learning was best with a conceptual map.

Typically, concept mapping is performed for several purposes (Lanzing, 1997):

- to generate ideas (brainstorming, etc.);
- to design a complex structure (long texts, hypermedia, large web sites, etc.);
- to communicate complex ideas;
- to aid learning by explicitly integrating new and old knowledge; and
- to assess understanding or diagnose misunderstanding.

The idea of *knowledge maps* and *knowledge mapping* in the knowledge management field can be analogous to the use of concept maps and concept mapping. According to Wright (1993), a knowledge map is an interactive, open system for dialogue that defines, organizes, and builds on the intuitive, structured and procedural knowledge used to explore and solve problems. It is an active technique for making contextual knowledge representable, explicit and transferable to others. In knowledge management terms, knowledge mapping relates to conceptual mapping in a very direct way. Specifically, the objective of knowledge mapping is to develop a network structure that represents concepts and their associated relationships in order to identify existing knowledge in the organization (in a well-defined area) and determine where the gaps are in the organization's knowledge base as it evolves into a learning organization.

At Texas Christian University (Newbern and Dansereau, 1993), a knowledge mapping system has been developed. They view a knowledge map as a two-dimensional diagram which conveys multiple relationships between concepts using nodes, links, and spatial configuration.

The link labels for the knowledge maps are:

	NAME	SYMBOL
Descriptive Relationships:	CHARACTERISTIC	C—>
	PART	P—>
	TYPE	T—>
Dynamic Relationships:	INFLUENCES	I—>
	LEADS TO	L—>
	NEXT	N—>
Instructional Relationships:	ANALOGY	A—>
	SIDE REMARK	S—>
	EXAMPLE	E—>

Spatial configurations of the knowledge maps could be in hierarchies, clusters, or chains. Knowledge maps can also take the form of overview maps, detail maps, and summary maps. Newbern and Dansereau (1993) developed a relationship-guided search to generate a knowledge map:

A. Make a list of important concepts or main ideas. Save this Concept List.
B. Pick one concept as a starting node for the map. Put the node in a central location on the paper.
C. Ask the following questions and draw the links on the map. Be sure to label the links before you move on.
   1.   Can this node be broken down into different types? (Descriptive link label=T)
   2.   What are the characteristics of each type? (Static link label=C)
   3.   What are the important parts of each type? (Static link label=P)
   4.   What are the characteristics of each part? (Static link label=C)
   5.   What led to the starting node? (Dynamic link label=L)

6. What does the starting node lead to? (Dynamic link label=L)
7. Which things influence the starting node? (Dynamic link label=I)
8. What does the starting node influence? (Dynamic link label=I)
9. What happens next, or what does this lead to? (Dynamic link label=N/L)
    Elaborate the map by using analogy links or example links.
D. Pick a new node from the list to start a new map by repeating step C.
E. As you end the session, review the maps and include any instructional nodes (side comments, definitions, or analogies).

These nodes and linkage connections in a knowledge map may be analogous to the activation of those same ideas in the expert's memory (Wiig, 1993).

To assist in developing these knowledge maps, various knowledge mapping tools are being developed. Some examples include The Brain and WisdomBuilder. The Brain, by Natrificial Software Technologies (whose Version 1.5 can be downloaded from the web site—www.thebrain.com), is a tool to help visualize and express valuable relationships between your information and knowledge. Another tool to aid in the knowledge mapping development and analysis is WisdomBuilder, by WisdomBuilder Inc. (*www.wisdombuilder.com*; Liebowitz (1999)).

Through the analysis and reporting stages of WisdomBuilder (1998), the «Connections» tab allows the user to find all of the paths in the knowledge repository between any two category items. The Paths screen in WisdomBuilder consists of the display area where icons representing category items and links representing the relationships between the category items are displayed. The relationship lines are color-coded to indicate the most direct link (red), the longest link (black), and the intermediate lengths (blue). The Link Notebook tab in WisdomBuilder provides an interface to an optional data visualization package, Link Notebook, produced by i2, Inc.

CREATING KNOWLEDGE MAPS FOR CATEGORIZING KNOWLEDGE MANAGEMENT TOOLS USING WISDOMBUILDER

In the "Knowledge Management and Knowledge Organizations" course, taught in the Spring 1999 semester in the Department of Information Systems at the University of Maryland-Baltimore County, students were asked to identify, classify, and categorize existing knowledge management tools and use WisdomBuilder to help create the knowledge maps for aiding in the identification and categorizing process.

WisdomBuilder uses a four stage process: Requirements, Collection, Analysis, and Reporting. In the requirements phase, one creates one's own cataloging structure based on how one needs to analyze the information. WisdomBuilder allows the partitioning of these requirements into separate databases (called Requirement Sets) so that one can either work in private or as part of a team.

Collection then follows whereby based on the recorded requirements, WisdomBuilder directs the searching of internal and external data sources for relevant information. Files can be selected individually or in groups for review. Once selected, the Review step then follows to review the selected files based on a personal dictionary created by the user.

After the Collection phase, the next stage is Analysis. In the Analysis phase, the collected information is analyzed, compared, related, and understood in terms of the requirements. During the Analysis phase, WisdomBuilder retrieves the original Research Items through any of its related items (Interest List) found during the scanning performed in the Collection phase. Equally important, WisdomBuilder allows one to create relationships between any of the 7 default categories (Research, Requirements, People, Organizations, Places, Events, and Products) to capture one's own knowledge and analysis results

The Link Notebook tab in WisdomBuilder provides an interface to Link Notebook, produced by i2, Inc. WisdomBuilder, through the requirements and information that have been developed, collected, and analyzed, will then use a proprietary artificial intelligence algorithm to develop the knowledge map indicating the relationships that can be inferred between the nodes or objects. Figure 1 shows an example of determining possible criminal relationships using WisdomBuilder.

SUMMARY

Developing knowledge maps as part of a knowledge management methodology has similarities to the conceptual mapping community. Typically, a knowledge map is created as part of a knowledge audit. Tools, like WisdomBuilder, can be used to help represent, organize, and structure knowledge via a knowledge mapping capability.

REFERENCES

Lansing, J. (1997). The Concept Mapping Homepage, University of Twente, The Netherlands, www.to.utwente.nl/user/ism/lanzing/cm_home.htm.

Liebowitz, J. (Ed.) (1999). *The Knowledge Management Handbook*, Boca Raton, FL: CRC Press.

Liebowitz, J. (2000). *Building Organizational Intelligence : A Knowledge Management Primer*, Boca Raton, FL: CRC Press.

Liebowitz, J. and Beckman, T. (1998). *Knowledge Organizations: What Every Manager Should Know*, Boca Raton, FL: CRC Press/St. Lucie Press.

McDonald, S. and Stevenson, R. (1999). Spatial Versus Conceptual Maps as Learning Tools in Hypertext, *Journal of Educational Multimedia and Hypermedia*, 8(1), AACE, Charlottesville, VA.

Newbern, D. and Dansereau, D. (1993). Knowledge Maps for Knowledge Management, in K. Wiig (Ed.), *Knowledge Management Methods*, Arlington, TX: Schema Press.

Wiig, K. (1993). *Knowledge Management Methods*, Arlington, TX: Schema Press.

WisdomBuilder, Inc. (1998). Getting Started With the Desktop Edition of WisdomBuilder, Columbia, Maryland.

Wright, R. (1993). An Approach to Knowledge Acquisition, Transfer, and Application in Landscape Architecture, University of Toronto, Canada, www.clr.toronto.edu/PAPERS/kmap.html.

Chapter 4

Knowledge Management System: A Case Study of RDCIS Laboratories

R.K. Jha, K.K. Mallik, and R.N. Mukherjee
Steel Authority of India Limited, India

Knowledge Management System, with its database consisting of details of equipment capability, test methods, references and expertise of individuals is introduced in RDCIS laboratories through existing wide spread LAN on windows NT platform. Being a R&D organisation, both codification and personalisation strategies were adopted carefully to reuse and share the knowledge efficiently. This involves capturing of inherent knowledge and storing it in a web based hyperlinked information system so that it can be retrieved whenever and wherever needed. A two layer K M platform, based on Distributed interNetApplications of Microsoft has been designed and implemented successfully for this purpose. Significant improvement has been noticed in effective utilisation of equipment potential through systematic approach of knowledge sharing beside continuous enrichment of data bank.

INTRODUCTION

In today's fast changing global market, success is no longer tied to the traditional inputs of labour, capital or land. The new critical resource is inside the minds of employees known as **Knowledge**. The concept of knowledge management is essentially to capture the inherent learning locked inside human brain and convert it to explicit knowledge,[1] which can be reused in future easily.

Previously Published in *Challenges of Information Technology Management in the 21st Century* edited by Mehdi Khosrow-Pour, Copyright © 2000, Idea Group Publishing.

The Research & Development Centre for Iron and Steel (RDCIS), a corporate R&D unit of Steel Authority of India Limited (SAIL), is equipped with more than 350 advanced scientific and analytical equipment with 5 pilot facilities under 15 major laboratories. These equipment encompasses the entire spectrum of diagnostic and research tools, from testing of raw materials to finished steel products. RDCIS is a pioneer in selecting, developing, adapting and implementing cost-effective iron and steel making technologies. The research activities at RDCIS are broadly divided into four technology areas such as Iron, Steel, Product and Automation. All these areas share laboratory equipment and facilities which are diverse in nature for carrying out experiments. Therefore, it calls for an appropriate Knowledge Management System (KMS) for maximising utilisation of these equipment and retaining the knowledge & expertise gained in a systematic manner so that it would benefit the organisation in the long run.

FOUNDATION OF KNOWLEDGE MANAGEMENT SYSTEM

The main purpose of KMS in RDCIS was to codify, store and disseminate information about laboratory equipment facilities and support sharing of knowledge resources in respective fields which have been built through years of R & D experience. Both codification and personalisation[2] strategies were adopted in designing the basic structure of KMS. In codification strategy the knowledge or information is codified using standard document preparation software and stored in databases, where it can be accessed and used easily by anyone in the organisation, whereas in personalisation strategy, the knowledge is closely tied to the person who developed it and is shared mainly through direct person-to-person contacts. Merits and demerits of these strategies were carefully examined before designing the KMS model and has been accomplished through a sequence of activities which encompasses:

- Identification / selection of laboratory equipment
- Building of knowledge database in respective areas
- Procedure for data capture and packaging
- Selection of methodology for sharing and transfer of data
- Building of KM platform and services
- Measurement of success and failure of KMS

Identification / Selection of Laboratory Equipment

Laboratory equipment were identified by considering the nature of research activities pursued at RDCIS. These were classified under six major categories such as charterisation of raw material, iron and steel making technology, testing and evaluation of steel product attributes, process automation and software development, application engineering, pollution and environmental study. Some of the important equipment under above categories were spiral classifier, pneumatic floatation unit, fisher coal analyser, giesseler plastometer, pilot coke oven, 100/300 kg induction furnace, high temperature viscometer, C-S analyser, O-N analyser, gas chromatograph, x-ray fluorescence spectrometer, optical emission spectrometer, scanning auger micro probe, electron probe micro analyser, scanning electron microscope, transmission electron microscope, x-ray diffractometer, image and particle size analyser, PLC and micro-processor development laboratory, computer networking and software development laboratory etc.

Building of Knowledge Database

Teams of in-house experts were engagged to prepare database on accumulated knowledge of R&D experience. This included development of new product and process, special test methods involving sophisticated scientific and analytical equipment, noteworthy results of innovation, development of new/useful application program, development of new instrument /equipment, automation of process equipment etc. As the building of knowledge database was a continuous process, researchers were continuously encouraged to contribute through a standard procedure. Each contribution is examined and suitably modified before being stored in KM database. Additionally, a directory of experts from various academic and R&D institutions was maintained for person to person sharing of high level tacit knowledge in respective fields.

Data Capture and Packaging

Information about laboratory equipment were compiled through a standard format and stored in KM database. This included primary capability of equipment, its basic function, list of application programs, sample details, special test methods & pre-requisites and finally results & references. Data compilation was carried out in Hyper Text Markup Language (HTML)[3] format so that linking with other details could be made possible. A typical example of data capture format is shown in Figure 1.

Methodology for Sharing and Transfer of Data

Laboratory equipment facilities covering four major technology areas such as Iron, Steel, Product and Automation, constitute major chunk of useful information in KM database. Each area consists of several small functional group work in tandem to meet several organisational goals were interconnected through a LAN system. Codified information were essentially shared among the groups through web services. Besides there were other popular services in which data transfer

Figure 1: Data capture form for equipment details in HTML format.

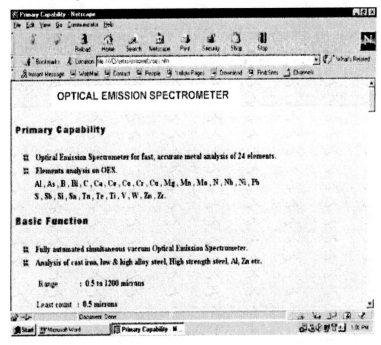

Figure 2: K M network showing interconnected functional laboratories of RDCIS

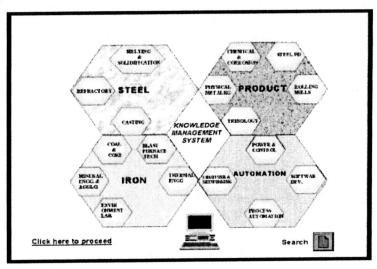

was managed efficiently. Figure 2 shows basic structure of KM network where large cache of documents was searched through popular search engines allowing people to find and use the documents easily.

Figure 3: Homepage of Knowledge Management System developed in Frontpage 98.

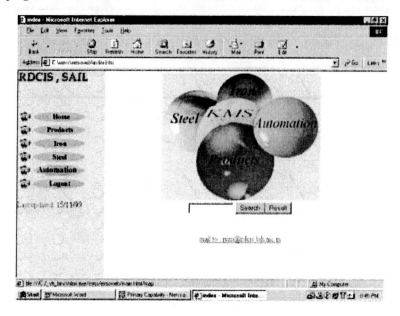

Building of K M Platform & Services

The existing corporate wide computer LAN system was used additionally as KM network. A two-tier KM platform has been designed which was based on Distributed interNet Applications Architecture (DNA)[4] of Microsoft. The KM platform provides System Service, built on Windows NT / Workstation and Knowledge Service built with Backoffice components.

System Services provide web services, directory services, security, communications, distributed transaction management and network administration tools. It essentially consists of Windows NT 4.0 server with the NT 4.0 option pack, which includes Internet Information Server 4.0, Microsoft Transaction Server 2.0, Microsoft Message Queue Server 1.0, and Routing & Remote Access Server.

Knowledge Services facilitate all the primary goals of knowledge management through a set of services such as search & retrieval, analysis, collaboration, workflow, data management etc. Navigation of KM database was made relatively simple through the homepages of different areas where several common KM scenarios in the form of application templates and Frequently Asked Questions (FAQ) - Answers has been formulated. Figure 3 shows the homepage of KM system linking four functional areas developed in MS frontpage98. A special directory of experts in each area has been created which can be scanned to find out previous contribution on a specific topic. These experts can be consulted directly by e-mail, telephone or fax. for solving problems.

Measurement of Success and Failure of KMS

The success of any KM system depends heavily on people who use it, and obviously people need incentives to participate in the knowledge sharing process[5]. Firstly, in RDCIS access to KMS has been made very simple and people were encouraged to contribute in their areas of specialisation. The efforts of individuals were recognised through citation and award. The KM system administrator, besides managing the database and the network, monitors frequency of visit to each site by different user groups and generate a weekly report. This report indicates that on an average each site is visited at least twice a week, which is quite good for a new KM system. Person-to-person high quality information sharing often results in good understanding of a technological problem and outcome of such exercise lead to development of new product/process, filing of patents or publications. These activities are highly recognised in RDCIS, so that it motivates others.

RESULTS & DISCUSSIONS

Introduction of KM system in an R&D organisation is much more challenging compared to a consulting or a manufacturing firm because of its wide area of activities, with varied interest and expertise among the people. Hence, it calls for appropriate selection of KM strategy to capture vast pool of knowledge and develop a system to retain the same in a systematic manner that would benefit the organisation. KM system at RDCIS, provide detailed information about each equipment vis-à-vis competing technique available in the laboratory, which helps in selection and judicious use of equipment potential for undertaking a metallurgical investigation. For example, there are several equipment for elemental analysis of steel sample namely X-ray Fluorescence Spectrometer (XRF), Spark Optical Emission Spectrometer (OES), Inductively Coupled Plasma (ICP), Mass Spectrometer ICP, Wet Chemistry, Atomic Absorption Spectrometer (AAS) etc. A user can easily retrieve all the important information of equipment such as accuracy level, type of sample required, analysis time (slow/fast), equipment availability etc. from KMS to decide which equipment would be most suitable for a specific test. Additionally, several case studies on metallurgical investigations were compiled where various equipment and facilities such as chemical analysis through OES, optical microscopy, hardness, tensile, charpy , high cycle fatigue tests were used for failure analysis of steel samples. These knowledge can be re-used by the organisation in future and stored as white papers.

Although, concept of knowledge management can be applied to all the areas of activity in RDCIS, to begin with it was limited to R&D laboratories. Some of the immediate benefits of KM implementations were as follows:

- Systematic approach of knowledge sharing brought visibility among the workers
- Dissemination of equipment capabilities leading to full exploitation of equipment potential
- Curtain raiser of laboratory facility, helped the users to come up with specific test request
- Encouraged innovation - finding and nurturing new ideas, and bringing people together for brainstorming & collaboration
- Access to manufacturer application expertise through Internet

CONCLUSION

No such system so far been developed that can capture the often hidden or tacit insight of employees and convert them into specific, actionable know-how that can be transferred to others. The basic purpose of KM was to capture and express expertise in a way that can be easily accessed and used by others. In RDCIS, KM system has been introduced in its well-equipped laboratories using existing computer LAN with a minimum expenditure. There is further scope for improvement with regard to assimilation of new technologies in various fields and codify them for reuse. This requires meticulous planning and execution with some higher level of IT inputs that will reduce cost in the long run and thus making it an essential tool for any research laboratory.

ACKNOWLEDGEMENT

The authors are grateful to the management of R&D Centre for Iron & Steel, SAIL for support and guidance in pursuing the project. The help extended by numerous colleagues for creation of KM database is gratefully acknowledged.

REFERENCES

Hansen, M. T., Nohria, N. and Tierney, T. (1999). What's your strategy for managing knowledge, p.106-116, *Harvard Business Review*, March-April.

Knowledge Management at Lotus (1998). Lotus Development Corporation.

Microsoft Knowledge Management website, http://www.microsoft.com/dns/km.

Nonaka, I. and Takeuchi, H. (1990). The knowledge creating company.

The Knowledge Management Consortium International website, http://www.km.org.

Chapter 5

Three Problems of Organizational Memory Information Systems Development

Fons Wijnhoven and Kees van Slooten
University of Twente, The Netherlands

Organizational memory information systems have a diversity of contents and may need a variety of information technologies. To cope with this diversity, OMIS requires specific development methodological guidelines. First the OMIS's objectives have to be stated in organizational functional requirements. Second, the conceptual OMIS model has to be defined at a high level in terms of organizational memory subsystems, and a diversity of modelling techniques are required to develop these subsystems. An OMIS also may profit more from a description of its technological and organizational infrastructure than from a business-led architecture definition. An OMIS needs clear role definitions of its stakeholders, an organizational (improvisational) change scenario, and a non-linear systems procurement scenario. Much of OMIS development happens in its use-stage. Consequently OMIS development has to cope with high levels of complexity, diversity and organizational and IT developments. Several suggestions for further research complete the paper.

Previously Published in *Challenges of Information Technology Management in the 21st Century* edited by Mehdi Khosrow-Pour, Copyright © 2000, Idea Group Publishing.

ORGANIZATIONAL MEMORY INFORMATION SYSTEMS

An OMIS is an information system containing all kinds of knowledge and information in some more or less coherent way (Stein & Zwass, 1995; Wijnhoven, 1999). Technically, an OMIS may be realized by several subsystems that may be technologically integrated in one package, or may be more loosely coupled by intranet links or intersubsystem interfaces (Gaines, 1994; Stein & Zwass, 1995; Wijnhoven, 1999). Personally, an OMIS provides support to a person's memory and helps to associate thoughts and information without any physical (IT or organizational) hindrance (Stein & Zwass, 1995). Therefore, OMIS-use has to cope well with human aspects of the OMIS-person interactions in its design and implementation. Organizationally, an OMIS is an extension of memory of organization members by electronic access and sharing of data and knowledge, and facilitating search and transfer of memory among organization members (Stein & Zwass, 1995; Wijnhoven, 1998). Like with any information system, an OMIS is expected to help the handling of certain information for specific organizational goals and functions.

OMIS is technologically not really new, but the concept is. The innovation is summarized in the following statements:

1. OMIS provides an *integration of organizational memory content* by easing the linking and transfer of information among people and different information systems. This issue is typical for OMIS as has been mentioned before by Stein & Zwass (1995), Wang (1999), and Weiser & Morisson (1998). It is not unique for OMIS, as different kinds of groupware (Enterprise Resource Planning systems, electronic commerce systems and group decision support systems) share this challenge. It is nevertheless a challenge.

2. OMIS handles a *diversity of memory contents* (varying from very formal to very informal, and from abstract to concrete; Boisot, 1998; Stein, 1995) in a seemingly united system. Because people are used to handle different kind of memory, with very different levels of abstraction and codification, an organizational memory system would not be a memory system if this would not be enabled (Weick, 1979). This means that systems with very diverse contents will require very different technologies (media) and content representation methodologies. Together with the requirement of integration this makes OMIS development very complex.

3. A memory has two features that an OMIS should try to emulate to be effective in memory processes: (1) much of a person's memory is personal and not overt, and (2) it is constantly changing as a consequence of learning. For OMIS this implies that it should be as close as possible to the user's mind and support

learning. We introduce the term "*closeness*" here to refer to the proximity of a user's memory and the OMIS. It is obviously true that this is hard to realize. Integration, diversity and closeness are three big challenges for information management in the context of OMIS.

This chapter will deliver specific methodological insights for coping with the integration, diversity and closeness challenges of OMIS. As such, this paper fills in a design methodological link between conceptual OMIS papers (Stein & Zwass, 1995; Wang, 1999), cases studies (e.g., Weiser & Morrison, 1998, on project memories), and organizational change oriented studies (Orlikowski & Hofman, 1997; Wijnhoven, 1999). This paper will treat these three OMIS challenges theoretically and will further define problems of OMIS development.

INTEGRATION OF MEMORY RESOURCES

An OMIS contributes to the goals of the context where it is applied. In this sense OMIS content might contribute to the following organizational functions: integration, adaptation to the organizational environment, goal attainment, and pattern maintenance or cohesiveness of a social system (Stein & Zwass, 1995). These functions, according to Stein and Zwass, require four types of OMIS subsystems. The integrative subsystem must provide multilocal and instantaneous access to shared information. This requires systems that integrate memory over time and space. The adaptive subsystem includes boundary-spanning systems to recognize, capture, organize, and distribute memory about the environment to the appropriate organizational actors. The goal attainment subsystem assists organizational actors in planning and control by templates of the context-plan-result nature, expert planning knowledge, evaluation models, and company performance data. The emphasis of the pattern maintenance subsystem is on the human resources. "Pattern" pertains to the attitudes, values, norms of members of the organization, personal routines, and personal knowledge. Effective organizations "maintain" values, attitudes, and norms that contribute to corporate cohesion and morale. Systems for this function could contain the work history of individuals, with emphasis on project descriptions, capabilities, skills, and aspirations, training programs, and systems for the preservation of organizational protocols and the values implicit in them.

For each of these subsystems there are several software products on the marketplace. Several problems of realizing these subsystems however still exist. A first problem is how to prioritize and schedule the OMIS subsystem creating projects. Second, an organization may have to understand what it really needs and what is infeasible for them. This means that depending on an organization's conditions the development of a specific OMIS subsystem may not make much sense, and that the other three subsystems should be developed in a specific sequence. Finally, an organization may have to decide on the possible linkages among the subsystems. In some cases everything may be well developed in one software environment, and in other cases this is not feasible (e.g., Lotus Notes will not allow to develop an expert system in its own environment). It may also be that linking data of a finance group and an operational management group may go into conflict with certain administrative rules.

The four organizational requirements of an OMIS may help to define a specific OMIS-project. What project is selected at a certain period of time is the result of balancing priorities, limited resources and capabilities. An extra complication, like in any information systems planning, is the shifting of goals (functions pursuited) and organizational learning during the project (leading to improved insights in needs and solutions). To start OMIS development, however, it is required to have some concrete objectives within a domain that is clearly supported by specific users, the management, and IS-professionals (Damsgaard & Scheepers, 1999). Like organizational memory itself, the bottom up development is most fundamental and top down definitions only give superstructural (ideological and motivational) guidance (cf. Wijnhoven, 1999). These initiative domains may be for instance project groups (cf. Weiser & Morrison, 1998), departments and social groups (Anand, Manz & Glick, 1998), social networks (Harvey & Smith, 1996), and sales & service groups (Quinn, 1992). Identifying an initiative group may also be based on a core competence policy definition, but generally speaking a top down starting up of these groups is difficult because many OMIS projects failed because the memory content owners were not ready for it (Hansen et al, 1999). Because much of the memory is tacit and personal (Nonaka & Takeuchi, 1995), and knowledge-intensive business domains are hard to define explicitly (Mintzberg, 1983), OMIS development without explicit leadership of the memory content owners is mostly not feasible.

Organizational memories have very diverse information and knowledge contents. Information consists of *concrete* registrations of events and thoughts, whereas knowledge consists of the more *abstract* explanations, predictions or technologies. As has been stated by Nonaka & Takeuchi (1995) and many others, these memory elements may be *tacit* or *explicit*. Tacit knowledge and information consists of feelings, uncertain statements, non-scientific beliefs, often also non-expressed. Explicit knowledge and information consists for instance of defined rules of handling problems (technology), databases, optimization routines and models. These diverse types of memory elements require different types of information systems and different types of modelling (Boisot, 1998; Nilsson et al, 1999; Shariq, 1998). We classify some existing methods and techniques for systems design along these two dimensions, so that the reader may apply Table 1 as a selection device for method engineering.

Table 1: Dimensions and elements of the OMIS Infrastructure. The greater the representation of these items, the higher the OMIS infrastructure level Source: Wijnhoven, 1999.

Dimension	OMIS-infrastructure elements
Human infrastructure	IT experts' experience with OMIS development IT experts' experience with type of relevant scenario Users' experience with IS development involvemen Users' general knowledge of relevant IT components and services Managers' experience with IS development projects Management of the costs and benefits
Omis IT components	Use of one or more of the following information technologies for OMIS purposes: databases, expert systems, decision support and modelbases, groupware, internet applications and sites Technological linkages among components of OMIS
IT services	Communications Management Management of OMIS-relevant applications Data management of the whole OMIS Standards Management User support (including education) Services Management Security Management IT R&D

The following lessons, deviating from traditional IS development, are found regarding the integration aspect.

1. OMIS must be ex ante evaluated with respect to their organizational function. This also specifies requirements for OMIS subsystems.
2. OMIS often develop from bottom up initiatives and some direction provided by superstructure statements.
3. OMIS content is very diverse, which complicates the combination of all relevant content. Combining all content may be infeasible and possibly also not required depending on organizational rules of content sharing. The organizational function typology of Stein and Zwass is most valuable in reducing the complexity of OMIS development at the subsystem level and OMIS organization.
4. An OMIS requires a diversity of methods and techniques for the design of its subsystems, depending on the abstractness and codification level of its memory contents.

Table 2: Some examples of methods for OMIS subsystem design

Knowledge/-abstract	Ethnomethodology for process analysis (cf. Suchman, 1987). Semantic analysis for conversation analysis (cf. Stamper et al 1988).	Model base design (cf. Turban, 1995). Workflow optimization routine modelling (cf. Scheer, 1998). BPR (cf. Davenport & Short, 1990). Expert system design (e.g. KADS) (cf. Tansley & Hayball, 1995; Turban, 1995; Kerr, 1991).
Information/-concrete	Flat files (no methodology). Doc systems with associative linking of docs (hypertext systems) (cf. Conklin, 1987).	Database design (cf. McFadden & Hoffer, 1994). Doc systems with firm structure (library systems) (Barthès, 1994; Gaines, 1994).
	Uncodified memory/Tacit knowledge	*Codified memory/explicit knowledge*

COPING WITH DIVERSITY

Many types of IT-components exist that can help in realizing OMIS. Basic in a classification of these is the extent to which they store and process memory, versus the extent to which they only handle information about memory (the real memory than is stored on another medium, e.g., paper or in a person's head) (Hansen et al, 1999). OMIS may require several IT-components to be integrated to an open memory infrastructure. This infrastructure is like a "jigsaw puzzle" of loosely coupled components (Gaines, 1994) because that is the way the individual major sub-components (hypermedia, databases, Group-Ware, etc.) may be designed, implemented and used.

Following Broadbent et al. (1996) IT infrastructure is the basic IT-capability (technical as well as human) that is shared in any given organization. The basis of this infrastructure is the IT components, such as computers and communication technology. Superimposed on these components is a second component set containing a set of shared services for the running of effective applications, namely (1) Communication management (networks), (2) Application management, (3) Data management, (4) Management of standards, (5) IT education management, (6) Services management, (7) Security and (8) IT R&D. The IT components are employed in useful services via the application of the human IT infrastructure components: knowledge, skills and experience, time, and problem-solving tools.

The OMIS-infrastructure maturity thus has three types of components: human infrastructure with respect to OMIS development, IT components, and IT services. Table 2 lists some typical OMIS-infrastructure elements.

The development of this IT capability will not go over a fortnight, and needs a clear longer term ambition statement, called the superstructure (Wijnhoven, 1999) (cf., Ang et al., 1997, for an example in an insurance company).

The following consequences in deviation from traditional IS development exist in the context of managing OMIS technological diversity:

1. With respects to skills, the information systems experts in the OMIS context should be able to handle a diversity of technologies.
2. With respect to services high demands are needed to realize the knowledge sharing, the security, the user support for OMIS.
3. With respect to OMIS IT components, a very high diversity of software will need to be managed.

CLOSENESS

According to Stein (1995) a typical characteristic of any memory is the disjunction of its creation and its use. "With memories, the coupling between sender and receiver is weak because transmission is one-way and temporal distance is significant (Stein, 1995, p. 22)." This problem may be weak when the memory content can be defined unambiguously and its meaning may be very stable through time. This is the era where formal knowledge elicitation may be most effective (e.g. in applications in natural sciences and some technological applications). Much memory content is however difficult to define unambiguously (particularly when tacit) and may change rapidly as a consequence of learning (e.g., in very innovative fields) or changes in the represented objects (e.g., in very highly competitive environments). These last three situations may require the OMIS content to change frequently. If they are not able to do so, they will quickly loose relevance for what people really think (closeness reduction). As a consequence it may be difficult to predict information requirements for many OMIS subsystems and the development process may extend over the user stage of the system (cf., Käkölä & Koota, 1999; Stein & Zwass, 1995; Wijnhoven, 1999). Consequently, the development process may need to deviate from the commonly used business driven scenarios. The business driven scenario (cf., Earl, 1993) first wants to articulate objectives and tasks for an information system, and from there proceed with the steps of analyzing and modelling of information needs, defining the hardware and software requirements and finally install and deliver the system to the users (possibly with some additional training). A clear workbreakdown structure is typical for the business driven scenario and clear deliverables and end terms for the project are defined.

Analysis of content needs, especially in case of OMIS, might be hard, because large volumes of memory are tacit. Especially important in this respect is that in the use stage, and not earlier, people might discover the possibilities and real objectives of OMIS. The IT architecture might be difficult to define, because OMIS developments might take many years and will possibly be never completed. Often, many choices and activities might emerge spontaneously by users who want to explore opportunities of a certain technology. Obviously, an OMIS development scenario needs an organizational change scenario emphasizing improvisation and learning instead of planned (anticipated) change (cf. Neilson, 1997; Orlikowski & Hofman, 1997). Orlikowski & Hofman distinguish between improvisational processes: emergent change and opportunity-based change. Emergent changes arise spontaneously from local innovation and are not originally anticipated or intended. An example is the installation of email intentionally to facilitate communication, but allowing the creation of grapevines and the dissimination of rumors. Opportunity-based changes are changes that are not anticipated but are introduced purposefully and intentionally during the change process in response to an unexpected opportunity, event, or breakdown. An example is that after installation of WWW for a company, people start to explore WWW opportunities for internal knowledge sharing.

Besides of an organization change scenario, OMIS also requires a non-linear system procurement strategy. This non-linear procurement strategy may be of three types (Van Slooten & Schoonhoven, 1996):

1. Incremental development. Often the nucleus of the OMIS including one or more subsystems is developed first. After introducing that part of the system to the users, the development of another part is started immediately.

2. Stroke-wise development. After every development stroke, it is checked whether the developed subsystem prototype satisfies the expectations and requirements of the users. The required changes are implemented during the next development stroke. The whole system is made ready for use during a final development stroke.

3. Evolutionary development. During evolutionary development a complete system is developed, after which it is used. Based on experiences with the use of the system further development is undertaken, which means that the system evolves. Every version or release of the system is complete, which means that the user is provided with sufficient functionality for the time being. Only one delivery is planned for the current project, which is different from incremental development. A final number of releases may not be determined beforehand.

Because these non-linear scenarios are most important for OMIS and the creation of its closeness, they also imply other role definitions of people in the scenario. In the planned scenario, the goals and processes of the project will be clear and a project manager (supported by a champion) will be clearly leading throughout the whole development process. In non-planned scenarios, the responsibilities may shift during the process and different stake-holders (users, the management and the IT experts) might be leading.

Because an OMIS develops especially after its launch, one vital issue to be designed is the responsibilities for the maintenance and quality of the OMIS and its content. This explicitly links the memory elements to organizational functions that have main responsibility, permission to contribute, rights of being informed about the status of the OMIS content, and access to content. Maintenance requires extensive user involvement, the effective role of IS management thus may need redefinition and should especially include advocacy and facilitation (Markus & Benjamin, 1996; Wijnhoven, 1999). These capabilities may be scarce among IT-professionals and users might have insufficient time and priorities to deliver and maintain the memory. When the memory contents required of an OMIS are difficult to codify, the process will be strongly led by the memory owners and OMIS-users themselves, and the definition of deliverables will be hard as well. In case these requirements are easy to define, the project will be led by the management or information systems experts. In some cases IT-professionals will first create a sufficient infrastructure (e.g., office systems and Web environment) and after handling over this to the users will only facilitate effective use. In some cases these IT professionals therefore need advocacy qualities or the management will act as advocate of change (Markus & Benjamin, 1996). Also the knowledge management strategy of the organization may lead to given leading, advocate, facilitator, expert or follower roles to the three stakeholders. If a company follows a codification strategy of knowledge management (Hansen et al., 1999), the attempt will be to put as much knowledge of persons in person-independent systems. These requires the management as advocate and leader, the IT professionals as experts, and the users as followers. When following a personalization strategy, a firm may give the leading role to the users, the management as advocate (motivating the users to use the system) and facilitator (supplying money, computers, and support) and the IT people as facilitators who really understand the users requirements. Finally, the realization of these maintenance processes requires that the OMIS subsystems are transparant with respect to its content and have sufficient flexibility to change (Kakola & Koota, 1999).

As conclusions to closeness, the following consequences for OMIS are found:
1. Closeness requires an OMIS development scenario that is integrated in a broader organizational and technical change context. Consequently, besides of planned change also emergent and opportunity-based change need to be managed effectively.
2. Most of the development of the system occurs in its usage stage, by incremental, stroke-wise and evolutionary scenarios This complicates the exante definition of deliverables and end results of a project.
3. Creating closeness often requires intense user participation and leadership, and IT-professionals that want to advocate the system and facilitate its users. These capabilities may be scarce among IT experts and its management, and probably has high consequences for the training of leading people in OMIS development (Markus & Benjamin, 1996).

4. The evolutionary development of OMIS requires high transparancy, flexibility and maintainability of systems. The realization of these requirements is at an initial stage of development at the moment (Käkölä & Koota, 1999).

CONCLUSIONS ABOUT OMIS DEVELOPMENT

These insights about OMIS have lead to the following lessons for OMIS development:

- An important difference between OMIS and other types of information systems is OMIS' ambition for integrated systems. Integration must be attuned to the OMIS functions (integration, adaptation, goal attainment, and pattern maintenance). The complexity of this process may require a bottom up approach, initiated by an initiative group and possibly supported by a superstructure and infrastructure OMIS-policy.

- The diversity of the OMIS content requires applying different technologies and different analysis and design techniques. These techniques may have to be selected based on the codification and abstraction level of the contents. Additionally, however, these development activities require conceptual cohesion as far as organizationally required and technologically feasible.

- Because OMIS is so large and so closely related to an everyday aspect of human life (memories), it has to be carefully attuned to the organizational environment where it has to become part of. This means that special attention has to be paid to the organizational change aspects of OMIS development. This may require non-linear organization-IS development (improvisational) scenarios, and non-linear subsystem procurements (incremental, stroke-wise and evolutionary). Because OMIS is an organic part of an organization, it should be able to evolve with the developments of the organization. This requires role definitions among its users, IS professionals and the management, which may also change during the development process, and flexibility of the OMIS.

Despite these insights, much about OMIS development is still open for debate and this field also offers many opportunities for valuable research.

REFERENCES

Anand, V., Manz, C. C., and Glick, W. H. (1998). An organizational memory approach to information management. *Academy of Management Review*, 23(4): 796-809.

Ang, K.-T., Thong, J. Y. L., and Yap, C.-S. (1997). It Implementation Through the Lens of Organizational Learning: A Case Study of INSUROR. *Proceedings of the Eighteenth International Conference on Information Systems*. (December), Atlanta, Georgia: 331-348.

Barthès, J. A. (1994). Developing integrated object environments for building large knowledge-based systems. *International Journal of Human-Computer Studies*, 41: 33-58.

Boisot, M. H. (1998). *Knowledge Assets: Securing Competitive Advantage in the Information Economy*. New York: Oxford University Press.

Broadbent, M., Weill, P., O'Brien, T., & Siong Neo, B. (1996). Firm context and patterns of IT infrastructure capability. *Proceedings of the Seventeenth International Conference on Information Systems* (Cleveland Ohio, December): 174-194.

Conklin, J. (1987). Hypertext: An Introduction and Survey. *IEEE Computer*, 20(9): 17-20; 32-41.

Davenport, Th. H. & Short, J. E. (1990). The new Industrial Engineering: Information Technology and Business Process Redesign. *Sloan Management Review* (Summer): 11-27.

Earl, M. J. (1993). Experiences in strategic information systems planning. *MIS Quarterly*: (March): 1-24.

Gaines, B. R. (1994). Class library implementation of an open architecture knowledge support system. *International Journal of Human-Computer Studies,* 41: 59-107.

Harvey, C. F. & Smith, P. (1996). An Information System to improve Organisational memory. In J.D. Coelho et al. (eds.), *Proceedings of the 4th European Conference on Information Systems*, (Lisbon, June): 553-570.

Kerr, R. (1991). *Knowledge-Based Manufacturing Management: Applications of Artificial Intelligence to the Effective Management of Manufacturing Companies*. Sydney: Addison Wesley.

Markus, M.L., & Benjamin, R. I. (1996). Change agentry: the next IS frontier. *MIS Quarterly*, (December): 385-407.

McFadden, F.R. & Hoffer, J.A. (1994). *Modern database management* (4th ed.), Redwood City, CA: Benjamin/Cummings.

Mintzberg, H. (1983). *Structures in Fives: Designing Effective Organizations*. Englewood Cliffs, N.J.: Prentice-Hall.

Neilson, R. E. (1997). *Collaborative Technologies and Organizational Learning*. Hershey, PA: Idea Group.

Nilsson, A. G. (ed.) (1999). *Perspectives on business modelling: understanding and changing organisation*. Berlin: Springer.

Orlikowski, W. J. & Hofman, D. J. (1997). An improvisational model for change management: the case of groupware technologies. *Sloan Management Review* (Winter): 11-21.

Quinn, J. B. (1992). *Intelligent Enterprise: A Knowledge and Service Based Paradigm for Industry*. New York: The Free Press.

Rumbaugh, J. et al. (1991). Object-Oriented Modelling and Design. Englewood Cliffs N.J.: Prentice-Hall.

Scheer, A. W. (1998). *ARIS: Business Process Frameworks* (2nd ed.), Berlin: Springer.

Shariq, S. Z. (1999). Sense Making and artifacts: an exploration into the roles of tools in knowledge management. *Journal of Knowledge Management*, 2(2): 10-19.

Stamper, R., Althaus, K. & Backhouse, J. (1988). Measur: Method for Eliciting, Analysing and Specifying User Requirements. In T. Olle, A.A. Verrijn-Stuart & L. Bhabuta (eds.), *Computerized Assistance During the Information Systems Life Cycle*, pp. 67-115. Elsevier Publ.

Stein, E. W. (1995). Organizational memory: Review of concepts and recommendations for management. *International Journal of Information Management*, 15(2): 17-32.

Stein, E. W. & Zwass, V. (1995). Actualizing organizational memory with information systems. *Information Systems Research*, 6(2): 85-117.

Suchman, L. A. (1987). *Plans and situated actions : the problem of human-machine communication.* Cambridge [etc.]: Cambridge University Press.

Tansley, S. W. & Hayball, C. C. (1995). *Knowledge-Based Systems Analysis and Design-A KADS Developer's Handbook.* Sigart bulletin: a quarterly publication of the Special Interest Group on Artificial Intelligence, vol. 6.

Turban, E. (1995). *Decision Support and Expert Systems: Management Support Systems* (3rd ed.), Englewood Cliffs, N.J.: Prentice-Hall.

Van Slooten, K. (1996). Situated Method Engineering. *Information Resources Management Journal*, 9(3): 24-31.

Van Slooten, K. & Schoonhoven, B. (19960. Contingent Information Systems Development. *Journal of Systems and Software*, 33: 153-161.

Wang, Sh. (1999). Organizational Memory Information Systems: A Domain Analysis in the Object-Oriented Paradigm. *Information Resources Management Journal* (April-June): 26-35.

Weick, K. E. (1979). *The Social Psychology of Organizing.* Reading, MA: Addison-Wesley.

Weiser, M. & Morrison, J. (1998). Project memory: Information management for project teams. *Journal of Management Information Systems*, 14(4): 149-166.

Wijnhoven, F. (1998). Designing organizational memories: concept and method. *Journal of Organizational Computing and Electronic Commerce*, 8(1): 29-55.

Wijnhoven, F. (1999). Development scenarios for OMIS. *Journal of Management Information Systems*, 16(1): 121-146.

Chapter 6

An Empirical Study of Knowledge and Organizations

Andrew Doswell and Vivien Reid
Glasgow Caledonian University, Scotland

An empirical investigation into perceptions about the handling of knowledge in organisations. The findings are based on replies to a non-random postal questionnaire based survey. The respondents were the senior human resource management (HRM) and information technology (IT) specialists at the 60 largest Scottish companies (as measured by market capitalisation). The findings in the main confirm both ideas in the literature in general and the findings and conclusions from previous studies including Alavi, and Leidner (1999). In addition some new aspects are reported which can be construed as showing support for the idea of professional groupings holding onto knowledge and for the existence of ambivalence towards the emphasis placed on the role of IT in conducting KM.

INTRODUCTION

Bibliometric studies (Ruggles, 1998; Scarborough et al, 1999) show a considerable growth in knowledge management literature since the late 1980s. Although on simple reflection the fundamental importance of knowledge,

> "Every human activity, child-rearing, hunting, farming and crafts, no less than administration, research and government depends on the use and transmission of skills and knowledge." (Parker, 1994)

Previously Published in *Challenges of Information Technology Management in the 21st Century* edited by Mehdi Khosrow-Pour, Copyright © 2000, Idea Group Publishing.

and its attendant economic impact, "Knowledge is our most powerful engine of production" (Marshall, 1890) may be obvious, the study of knowledge as a business topic has been patchy and sporadic.

Until recently the only area of consistent knowledge work has been the development of copyright and patent law. This was conducted to protect some aspects of the exploitation of knowledge to help overcome some impediments to knowledge diffusion:

> "... the obstetrical forceps, introduced by a French Huguenot, William Chamberlen (c 1540-96), ... Chamberlen kept the instrument a family secret, passing it on to his son, Peter, who passed it on to his son, Peter (1601-83), who passed it onto his son Hugh (1630-1720). When called to a confinement, they supposedly hid the forceps m a box to preserve their trade secret..." (Porter, 1997: 232)

BACKGROUND AND LITERATURE REVIEW

A frequent starting point for a discussion of the business and economic importance of knowledge is Bell (1976) with his emphasis upon the growing importance of a scientific approach to knowledge discovery and the role IT has to play. Although Bell's work has been "indicted on a number of counts" (Blackler, Reed, and Whitaker, 1993) it retains its influence. The next well-recognised staging post is Drucker's vision (1989) of knowledge worker based organisations. There then starts what becomes an avalanche of texts dealing with knowledge and various knowledge related ideas such as "systems" and "learning organisations": Senge (1990), Nonaka (1991), Peters (1992), and Drucker (1993) leading to Swan's comment that *now* there is considerable consensus that 'knowledge' is an increasingly important business topic (1999).

Examination of the literature content shows immediately considerable confusion about what knowledge is and considerable debate over its relationship to data and information. This has provided (Godbout) "a challenge in semantics" with Starbuck noting "knowledge itself is almost as ambiguous an idea as value or importance, and it has many guises" (1992) and Alvesson commenting "knowledge easily becomes everything and nothing" (1992). But as well as confusion there is broad agreement on some issues.

First, whereas historically firms did not need to manage knowledge because there was a sufficient natural flow (Ruggles, 1998), now knowledge management is important because of factors including growing international competition, changing requirements of customers, and rapid economic changes (van der Spek, and de Hoog, 1994). Ruggles' argument echoes a comment of Tricker made 20 years earlier with respect to information that it *was* like sunlight to Victorian botanists, there or not there, but something about which nothing could be done (Tricker, 1982).

Second, a recurrent theme is of the difficulties of dealing with personal tacit knowledge and its transfer. For example if knowledge is personal and cannot be represented its transfer or sharing becomes problematic (Collins, 1997). Scarborough (1997: 202) summarises the knowledge based view literature of the firm as seeing knowledge as being overwhelmingly important, but recognising that there are different types of knowledge with different degrees of transferability, with especial difficulties being associated with tacit knowledge. If knowledge is personal it creates some difficulties for IT approaches as they need to be able to codify knowledge so that it can be handled by computer languages (such as Prolog), or applications (can chess be played without knowledge?), or in databases.

Third, there are motivation and cultural difficulties as well as technical problems. For the individual holding knowledge, the value of the knowledge decreases as more people have it, but organisationally it may be beneficial to have knowledge shared. There is evidence that in business settings where knowledge is thought to be highly important, highly individual financial reward may be practised (Robertson, 1999).

In summary, the attempts to manage knowledge have, it is widely accepted, caused contradictions to surface including:

1) the tension between personal tacit esoteric knowledge and its codification and publication (Schultze, 1998);

2) the contrasting views of knowledge as Cognitive or Community based (Newell et al., 1999); and

3) the real value of *further* knowledge acquisition as it may lead to increased ambiguity, uncertainty, and increased responsibility to use wisely (Schultze, 1998) all of which have costs.

The literature can be seen as containing three distinct strands: personal evangelic campaign and vision, empirical work based on case studies, empirical work based on surveys.

Although the evangelic strand may use anecdotal evidence of what is happening (see for example Hammer's original business process reengineering evangelism or Stewart's revealing of the practice of knowledge related activities) it is empirical work where practical experience might be expected to be reported on and analysed. In the case studies there is often an emphasis upon large firms of North American origin (for example, Wah, 1999). In this literature there is a strong emphasis upon computer technology and much of the material could be seen as re-labelled IS case studies of "how to introduce computer systems" with emphasis upon inter- and intra- nets. The survey based strand consists of two reported studies, Ernst and Young (undated), and Alavi and Leidner (1999).

For the Ernst and Young survey, 430 executives responded to "Twenty Questions on Knowledge in the Organization." The questions were divided into four major categories: The case for managing knowledge, the levers of KM, challenges to overcome, and gaining the knowledge advantage.

Alavi and Leidner's survey used a non-random sample of 109 participants (respondents included chief information officers, and information systems managers, as well as general executives) who were on an executive development programme conducted in July 1997. The participants were from twelve countries and from organisations with significant IT investments. The questionnaire contained 13 questions and consisted of short answer questions as well as multiple choices. A total of 50 usable responses were received, a response rate of 45.8 percent.

As a result of the literature review the authors decided to conduct some exploratory field work. The broad objective of the work was to investigate the extent to which some of the topics and themes evident in the literature could be detected empirically in organisations. Attention was to be focused upon ideas emerging from previous empirical work, particularly the two surveys identified.

METHODOLOGY

Empirical data can be gathered in a number of ways as discussed in many introductory texts on research methods. It was decided to obtain data from a variety of sources with a particular objective of investigating any variation in response due to contingent factors such as experience and organisational role of the respondent.

A schedule of questions was developed. As well as being original, the questions were adopted and adapted from the questionnaires already conducted or, in the case of Coakes and Sugden (undated), reported as being underway. Questions from existing sources were modified in particular in terms of format to give a standardised format. The main focus of original questions were concerned with various aspects of the respondents such as educational and work experience. These questions were asked in order to assist in any search for possible associations to reported individual attitudes to KM or to reported attitudes to organisational responses to KM.

The complete questionnaire was 7 pages long and, it was estimated could be completed in 10 minutes. The questionnaire was piloted using postgraduate students who were employed in various information or administrative roles in organisations, and then revised. The revised questionnaire was then trialled using contacts who provided work-experience placements for students from another information related postgraduate programme, and revised again in the light of these responses. All of the responses were of a minor nature. The newly revised questionnaire was then posted out, with reply-paid envelopes, to named senior HR and IT specialists. The names of individuals were identified by prior telephone contact. The individuals were selected from Scotland's 60 largest (by capitalisation) firms. A rich mixture of sectors was covered.

Firms in Scotland were chosen because it was hoped that a higher response rate might be achieved (because of the university's Scottish connexion) and because by using a Scottish base possible cultural differences in attitudes to KM might be seen.

Data was analysed in parallel and independently by the authors and consensus then reached, through discussion, upon its meaning.

RESULTS AND DISCUSSION

120 questionnaires were sent out in July and by mid-August 25 responses had been received representing 42% of the organisations in the survey without any reminders being sent out. Responses continued to be received through September to November as the paper was being drafted, these additional responses were scanned for evidence of obvious major disagreement with the ideas which had already been drawn – none were found.

Because of the number of areas questioned a significant amount of data was captured and can be interpreted in a variety of ways. The process of analysis and interpretation is on-going. For this work the focus is on the respondents' views of the importance of knowledge to their employing organisation, and how it is handled and used in that organisation.

The first questions discussed here were intended to gain a view of the organisation's operating circumstances and to see if there was any connexion to the perceived importance of knowledge.

Respondents were asked to assess the competitiveness of their market using a 1 (stable) to 7 (highly competitive) scale. The mean response was 5.8, with 63% of respondents rating competitiveness at 6 or higher. Although of course quite what the meaning of an answer such as "6" is to the question "How competitive is your market?" is subject to some vagueness, nonetheless clearly a majority of respondents considered their market to be very competitive. As this work is not reporting a longitudinal study it cannot be said that market competition has increased but clearly the well expounded concept in the literature of competition being an important factor [see for example Castells, 1996] has at least an echo in the experience of most respondents.

A second question examined attitudes to "information as an output". Using the same 1 (information is not an output) to 7 (information is an output) question format, the mean response was 5.7, with 67% recording an answer at 6 or higher, indicating a high level of agreement with the proposition. As shown in the table in the previous section there was a mixture of firms in the survey, some of which would not traditionally have been thought as being concerned with information as output. Again however in line with much of the literature, clearly many respondents considered that information is a major part of their output irrespective of their nominal industrial sector.

In response to questioning about the importance of specialised knowledge, there was even greater agreement. The mean response was 6.4, with 81% returning a 6 or higher. This kind of response again reflects the main body of the KM and related literature. Two interesting aspects emerged from further analysis. All the respondents who came from organisations considered to be in *stable* environments rated specialised knowledge as being very important. Intuitively one might have expected stable market conditions to generate a lack of importance in specialised knowledge. But one could generate a hypothesis of powerful professional groups generating, in their own interests (particularly of preserving the value of their knowledge and reducing the amount of new knowledge acquisition required), a stable market [Starbuck, 1992]. One respondent from an organisation reported as being in a highly competitive market saw specialised knowledge as being unimportant, this can be explained in terms of organisations dealing with commodity products and services where factors such as, for example, location may be much important than anything else.

Respondents were asked to identify the variation of level and depth of knowledge across the organisation. Clearly there must always be some variation in the knowledge possessed by individuals and the mean response was 4.8 (the scale mean being 4). As with the previous question further analysis showed that all the respondents who saw the variation in knowledge across the organisation as being high (rated as 6 or more) included all those from organisations which considered themselves to be in a stable market. This could also be explained in terms of a professional organisational elite. Additionally all those organisations where respondents saw information as *not* being an important part of the output also recorded high levels of knowledge variation across the organisation. In organisations which do not have significant information content in their output, no benefit is seen in distributing knowledge - organisations are concerned with efficiency of production not market responsiveness.

Related to knowledge variation across the organisation, is knowledge sharing and transfer. The difference between the degree to which it is believed that knowledge should be and is transferred (mean values) is 6.3 (85% rated 6 or higher) to 4.2 (10% rated 6 or higher). But as with almost any overall analysis there are exceptions. Although 90% of respondents considered there should be significantly more knowledge transfer, 10% thought either the degree of transfer was just right or that there was too much.

Respondents were asked to rate the importance of specialised knowledge in various organisational activities and areas. Using a 1 to 7 scale, the mean responses for the 8 areas divided into three categories as shown in Table 1:

Table 1

Mean value	Area
6.0	Competitors, computer information systems
5.6	Marketing, customer services, business partners
5.0	Internal activities, human resources, suppliers

These overall responses suggest a strong interest in expertise in competitors and computer information systems which, along with the middle ranking activities, are concerned with externalities whilst the areas concerned with internalities or agents who are, perhaps, seen as being dependent (suppliers) there is significantly less interest. These findings are similar to those of Alavi and Leidner, (1999).

Respondents were asked to assess how important People, Process, Technology, and Culture were in handling knowledge and to compare this with their assessment of how their organisation rated these factors were. The table of mean results show there is consistently a gap between what respondents think the importance is and how they consider the organisation values the same factors. The organisational valuation is always considered to be less than that which is "really" appropriate. But the gap is much less for technology than for the other factors. This seems to run counter to the response to the previous question where specialised knowledge in computer information systems is seen as being important. Apart from technology, the order of importance is the same for what respondents think "should be" and is, Table 2.

Table 2

	Respondents' view	Respondents' view of organisation's view	Difference
People	6.5	5.2	1.3
Process	6.3	4.8	1.5
Technology	5.9	5.3	0.6
Culture	5.9	4.4	1.5

Because of the suggestion of some dissonance between the answer to this question and the preceding one, further analysing was carried out, by categorising the respondents into those who consider the organisation response as: too much, just right, or too little. This analysis with the results in percentage values gives, as shown in Table 3 (Note, rows total to 100%).

Table 3

Company response is	Too much	Just right	Too little
People	5	20	75
Process	5	20	75
Technology	20	25	55
Culture	5	40	55

It is apparent that whilst in all cases a majority of respondents think the organisations' responses are too little. But in the case of technology a significant minority consider the organisation response to be excessive, with nearly half the respondents report the technology emphasis as being either to much or just right. Additionally, a large minority consider company response to Culture to be "just right." It is the area of people and process where a large majority of respondents think organisational response is inadequate.

Finally some general questions were asked about KM. Respondents were asked to assess knowledge could be better managed and whether only lip service was being paid to ideas of KM. As far as better KM management was concerned, the response was "Yes," but not overwhelmingly so. The mean response was 5.5, with 55% rated 6 or higher. No discernible association between the pattern of responses here and responses to any other question could be detected. With respect to only lip service being paid to the ideas of KM, respondents thought this was not the case but again the average response was not overwhelming: the mean was 4, with 45% rating a 3 or less. This could be interpreted as showing that respondents recognising that in spite of various failings, the respondents recognised that KM is difficult and that organisations where KM is said to be being practised are making a genuine attempt. Again there are respondents who disagree. For those who perceive that only lip service is being paid there is no clear pattern of association with other responses. Equally for those respondents who believe *strongly* that management is committed to KM there is also no clear pattern of association with their other responses.

CONCLUSIONS AND FUTURE RESEARCH

At this preliminary stage of reporting, the main ideas and themes in the literature are supported by the findings of this survey. These findings are from organisations outwith much of the literature, which tends to concentrate on very large, often North American based, companies. The evidence here suggests that concerns with KM are just as much evident in firms in a Scottish setting and covering much more than the classical area of professional service firms. Many of the findings correspond to those reported by Alavi and Leidner. This similarity may be reassuring but it does also prompt a question worth investigating. Do those respondents with more recent and higher qualifications respond more in line with the "accepted" views in the literature than others? And do they do this because they have been more exposed to current thinking? Are the perceptions and attitudes they report "true?" Although designed to assess this point the response rate for this survey is unfortunately insufficient to allow any sensible judgement to be made.

All the respondents who came from organisations considered to be in *stable* environments rated specialised knowledge as being very important. Initially one might have expected stable market conditions to generate a lack of importance in specialised knowledge. But powerful professional groups could generate, in their own interests, particularly of preserving the value of their knowledge and reducing the amount of new knowledge acquisition required (Starbuck, 1992), a stable market. Additionally organisations rated as having high knowledge variation (rated as 6 or more) included all those from organisations which considered themselves to be in a stable market. This could also be explained in terms of a professional organisational elite. Also all those organisations with information as *not* being an important part of the output also recorded high levels of knowledge variation across the organisation. Here apparently no benefit is seen in distributing knowledge. An image is generated of organisations concerned with efficiency of commodity production rather than market responsiveness. And this it seems can be applied even to organisations reported as being in a highly competitive market where specialised knowledge is not seen as being unimportant. Here again there are organisations dealing with commodity products and services where factors such as, for example, outlet location may be much important than anything else.

Whilst considering specialised knowledge in IT to be important, more so than other factors such as human resources for example, simultaneously a significant minority considered there to be excessive organisational "fixation" upon IT. This perhaps give some credence to Newell et al.'s (1999) suggestion of an IT versus Community model of knowledge, however it has to be noted that the total of respondents who reported either "too much" or "just right" amounts of effort focused upon technology and *culture* were the same. The areas of most concern for respondents were "people" and "process", this message carries echoes of business process re-engineering (BPR) concerns and underlines the danger of over emphasising a general concept of corporate culture.

This work is going to be continued by following up with respondents who have indicated willingness to provide further data. The concern with this aspect of the work will be to gain richer insights into the responses already provided. In the same vein of gaining a richer insight into the practice of KM, a longitudinal case study is planned.

REFERENCES

Alavi, M., and Leidner, D. L. (1999). Knowledge management systems: issues, challenges, and benefits, *Communications of the Association for Information Systems*, 1(7), February.

Alvesson, M. (1992). Leadership as social integrative action A study of a computer consultancy company, *Organisation studies*, 13(2), 185-209.

Blackler, F., Reed, M., and Whitaker, A. (1993). Editorial introduction: Knowledge workers and contemporary organizations, *Journal of Management Studies*, 30(6), 851- 862.

Coakes, E., and Sugden, G. undated, http://www.wmin.ac.uk/~coakese/knowledge/survey.

Castells, M. (1996). *The Rise of the Network Society*, Oxford: Blackwell

Collins, H. M. (1997). Humans, machines, and the structure of knowledge, In R. L. Ruggles (Ed.), *Knowledge Management Tools*.

Drucker, P. (1989). *The New Realities*, Butterworth-Heinemann.

Drucker, P. (1993). *Post-Capitalist Society*, Butterworth-Heinemann.

Ernst and Young LLP (undated). http://www.businessinnovation.ey.com/research/kowle/survey/survey.html.

Godbout, A. J. (undated). State of the KM art: Lessons learned from early adoptions of Knowledge Management, Technical Document No TD99-103, Godbout Martin Godbout & associates.

Marshall, A. (1890). Principles of Economics, quoted at the start of the Introduction of the documentation supporting the UK government's White Paper, Our competitive future: Building the knowledge driven economy, 1998, Cm 4176, London: HMSO.

Newell, S., Swan, J., Galliers, R. and Scarbrough, H. (1999). The intranet as a knowledge management tool? *Proceedings Information Resources Management Association International Conference*, May 16-19, 613- 619, Hershey, PA.

Nonaka, I. (1991). The knowledge-creating company. *Harvard Business Review*. November/December.

Parker, T. M. (1994). Information, power and the view from nowhere, 217. In L. Bud-Frierman (Ed.), *Information Acumen,* London: Routledge

Peters, T. (1992). *Liberation Management*, Macmillan,

Porter, R. (1997). *The Greatest Benefit to Mankind*, London: HarperCollins.

Robertson, M. (1999). Expert consulting: a case of managed autonomy, 13-23, in Scarborough and Swan.

Ruggles, R. L. (1997). *Knowledge Management Tools*, Boston, MA: Butterworth-Heinemann.

Ruggles, R. (1998). Why knowledge? Why now?, http:/www.businessinnovation. ey.com.

Scarbrough, H. (1997). Business process re-engineering & the knowledge-based view of the firm, 199 - 216, in *Proceedings of the business process track, British academy of management conference*, 8 -10 September.

Scarborough, H. and Swan, J. (eds.) (1999). Case studies in knowledge management, London: Institute of Personnel and Development.

Scarbrough, H., Swan, J. A. and Preston, J. (1999). Knowledge management: a literature review, London: Institute of Personnel and Development.

Schultze, U. (1998). Investigating the contradictions in knowledge management, *Proceedings of the IFIP conference on Information Systems*, December, 155-174, Helsinki.

Senge, P. M. (1990). *The Fifth Discipline*, Doubleday.

Starbuck, W. H. (1992). Learning by knowledge-intensive firms, *Journal of Management Studies*, 29(6), 713 – 740

Swan, J. (1999). Introduction, in Case studies in knowledge management, IPD, London, Scarbrough H, J Swan (eds).

Tricker, R. I. (1982). *Effective Information Management*, Beaumont Executive Press, Oxford.

van der Spek, R., and de Hoog, R. (1994). Towards a methodology for knowledge management, Technical note, Knowledge Management Network.

Wah, L. (1999). Making knowledge stick, Management review 88, 5,May.

Chapter 7

Facilitating Sensemaking in Knowledge Integration within Geographically Dispersed Cross-Functional Teams

Thekla Rura-Polley and Ellen Baker
University of Technology, Sydney, Australia

Igor T. Hawryszkiewycz
University of Technology, Sydney, Australia

This paper looks at knowledge management within geographically dispersed, cross-functional teams. In particular, it describes an electronic knowledge management system, LiveNet, that combines support for rational innovation processes with collaborative support mechanisms. These collaborative support mechanisms extend previously available group support systems by incorporating sensemaking tools.

INTRODUCTION

The creation and integration of knowledge within organizations have been recognized as an essential competitive advantages in dynamic industries. Grant (1996: 377) suggests that knowledge "accounts for the greater part of value added" and that "the barriers to the transfer and replication of knowledge endow it with strategic importance.." This is especially true for knowledge-intensive organizations, such as consultancies and, investment services. Such organizations recognize the importance

Previously Published in *Challenges of Information Technology Management in the 21st Century* edited by Mehdi Khosrow-Pour, Copyright © 2000, Idea Group Publishing.

of improving their ways of managing existing knowledge and creating new knowledge to gain competitive advantage in volatile environments. Knowledge creation in this context includes the creation of new products, services, and ideas. It requires the capture and combination of both tacit and explicit knowledge from a number of specialized areas and experts. For example, Xerox developed a Web site for its technical representatives to allow them to post their tips and insights, or receive feedback. The Web site acts as a way to test ideas, collect evidence, and allow electronic discussions about ideas. This process also allows a peer-review team to validate or refine ideas, and if a consensus is not reached quickly an expert may be called in as referee. Tips that are validated will subsequently be posted for worldwide distribution (Brown, 1999).

One issue that has scarcely received research attention within organizational knowledge integration concerns the process of sensemaking (Weick, 1995). When making sense, individuals rationalize phenomena that do not appear to be inherently sensible at first sight, using the categories available to them in their everyday organizational languages and modes of rationality. Sensemaking is a crucial organizational capacity. As Brown (1999) has observed, managers increasingly engage in making sense rather than products for their stakeholders. They interpret the market, the forces shaping the competitive landscape, and the risks and opportunities presented to their company.

As Grant (1996) observed, most research on knowledge integration issues has focused on cross-functional teams in new product development. In many cases, cross-functional project teams involve geographically dispersed members. For example, film production increasingly involves electronically facilitated, remote collaboration, with team members dispersed all around the world (Mizer, 1994). Knowledge integration in general, and sensemaking in particular, can be problematic in such geographically dispersed, cross-functional teams. Firstly, sensemaking must translate individual, departmental, and functional knowledge into team-based knowledge. This can be difficult in cross-functional teams where language and meaning differ greatly across functions, the language of accounting differs markedly from that of manufacturing engineering. Communication, let alone sensemaking, within cross-functional teams is often complicated, since effective communication relies on common language and shared meanings. Secondly, sensemaking in cross-functional, face-to-face teams is generally supported by non-verbal and contextual cues. In geographically dispersed teams, such facilitators of sensemaking are often missing, especially where dispersed teams rely on electronic means of communication. According to Weick (1985: 51), electronic representations are often flawed, because the data "contain only what can be collected and processed through machines. That excludes sensory information, feelings, intuitions, and context" – all of which are important for sensemaking.

A variety of group-support tools exists to facilitate cross-functional collaboration electronically, either within one locality or across several localities (Huseman and Miles,

1988). Most of these do not include any sensemaking facility and this may be because, as Tenkasi (1999) among others (Lyytinen, 1987; Boland et al., 1994) argues, that the prevailing technologies draw upon models from decision theory rather than upon interpretative approaches to organizations and organizational actors. Thus, they support the creation of knowledge through collating information on certain parameters, similar to collating personal preferences in electronic decision-support systems. They rely on rational actors and objectivity of information and knowledge. They support neither the situatedness nor subjectivity of knowledge nor the framing of the knowledge arena, all of which have to be explicit before knowledge can be created and shared in cross-functional teams.

Some authors propose that reliance on decision theory has hindered the development of information technology which is capable of supporting sensemaking processes in organizations (Feldman and March, 1981; Boland et al., 1994). Also, most researchers into group-support systems have favored problem definition rather than problem framing. Their research has focused on "answers rather than questions, outcomes rather than inputs, and structure rather than process" (Weick and Meader, 1993: 231). This leads to problems, because "in real-world practice, problems do not present themselves to the practitioners as givens. They must be constructed from the materials of problematic situations which are puzzling, troubling, and uncertain" (Weick, 1995: 9). In other words, problems are shaped by, and in turn shape, sensemaking,. a set of activities that occurs prior to the decision-making stage.

In this paper we report research on designing and evaluating electronic support technologies for facilitating effective cross-functional knowledge integration. These support technologies includes sensemaking modules and can be used when team members are in the same location or in different locations. The electronic collaboration tool, *LiveNet* (available at http://livenet.socs.uts.edu.au), is based on a paradigm called "workspace networks" (Hawryszkiewycz, 1998). One reason for adopting the workspace paradigm is that it allows evolution by utilizing the creation of new workspaces linked through a workspace tree, as new opportunities and ideas emerge. We are looking at ways in which work can grow in unanticipated directions, rather like having to build new spaces for new ideas or processes, and this may seem unfamiliar to some users at first. *LiveNet* provides an interface where users define their knowledge goal, and the system sets up the necessary collaborative workspace. The interface includes the knowledge sources and the interactive services to support knowledge integration and sensemaking. Currently, *LiveNet* includes two basic sensemaking modules which evolve around issues of shared terminology and frames of reference (Bolman and Deal, 1997).

Knowledge Integration in Cross-Functional Teams

Knowledge integration concerns itself with combining, incorporating, and extending knowledge created within separate communities of knowing (Boland and Tenkasi, 1995) or practice (Brown, 1999). It is an important element in innovation processes (Brown and Eisenhardt, 1995) which often rely on the integration of knowledge in cross-functional teams to speed up the innovation process as well as to increase the likelihood of success for new products or services. Team members from different functions, i.e., different communities, contribute their particular expertise to create a new product or service.

A cross-functional team includes not only the people, but also the records of activities, stored repositories of documents, recorded decisions, implicit or explicit dictionaries of shared terminology, symbols, rituals, records of shared past experiences and so on. Within the team, members share knowledge and experiences, create artifacts, and develop shared terminology. Membership in a team can be quite varied and often transient, with recognized experts as well as novices or apprentices. The team may share responsibilities and establish governance structures to define permitted and required actions that team members may take. Novices may have reduced access for making global changes to defining concepts and terms ofr reference, more often the responsibility of experienced members.

Reaping the benefits of using cross-functional teams, is not guaranteed, because sensemaking across communities can be difficult. Each community deals with a specialized aspect of knowledge and develops its own knowledge about organizational issues, its own approaches to solving problems, and its own modes of rationality. Moreover, each community uses its own terminology and methods of communication which may not correspond with those used by another community. Bechky (1999) showed that design engineers used different terms than assembly workers, and when the two groups used a common term,, the term actually referred to different objects. The technicians, located organizationally between the design engineers and the assembly workers, brokered knowledge transfer between these groups in order to create new products successfully. These technicians made sense of, and for, the other communities. Translating this function of sensemaking within knowledge brokering into a knowledge management system presents a challenge.

Knowledge Integration within *LiveNet*

LiveNet, is designed to support knowledge integration within local or geographically dispersed cross-functional teams by facilitating sensemaking. The major modeling terms are based on ideas from soft systems methodologies. They are combined as shown in Figure 1 and include the activity, role, and artifact. Activities, shown as cloud-like shapes, are organizationally recognized in that they produce some output, which is then used in other activities. Artifacts are represented by rectangular boxes and roles by their names. An arrow from an artifact to an

Figure 1: A Cross-functional Product Development Process in LiveNet

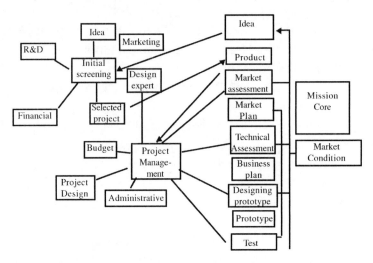

activity means that this activity uses, but does not change, the artifacthere. An arrow from an activity to an artifact means that the activity may change the artifact. Links between roles and activities mean that people who undertake these roles participate in the activity. Figure 1 describes a set of activities that can be used in a product-development process. Other organizational processes could be modeled similarly.

Each activity in Figure 1 produces some output, which may be used in other activities. The way that these activities are carried out is usually collaborative in nature and often cannot be strictly predefined. The activities are dependent on each other but not necessarily sequential. The emphasis is not on sequencing but concentrates on the activities, their participants, and the outputs that they produce. The sequencing relationships between activities are represented by transition diagrams which should not be viewed as workflows, but simply as events in one activity that could initiate actions in another.

Initial actions in most knowledge processes involves accessing explicitly stored background and sharing experiences, typically narratives which provide understanding of a particular community of knowing. Such experiences and insights are often shared during discussions, and can sometimes be captured in discussion databases, providing a form of externalizing tacit knowledge. Further actions interpret such captured information and progress to a new action, that is produce the explicit output document.

Combining stored knowledge with agent systems provides improvements to collaboration processes. Two kinds of agencies (Verona, 1999) have been found useful – technical agency and process agency. The technical agency primarily assists users in gathering both the information and the people needed to accomplish the workspace goal. Events within workspaces may be directed to agents that can perform a number of tasks. Process agency may be expressed by agents that facilitate workflows (Hawryszkiewycz and Debenham, 1998) through basing plans on the status of workspaces and the organizational state when events are occurring, and creating new workspaces. When combined, the technical agents provide users with a workspace that contains access to information and actions needed by the knowledge worker. The process agency then directs any outcomes from a workspace to other related workspaces.

Sensemaking is perhaps the most difficult of all processes to explain. It uses tacit knowledge possessed by community members to construct the new artifact. Again, guidelines and checklists are often developed at this stage to give guidance to novices, also providing a way of externalizing tacit knowledge. Nevertheless, the capture of such cognitive tacit elements in explicit form poses a challenge to any developer. In *LiveNet* we use formal and informal discussions, chat rooms, integrated background information, document support as well as pre-defined procedures such as goal setting, milestone definitions, terminology databases etc. to assist in these processes.

Facilitating Sensemaking in *LiveNet*

Sensemaking modules within *LiveNet*, are based on three theoretical perspectives. The first perspective is based on Weick's (1993, 1995) sensemaking approach. He understands sensemaking as "a process that is grounded in identity construction, retrospective, enactive of sensible environments, social, ongoing, focused on and by extracted cues, and driven by plausibility rather than accuracy" (Weick, 1995: 17). He uses these characteristics "to investigate what sensemaking is, how it works and when it can fail" (Weick, 1995: 18). His concept of sensemaking is grounded in identity construction; sensemaking is affected by and affects the recurrent and often changing definition of self of the sensemaker. As Weick (1995: 18) observes, "depending on who I am, my definition of what is 'out there' will also change." An individual's, perception of self and the contexts, in which he or she is placed, locally and temporally, are all intrinsic to sensemaking. However, Weick (1995) also views sensemaking as a social activity, acknowledging the impact of others. Through interaction with others, sensemakers can compare multiple sources of data, ponder the results, and place the confusing event or information into context (Weick and Meader, 1993).

Sensemaking in cross-functional collaborations involves not only many individuals with different prior experiences and contextual information, but also individuals who represent different functions, expertise, and modes of rationality (Boland and Tenkasi, 1995). The communication literature has shown that sensemaking failures often occur not just because of different general languages, but because participants use differing definitions of essential terms or different terminology. For instance, when an information systems analyst uses the term "top-down-approach," she may refer to a method for developing systems by first defining the top-level functions in terms of lower functions, which are then successively expanded in terms of the next lower level of functions until a basic implementation is reached; while the human resource specialist understands it to mean a change process that starts at the senior management team and filters down through the organization.

In face-to-face collaborations, miscommunication will become evident very quickly in the confused looks of the participants and through other contextual cues. In electronic collaborations such cues are missing. Therefore, Weick and Meader (1993: 232) thought it essential for an electronic collaboration "to construct moderately consensual definitions that cohere long enough for people to infer some idea of what they have, what they want, why they can't get it, and why it may not be worth getting in the first place."

Developing shared terminology is also an important element in the second perspective on sensemaking – Boland and Tenkasi's (1995) work on perspective making and taking. They (1995: 356) define perspective making as a "process whereby a community of knowing develops and strengthens its own knowledge domain and practice.". Perspective taking is a process where organizational knowledge emerges out of "exchange, evaluation and integration of knowledge" (Duncan and Weiss, 1979). It involves a range of inferential and judicative processes which open the process to systematic errors and biases (Boland and Tenkasi, 1995). Language usage and narrative are particularly important. Dougherty (1992) writes that perspective taking processes in cross-functional product development teams failed because members interpreted and understood linkages between technology and marketing qualitatively differently. Different departments had different internally consistent and coherent thought worlds. Members of a cross-functional team worked from their departmental thought worlds and assumed they knew the entire story; however, each story told within the team differed substantially from one another. Successful perspective taking involves "an increased capacity for communities of knowing to take each other into account within their own language games, and to construct new language games for their interaction" (Boland and Tenkasi, 1995: 359). Thus one important activity to facilitate sensemaking in cross-functional teams collaborating electronically is providing a tool that allows the development of shared terminology. The first sensemaking activity that *LiveNet* provides involves a database of key terms and definitions, as well as a means for discussing the terminology and definitions database, so that participants are able to develop a shared terminology and enrich and refine their knowledge and collaboration.

Our third perspective on sensemaking comes from Bolman and Deal's (1997) work on frames of reference and reframing. They list four frames that managers might use when making sense of organizations: the structural frame, the human resource frame, the political frame and the symbolic frame. Individuals interpret events in different ways depending on the frames that they adopt. Managers emphasizing the symbolic frame may, construct and convey meaning through symbols, and ceremony. Managers who think more in structural terms may convey meaning through organizational charts and chains of command. Framing and reframing have important implications for sensemaking, since sensemaking also includes "the standards and rules for perceiving, interpreting, believing, and acting that are typically used in a given cultural setting" (Sackman, 1991: 33).

In collaboration, individuals need to be aware of their own preferred frame as well as being capable of reframing an event: "effectiveness deteriorates when managers and leaders cannot reframe" (Bolman and Deal, 1997: 5). Reframing, or deliberately viewing events and problems from different perspectives, broadens cognitive perceptions, and helps to identify appropriate courses of action (Bolman and Deal, 1997). The ability to reframe is especially important in cross-functional collaborations where participants may prefer the frame of reference most closely related to their own professional expertise. *LiveNet* incorporates a module that allows participants to uncover their own latent frames of reference, as well as those of others.

Supporting the Development of Shared Terminology in *LiveNet*

The module that supports the development of shared terminology involves a database of key terms and definitions, as well as a means for discussing the database contents. This database is created through a discussion where users can ask for clarification and discuss connotations and meanings within the specific context of their team's tasks. Within *LiveNet*, we caution users about the occurrence of similar terminology in different disciplines and suggest that collaborators set up a separate discussion in which definitions can be agreed upon and questions can be more comfortably raised about what specific words mean.

Analyzing Underlying Frames of Reference in *LiveNet*

The second sensemaking module is guided by the experience of Kabanoff et al. (1995) who developed a computer-aided content-analysis system for categorizing organizational values embedded in text documents. They constructed a content dictionary and text-analysis program that counted the number of hits per sentence where phrases in their dictionary matched the text documents under study. Content analysis offers the advantage of utilizing non-obtrusive, naturally occurring text documents for examining organizational actions and processes. Such text documents accumulate over time and allow longitudinal analyses. According to Kabanoff et al. (1995), computer-aided analysis offers the additional advantage of precision, since the coding rules are always followed in the same way. *LiveNet* is designed to give instantaneous electronic feedback on underlying frames of reference. The challenge is to develop exhaustive, reliable, and valid dictionaries that are sufficiently context sensitive to decrease the likelihood of false hits.

Our module utilizes Bolman and Deal's (1997) work on frames of reference and reframing, in particular a dictionary of words typical of each frame of reference. Terms such as "goal," "plan," and "role" are associated with the structural frame; "motivate," "trust," and "relationship" with the human resource frame. We drew on electronic discussions among students in order to include colloquial terms as well. We also specifically looked for words that would be typical of the discussion style among practitioners: words such as "template" and "automate" (structural frame); "burnout" and "helpful" (human resource frame); "hammered" and "revolution" (political frame); and "decode" and "connotations" (symbolic frame). We supplemented these terms with indices that Palmer (1999) developed in his study of metaphor usage among managers. He analyzed a large number of metaphors with respect to the Bolman and Deal (1997) frames and validated the resulting dictionaries with the help of an international panel. In addition to these strategies, two researchers scanned a number of introductory management texts for keywords used regarding organizational phenomena related to each of the four frames, and added those to the dictionaries.

All the words and phrases were assessed for computer-aided processing, the main change being the elimination of terms which had more than one meaning.

Figure 2: Analyzing underlying Frames of Reference

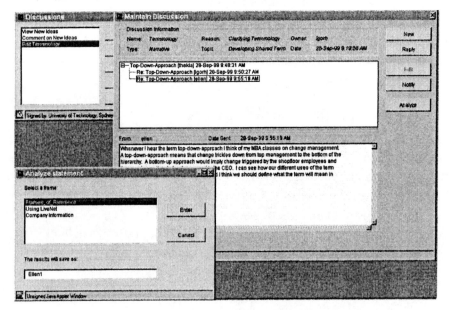

Such words may be processed by humans who would take the context into account, but would yield erroneous categorizing by the computer. Another modification involved the addition of all variations of a term, e.g., motivate, motivated, motivates, motivation.

This module allows participants to uncover their own latent frames of reference, as well as those of others. At any time a workspace user may request an analysis of the frames of reference to be carried out on a given portion of the electronic discussions or documents, and the analysis is conducted immediately. Thus the module provides instantaneous electronic feedback on the frames of reference being used within a particular discussion or by a specific participant. Figure 2 shows an example of the process.

CONCLUSION

In this paper we have explored how knowledge management in general, and sensemaking in particular, can be supported electronically in geographically dispersed, cross-functional teams via *LiveNet*. Tthree major aspects of effective knowledge management in geographically dispersed, cross-functional teams include, (1) providing a workspace for knowledge sharing among communities of knowing or practice; (2) supporting flexible team formation and evolving structures and governance forms; and (3) facilitating sensemaking processes among members. *LiveNet* brings together members from different communities within one workspace, provides them with the ability to locate needed information quickly, and supports this process with an agency structure that understands the best way to achieve cross-functional goals. Members can re-define their tasks dynamically as they evolve, and *LiveNet* supports the building of relationships amongst the members within a workspace network. *LiveNet* assists the development of shared terminology as well as making underlying frames of reference explicit. Appropriate agents can facilitate coordination and sensemaking processes and thereby improve communication and collaboration.

REFERENCES

Bechky, B. (1999). Creating shared meaning across occupational communities: An ethnographic study of a production floor. Paper presented at the *Academy of Management Meetings*, Chicago, IL.

Boland, R.J. and Tenkasi, R.V. (1995). Perspective making and perspective taking in communities of knowing. *Organization Science*, 6: 350-372.

Boland, R.J. and Tenkasi, R.V. (1995). Perspective Making and Perspective Taking in Communities of Knowing, *Organizational Science*, 6(4), July-August.

Boland, R.J., Tenkasi, R.V. and Te'eni, D. (1994). Designing information technology to support distributed cognition, *Organization Science*, 5: 456-475.

Bolman, L.G., and Deal, T.E. (1997). *Reframing Organizations: Artistry, Choice and Leadership* (2nd ed.), Jossey-Bass.

Brown, J.S. (1999). Sustaining the ecology of knowledge. *Leader to Leader*, 12 (Spring): 31-36.

Brown, S.L., and Eisenhardt, K.M. (1995). Product development: Past research, present findings, and future directions. *Academy of Management Review*, 20: 343-376.

Carrol, J.M. and Rosson, M.B. Network Communities, Community Networks, CHI98 18-23 April.

Dougherty, D. (1992). Interpretive barriers to successful product innovation in large firms. *Organization Science*, 3: 179-202.

Dourish, P. (1998). Using Meta-level Techniques in a Flexible Toolkit for CSCW Applications, *ACM Transactions on Computer-Human Interaction,* 5(2), June, pp. 109-155.

Duncan, R. and Weiss, A. (1979). Organizational learning: Implications for organizational design. In L. Cummings and B.M. Staw (Eds) *Research in Organizational Behavior 1.* Greenwich, CT: JAI.

Feldman, M.S. and March, J.G. (1981). Information in organizations as signal and symbol. *Administrative Science Quarterly*, 26: 171-186.

Grant, R.M. (1996). Prospering in dynamically-competitive environments: Organizational capability as knowledge creation. *Organization Science*, 7: 375-387.

Grant, R.M. (1996). Prospering in Dynamically-competitive Environments: Organizational Capability as Knowledge Integration, *Organization Science*, 7(4), July, pp. 375-387.

Greiner, C., Hawryszkiewycz, I.T., Rose, T., and Fliedner, T.M. (1996). Supporting Health Research Strategy Planning Processes of WHO with Information Technology, *Proceedings of the GI-Workshop on "Telecooperation systems in decentralized organizations"* Berlin, March 22-23, pp. 121-145, ISSN 0943-1624.

Hansen, M.T. (1999). The Search-Transfer Problem: The Role of Weak Ties in Sharing Knowledge across Organizational Sub-Units, *Administrative Science Quarterly*, 44, pp. 82-11.

Hawryszkiewycz, I.T. (1998). Extending Workspaces for Knowledge Sharing, World Computer Congress, IFIP98, Vienna-Budapest (to be presented).

Hawryszkiewycz, I. T. (1998). Extending workspaces for knowledge sharing. In: R. Traunmuller and E. Csuhaj-Varju (eds.) *Proceedings of the XV. IFIP World Computer Congress, IFIP98,* Vienna-Budapest: 77-88.

Hawryszkiewycz, I.T. and Debenham, J. (1998). A Workflow System Based on Agents. *Ninth International Conference on Database and Expert Systems,*

DEXA98, Vienna, pp. 135-144.

Huseman, R.C. and Miles, E.W. (1988). Organizational communication in the information age. *Journal of Management*, 14: 181-204.

Jones, C.T., Hesterly, W.S., and Borgatti, S. P. (1997). A General Theory of Network Governance: Exchange Conditions and Social Mechanisms. *Academy of Management Review*, 22(4), October, pp. 911-945.

Kabanoff, B., Waldersee, R. and Cohen, M. (1995). Espoused values and organizational change themes. *Academy of Management Journal*, 38: 1075-1104.

Kuczmarski, T.D. (1997). Innovation: Leadership Strategies for the Competitive Edge, IL: NTC Business Books.

LiveNet – http://linus.socs.uts.edu.au/~igorh/workspace/explore/livenet.htm.

Lyytinen, K. (1987). Two views of information modeling. *Information Management*. 12: 9-19.

Mizer, R.A. (1994). From post-production to the cinema of the future. *SMPTE Journal*, December: 801-804.

Nonaka, I. (1994). A Dynamic Theory of Organizational Knowledge Creation, *Organization Science*, 5(1), February, pp. 14-37.

Palmer, I. (1999). Framing managers' experiences of collaboration: A metaphor-based analysis. Under review at *Journal of Management Inquiry*.

Riggins, F.J. and Rhee , H-K. (1998). Developing the Learning Network Using Extranets, *Proceedings of the Thirty-First Hawaiian Conference on Systems Sciences.*

Sackman, S.A. (1991). *Cultural Knowledge in Organizations*. Newbury Park: Sage.

Szulanski, G. (1996). Exploring Internal stickiness: Impediments to the transfer of best practice within the firm, *Strategic Management Journal*, 17, Winter Special Issue, pp. 27-43.

Tenkasi, R.V. (1999). Information technology and organizational change in turbulent environments. Symposium presented at the Academy of Management Annual Meeting, Chicago, IL.

Verona, G. (1999). A Resource Based View of Product Development, *Academy of Management Review*, 24,(1), pp. 132-142.

Weick, K.E. (1985). Cosmos vs. chaos: Sense and nonsense in electronic contexts. *Organizational Dynamics*, 14(2): 51-64.

Weick, K.E. (1993). The collapse of sensemaking in organizations: The Mann Gulch disaster. *Administrative Science Quarterly*, 38: 628-652.

Weick, K.E. (1995). *Sensemaking in Organization*. Thousand Oaks: Sage.

Weick, K.E. and Meader, D.K. (1993). Sensemaking and group support systems. In L.M. Jessup and J.S. Valacich (eds.) *Group Support Systems*: 230-252. New York: Macmillan.

Chapter 8

Evaluating Organizational Patterns for Supporting Business Knowledge Management

Danny Brash
Stockholm University, Sweden

Nikos Prekas
University of Manchester Institute of Science and Technology (UMIST)

Georges Grosz and Farida Semmak
Universite Paris 1, Paris, France

One approach to managing business knowledge is to generalize problems and solutions within the context they appear, to enable reuse. We have applied a pattern framework adopted from software development, in a project for managing business knowledge. The pattern development process has included the evaluation of the suitability of "candidate" patterns. We present criteria for considering and measuring suitability, since not all knowledge is suitable for reuse.

INTRODUCTION

In this chapter, we discuss reuse of business knowledge using a patterns-based framework that draws on the Enterprise Knowledge Development (EKD) methodology, Bubenko et al. (1997) and Loucopoulos et al. (1997), and on the application of EKD in the case of deregulation in the Electricity Supply Industry (ESI) sector. This work is part of the ELEKTRA project aiming to tailor EKD to man-

Previously Published in *Challenges of Information Technology Management in the 21st Century* edited by Mehdi Khosrow-Pour, Copyright © 2000, Idea Group Publishing.

aging change in ESI companies and to discover patterns of change management for reuse. The paper is based on two project reports and follows on from Prekas et. al (1999) and Brash, Stirna (1999).

Our work is based on the assumption that not *all* knowledge should be documented and reused. How do we decide then what is a suitable? Suitability has to do with both the usage and knowledge parts of a description of the knowledge.

BACKGROUND TO PATTERNS

Recently, there has been increasing interest in the use of patterns in software development focussing on these ideas:

1. A pattern relates a *problem* to a *solution* to this problem.
2. In pattern identification,
   - not so much to recognize the commonalties among elements but to identify the distinguishing criteria and
   - find the unique characteristics of a problem that distinguishes it from other similar problems.

For the pattern to be effectively reusable, it should satisfy certain criteria, by being a self-contained logical system that is capable of stating that:

1. a problem exists within a stated range of contexts, and
2. in the given context, a solution resolves the given problem.

Therefore, a pattern should possess the following minimum set of properties. It defines the:

- *problem* and the *forces* that influence it that must be resolved. Forces refer to any goals and constraints that characterize the problem.
- concrete *solution* that represents a resolution of all the forces characterizing the problem.
- *context* that refers to a recurring set of situations in which the pattern applies.

THE ELEKTRA PROJECT

Due to EU directives toward deregulation as well as market, political and social pressures, electricity companies must react to and manage change. The experiences of two electricity companies suggested that this carried out in an unstructured manner, and is situation-dependent.

We address one of the project objectives, "to discover generalized patterns of change management for reusing them in similar settings in other electricity companies". One task, (the focus of this chapter) in achieving this objective is that the patterns be evaluated to ensure their relevance and completeness for solving specific ESI problems.

ELEKTRA patterns describes regular, repeatable characteristics; formal organizational and informal or contractual relationships, responsibilities, work practices etc.

Figure 1: The product-process cycle in change management

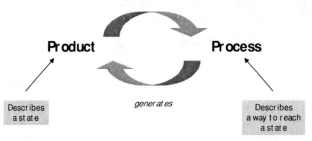

To systematically deal with change management, we impose the product-process cycle (Figure 1) upon the change activity. An initial state of affairs gives rise to an intention for change that leads to a new state of affairs through alternative ways of achieving change. The way of conducting the change is the *process*, while the states that we start from and arrive to are the *products*.

We ensure repeatability of the cycle by involving the identification of possible products or states that can be of interest to other ESI companies and of repeatable processes that can be followed to reach these states, leading to the definition of two pattern types:
- *Product patterns,* describing a state of affairs, i.e., a way in which an enterprise can conduct its business.
- *Change process patterns* modeling the change process and expressing how a transition from one state to another can be achieved.

To aid reuse, a mechanism for knowledge representation is made, distinguishing between the *body* of a pattern, that is effectively reused and its *descriptor,* providing sufficient information about the pattern and to describe the context in which the body can be reused. This separation allows for distinguishing the *knowledge perspective* from the *usage perspective*.

We use a conceptual modeling approach based on the presentation of the pattern body as EKD models. For the descriptor, we developed an aggregation of a *signature,* describing in what situation it is relevant to reuse the pattern and the *guidelines*, recommendations for "how to reuse."

PATTERN EVALUATION

In Prekas et al. (1999), we defined the pattern utility and structure and development process. The latter includes, elicitation, evaluation of suitability, documentation and verification.

The evaluation process consists of grading the pattern, deciding on suitability and, correction if needed. Evaluation is based on three criteria, *Usefulness, Quality and Cost,* each decomposed into sub-criteria, covering the two types of evalua-

Table 1: Evaluation sub-criteria of usefulness

Usefulness
Degree of triviality: The degree to which it addresses a problem of importance to the business.
Grade of implementability: The extent to which it is practical, implementable and compatible with business strategies.
Degree of confidentiality: The degree to which it discloses sensitive business information.

Table 2: Evaluation sub-criteria of quality

Quality
Degree of complexity: Considering the number of domain concepts and ideas it contains.
Addition of value: Local and global benefits accruing to the business with implementation.
Level of genericity: General enough to be applicable in other ESI companies.
Grade of understandability: The degree to which it is easy to comprehend by decision-makers and/or domain experts.
External compatibility: The extent to which other companies can use it taking into account national, business and organizational cultures, and ways of working.

Table 3: Evaluation sub-criteria of cost

Cost
Level of experience required for its use: The degree to which it is perceived to be difficult to use and implement.
Economic feasibility of the proposed solutions: The expected economical, political and social costs of implementation.

tion; adherence to the pattern framework and the knowledge contents as described in Tables, 1, 2 and 3 below.

Suitability of the Pattern

The decision on further development of a pattern is based on a numerical global rating, based on the criterion scores with a numerical value 0,1 or 2 associated to each criterion. The evaluation can be performed either on the top three criteria or on the sub-criteria. For the criterion **cost**, values are in ascending order (a high cost is not a positive feature for a pattern). The global rating of each pattern is the sum of the numeric values of each criterion, from 0- 6.

Further development

- *Acceptance of the pattern:* If the global rating of a candidate pattern is greater or equal to 4.
- *Corrective actions needed:* If the global rating of a candidate pattern is below 4 and greater than 2, it will need to be adjusted. Depending on the criterion that has a "low" marking, its sub-criteria must be considered and where the answer is not positive, actions must be undertaken.

Table 4: Questions associated with the evaluation sub-criteria

Usefulness:
Degree of triviality: Q1: Is the pattern trivial?
Grade of implementability: Q2: Is the pattern easy to implement?
Degree of confidentiality: Q3: Is the pattern confidential?
Quality:
Degree of complexity: Q4: Is the pattern simple?
Addition of Value: Q5: Is the pattern of a good additional value?
Level of genericity: Q6: Is the pattern applicable to other ESI companies?
Grade of understandability: Q7: Is pattern easy to understand?
External compatibility: Q8: Is the pattern applicable to other countries?
Cost:
Level of experience in their use: Q9: Is the pattern easy to use?
Economic feasibility of the proposed solutions: Q10: Is the solution of the pattern feasible?

- *Rejection of the pattern:*If the global rating of a candidate pattern is less or equal to 2. No further refinement is performed.

  The Set of Questions Associated to each Evaluation Sub-criterion

  For every sub-criterion, there is a question to be answered by Yes or No, according to Table 4 below.

Decision Tables Associated to Evaluation Criteria

The following decision tables aim to determine the value of each criterion, depending on the answers provided to the questions listed above.

The second line of Table 6 provides an entry for each possible arrangement of the answers to questions 1 and 2. The second column provides the possible answers for question 3. The grading of the criterion "Usefulness" is obtained by taking the value given in the cell that corresponds to the answers to questions 1, 2 and 3.

Table 5: Decision table for the sub-criterion cost

Cost		Question 9	
		Yes	No
Question 10	Yes	High	Medium
	No	Medium	Low

Table 6: Decision table for the sub-criterion usefulness.

Usefulness		Question 1, Question 2			
		Yes Yes	Yes No	No Yes	No No
Question 3	Yes	Low	Low	Medium	Low
	No	High	Low	High	Medium

Table 7: Decision table for the sub-criterion quality

Quality		Question 4, Question 5, Question 6							
		YesYesYes	YesYesNo	YesNoNo	YesNoYes	NoYesYes	NoNoYes	NoYesNo	NoNoNo
	Yes Yes	High	High	Med.	High	Med.	Med.	Med.	Low
Quest. 7	Yes No	High	Med.	Low	Med.	Med.	Low	Low	Low
Quest. 8	No Yes	High	Med.	Low	Med.	Med.	Low	Low	Low
	No No	Med.	Med.	Low	Low	Low	Low	Low	Low

An Example of Pattern Evaluation

We present, the Meter Reading product pattern, explaining how collecting data about customer consumption of electricity is performed. The evaluators had technical/operational knowledge and a view of how electricity companies handle the issue. The pattern was based on the following problem/solution pair:

Problem: ESI companies must measure electricity consumption of their customers.

Solution: Use human meter readers to perform the meter reading task. Produce meter-reading routes through customer areas; assign these routes to individual meter readers. Upon collection of meter reading data (MRD), group these data and initiate billing process.

The body was produced in terms of the roles necessary to fulfil the meter reading operations and the actors to whom these roles are assigned (Figure 2).

The participants voted on the criteria, Usefulness, Quality and Cost. For usefulness and quality, it was desirable to have a high marking; for cost, the lowest one, as discussed previously. This pattern achieved a mean of 2 for usefulness, 1.67 for quality and 0.33 for cost. These reflect that the:

- pattern represents an essential activity in every ESI company (usefulness marking).
- level of abstraction was sufficient so as to represent a generic solution without being too company-specific or too generic and thus trivial (quality marking).
- cost of implementing this solution is low (cost marking).

Figure 2: The first draft of the 'Meter Reading' pattern

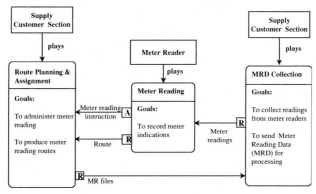

CONCLUSIONS

When using a framework for managing knowledge for reuse, a precondition is the ability to decide whether specific knowledge fits into the framework in terms of its usage or contents. We have presented a way of working with the pattern evaluation, with the framework being a way to capture and document business knowledge. We believe in the potential for this approach.

REFERENCES

Brash D., and Stirna, J. (1999). Describing Best Business Practices: A Pattern-based Approach for Knowledge Sharing. *SIGCPR 1999 Conference on Managing Organizational Knowledge for Strategic Advantage: The Key Role of Information Technology and Personnel*, New Orleans, Louisiana, April 8-10.

Bubenko, J., Brash, D., and Stirna, J. (1997). *EKD User Manual*. Department of Computer and Systems Sciences, Stockholm University.

Loucopoulos, P., Kavakli, V., Prekas, N., Rolland, C., Grosz, G., and Nurcan, S. (1997). *Using the EKD Approach: The Modeling Component*.

Prekas, N., Loucopoulos, P., Rolland, C., Grosz, G., Semmak, F., and Brash, D. (1999). Using patterns as a mechanism for assisting the management of knowledge in the context of conducting organizational change. *10th International Conference and Workshop on Database and Expert Systems Applications, DEXA '99*, August 30 - September 3, University of Florence, Florence.

Chapter 9

ERP-Based Knowledge Transfer

Zoonky Lee and Jinyoul Lee
University of Nebraska-Lincoln

Tim Sieber
Lincoln, NE

Enterprise Resource Planning (ERP) is an enterprise-wide package that tightly integrates all necessary business functions into a single system with a shared database. The implementation of ERP entails that business knowledge incorporated in the basic architecture of the software package is transferred into the adopting organization. This article investigates how organizational-specific requirements and technology constraints inherent in the software package interact in this knowledge transfer process. In-depth interviews, process analysis and documentation analysis are used to analyze the early implementation stage of ERP. The results conclude that the visible knowledge in the business process from the ERP package is compulsorily transferred into the organization along with business rules inherent in the process due to the process automation, the cross-functional nature of ERP package and limited flexibility of the package. The results also suggest that organizational adaptive capability of role and responsibility redistribution, development of new types of required knowledge and a different knowledge structure in the organization will internalize these standardized processes into business routines that will give a competitive edge.
This article provides a new angle of adopting ERP in an organization, and contributes to a better understanding of competitive advantage based on

Previously Published in *Challenges of Information Technology Management in the 21st Century* edited by Mehdi Khosrow-Pour, Copyright © 2000, Idea Group Publishing.

process knowledge when standardized business processes are implemented in an organization.

INTRODUCTION

Transfer of knowledge has been an important topic in management literature. Sometimes, the issue arises in the form of transferring best practices in multinational corporations when they transfer accumulated knowledge of headquarters to new foreign affiliates (Ghoshal and Nohria, 1989; Gupta and Govindarajan, 1991; Kogut and Zander, 1993). At other times, it becomes an issue of transferring technology, business processes and best practices inside the firm (e.g., Argote, 1999).

As more and more companies are implementing Enterprise Resource Planning (ERP) systems in their organization, the issue of knowledge transfer comes in a different format. While customization is not impossible, the broad scope and close connectivity of all related functions makes the customization very costly for any implementation of ERP (Davis, 1998). This high cost and long implementation process lead most organizations to align their business processes with functionality provided from the ERP. According to Forrester Research, only five percent of organizations among Fortune 1000 companies purchased an ERP application and customized it to match their business process (Davis, 1998). Therefore, the implementation of ERP entails taking the business model around the package (Slater, 1998). In other words, business knowledge incorporated into the basic architecture of the software is transferred into the adopting organization.

The article is a part of longitudinal study based on an ERP implementation at the University of Nebraska. From an in-depth analysis of this early stage of implementation, we are particularly interested in how organizational-specific requirements and technology constraints inherent in the software package interact in the knowledge transfer process. The findings will contribute to a better understanding of competitive advantage based on process knowledge when standardized business processes are implemented in the organization.

KNOWLEDGE TRANSFER OF BUSINESS PROCESSES

Can knowledge be transferred when business processes are mapped and imitated? If so, what knowledge is transferred and what is not? One important step in answering these questions is to understand the difference in business processes. Brown and Duguid (1991) presented two different views of work: canonical and noncanonical. Canonical practice, based on an abstract representation of the organization, originated with Taylor's scientific management where complex tasks are mapped to a set of simple canonical steps. Noncanonical practice, on the other hand, is what actually happens in the work. It is the informal processes about the relationship and communication of practices and coordination.

Workers in the organization construct learning in the community of practice (Lave and Wenger, 1991), deviating from formal organizational rules and procedures. A similar classification of processes can be found in Sachs' (1995) "organizational, explicit" and "activity-oriented, tacit" views. The organization-based view—represented by sets of defined tasks and operations—differs from the activity-based view that determines how employees actually make the business function more effective. Sachs also observed it is through these workers' relationships in "communities" and within their human systems that problems are discovered and resolved, and work is effectively accomplished.

What can be derived from this conceptual clarification is ERP-based knowledge transfer has two different aspects. On one hand, the knowledge transfer is based on canonical processes: the reference models contained in ERP systems are visible, formal chains of activities represented by process modeling tools. There is no collaborative social arrangement such as narration, communication and collaboration between a source and a recipient in this knowledge transfer process. In ERP-based knowledge transfer, business processes are packaged in the software. Studies have shown the degree of codification has a strong relationship with the speed of transfer (Zander and Kogut, 1995). Similarly, Szulansk (1996) reports that "casual ambiguity" in knowledge is more difficult to transfer than well-understood knowledge.

The second aspect of ERP-based knowledge transfer refers to the non-canonical part of knowledge associated with the reference models. Previous studies in knowledge transfer found that knowledge transfer inherits the property of stickiness (Szulanski, 1996) and embeddedness (Badaracco, 1991), a difficult-to-migrate portion of organizational knowledge which is deeply embedded in complex social interactive relationships within organizations. Other studies have reported that knowledge transfer is best achieved through intimate communication or relationships such as franchise (Darr, Argot and Epple, 1995), research alliance (Powell, Koput and Smith-Doerr, 1966) and strategy alliance (Uzzi, 1996) between a source and a recipient. Since there is no source to transfer the knowledge in this case, the ability of a recipient to adjust their existing business fundamentals (e.g., culture, norm and values, etc.) to the invisible part of principles embedded in the business models will play a crucial role in this type of knowledge transfer.

RESEARCH METHOD

On July 1, 1999, the University of Nebraska's four-campus system started to use SAP R/3 for its external and internal accounting functions as well as its purchasing and inventory functions. This study is based on the observation of a three-month in-depth analysis during early implementation on the University of Nebraska-Lincoln campus.

The study is based on in-depth interviews, process analysis and documentation analysis. Among the many different functions implemented, this study focuses on the purchasing function as it has a limited system modification process (so, more business process changes). This provides a relatively clear case of direct knowledge transfer from the ERP package. Additionally, the function is relatively easy to understand is similar across different organizations and the process is cross-functional as it impacts end users as well as the accounts payable and purchasing departments.

First, old and new processes were mapped and analyzed. Both existing documents and interviews were used to identify discrepancies between the designed process and the process actually being implemented. Six interviews were conducted with two persons in each area impacted by the process (e.g., users, purchasing and accounting payable department). Each interview lasted 60 to 90 minutes. All interviews were recorded with permission of the interviewees and transcribed at a later date. The format of the interviews was semi-structured-prepared questions were asked and answered in an open-ended manner.

ANALYSIS
Analysis of Old Process vs. New Process

For the purchasing function, the University adopted standard ERP processes that were different in many aspects from the old processes. Figure 1 shows the two processes.

One primary difference between the two processes is the new process is computer-based, while the old process is paper-based. In the old process, for instance, the purchasing department (PU) hand entered a purchase order based on a requisition submitted manually by user departments (USER). In the new process, a requisition is entered and electronically stored by USER. PU creates a purchase order instantly by just clicking several buttons in the computer as the same information is forwarded directly from the requisition to the purchasing order.

The difference in the two processes is not limited to automation. One of the most distinctive improvements is elimination of the invoice matching process by the accounts-payable department (AP). This was probably the most time-consuming process in the entire purchasing process. In the old process when USER received goods, USER received a copy of the receipt and sent it to AP. AP then matched it to a copy of the original purchase order received from PU and an the

Figure 1: Purchasing Process
  (a) Old Process Flow   (b) New Process Flow

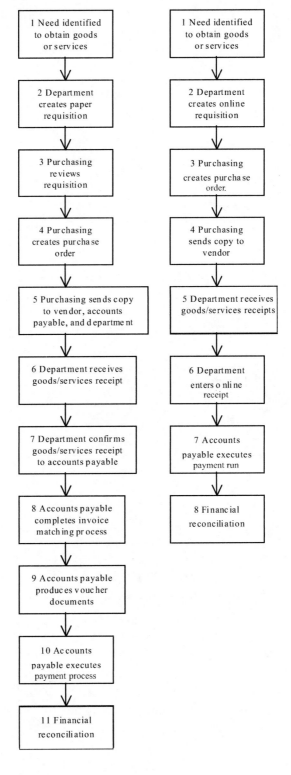

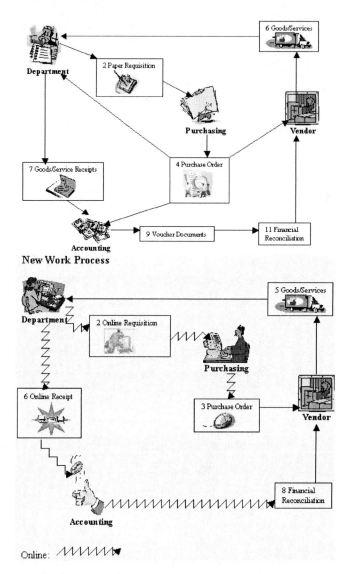

Old Work Process

New Work Process

Online: ∕∖∕∖∕∖∕∖►

invoice from the vendor. The payment process was then executed. In the new process, USER verifies the goods they receive with an electronic invoice, and then AP executes the payment process.

Analysis of Interviews

Overall, users are mostly required to follow the business processes inherent in the ERP package due to the following three reasons: the process being automated, limited flexibility of the package and cross-functional nature of the package. First, the automation process makes people involved in the purchasing process follow standards as designed. When many tasks were paper-based, people had much more flexibility. When USER sent a requisition, for instance, PU sometimes talked with vendors first before requesting USER to modify the requisition. Now once a requisition is entered into the computer system, it is logged and PU generates a purchasing order directly. The inherent business rule behind the process in fact gives less flexibility to PU.

Secondly, limited technical flexibility in ERP package also enhances people to accept processes and rules inherent in the package. While the project implemention team tried to apply the functional model in the ERP package directly to the new process, not all organizational requirements were compatible with the new business processes provided with the package. However, due to the limited technical flexibility in the package, the University had to reconcile their process within the flexibility offered from the ERP package.

Finally and most importantly, the cross-functional nature of the ERP package enforces people to follow the business processes as they are all interconnected by the system. Under the old system, departments were very loosely coupled. Under the new system, however, all inputs and outputs are tightly connected. The cross-functional interconnectivity requires people around the process to have more cross-functional knowledge in the process. The requirements of a broader scope of knowledge also make people actively seek knowledge sources for their inquiries. This seeking process generates an organization atmosphere to weight the organizational meta-knowledge, or knowledge about who knows what knowledge.

While the nature of the ERP package enforce users to accept business processes and rules provided from ERP, the enforcement also leads to different types organizational requirements. These include role and responsibility redistribution, new types of required knowledge to people around the process and a different knowledge structure in the organization. After the ERP implementation, people in PU and AP generally believed their jobs were deprived. Especially the people in AP as their important matching processes were removed. AP users felt helpless and a higher-than-expected turnover rate was reported. After recognizing the problem, the University recently assigned the purchasing audit function—formerly completed by the State government—to AP.

CONCLUSION

The analysis demonstrates that non-canonical business rules inherent in the package accompany the canonical part of business models in ERP adoption. Due to process automation, the cross-functional nature of ERP package and limited flexibility of the package, users of the ERP package are practically enforced to accept the business processes and business rules inherent in the ERP package. This result is consistent with other technology based knowledge transfer. In their study of knowledge transfer in the manufacturing plant, Epple et al. (1996) noted that embedding knowledge in technology is a very powerful and effective way of knowledge transfer.

The results also suggest that while new requirementsbased on the ERP adoption, come into a challenge, organizational capability to adapt to the new rules can make its process more competitive than others. In other words, although the ERP restricts organizational flexibility to deviate from the standardized rules prescribed in the package, the way to internalize the standardized rules can be different across adopting organizations. In dealing with the issue to redefine the roles and responsibilities, organizations might take a broader set of options from "leave it as it is" to "actively restructure the organization to redistribute roles and responsibilities." The same is true for new requirements of different knowledge and different knowledge structures. Organizations can develop a new training program to imbue more cross-functional knowledge into the organizational members. Organizations can develop a new knowledge management system that will provide knowledge about who knows what information.

The business process becomes one of the most important competitive resources of the organization (Camp, 1995). Implementing the ERP package implies most business processes in the organization will be affected. Organizations should understand what knowledge will be and should be transferred into the organization when they accept business processes stored in the ERP package. Organizations should understand how they still make firm-specific business processes to provide them with a competitive advantage while accepting industry standardized business processes. This research is an explorative study to answer some of the questions.

In summary, the results show the visible knowledge in the business process from the ERP package is compulsorily transferred into the organization along with business rules inherent in the process. The results also suggest that organizational adaptive capability will internalize these standardized processes into business routines that give a competitive edge.

REFERENCES

Argote, L. (1999). *Organizational Learning Crating, Retaining and Transferring Knowledge*, Kluwer Academic Publishers.

Baddaracco, Jr., J. L. (1991). *The Knowledge Link: How Firms Compete through Strategic Alliance*, Boston: Harvard Business School Press.

Brown, J. S., and Duguid, P. (1991). Organizational Learning and Communities of Practice: Toward a Unified View of Working, Learning, and Innovation, *Organization Science*, 2(1), February, pp. 40-57.

Camp, R. (1995). *Business Process Benchmarking: Finding and Implementing Best Practices*, Milwaukee, WI.

Davis, J. (1998). Scooping up vanilla ERP (off-the-shelf versus customized software)(Technology Information), *InfoWorld*, November 23, pp. 1.

Darr, E., Argote, L., and Epple, D. The Acquisition, transfer and depreciation of knowledge in service organizations: Productivity in Franchises, *Management Science*, 41, pp. 1750-1762.

Ghoshal, S., and Nohria, N. (1989). Internal Differentiation Within Multinational Corporations, *Strategic Management Journal*, 10, pp. 323-337.

Gupta, A. K., and Govindarajan, V. (1991). Knowledge Flows and the Structure of Control Within Multinational Corporations, *Academy of Management Review*, 16, pp. 768-792.

Kogut, B., and Zander, U. (1993). Knowledge of the Firm and the Evolutionary Theory of the Multinational Corporation, *Journal of International Business*, 24, pp. 625-645.

Lam, A. (1997). Embedded Firms, Embedded Knowledge: Problems of Collaboration and Knowledge Transfer in Global Cooperative Ventures, *Organization Studies*, 18(6), pp. 973-996.

Lave, J., and Wenger, E. (1991). *Situated Learning: Legitimate Peripheral Participation*, Cambridge, England: University Press.

Li, C. (1999). ERP packages: What's next?, *Information Systems Management,* 16(3), Summer, pp. 31-35.

Powell, W., Koput, K., and Smith-Doerr, L. (1996). Interorganizational Collaboration and the Locus of Innovation: Networks of Learning in Biotechnology, *Administrative Science Quarterly*, 41, pp. 116-145.

Sachs, P. (1995). Transforming Work: Collaboration, Learning and Design, *Communications of the ACM*, September, 38(9), pp. 36-45.

Szulanski, G. (1996). Exploring internal stickiness: Impediments to the transfer of best practice within the firm, *Strategic Management Journal*, 17, Winter Special Issue, pp. 27-43

Uzzi, B. (1996). Sources and Consequences of Embeddedness for the Economic Performance of Organizations, *American Sociological Review*, 61, pp. 674-698.

Zairi, M. and Ahmed, P. K. (1999). Benchmarking maturity as we approach the millennium? *Total Quality Management*, 10(4&5), pp. S810-S816.

Zander, U., and Kogut, B. (1995). Knowledge and Speed of the Transfer and Imitation of Organizational Capabilities: An Empirical Test, *Organization Science*, 6(1), January-February, pp. 76-92.

Chapter 10

Knowledge Management in U.S. Federal Government Organizations: Can It Work?

J. Judah Buchwalter
University of Maryland, Baltimore

Knowledge management (KM) is an active and growing field. One of the key factors of KM is its dependence on a culture that will support KM activities. Some of the activities that are extremely culture dependent are the sharing and acceptance of knowledge between individuals and organizations. The question to be answered is whether U.S. federal government (hereafter referred to as "government") organizations, which are notorious for the lack of this type of culture (although not all), can accomplish KM at all or just need a different approach that has not been defined previously? In this research, we will propose to use government initiatives to entice the organization into creating the culture needed for KM. We will also propose a way to effect changes in the culture by implementing a social initiative that has proven successful in other organizations. The combination of these two activities is expected to create a culture that is viable for KM to flourish even in the infamous government organization.

INTRODUCTION

Knowledge management (KM) is the process whereby knowledge (both explicit and implicit), which is contained in an organization, is distributed to other

Previously Published in *Challenges of Information Technology Management in the 21st Century* edited by Mehdi Khosrow-Pour, Copyright © 2000, Idea Group Publishing.

people, in or outside of the organization in a controlled format. It is not just a document management system with a high-tech search engine, as many current vendors would like to portray it (Van der Spek and de Hoog, 1998). A goal of the KM process is to remove the dependency on individual people for knowledge, which will segregate the knowledge and the people. The accomplishment of this goal will enable any person to retrieve and use any of the knowledge that exists in the organization. The benefits derived from this process are numerous, for example creating more productive workers, alleviating the risk of lost workers, and realizing organizational value.

KM can be found to be taking a foothold in many organizations. Many information technology companies are promoting it as the cure for all kinds of organizational ills (Dataware TEchnologies, 1998; Swoyer, 1999; Van der Spek and Spijkervet, 1997). Even government organizations are taking active steps in the KM arena (Liebowitz, Rubenstein-Montano, McCaw, Buchwalter, Browning, Newman and Rebeck, 2000), for example the government's CIO council subcommittee on KM. Academia is doing scientific research in order to expose its capabilities and failings (Alavi, 1999; Weidner, 1999). Both of these efforts have found that culture plays a critical role in the entire KM process. Most KM frameworks and initiatives include some form of cultural input and/or strategy (Apostolou and Mentzas, 1998; Andersen, 1997; Holsapple and Joshi, 1997; Liebowitz et al., 2000; Marquardt, 1996; Seaman and Basili, 1994). The cultural factors, which are enumerated in these references, encompass the activities of sharing and accepting. The individuals with the knowledge are required to share it. Conversely, the people who require knowledge need to accept it. These activities appear to be simple social constructs that children are taught in pre-school and develop in elementary school. However, there are many obstacles, which stand in the way of such progress. Organizational structures, which are depicted as concretely defined boundaries and organizational culture, which can be defined as accepted customs, are some of the obstacles (Tierney, 1999). Many government organizations contain these obstacles for the other productive purposes. Therefore, research is required to identify whether existing KM methodologies can accomplish their goals in a government organization. Through the following research, which places a greater emphasis on specific areas of current KM methodologies and manipulating other government specific variables, we can accomplish KM in government organizations.

BACKGROUND

Knowledge management is dependent on more than just information technology (Marquardt, 1996). KM can be summarized to depend on process, culture, and technology (Weidner, 1999). As mentioned previously, KM frameworks include a substantial number of steps for social activities. Examining the KM frameworks summarized by Liebowitz, et al. (Marquardt, 1996), we can see the numerous activities that require social interaction. There are processes for:

- retrieving knowledge from people (tacit and non-tacit),
- internalizing knowledge, which is a form of learning,
- combining knowledge, and
- transferring knowledge to people.

All of these actions rely on some form of sharing and interaction that must occur between individuals of an organization. We must ascertain to what extent the attributes supporting KM exist in an organization. Numerous KM methodologies (Marquardt, 1996) have documented the initial step of KM as a knowledge audit or some variant of a cultural assessment to identify the strengths and weaknesses in an organization. The output from this document will provide the needed insight into the organization and its abilities to provide the elements needed for knowledge management activities. In the case where the organization is lacking the social constructs needed for successful KM, a plan can be developed to introduce the needed culture. In the case where the knowledge or information technologies are lacking, a plan can be created to fulfill that need.

The first part of the cultural assessment must be documentation of the existing organizational culture. This step will educate the KM implementers to the type of culture that is currently active, for which they can build a consensus (Wielinga, Sandberg and Schreiber, 1997). A culture that is rich in human interaction is much different than one where people only talk with each other when a meeting is scheduled, in other words by appointment. A culture where there is a lot of face-to-face communication is very different from one where most communication is via phone or e-mail. This information will make a significant difference in the approach that is used to implement KM in the organization.

Some cultures are very strict where people follow well-defined rules and protocols. Also, hierarchies are in place to which people must conform (Seaman et al., 1994). Some cultures are much more flexible and the only issue is the bottom-line, whether the job gets done. The former culture requires well-developed and appropriate activities for KM to work. The latter culture can usually deal with whatever is thrown at it. All of these nuances must be collated and understood. As Seaman (1994) details, "…organizational structure within which the process executes has a profound effect on its outcome."

Upon completion of this familiarization step, the organization should perform an on-site inspection. Only after the KM implementer has an understanding of the organizational culture can a process of detailing the culture begin. In the case of a strict culture, meetings have to be scheduled in order to produce high turnout as opposed to a flexible culture where ad-hoc interviews and focus groups can be initiated. In the case of a face-to-face culture, focus groups and in-person interviews are needed as opposed to a more disengaged culture where independent surveys can accomplish the task. In whichever culture the assessment is done, in-depth understanding of the organization will only be derived through individual interviews and focus groups.

The aforementioned examples of differences in organizational cultures are applicable to more than just the initial assessment. These representations are the underpinnings of how a culture works and, therefore, how interaction, as required by KM, will take place. In some cases, there is another facet that could be a key point and a formidable obstacle. Some organizations proclaim to be of one cultural breed while they really abide by another. This situation can be made even more difficult because, before the culture can be changed, the people need to be made aware of the purpose for the changes to occur (Wielinga et al., 1997). As Schein (1992) details, there are many layers to any culture and each one needs to be revealed for clarity of the environment.

The organizational literature abounds with analyses of organizations and how to manipulate them. In this paper, we will restrict ourselves to current examples of organizational changes that are being achieved, inside and outside of the government. At NASA (Karlin, 1999), there is a new initiative called the Intelligent Synthesis Environment (ISE) whereby the organizational culture at NASA will be modified to create a synthesis of scientists and engineers. The concept of the ISE is to create collaborative efforts between diverse workers in strictly structured organizations. In addition to these restrictions, the workers are scattered across remote geographic locations. NASA realizes that the established culture must be changed to accomplish their goals (Karlin, 1999). It is not enough to just throw new technology at the problem. Actually, new technology alone may just worsen the situation.

NASA has recognized that changing a culture, especially a strict culture as is found in many government organizations, is not a simple overnight task. Therefore, one of the main tasks of the ISE is to "revolutionize cultural change"(Karlin, 1999). Through the use of training and education, NASA plans to initiate cultural change for the goals of ISE. They also plan to change management practices. Management practices are always the critical factor for any new implementations in an organization (Andersen, 1997; Carlson, Kahn and Rowe, 1999; Dataware Technologies, 1999; Swoyer, 1999; Wielinga et al., 1997). However, a government organization differs from private industry where the boss is the boss. In a government organization there are many bosses. The executive branch of government delineates processes for many agencies. The legislative branch of government (i.e. Congress) makes laws that government agencies must follow. Therefore, there are other items, which can be used to effectuate or encourage a government agency to follow a specific strategy. In summary, NASA demonstrates how organizational changes can be used to improve productivity.

Another approach towards this goal is described by Carlson et al. (1999). It is called Organizational Imperative. In this approach, there is some type of impetus at the organizational level that causes changes to occur in the organization to improve the processes. These could be management decisions, active participation in key positions, and/or technology strategies. They (Carlson et al., 1999) specifically remark that organizations with similar cultures could be used to test this approach. This will be the goal of our research to be defined in this paper.

Tierney (1999) provides numerous examples of companies that have changed their business strategies to incorporate knowledge management activities through changes in their culture. McKinsey, a consulting firm, makes business changes by "…supporting a culture …" that is imperative to their strategy. Bain & Company, a London based consulting firm, also has made changes in their organizational structure to improve the business strategy and products.

PROBLEM

The general lack of a culture, which supports knowledge management, is the primary obstacle for government organizations. The previously mentioned characteristics of sharing and openness are very few and far between in government organizations. Also, as described above, even where claims of open-door policies are made, the management body disdains any activities that do not follow the hierarchical structure. In some circumstances, a strict organizational structure is beneficial. However, if we look at the current efforts in the executive and judicial branches of government, we may see a different necessity. Fletcher (1999) lists numerous current legislative and executive activities that are specifically targeted at improving federal government performance. If we look at the long list of executive initiatives, e.g. the National Performance Review (1993), the National Partnership for Reinventing Government (http://www.npr.gov/), the Government Performance Results, and the Federal Information Technology executive order (Fletcher, 1999), we can see that even the government leadership has recognized a problem in government performance. A look at the National Performance Review's web-site (http://www.npr.gov/links/) displays a long list of initiatives towards the goals of NPR. Critical steps in these initiatives are the capturing and dissemination of information and the redesign of organizational dynamics, which are underlying conditions of knowledge management.

The legislative branch of the federal government is also very active with these issues. The Chief Financial Officers Reform Act of 1990, the Government Performance and Results Act of 1993, the Government Management Reform Act of 1994, the Paperwork Reduction Act of 1995, the Information Technology Management Reform Act of 1996, and the Clinger-Cohen Act of 1996 are examples of federal legislation to improve the performance of federal agencies via changes in organizational structures and policies. Even legislation in other areas like the Computer Matching and Privacy Protection Act of 1988 address issues of improving the way government organizations manage their information technology and organizational performance.

In summary, given the troubled state of federal government organizational structures that exist today, as evidenced by the high number of initiatives and legislation to improve the current condition, a specialized strategy is required to implement knowledge management in any organization that emulates a typical U.S. federal government agency's culture.

PROPOSAL

This study proposes a solution that is targeted for organizations like the federal government. This strategy will put an emphasis on the cultural and organizational steps of KM. Furnishing the correct culture for KM to succeed is the first hurdle for these types of organizations. However, changing a culture in a government organization where people are permanent employees, there is a strict organizational structure, and directives come from numerous sources is a formidable obstacle. Therefore, this study will investigate the following three steps (1) a focused approach to KM, (2) government specific inducements, and (3) a social process to change an organization's culture in order to accomplish its goals.

As Fletcher (1999) indicates, government organizations are now doing business in the format of commercial businesses. Therefore, a business assessment is required to develop the requirements, priorities, and goals for this activity. Numerous KM methodologies recognize this step as the building block for any KM effort (Marquardt, 1996). The output of this first step may provide many areas or the entire organization as a target area for the KM effort. Applying a KM effort to an entire organization is a formidable task that is not recommended (Dataware Technologies, 1998; Van der Spek et al., 1997). However, if an isolated section of an organization is targeted many organizational inter-relationships will not be covered, which will leave questions and omit information flow. Therefore, this study will choose one problem in the organization and address it from end to end. Dividing each piece of the problem into smaller tasks and/or working with each part of the organization individually can make this task complete.

The next stage in the KM methodology is to conduct a knowledge audit (KA) in order to identify the requirements for the KM process that will solve the business problem. The knowledge audit will provide the sources and destinations of knowledge in the organization (Moore, 1999). The KA will supply the organizational structure (e.g. hierarchical/flat, strict/loose) and the flow of knowledge within and outside of the organization. In a government organization, it will also provide the agency's specific initiatives and plans. These outputs will be available due to legislation such as the GPRA (Fletcher, 1999) which require agencies to create an Annual Performance Plan(APP). The KA will also supply the knowledge leaders. These are the people who others turn to for answers to questions and reliable knowledge. It is with these outputs that this study will move on to its next step.

The next step in this study will be to formulate a list of executive and legislative government initiatives that are applicable to the government agency under study. This list will then be used to address the targeted problem from the previously described business assessment and knowledge audit. For each problem that has been assessed, there will be a reference to the government initiatives that require reforming the given problem. With this list in hand, the KM implementers should be able to go into any government manager's office and find an open hand (fiscally speaking) and ear for any initiative which they suggest. Government managers are more than eager to support projects that fulfill their responsibilities to implement the programs coming from the executive and legislative branches, especially when they can be clearly tied to them. In this step, the KM implementers will accomplish the crucial step of buy-in from management that only too few projects are able to muster. Any KM initiative will only work with this critical piece in place.

The final step for this study will be to target the knowledge leaders in order to effectuate change. After defining the problem and requirements in step one, we moved on to step two where we acquired upper management approval. In this final step, before implementation of the KM activities, there is a need to infiltrate the current culture and initiate change. Although this step and the previous steps are all part of an overall KM framework, there is a difference between the preparatory work for the management of knowledge and the actual management activities that work directly with the knowledge. This step is a crucial move into the organization. Even with management buy-in, there still are hurdles to surmount in order to affect the individuals and processes within an organization. People are reluctant to change and, by nature, will fight to continue with the pervasive culture.

However, as in any organization, the strict hierarchical type of organization, has leaders and followers. This paradigm is applicable to knowledge as well. Knowledge leaders are defined as the people others turn to in the organization to answer their questions at least three times in a week. If the knowledge leaders can be influenced to promote the culture that is required for the KM initiative, then the rest of the organization will follow them. When the followers in the organization obtain knowledge and watch the leaders, then their opinions and beliefs will be influenced. These influences can then effectuate change in the culture of the organization.

The key is to find a way to influence the knowledge leaders. Some suggestions that can be experimented with are showing the knowledge leaders respect and seniority and requesting their input. Other social endeavors can be implemented to accomplish this goal. The most important objective is to find a way to have the appropriate culture for KM dispersed through the organization.

SUMMARY

Knowledge management is not just a technology project. KM relies on organizational structures and culture to meet its goals. Therefore, there is a very heavy dependency on the specific organization or at least the specific type of organization, where the KM initiative is being implemented. In an organization with a culture that promotes the underlying requirements of KM there are very few organizational or cultural issues that must be dealt with. However, if KM is being proposed in an organization that has a culture, which opposes KM requirements, then a specialized approach is required.

This study offers a methodology to effectuate change in an organization's culture via a three step process that can be added to common KM frameworks (Moore, 1999). The three steps entail using aids that are familiar and common to the organization in order to effectuate change therein. The goal of this study is to accomplish a knowledge management initiative in an organization that would not be expected to accomplish the task.

ACKNOWLEDGEMENT

This work was partially funded by the Social Security Administration.

REFERENCES

Alavi, M. (1999). Knowledge Management Systems: Issues, Challenges, and Benefits, *Communications of the Association for Information Systems,* 1(1).

Andersen, A. (1997). http://www.arthurandersen.com/aabc.

Apostolou, D., and Mentzas, G. (1998). Managing Corporate Knowledge: A Comparative Analysis of Experiences in Consulting Firms, *Second International Conference on Practical Aspects of Knowledge Management*, Basel, Switzerland, 29-30, October.

Carlson, P. J., Kahn, B. K., and Rowe, F. (1999). Organizational Impacts of new Communication Technology: A Comparison of Cellular Phone Adoption in France and the United States, *Journal of Global Information Management*, 7(3), Hershey, PA: Idea Group Publishing.

Checkland, P. B. (1992). From Framework Through Experience to Learning: the Essential Nature of Action Research, in *Proceedings of the Second World Congress on Action Learning*, 1-7 (14-17 July).

Dataware Technologies (1998). Seven Steps to Implementing Knowledge Management in Your Organization (Corporate Executive Briefing, http://www.dataware.com , 1998).

Dataware Technologies (1999). Software for Knowledge Management, seminar, April 28.

Fletcher, P. (1999). Governmental Information Systems and Emerging Computer Technologies, *Handbook of Public Information Systems*, M. Dekker (in press).

Holsapple, C., and Joshi, K. (1997). Knowledge Management: A Three-Fold Framework (Kentucky Initiative for Knowledge Management [Paper No. 104], July 1997).

Karlin, J. (1999). NASA's Intelligent Synthesis Environment(ISE), NASA [white paper], KMCI-GWA, May 5.

Liebowitz, J. (1999). (Ed.), *The Knowledge Management Handbook,* Boca Raton, FL: CRC Press.

Liebowitz, J. (2000). *Building Organizational Intelligence: A Knowledge Management Primer,* Boca Raton, FL: CRC Press, in press.

Liebowitz, J., and Beckman, T. (1998). *Knowledge Organizations: What Every Manager Should Know*, Boca Raton, FL: St. Lucie/CRC Press.

Liebowitz, J., Rubenstein, B., and Buchwalter, J., et al. (1999). Developing a Knowledge Management Methodology, submitted for publication May.

Liebowitz, J., Rubenstein-Montano, B., McCaw, D., Buchwalter, J., Browning, C., Newman, B., and Rebeck, K. (2000). The Knowledge Audit, *Journal of Knowledge and Process Management* 7(1-2), John Wiley.

Liebowitz, J., Rubenstein-Montano, B., McCaw, D., Buchwalter, J., Browning, C., Newman, B., and Rebeck, K. (2000). *The Knowledge Audit, Knowledge and Process Management* 7(1-2).

Marquardt, M. (1996). *Building the Learning Organization*, McGraw Hill.

Moore, C. R. (1999). Performance Measures for Knowledge Management, in J. Liebowitz (Ed.), *The Knowledge Management Handbook*, Boca Raton, FL: CRC Press.

O'Dell, C. (1996). A Current Review of Knowledge Management Best Practice, Conference on Knowledge Management and the Transfer of Best Practices, *Business Intelligence*, London.

Saint-Onge, H. (1999). Knowledge Management, in *Proceedings of the 1998 New York Business Information Technology Conference*, TFPL, Inc., November.

Schein, E. H. (1992). *Organizational Culture and Leadership*, San Francisco, CA: Jossey-Bass Publishers.

Seaman, C. B., and Basili, V. R. (1994). OPT: Organization and Process Together, *AAAI Symposium on Computational Organization and Design*, March.

Smith, B. (1999). Personal communication. *American Management Systems*, Feb. 23.

Swoyer, S. (1999). Defining Knowledge Management in the Enterprise, *ENT*, 4(10), May 19.

Tierney, T. (1999). What's Your Strategy for Managing Knowledge? *Harvard Business Review*.

Van der Spek, R., and Hoog, R. de (1998). *Knowledge Management Network*, U. of Amsterdam, The Netherlands.

Van der Spek, R., and Spijkervet, A. (1997). Knowledge Management: Dealing Intelligently with Knowledge, in J. Liebowitz and L. Wilcox (Eds.), *Knowledge Management and Its Integrative Elements*, Boca Raton, FL: CRC Press.

Van Heijst, G., Van der Spek, R., and Kruizinga, E. (1997). Corporate Memories as a Tool for Knowledge management, *Expert Systems with Applications* 13(1).

Weidner, D. (1999). Summary of KM Framework by Phase, KMCI-GWA [handout], May 5.

Wielinga, B., Sandberg, J., and Schreiber, G. (1997). Methods and Techniques for Knowledge Management: What has Knowledge Engineering to Offer? *Expert Systems with Applications* 13(1).

Chapter 11

A Conceptual Model of Collaborative Information Seeking

Ric Jentzsch and Paul Prekop
University of Canberra, Australia

Past research into information seeking has generally focused on the information seeker as an individual, and examined the activities, roles, behaviours, methods and processes an individual uses to locate and gather information. Little work has been done examining the information seeker as a group, that is, collaborative information seeking. The goal of the research described in this paper is to examine collaborative information seeking, suggest a conceptual model for collaborative information seeking and relate that model to current information technology initiatives. The potential value of collaborative information seeking can be seen (not limited to) in such information technology initiatives as computer supported collaborative work (CSCW), knowledge management, and electronic commerce.

INTRODUCTION

The aim of this paper is to present information seeking within a collaborative context, suggest a conceptual model of collaborative information seeking, and suggest the application of the model in an information technology context.

Information seeking exists on a continuum ranging from individual information seeking, through shared information seeking, and into collaborative information

Previously Published in *Challenges of Information Technology Management in the 21st Century* edited by Mehdi Khosrow-Pour, Copyright © 2000, Idea Group Publishing.

seeking. During individual information seeking, the information seeker interacts with no one during the information seeking activity. During shared information seeking, the information seeker interacts with external agents or systems, in the way of social navigation (Jentzsch, 1999) that helps select information sources and aids in the gathering of the needed information. During collaborative information seeking, multiple information seekers work together throughout all stages of the information seeking activity in finding and retrieving information.

STUDY OF INFORMATION SEEKING

Formal research into information seeking has been conducted for more than 50 years, and has progressed from the initial views of information seeking as a mechanistic goal driven process, through to current cognitive and behavioural views of information seeking (Ellis, 1989). Information seeking forms an important part of many human activities, ranging from decision making and problem solving through to resource allocation and system management (Rouse and Rouse, 1984). As an area of research, information seeking crosses many disciplines, such as psychology, library and information science, management information systems, knowledge management, and information technology. Each discipline has it own set of models, perspectives and assumptions that attempt to define and describe information seeking (Brown, 1991).

Collaborative information seeking, that is information seeking as performed by a group of information seekers, has not been examined in detail by previous researchers or has it been well considered in the commercial world. As a result, there is little in the way of information technology to support information seeking when performed by two or more information seekers in a collaborative group environment.

Information seeking has been described and discussed from various view points and using various terms. For example the concepts presented in information literacy research encompasses all the skills and tools needed to find, understand, absorb, and essentially *use* information (Bruce, 1996; Mutch, 1997; Snavely and Cooper, 1997). Existing models of information seeking offer different perspectives on how information seeking can be described, and what activities, steps or actions constitute the information seeking activity (Westbrook, 1993; Kuhlthau, 1991; Ellis, 1989; Dervin, 1983; Cheuk, 1998; Court, 1997; Leckie, Pettigrew and Sylvain, 1996; Brown, 1991). Some of these models assume information

Figure 1: Information Seeking Continuum

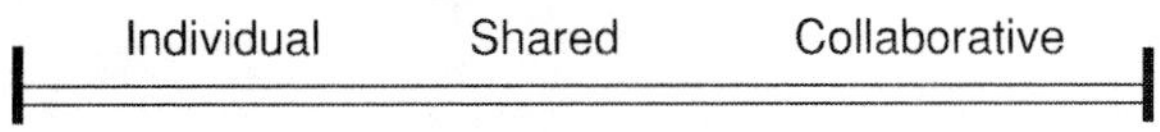

| Individual | Shared | Collaborative |

seeking is a linear process (Vickery and Vickery, 1987; Westbrook, 1993; Kuhlthau, 1991). Some authors assume it is a reactive process (Dervin 1983) or is based on information seeking situations (Cheuk, 1998; Court, 1997). Other authors assume information seeking is a synergistic activity, where the various elements of the information seeking activity interact in parallel (Brown, 1991; Leckie et al., 1996).

COLLABORATIVE INFORMATION SEEKING

Using the model of information seeking in Figure 2, information seeking is not a simple mechanical process. It is affected and influenced by the information seeker's cognitive abilities, awareness and experiences with the information sources, and the information seeker's past information seeking experiences. The nature of the information seeking activity is shaped by the nature and environment of the information seeker. The main argument this paper makes is that collaborative information seeking is different from information seeking performed by an individual working alone, because the group, as an information seeker, alters and affects the information seeking activity. A few authors, noticeably Narayanan, et al. (1999), acknowledge that group or collaborative information seeking is different to individual information seeking.

Figure 2: Conceptual Model of Information Seeking

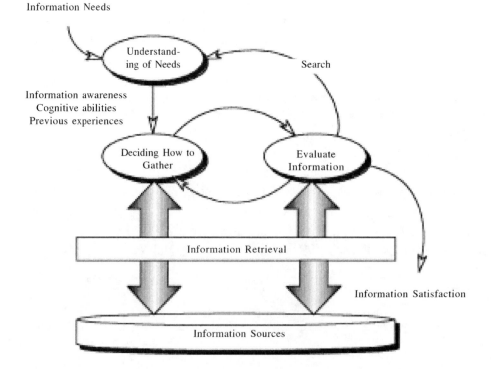

Interactions within Information Seeking

Information seeking is viewed and described from various perspectives. It can be examined from a conceptual perspective, it can be examined in terms of its context, and it can be examined in terms of the information gathered, or the sources used. Following are some of those perspectives.

No Interactions. Research by Court (Court et al., 1995a; Court, et al., 1995b; Court, 1997) shows the information seeker is completely self contained and has no interactions with external agents or systems.

A Client-Service/Service provider interaction. This involves the information seeker articulating a set of information needs, or a well developed information retrieval query to some type of external agent (Vickery and Vickery, 1987; Kuhlthau, 1993; Lancaster and Warner, 1993). Alternatively, the agent may be an information system, in the form of a database, or an index service, or bibliographic system, an Intranet or Extranet or some other system. In this case, information seekers articulate their information seeking query to a system for retrieval (Belkin, 1980).

A Group/Collaborative interaction. This form of information seeking exists within a group of information seekers. This is the perspective that is discussed in this paper.

Research Design

Within information seeking research, quantitative approaches often focused on user studies, and gathering and analysing the information seeker's view on particular sources or particular information (Cheuk, 1998; Gralewska-Vickery, 1976; Leckie et al., 1996; Tseng and Atkin, 1997) through to building profiles of users' attitude to information, and their information seeking personalities (Palmer, 1991; Bonner et al., 1998).

Qualitative research methods ranged from the interview approach of Ellis (1989), through to the observational, almost ethnographic approaches of Kuhlthau (1991) and Palmer (1991). There have also been attempts to combine both; Palmer's (1991) work on building an understanding of information seeking personalities combines both qualitative and quantitative methods.

What seemed to emerge as the major difference between previous studies on information seeking using a qualitative approach and previous studies on information seeking using a quantitative approach, was the degree to which the context of the phenomenon under study was included. As Kaplan and Duchon (1988) point out, the "immersion in context is a hallmark of qualitative research methods and the interpretive perspective on the conduct of research" (Kaplan and Duchon, 1988).

INFORMATION SEEKING

The conceptual model developed in this research and shown in Figure 2, is not intended as an empirically tested model of information seeking. This model servers as a basis for the development of the collaborative information seeking model and codifies many of the existing information seeking models. The model presented in Figure 2 further serves as a device to bring together a wide collection of research material describing information seeking into a coherent description of the activity. This model also serves as a beginning point of how information technology and collaborative information seeking can and will need to work together.

A Model of Information Seeking

An understanding of collaborative information seeking can provide insights and understanding that is needed to influence the development of information technology applications in support of various types of information seeking that is done in modern organisations. The model in Figure 2 codifies various information seeking research perspectives. The relationship between the elements of information seeking is also shown.

Information Needs

The information seeking activity can be seen as beginning with some state of information need. The concepts of information needs is well presented in literature. Westbrook (1993) describes the information seeking activity as beginning with a *needing* stage. For Westbrook (1993), needing is the state of acknowledging a need for some type of information.

For Kuhlthau (1991, 1993) information seeking begins with an *initiation* stage. During this stage, the information seeker first becomes aware of the need to gather information. The task during this stage is to recognise the initial need for information.

Sutcliffe and Ennis (1998), in their cognitive model of information seeking illustrate the information seeking activity as beginning when the information seeker encounters an "external task information problem" (Sutcliffe and Ennis 1998). For Sutcliffe and Ennis (1998), this is an external task.

Cheuk (1998) found that much of the information seeking activities performed by engineers was a result of information seeking situations. Cheuk found that the engineers tended to develop patterns of information seeking behaviours as a result of past information seeking situations, and tended to re-use these patterns in similar information seeking situations.

Leckie et al. (1996) examined the information seeking needs of professionals (specifically, doctors, lawyers and engineers) and found that there was a tight relationship between the professional's work role, the tasks that role included, and the type of information needed. Leckie, et al. (1996) further describes professionals as adopting one of five professional roles; service provider, administrator/manager, researcher, educator, and student.

Understanding of Needs

This stage of the information seeking activity has been identified and defined by several authors from the view point of an individual. Westbrook's (1993) *starting* stage describes the point at which the information seeker moves from having an information need to being able to deciding how best to meet that need. Westbrook points out that the process of moving from acknowledging a need to developing ways of articulating it is often ill defined (Westbrook 1993).

Brown (1991) describes the information seeking activity as beginning with a perceived need and moving through activities that work to satisfy that need. Sutcliffe and Ennis's (1998) *identify problem* and *articulate needs* stages, encompass the activities described here as being important for building an understanding of an information need. Belkin's (1980) anomalous state of knowledge (ASK) model describes many of the properties of information needs, and how they can be understood and articulated by the information seeker. Within the ASK model, information seeking needs can be seen as existing on two dimensions, the cognitive and the linguistic dimension (Belkin, 1980; Belkin et al., 1982a; Belkin et al., 1982b).

Deciding How to Gather

This stage of the information seeking activity is well represented in literature. In Westbrook's (1993) description of her *working* stage, she describes many of the activities that are a part of the deciding how to gather stage of the information seeking activity. Westbrook (1993) describes this stage of the information seeking activity as the most complex part of the process, encompassing all the activities and functions performed to gain or gather the needed information.

The *exploration* and *formulation* stages of Kuhlthau's empirically grounded model of information seeking, captures many of the elements of the deciding how to gather stage described here. Kuhlthau (1991) characterises the exploration stage as feelings of confusion, uncertainty and doubt.

Most of the information seeking behaviours described in Ellis's behavioural model (Ellis, 1989; Ellis, Cox et al., 1993; Ellis and Haugan, 1997) describe activities information seekers perform during the deciding how to gather stage of the information seeking model.

Ellis's *chaining* behaviour describes the process of following citation connections between information sources. Ellis also describes information seekers as building and maintaining an awareness of available information sources in several ways. Both formal and informal methods are used. Ellis describes *browsing* as a very important visible form of the monitoring activity. Browsing is often used to maintain an awareness of developments, as well as gaining an overview of a new area (Ellis, 1989; Ellis, Cox et al., 1993; Ellis and Haugan ,1997).

Erdelez (1997) noted that accidental information discovery has generally been seen in two distinct models, browsing behaviours, and environmental scanning. Browsing generally describes what Erdelez calls the "don't-know-what-I-want-behaviour." It can be seen as a semi-directed or semi-structured form of information seeking where the information seeker will scan a collection of information sources, with no particular information seeking goal in mind. The second model of accidental information discovery is environmental scanning. Environmental scanning can be seen as a type of information acquisition that involves various information activities needed to keep abreast of new information, changes or developments in specific domains (Erdelez, 1997).

Erdelez (1997) (like other authors) points out, accidental information discovery is important to information seeking because it represents a major way for information seekers to find information within complex environments, and it also represents a major way for information seekers to maintain an awareness of potentially useful information sources.

As well as perceptions of quality, timeliness and relevance, the information seeker's personal preference also affects what information sources the information seeker would consider using. As Krikelas (1983) points out, individual information seekers have their own personal hierarchy of the types of information sources they prefer.

Information Retrieval

For Westbrook (1993) physically gathering or retrieving information forms a major part of her *working* stage. This stage describes all the activities the information seeker performs to gather the information identified as being important as a result of the previous stages of her information seeking model.

Kuhlthau's *collection* step of the information seeking activity describes the process of actually gathering the information selected. Kuhlthau describes the information seeker as having developed a clearer sense of what topic is being searched, and what information is needed (Kuhlthau, 1991; Kuhlthau, 1993).

As pointed out by (Vickery and Vickery, 1987) when physically gathering the needed information, the information seeker can employ a wide selection of well understood tools and strategies to gather the needed information. As with other information sources, issues of trust, reliability, availability, and awareness, all affect the use of people and electronic information source (Johnson, 1996).

Evaluate Information

The goal of *evaluating information* is where the information seekers evaluate the selected and gathered information against their initial information needs. As shown in Figure 2, this information seeking stage includes a link back to the start of the information seeking activity. If information seekers find that the information they have gathered fails to meet their initial information needs, they may move through the information seeking activity again.

Not all information seeking models include an evaluating stage. For Westbrook (1993), evaluating the information selected is part of her *working* stage. For Kuhlthau's, evaluating the gathered information forms part of her *collection* step. Leckie et al. (1996) see the evaluation of gathered information as part of their *outcomes* stage.

Information Satisfaction

Different authors have described the ending of the information seeking activity in a variety of ways. In their model of the information seeking activities of professionals, Leckie, et al. (1996) describes the information seeking activity as having an *outcomes* stage.

Dervin's (1983) sense-making model describes how an information seeker moves into a state of information need, performs information seeking activities to meet that need, before moving into a state of information satisfaction. The information seeking activity typically ends when information seekers enter this state (Dervin, 1983; Dervin and Nilan, 1986).

For Kuhlthau (1991), the information seeking activity ends with a formal *presentation* stage. During this stage of the information seeking activity, feelings of satisfaction or dissatisfaction are common. Thoughts often involve a synthesis of new information, with information already known (Kuhlthau, 1991; Kuhlthau, 1993).

Ellis describes the information seeking activity ending with a specific *ending* behaviour. This behaviour generally includes the activities carried out at the end of the project (rather than at the end of a specific information seeking activity). For most of the information seekers examined in Ellis et al. (1993) and Ellis and Haugan (1997) the end of a project involves a write up of results and findings.

A CONCEPTUAL MODELING OF COLLABORATIVE INFORMATION SEEKING

Research into information seeking has focused primarily on individual and shared information seeking, with little research being done in examining collaborative information seeking. This conceptual model was derived using Grounded Theory (Martin and Turner, 1986) applied to the preliminary analysis of interviews of a collaborative work group and virtual collaboration exercises conducted in 1995 and 1996 (Jentzsch, 1996) with subsequent surveys conducted in 1997 and 1998, and on a collaborative project in 1998-1999.

Overview of Collaborative Information Seeking

Collaborative information seeking can be seen as consisting of three main elements: the roles, the patterns and the contexts in which the roles and patterns exist. At its essence collaborative information seeking is seen as the interactions of a group of representatives, each adopting one or more information seeking roles. These roles and the interactions between them exists within virtual and physical contexts. The collection of actions, interactions and behaviours clustering together is described as an information seeking pattern. These essential elements of collaborative information seeking, and their relationship is shown in Figure 3.

Roles are the grouping together of the behaviours, actions and responsibilities group members have and perform. Within this model of collaborative information seeking, roles are both formally assigned as well as being assigned or adopted by group members through both explicit and tacit negotiation.

Roles are enacted by representatives that are drawn from the structural context. This structural context affects the way the representatives will enact the different roles that they fulfil. The analysis of a 1998-1999 project where the mem-

Figure 3: A Model of Collaborative Information Seeking

Collaborative Information Seeking Context

Information Context

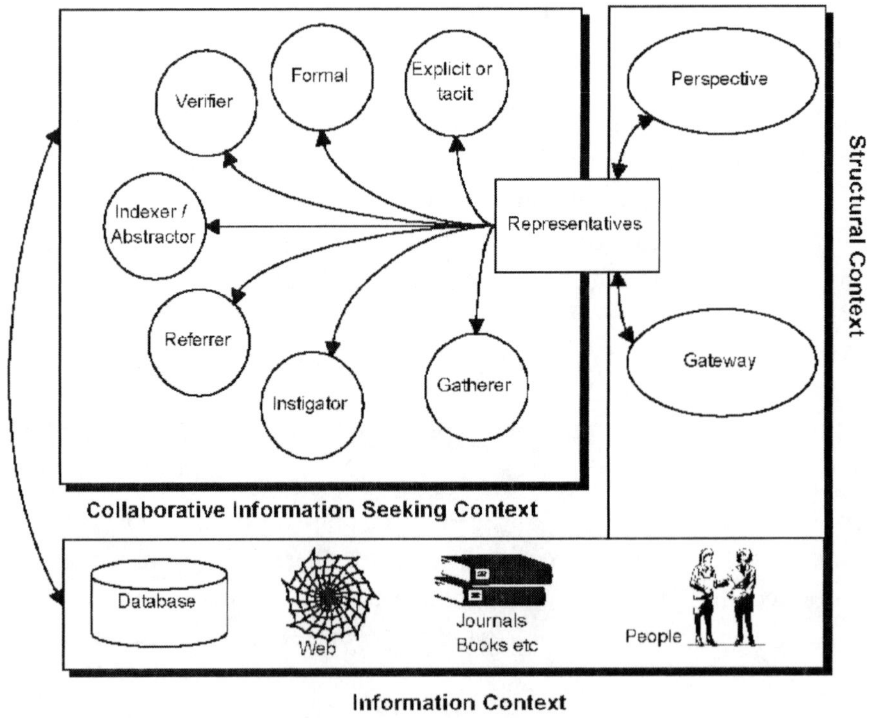

bers worked in a collaborative information seeking environment has shown that the information seekers adopted one of five roles. The five information seeking roles that each representative may adopt are:

- information referrer,
- information gatherer,
- information verifier,
- information seeking instigator, and
- information indexer / abstracter.

Two additional administrative roles were identified from the study that are important to the collaborative information seeking process. These administrative roles are the formal administrator and the explicit or tacit negotiated manager. Both these administrative roles are concerned with the management of the collaborative information seeking group.

As shown in Figure 3, collaborative information seeking can be seen as being affected by three different contexts, the *collaborative information seeking context*, the *information context* and the *structural context*. The collaborative information seeking context is where the collaborative activity of information seeking takes place. Each representatives can adopting one or more collaborative information seeking roles at any point in time.

The second context, the structural context, describes where each representative is drawn from. The context they bring can be described as their *structural perspective* and *structural gateway*. The representative's structural perspective and structural gateway influence and affect how each representative performs the roles they assume within the collaborative information seeking context.

The final context, the information context, contains the information that is sought by the collaborative information seekers. There is often a very tight relationship between the information and structural context. Also note that the information context covers a wide range of information sources.

Context and Representatives

Context is an important part of the model of collaborative information seeking model. Context not only represents where activities take place, as in the collaborative information seeking context, but also where the representatives who enact the different information seeking roles are drawn from. Context describes the collection of events, histories, culture, knowledge, and understanding, which exist together at a point in time, in which actions occur or in which people exist (Dervin, 1996; Sonnenwald, 1999).

Information Seeking Patterns

Within the collaborative information seeking model, the term information seeking patterns is used to describe groupings of information seeking behaviour that appear frequently within the collected data. Information seeking patterns describe how a work group or group of individuals work together to perform the various actions of collaborative information seeking. The information seeking patterns illustrate how the contexts and roles work together to gather information.

Seeking patterns in collaborative information seeking is divided into five areas. These five areas are:

- seeking by provocation,
- seeking by recommendation,
- seeking by direct questioning,
- seeking by advertising representation, and
- seeking by trading advertisements.

Seeking by Provocation

Representative members of a group draw on their structural perspective and gateway during information seeking discussions. The outcome is intended to be a well defined information need.

Information Seeking by Recommendation

This pattern is tied very tightly to the information referrer role described previously. The important characteristic of this information seeking pattern is the unsolicited nature of the information, or information references, forwarded by the information referrer.

Direct Questioning

The direct questioning information seeking pattern is the most intuitive of all the information seeking patterns discussed. This pattern describes a form of information seeking which is driven by the information seeking instigator.

Advertising Representation

The advertising representation pattern is not so much about seeking information, as it is about providing potential paths by which to seek information.

Trading of advertisements

The final form of advertising representation that emerges. This is where representative members of the group or even outside of the group, act as information gatherers or information indexers/abstracters.

Knowledge and Information Management Technology

When dealing with complex information held within a large organisation, information is often found through the use of interpersonal contacts also referred to as social navigation. The understanding of how information seekers build and maintain their awareness of interpersonal contacts may help address the tacit knowledge problem which current information and knowledge management technology may face.

The one necessary prerequisite for current forms of information and knowledge management is that the information or knowledge they deal with is explicit, that is, the information or knowledge they manage can be independently (free from its owner or creator), expressed in some shared and recordable form. The form may vary from structured database records, unstructured text, graphical representations, through to production rules, or semantic networks, and so on. However, research into information and knowledge within organisations has shown that information and knowledge can also be described as tacit (McAulay et al., 1997; Polanyi, 1966). Tacit information or knowledge, is information or knowledge which is often personal, often context-specific, hard to formulate, hard to communicate and very difficult to express in some shared, recordable form. Traditional forms of information and knowledge management may be unable to deal with this style of information or knowledge (McAulay et al., 1997; Nonaka and Takeuchi, 1995).

Computer Supported Collaborative Work

Within the area of computer supported collaborative work (CSCW), the understanding provided by the collaborative information seeking model developed in this paper may impact in several ways. The understanding of how and why people act as information sources may provide ways of building a better awareness of other organisational members, and the information, knowledge and experience they have.

FUTURE WORK

A major limiting factor of the collaborative information seeking model developed and described in this paper, is its scope. The model can only reliability be said to describe collaborative information seeking in a generic context. Ideally additional work needs to on validating the conceptual model.

The second major limitation of the research is the ability to collect data and test the data on a variety of situations. To do this requires the cooperation of industry, government, and other organisations that have team projects (virtual and physical) that are willing to let the teams be studied as they go about collaboratively seeking information.

Finally it would be naive to suggest that this model would fit all situations. Even in the ones that it was derived from there exists questions that can not be answered. For example, in the global virtual teams, not every member of the team across all political boarders responded to the survey that were distributed. This also brings up the question of cultural differences in collaborative information seeking, (as well as several others) an area that is not covered in this paper.

CONCLUSION

The data collection methods used failed to capture many of the subtleties of the information seeking patterns. As a result not all patterns could be reliably described within the context of conceptual model of collaborative information seeking as presented in Figure 3. Alternative additional data collection methods, for example an ethnographical approach performed on a variety of live collaborative information seeking activities followed up by surveys and interviews may provide more detailed data that can be used to revise or validate the model with a higher level of confidence.

REFERENCES

Belkin, N. J. (1980). Anomalous States of Knowledge as a Basis for Information Retrieval. *Canadian Journal of Information Science* 5.

Belkin, N. J., Oddy, R. N. and Brooks, H. M. (1982a). ASK For information Retrieval: Part I Background Theory. *Journal of Documentation* 38(2).

Belkin, N. J., Oddy, R. N. and Brooks, H. M. (1982b). ASK For Information Retrieval: Part II. Results of a Design Study. *Journal of Documentation* 38(3).

Bonner, M. M., Casey, E., Greenwood, J., Johnstone, D., Keane, D., and Huff, S. L. (1998). Information Behaviour - A Preliminary Investigation. *IRMA International Conference*, Boston, MA: Idea Group Publishing.

Brown, M. E. (1991). A General Model of Information-Seeking Behaviour. *Proceedings of the ASIS Annual Meeting, American Society for Information Science*.

Bruce, C. (1996). *The Seven Faces of Information Literacy*. Adelaide, Auslib Press.

Cheuk, W. (1998). Exploring Information Literacy in the Workplace: A Qualitative Study of Engineers Using the Sense-Making Approach. *International Forum on Information and Documentation* 23(2).

Computerworld (1999). Rolling Out the Web carpet. http://www.computerworld.com. Sept 27.

Court, A. W. (1997). The Relationship Between Information and Personal Knowledge in New Product Development. *International Journal of Information Management* 17(2).

Court, A. W., Culley, S. J., and McMahon, C. A. (1995). A Methodology for Analysing the Information Accessing Methods of Engineering Designers. *Inter-*

national Conference on Engineering Design (ICDE'95), Praha, Czech Republic.

Court, A. W., Culley, S. J. and McMahon, C. A. (1995). Modelling the Information Access Methods of Engineering Designers. *International Conference on Design Theory and Methodology (DTM'95)*, Boston MA.

Dervin, B. (1983). An Overview of Sense-Making Research: Concepts, methods and Results to Date. *International Communications Association Annual Meeting*, Dallas, Texas, USA, OnLine, [http://communication.sbs.ohio-state.edu/sensemaking/art/artdevin83.html].

Dervin, B. (1996). Given a Context by any other name: Methodological tools for taming the unruly beast. *ISIC 96: Information Seeking in Context*, Tampere, Finland, Taylor Graham.

Dervin, B. and Nilan, M. (1986). Information Needs and Use. *Annual Review of Information Science and Technology*. M. E. Williams, American Society for Information Science, 21.

Ellis, D. (1989). A Behavioural Approach to Information Retrieval System Design. *Journal of Documentation* 45(3).

Ellis, D., Cox, D. and Hall, K. (1993). A comparison of the Information Seeking Patterns of Researchers in the Physical and Social Sciences. *Journal of Documentation* 49(4).

Ellis, D. and Haugan, M. (1997). Modelling the Information Seeking Patterns of Engineers and Research Scientists in an Industrial Environment. *Journal of Documentation* 53(3).

Erdelez, S. (1997). Information encountering: a conceptual framework for accidental information discovery. *International Conference on Research in Information Needs, Seeking and Use in Different Contexts*, Tampere, Finland, London: Taylor Graham.

Gralewska-Vickery, A. (1976). Communication and Information Needs of Earth Science Engineers. *Information Processing and Management* 12.

Jentzsch, R. (1996). Global Virtual Collaboration - an Australian Experience, *Seventh Australian Information Systems Conference*, 11 - 13 December, Hobart, Tasmania.

Jentzsch, R. (1999). A Model and Application of Social Navigation of Information, *IRMA'99 Conference* 16 – 19 May 1999, Hershey, PA, USA.

Johnson, J. D. (1996). *Information Seeking: An Organisational Dilemma*. London: Quorum Books.

Kaplan, B. and Duchon, D. (1988). Combining Qualitative and Quantitative Methods in Information Systems Research: A Case Study. *MIS Quarterly* 12(4).

Krikelas, J. (1983). Information-Seeking Behaviour: Patterns and Concepts. *Drexel Library Quarterly 19*, 5(20).

Kuhlthau, C. C. (1991). Inside the Search Process: Information Seeking from the User's Perspective. *Journal of the American Society for Information Science* 42(5).

Kuhlthau, C. C. (1993). A Principle of Uncertainty for Information Seeking. *Journal of Documentation* 49(4).

Lancaster, F. W. and Warner, A. J. (1993). *Information Retrieval Today*. Arlington: Information Resource Press.

Leckie, G., Pettigrew, K. and Sylvain, C. (1996). Modelling the information seeking of professionals: A general model derived from research on engineers, health care professionals and lawyers. *Library Quarterly* 66(2).

Martin, P. Y. and Turner, B. A. (1986). Grounded Theory and Organisational Research. *The Journal of Applied Behavioural Science* 22(2).

McAulay, L., Russell, G. and Sims, J. (1997). Tacit Knowledge for Competitive Advantage. *Management Accounting*.

Mutch, A. (1997). Information Literacy: an Exploration. *International Journal of Information Management* 17(5).

Narayanan, S., Bailey, W., Tendulkar, J., Wilson, K., Daley, R., and Pliske, D. (1999). Modelling Real-World information Seeking in a Corporate Environment. *International Journal of Human Factors and Ergonomics in Manufacture* 9(2).

Nonaka, I. and Takeuchi, H. (1995). *The Knowledge Creating Company: How Japanese Companies Create the Dynamics of Innovation*. Melbourne, Oxford University Press.

Palmer, J. (1991). Scientists and Information: Using Cluster Analysis to Identify Information Style. *The Journal of Documentation* 47(2).

Polanyi, M. (1966). *The Tacit Dimension*. London: Routledge & Kegan Paul Ltd.

Rouse, W. B. and Rouse, S. H. (1984). Human Information Seeking and Design of Information Systems. *Information Processing and Management* 20(1-2).

Snavely, L. and Cooper, N. (1997). The information literacy debate. *Journal of Academic Librarianship* 23(1).

Sonnenwald, D. H. (1999). *Evolving Perspectives of Human information Behaviour: Context, Situations, Social Networks and Information Horizons*. Information Seeking in Context '98, London, Taylor Graham.

Strauss, A. (1987). *Qualitative Analysis for social scientists*. Melbourne, Cambridge University Press.

Sutcliffe, A. and Ennis, M. (1998). Towards a Cognitive Theory of Information Retrieval. *Interacting with Computers* 10(3).

Tseng, G. and Atkin, L. (1997). Information gathering by UK business school academic and research staff. OnLine Information 97: *21th International Online Information Meeting*, Oxford UK, Learned Information Europe Ltd.

Vickery, B. C. and Vickery, A. (1987). *Information Science in Theory and Practice*. Sydney: Butterworths.

Westbrook, L. (1993). User Needs: A synthesis and Analysis of Current Theories for the Practitioner. *RQ* 32(4).

Chapter 12

Information Manager/Librarian to Knowledge Manager: Change of Role

K. Nageswara Rao and KH Babu
Defence Research & Development Laboratory, India

Many organizations world over are embracing knowledge management systems for survival and to retain profitability. This trend is visible in the technology intensive businesses like biotechnology, computers and telecommunications and also in professions like legal, accountancy and management consultancy. A new breed of managers called "Knowledge Manager" has emerged to put the new system in place in the organizations. Information Managers and Librarians are increasingly drafted to fill the post of Knowledge Managers as their work is nearest to the job. This article covers the broad classification of knowledge and the mechanisms of its transmission and transformation. Finally the importance of human element in the Knowledge Management System is highlighted for the benefit of Information Managers and Librarians.

INTRODUCTION

In the last decades of the twentieth century a shift in economy from capital to information base is perceptible. The intellectual capital in an organization has come to be realized as its main asset. This has resulted in more emphasis being laid in the business organizations on generation and maintenance of intellectual capital. The system that deals with this aspect is termed "Knowledge Management (KM)."

Previously Published in *Challenges of Information Technology Management in the 21st Century* edited by Mehdi Khosrow-Pour, Copyright © 2000, Idea Group Publishing.

The urgency felt in many organizations to have a KM system in place is understandable. The well-established best practices, which were supposed to retain their effectiveness over time, are increasingly seen unable to retain their efficacy indefinitely. The knowledge, which is a key factor in competitive advantage, has become so dynamic and short-lived that its effective management has become an imperative necessity for the survival. KM is seen under the circumstances as the system, which helps the organization to retain its competitive edge or advantage in the fast changing economic environment. The rapid inroads made by Knowledge Management in the organizations dealing with biotechnology, computer software and telecommunications and in firms of lawyers, accountants and management consultants illustrate the point.

The work of Information Managers and Librarians in the organizations though far from identical with that of the newly created Knowledge Managers, is nearest to the work of the later. The Information Managers and Librarians have therefore become the choice of the management to fill the new post of Knowledge Manager. It is important for the Information Managers and Librarians who are traditionally associated with the activities of gathering, enhancing, structuring and distributing information to fully understand what is KM and how to develop a KM system and put it in place in the organization. It is in their interest to understand the developments in KM and apply its principles where appropriate or risk being marginalized as others, more efficient and flexible organizations are likely to step in to offer a knowledge service with clout (Keeling and Hornby, 1999). It is intended in this article to introduce salient features of KM to the Information Managers and Librarians.

KNOWLEDGE MANAGEMENT (KM) DEFINITIONS

According to Chambers 20th Century Dictionary Knowledge is "assured belief, that which is known, information, instruction, enlightenment, learning, practical skill, acquaintance, cognizance, etc." Management is the "manner of directing or use of anything." The definition of KM according to one of the experts is "Knowledge Management caters to the critical issues of organizational adoption, survival and competence in face of increasingly discontinuous environmental change. Essentially it embodies organizational processes that seek synergistic combination of data and information processing capacity of information technologies and the creative and innovative capacity of human beings"(Malhotra, 1999). Another definition is "In practice, Knowledge Management often encompasses identifying and mapping intellectual assets within the organization, generating new knowledge for competitive advantage within the organization, making vast amounts of corporate information accessible, sharing of best practices, and technology that enables all of the above - including GroupWare and intranets"(Barclay and Murray, 1997). KM is explained as "A business practice that focuses on harnessing knowledge and information and making it seamlessly available to all employees in an organization in order to enable them to do their job better"(Sukumar, 1999). It is seen from these definitions that KM encompasses two domains, physical and non-physical and two states, inanimate and animate. A professional Information Manager and Librarian who hitherto concerned himself more with Information Technology and its advancements has to go far beyond to uncharted areas like creativity, knowledge, mind set etc. of the people and become proficient in exploitation of the somewhat esoteric aspects of human nature for the organizational benefit. Herein lies the challenge to the new Knowledge Manager. He has to assume a proactive role and his focus has to shift to the individuals in the organization.

TYPES OF KNOWLEDGE

Depending on where it is residing Knowledge is classified into "Explicit" and "Tacit"(Nonaka and Takeuchi, 1995). The Explicit Knowledge is the knowledge that can be articulated in formal language including grammatical statements, mathematical expressions, specifications, manuals, etc., and can be transmitted across individuals formally and easily. This is the knowledge with which Information Managers and Librarians are familiar. The Tacit Knowledge, on the other hand, is hard to articulate with formal language or communicate. It is personal knowledge embedded in individual experience and involves intangible factors such as skill, perspective, know how, value system etc. It is subjective and is acquired by practice. Tacit Knowledge in many organizations has never been recorded though its existence is known to be at the core of organizational performance.

The crucial factor in the role change of Information Managers and Librarians to Knowledge Managers involves their understanding, capturing and transferring the tacit knowledge in the organization to explicit knowledge. While their familiarity with the management of explicit knowledge could be of help in the new role, it is by no means sufficient or substitute to the new skills demanded in the role of Knowledge Manager. Acquisition of new skills, attitudinal change, clear vision of organizational goals, better interpersonal relationships, proactive outlook etc., are some of the aspects involved in the process of conversion to Knowledge Manager.

HUMAN ELELEMT IN KNOWLEDGE MANAGEMENT

The present day business environments are not stable and predictable. In these environments, the traditional heuristics based solutions to problems are found to be far from satisfactory in many cases. Due to perceptual insensitivity of changing environments, the core competency of yesterday in an organization has become its bane in the form core rigidity. In order to match the variety and complexity of outside environment, the need to encourage the human imagination and creativity within the organization is becoming apparent.

The Information Technology (IT) based management is not adequately equipped to address and solve the problem of tapping the tacit knowledge available in the organization. The Knowledge Management scheme acknowledges and gives explicit recognition to tacit knowledge and related human aspects such as ideas, values, emotions, etc., in the process of tapping it for problem solving. The KM paradigm aims at capturing diverse perspectives in a situation rather than epitomize and simplify the contextual information for storage in IT enabled repositories. KM recognizes that the human beings are the best sensors to capture the nuances and complexity of the phenomenon and the changes occurring in the external environment. The reality so captured plays the key role in shaping the organizational response to a situation in the KM system.

In a culture where individual knowledge ownership is held in high esteem, the individual instinctively feels the power of knowledge. Sharing knowledge with others, in essence, is sharing power and in general this is not to the liking of the individuals. The tough task in putting in place any KM system is in persuading people to part with the critical knowledge in their possession and share it with others. In other words creating a culture of knowledge sharing. To make this task smooth the first step would be to convince, educate and demonstrate to the individual, the need and benefit that would accrue to the organization and eventually to the individual on such sharing. As an organizational policy, knowledge sharing should be rewarded and hoarding discouraged. It is however important not to forget the lessons of history in communism while dealing with individuals. Persuasion rather than punishment should be the modus operandi in this endeavor.

INFORMATION TECHNOLOGY (IT) IN KNOWLEDGE MANAGEMENT

The importance and use of IT in tackling the turbulence and complexity of external environments is well known. IT, however, cannot drive KM by itself though it plays a vital role in facilitating the adoption and success of a KM initiative in an organization. In the quest to outdo competition, the demand for increased capabilities and more sophisticated ways of utilization of IT is seen in the organizations. The leverage offered by the new IT is undeniable in easing the problems. It is also equally true that the advances in IT have brought new problems peculiar to its speed, versatility and ubiquity.

External Knowledge is the knowledge capital that has its origin outside the organization. Examples are outside experts, online databases, Internet, etc. Information Technology is adept in dealing with the knowledge external to the organization, though, of late enormous strides have been made in the adaptation of IT to internal networks. GroupWare, data warehousing and mining technologies etc. have become indispensable tools in the decision making process. It is important for a Knowledge Manager to give due weightage to the incorporation of IT advances in the systems designed for capturing knowledge be it internal or external. The complimentary nature of the internal and external knowledge to each other should never be lost sight of.

KNOWLEDGE TRANSMISSION AND TRANSFORMATION

It is important to understand how knowledge transmission and transformation takes place before attempting to put a KM system in place (Rao and Prakash, 1999). A prerequisite for the success of KM initiative is that a sense of urgency and a feeling of challenge should prevail in the organization for its adoption. Management has a key role to play here.

Tacit to tacit transmission takes place through personal interactions or socialization mostly in an informal way. For this to be effective a clear understanding of the tacit component of the knowledge is essential. Also, conducive environment at the location, be it inside or outside the organization should exist. Tacit knowledge conversion to explicit form occurs by an externalization process in which the tacit knowledge in the form of intuitive maps gets translated into recordable format consisting of visual and indexed maps. These maps facilitate common understanding and can be reused. The usage of knowledge so converted should be encouraged in workflow and problem solving.

While the organizations are experimenting with new ways of conversion of tacit knowledge to the explicit knowledge, the traditional methods should not be overlooked. Mentoring or apprenticing juniors to veterans, reward schemes etc., have proved their utility over eons and as such have to be encouraged besides the high-tech methods such as videotaping the actions and conversations of veterans etc.

The experience of some of the commercial organizations in India suggests that knowledge sharing amongst the personnel in an organization is not really a big problem and the workers do share their knowledge given conducive environment and work culture (Mullick, 1999). The firm Pricewaterhousecoopers experience brings out that the organizations which have an informal work environment that promotes sharing or which tailor their work environment in such a way that the employees cannot prosper without participating in knowledge sharing, stand the best chance of translating KM into a sustainable competitive advantage. The information flow in the organization should be smooth and the set up nonbureaucratic. Tata Consultancy Services (TCS) experience indicates that people willingly come forward to create shareable and reusable assets given the conscious encouragement by the firm. TCS recognized that proper KM infrastructure which facilitates conversion of knowledge into assets in extremely essential. The publicity given within TCS for contributions to knowledge sharing also acted as a major incentive for the individuals or teams. Lotus Development Corporation believes that with its understanding of groupware it has learned that people will share what they know and reuse the know-how of others if it is easy for them, and worth their while. The firm DBS Internet asserts that to enable knowledge sharing, one has to first change the mindset "knowledge is proprietary." It needs to be understood by all the workers in the enterprise that being part of a single entity, they have a shared destiny, which can be best achieved through knowledge sharing.

Explicit to explicit knowledge conversion is essentially a reconfiguration of existing explicit knowledge to more efficient methods and processes. The knowledge base of an organization is the collective information stored in a variety of systems like server based file system, client desktops, relational databases, mail data stores, data on internet etc. The KM systems should provide a seamless view of this data to the end user in a user-friendly way. The process of explicit to explicit conversion involves the categorization and organization of the knowledge base into a well structured base that is meaningful, intuitive and easy to use. The Information Managers and Librarians have an important role to play in defining the taxonomy of the knowledge base, in the development of metadata and more importantly the creation of controlled vocabulary that reflects the business of the organization. Explicit to tacit conversion of knowledge takes place as user repeatedly applies the explicit knowledge in his work. The peer force and the organizations work culture have an important role to play in this type of conversion.

ROLE CHANGE OF INFORMATION MANAGERS AND LIBRARIANS TO KNOWLEDGE MANAGERS

The choice of Information Manager/Librarian for the new post of Knowledge Manager in many organizations is no accident. The former is already carrying out an important part of the job of the later albeit with a different perspective. The activities, which an Information Manager/Librarian has to address in the process of conversion to Knowledge Manager are, capturing, cataloguing, retrieving and utilizing Knowledge capital of the organization (Speh, 1998).

The first step in a KM programme is to define and determine what constitutes the knowledge asset for an organization. As this is the foundation of KM system, it is essential that most experienced executives in the organization are in-charge of the activity. The components of the knowledge base of the organization are defined and identified at this stage. This is also referred to as knowledge audit. In knowledge audit a point of caution is to avoid the tendency to be highly technical in the kind of information collected. The business and marketing information also has to be given due importance in the overall interest of the business.

Capture Knowledge Capital

The process of capturing initially essentially involves going out there to the locations and working side by side with the possessors of the knowledge to extract the knowledge and add it to be knowledge capital of the organization. Subsequently suitable mechanisms have to be kept in place for this activity to occur automatically. Weeding out of obsolete knowledge is also an essential activity. It has to be carried out by experts periodically. Knowledge Management is concerned with separating the grain from the chaff and weeding out is as important for knowledge base development as addition of new knowledge. The process of capturing tacit knowledge calls upon the Information Managers and Librarians to foray into the study of subjects like psychology, administration, human resource development etc. to be effective in the task. This aspect has been endorsed by the authors like Hazel Hall (1999).

The captured data and information is stored across a variety of systems, which include intranet servers, desktops, relational databases, mail data stores like MS Exchange etc. Besides these, the information accessible in web sites on internet and external mail data sources also have to be considered as part of captured knowledge base. Generally the information both internal and external is too voluminous, poorly organized and not integrated. Also there is the problem of ensuring accuracy. The best people to access, index, evaluate, authenticate and send the information around the organization are the Information Managers and Librarians. The next step in KM initiative therefore concerns with how these professionals go about the task of cataloguing the knowledge capital.

Cataloguing Knowledge Capital

An essential requirement for effective use of knowledge base created following the knowledge audit is to catalogue and organize it in a way that is most meaningful to the end users. The classification scheme adopted should facilitate intuitive and easy end use. At the time of classification, metadata, which is information about information, should be created as it plays a very important part in retrieval of information and in delivering more focussed results.

In the context of structuring and classifying a knowledge base, the development of a controlled vocabulary is very important. The knowledge audit carried out initially at the beginning of KM initiative normally brings out new categories, which were not part of terminology so far used by the organizations. The development of comprehensive controlled vocabulary, which reflects the business of the organization, is very important for the dissemination and end use of knowledge. Knowledge Managers require varying degree of technical expertise in the use of Intranet, GroupWare, creation of home pages on intranet, knowledge maps and agent technology applications based on the categorized knowledge base. Their contribution in these areas is very critical for the success of the KM initiative.

Retrieve Knowledge Capital

Knowledge Manager has to act as a coach initially to help users in the use of enabling information technology for the retrieval of knowledge from the knowledge base. In a good number of organizations network structure with embedded system tools of Intranet technology and GroupWare products is used for knowledge sharing. The system has capability to incorporate content and content-rich interfaces, which are attractive to the users. While it is not possible for the Information Manager/Librarian turned Knowledge Manager to master all the technological skills needed to use the system capabilities fully, to some degree, depending on the organization set-up, he has to inculcate aptitude and learn about the IT system in operation in his organization.

Initially training has to be imparted to the user on navigation on the internal network. The navigation skills training must go beyond to know which button of a system causes the desired effect. It should impart solid knowledge of the vocabulary used and the content and organization of the knowledge base.

The advances in IT facilitate the integration of KM in the workflow process. Knowledge Manager uses these to match the content of the knowledge base with the user preferences, needs and history of past usage to develop a personalized capsule, which can be pushed periodically with updating on to user desktop. There are a number of similar capabilities available for the effective use of knowledge base.

Utilize Knowledge Capital

The KM system can change the business perspective of an organization only when the knowledge capital is utilized fully by the individuals in the organization. In a system designed to share information, collaboration and communication are critical. Collaboration is facilitated by the modern IT in the form of interactive audio and video sessions and shared applications. These sessions in their native format should be captured and after an audit made part of knowledge base. Transcribing these sessions into textual format is also a possibility. The aim is to deliver information in a coherent and easy to use form to the user for effective use in his/her workflow process.

The knowledge Manager has a catalytic role to play in the KM initiative of an organization. Besides him, few experienced personnel in the organization have to assume a new role and name "Knowledge Champion" to cascade KM up and down the organizational hierarchy. The knowledge Manager has to nurture and support a network of knowledge champions as a part of his job. Though the efforts of these pioneers the KM culture takes root in the organization and knowledge based communities emerge.

SUMMARY

KM initiative has evolved as a response to the complex business environment existing in the world. It is successfully practiced in some organizations. It is a fact to day that very few organizations support knowledge sharing or knowledge management through their culture. The implementation of KM initiative without reservations is a prerequisite for its success. The vision and resolve of the top management are crucial for the emergence of an organization as a KM organization.

Information Managers/Librarians have great promise to assume the role of Knowledge Managers. The conversion however is not simple. It requires enormous effort, change of mindset, work culture and learning of new skills. In the end such an effort is worth the while as knowledge Manager would be the most sought after person in the new set-up.

ACKNOWLEDGEMENT

The encouragement and support given by Mr. Prahlada, Director, DRDL, Hyderabad in promoting knowledge management systems in general and for preparing this article in particular are acknowledged.

REFERENCES

Barclay, R. O., and Murray, P. C. (1997). What is Knowledge Management? *Knowledge at Work.* http://www.knowledge-at-work.com/whatis.htm.

Hall, H. (1999). Knowledge Management Lecture Outline 3: KM the Organization Approach. http://www.bim.napier.ac.uk/~hazel/km/km_lec3.htm.

Keeling, C., and Hornby, S. (1999). Knowledge Management in the Networked Public Library. *Managing Information*, 6(8). http://www.aslib.co.uk/man-inf/current/article01.html.

Malhotra, Y. (1999). Knowledge Management for the New World of Business. *Journal of Quality & Participation*, 21(4); pp.58-80.

Mullick, P. (1999). Knowledge Management. *Information Systems Computerworld.* November 1-15.

Nonaka, I., and Takeuchi, H. (1995). The Knowledge-Creating Company: How Japanese Companies Create the Dynamics of Innovation. London: Oxford University Press, VIII pp.

Rao, A.L., and Prakash, S. (1999). Issues of Knowledge Management Architecture: Conceptual Framework: The crucial Beginning. *DATAQUEST*. Supplement Series, XVII(18); pp.10-13.

Speh, M. (1998). Knowledge Management in *Handbook of Special Librarianship and Information Work*. London: ASLIB; 145-157pp.

Sukumar, S. (1999). Technologies for Knowledge Management: Customer-Driven Solution Is The Key. *DATAQUEST*. Supplement Series, XVII(18); pp.14-17.

Chapter 13

Social and Cultural Barriers for Knowledge Databases in Professional Service Firms

Georg Disterer
University of Applied Sciences, Germany

Professional Service Firms (PSF), where professionals (consultants, lawyers, accountants, auditors, tax advisors, engineers ...) work, are interested in knowledge management, because their business is heavily dependent from the knowledge of their employees. Core asset is their ability to solve complex problems through creative and innovative solutions, the basis for this is their employees' knowledge. Therefore, PSF are on the forefront of knowledge management. Experiences show that Information Technology (IT) is only one dimension of knowledge management, more important are social, cultural, and organizational dimensions.[1]

INTRODUCTION

There is hardly a professional denying that the use of working documents and similar materials produced by others is wise. All PSF are trying to set up collections of knowledge acquired in projects or while processing cases in order to share it and conserve it for reuse. Sharing knowledge between colleagues improves the economical benefits of a PSF's expertise[2]. The network of professionals in most cases can arise significantly better professional advice than any individual. Sharing knowledge is critical for PSF, because "... knowledge and intellect

Previously Published in *Challenges of Information Technology Management in the 21st Century* edited by Mehdi Khosrow-Pour, Copyright © 2000, Idea Group Publishing.

grow exponentially when shared,"[3] otherwise individual professionals become "atoms of knowledge, and the firm just the sum of individuals."[4] Knowledge databases can address what is sometimes called the traditional weakness of PSF: "... narrow specialists who see only their own solutions, self-centered egoists unwilling or unable to collaborate with colleagues."[5] Knowledge databases (in any form) are seen as an instrument to foster sharing and collaboration. Only for greater clarity of the argumentation this paper concentrates on PSF; the same is true for other companies or departments in which knowledge is critical.

Although the benefits of sharing and reusing of knowledge are quite clear, many attempts to use knowledge databases failed the expectations: only a few databases are accepted as up to date, the special fields of expertise are covered only in fragments. The access is laborious and uncomfortable. Heterogenous sources (text, internal and external databases, journals, books, comments, codes of law) hardly can be integrated. Especially the lack of actuality and completeness causes massive quality risks if dealt thoughtless and unreflected.

Obviously there is an discrepancy between the expectations and actual benefits, independent whether professionals collect paper documents manually, whether librarians set up such collections, or whether knowledge databases are constructed and maintained by massive use of IT. We analyze the existing social barriers for knowledge databases.

WORRIES OF LOSS

The phrase said to be by Francis Bacon "knowledge is power" is well-known and intuitively correct for many situations. Anybody knowing something may use this knowledge by taking action and enforce his/her influence – those who do not own knowledge are deprived of such capacity to act or to influence. In business perspectives, this is true regarding knowledge about customers, competitors, suppliers, procedures, recipes, methods etc. For PSF the evaluation of special situations and the knowledge about effective solutions is critical. Transferring this knowledge means enabling colleagues to act and grants influence. In this sense someone who passes on knowledge looses the exclusiveness of influence, he/she share this possibility with colleagues. This will function only if there is no unnecessary hard competition between the professionals.[6]

However, the worry about another loss has to be obeyed: with the passing on a monopoly of knowledge is abandoned. Such monopolies tend to be cultivated since they suggest job security and the esteem of others. Anybody who possesses monopolistic knowledge probably wont get dispensable or replaceable easily. And, intelligibly: who wont be happy to be asked by colleagues as an "expert" with rare knowledge? Anybody who shares knowledge frankly probably deprives himself/herself of the chance to be asked. With databases, the value that is apportioned to the knowledge is passed over from the person to the database. These worries lead to the fact that knowledge is protected and hidden from others and from being compiled in collections and databases. Protecting and hoarding of knowledge means security. Overcoming professionals' natural reluctance to share presents some challenges.[7]

Moreover, knowledge sharing runs counter to values that our society impresses on individuals. There are deep cultural traditions that tend to discourage sharing. Even memories of school confirm the picture of a treasury that has to be protected and hidden. During examinations the use of shared potentials is castigated as a "crib" and attempts to deceive, what counts are the individually produced results. Establishing knowledge databases also means to overcome those memories.

FEAR OF AWKWARDNESS

Putting working results into a database also may be felt as revelation. Thus, a professional by providing his/her working results also proclaims that the knowledge has certain value and rareness. If this assessment is not shared by colleagues, e.g., if they consider the collected knowledge as worthless or useless, there is the risk that they devalue the professional in total. Also, even with greatest care it is almost impossible to avoid inaccuracy. Therefore, there is the risk to abandon such deficits to colleagues by providing knowledge in a database. Moreover some colleagues tend to hurriedly point out alleged necessary improvements just to emphasize their own expertise. If this is not clearly marked as a loyal supplement the impression of humiliation hardly can be prevented.

FEELING OF UNCERTAINTY

Providing working results in knowledge databases assumes that the results are not too general, not well known, and not too specific for the current case. The positioning on the scale of "general" to "specific" is not trivial at all and, thus, generates uncertainty. Especially younger professionals may feel uncomfortable. Additionally, a professional providing knowledge has no certainty who, when and for what purpose this knowledge will be used. The unconsidered and unreflected use of the database involve considerable risks of quality and liability. An reasonable consequence is not to part with knowledge in form of contracts, patterns, checklists etc. in order to guarantee a quality check by personal presence and guidance.

LACK OF TIME AND ENTHUSIASM

Preparing and providing of working results consumes a certain amount of time. The predominant working pressure often prohibits to sift the documents at the end of a project and to prepare them for provision in a database. And the benefits of the additional work usually wont be earned by oneself but by colleagues. So the relation between the effort a professional has to spend affording use some later time to a colleague often is not cogent enough to release the necessary working capacity and motivation. The personal profit occurs too uncertain, therefore the commitment for an investment into the database fails. Besides, in many professions the sift and preparation of documentation is considered as not very demanding and attractive, so that one likely passes over to more exciting and alleged valuable activities – and contributions to the knowledge database are left undone.

COUNTERMEASURES

Thus social barriers against the implementation of knowledge databases are quite manifold and to be taken seriously. It is evident that administrative procedures can only play a supportive role. A more strategic approach[8] is grounded on the differentiation between implicit and explicit knowledge.[9] Implicit knowledge is embedded in the experiences, insights, and values of individuals. Because this knowledge is difficult or impossible to articulate, it cannot be filled into a database. If the most valuable knowledge of a PSF is implicit, a strategy of personalization should support the communication between people. First step would be some yellow-pages, where experts for a given topic could be found, second step the installation of communication systems like Email, chat forums, conference systems, where knowledge can be transferred on a personal basis. With this strategy, some of the mentioned social barriers will be lowered.

A very different type of knowledge is explicit knowledge. This is conscious, articulated, coded knowledge – at least it is possible to articulate and codify it. This knowledge defines the identity and the intellectual assets of an organization independently of its employees. If the core value of a PSF is explicit knowledge, a strategy of codification is suitable, to share it through database access. With this approach all of the above mentioned social barriers must be addressed carefully.

Basic prerequisite is that the social barriers are recognized and investigated. Is there a common set of ethical standards and values among the professionals? Is there a sufficient consensus of accepted and non accepted working methods and habits? Is there a sufficient and balanced common feeling of certainty and risk? The goal is a working atmosphere and culture that rewards revelation of knowledge, appreciates individual efforts and encourages the responsible dealing with a knowledge database. Trust among the professionals and confidence in the responsible dealing is a prerequisite to provide knowledge openly.

The initiative for the construction of a knowledge database has to be companioned by arguments and messages that pick up the worries. The aim of the database has to be discussed in detail with all involved staff. Moreover, these discussions should have a sufficient official nature to gain credibility. The inclusion of such discussions in the agenda of official meetings and written elaborations on that raise more confidence than accidentally mentioning the topic by the way.

The very best way to support installation and sustained use of a knowledge database leads through the impact of examples. If senior professionals do not show their credence to the benefits of a database, why actually younger colleagues should think that their contributions are acknowledged? If there is not at least one senior professional actively and visibly contributing and using the database the project will be condemned to fail.

Similarly fears can be counteracted that providing working results in a database means that these results are free to be teared in pieces by colleagues. Especially early contributions should be accepted expressly and positively. Corrections, if necessary, rather should be played down or should be done discreetly. The professionals' experiences in providing working results and in using results of colleagues should picked up, expressed and discussed early. Comprehensive contributions to the database should be singled out for praise in order to emphasize the firm's appreciation of the efforts. Signs must be clear: knowledge sharing and contributions to the database are both valuable and valued by the firm.

There are some examples where industrial companies promise incentives and award prizes to the 'most eager' contributor. Also usage of the database could be rewarded: Texas Instruments is said to have an annual reward which is named "Not Invented Here, But I Did It Anyway". If this sounds strange for PSF, at least care should be taken that distinct contributions to the database will be recognized during evaluation and assessment of the professionals.

The above mentioned actions are working primarily towards a sharing culture that rewards contributions and usage of knowledge databases. The cultural measures will definitely have a predominant effect over administrative actions. Because of the limited space, only some these actions are outlined here. The quality risk, which raises from filling faulty documents into the database can be lowered significantly when every contribution must be seen and qualified from at least two professionals. Another simple administrative procedure is easy to implement: at the opening and closing of a project the professionals should be asked for basic information. Terms for the professional field of action and some keywords describing problems and solutions should be indispensable. Last but not least, in larger PSF one person must be responsible for the knowledge database and act as first contact, if any questions or problems arise.

SUMMARY

All issues of the discussion are independent from the way a firm organize its knowledge database, therefore independent whether professionals collect documents manually, whether librarians set up such collections, or whether databases are constructed and maintained by massive use of IT. From an IT perspective: there are some software packages which claim to be knowledge management tools. But without attention for the social barriers, any project to implement a knowledge database is condemned to fail.

NOTES

[1] Cf. Borghoff/Pareschi (1997) p. 835, Huang (1998) p: 581, Davenport (1997) p. 2, Reimus (1997) p. 9, Davis/Botkin (1994) p. 167.

[2] Cf. Huang (1998) p. 582, Quinn/Anderson/Finkelstein (1996) p. 75, Liedtka/Haskins/Rosenblum/Weber (1997) p. 50.

[3] Quinn/Anderson/Finkelstein (1996) p. 75, cf. Liedtka/Haskins/Rosenblum/Weber (1997) p. 53, Fitter (1999).

[4] Bonora/Revang (1993) p. 204, cf. Fitter (1999) p.8.

[5] Liedtka/Haskins/Rosenblum/Weber (1997) p. 58.

[6] Cf. Quinn/Anderson/Finkelstein (1996) p. 75.

[7] Cf. Quinn/Anderson/Finkelstein (1996) p. 75, Fitter (1999) p.8.

[8] Cf. Hansen/Nohria/Tierney (1999).

[9] Cf. Nonaka (1991), Nonaka (1994).

REFERENCES

Bonora, E.A., and Revang, O. (1993). A Framework for Analysing the Storage and Protection of Knowledge in Organizations, in P. Lorange et al. (ed.), *Implementing Strategic Processes*, Oxford/Cambridge.

Borghoff, U.M., and Pareschi, R. (1997). Information Technology for Knowledge Management, in *Journal of Universal Computer Science*, 835-842.

Davenport, T.H. (1997). Some Principles of Knowledge Management, www.itmweb.com/essay538.htm; access on 15.03.1999.

Davis, S., and Botkin, J. (1994). The Coming of Knowledge-Based Business, in *Harvard Business Review*, No. 5, 165-170.

Fitter, F. (1999). The Human Factor, in *KM Magazine*, 6/1999; www.kmmag.com/kmagn2/ km199906/featureb1.htm; access 08.11.1999.

Hansen, M.T., Nohria, N., and Tierney, T. (1999). What's Your Strategy For Managing Knowledge, in *Harvard Business Review*, No. 2, 106-116.

Huang, K.-T. (1998). Capitalizing on Intellectual Assets, in *IBM Systems Journal*, No. 4, 570-583.

Liedtka, J.M., Haskins, M.E., Rosenblum, J.W., and Weber, J. (1997). The Generative Cycle: Linking Knowledge and Relationships, in *Sloan Management Review*, No. 1, 47-58.

Nonaka, I. (1991). The Knowledge-Creating Company, in *Harvard Business Review*, No. 6, 96-104.

Nonaka, I. (1994). A Dynamic Theory of Organizational Knowledge Creation, in *Organizaion Science*, No. 2, 14-37.

Quinn, J.B., Anderson, P., and Finkelstein, S. (1996). Managing Professional Intellect, in *Harvard Business Review*, No. 2, 71-80.

Reimus, B. (1997). Knowledge Sharing Within Management Consulting Firms; www.kennedyinfo.com/mc/gware.html; access 09.02.1999.

Chapter 14

Web-Based
Knowledge Management

Ruidong Zhang, Ph.D.
University of Wisconsin-Eau Claire, USA

The importance of knowledge management has been recognized both in academia and in practice. Meanwhile, the web technology is being used as a new and common medium to support the collective nature of knowledge management. In this chapter, 4 types of web-based knowledge management models are identified and discussed. It is believed that more models exist and could be identified. Nonetheless, these 4 models are believed to be able to reflect the current level of web-based knowledge management, which can be basically described as content-based information retrieval and topic-oriented information association and organization. This chapter concludes that the current web-based knowledge management is at a lower level, and, the potential of the web technology based knowledge management has just started to be realized. The study of the models identified in this paper would provide insights on leveled knowledge management, what should be contained in a higher level of knowledge management system, and how knowledge management support systems can be technically implemented.

INTRODUCTION

In the recent years, the importance of knowledge management has been recognized both in academia and in practice. Organizations have started talking about knowledge management, organizational learning, organizational memory, and in-

Previously Published in *Challenges of Information Technology Management in the 21st Century* edited by Mehdi Khosrow-Pour, Copyright © 2000, Idea Group Publishing.

tangible assets. As an example, in the second Microsoft's CEO summit, which was held in May 99 and attracted more than 120 CEOs and other corporate executives from Fortune 1000, the keynote speech delivered by Bill Gates focused on the theme of "knowledge management." Gates outlined his vision through a term he coined - Digital Nervous System, which is an integrated electronic network that gives people the information they need to solve business and customer problems. According to Gates (1999), an effective Digital Nervous System should include access to the Internet, reliable e-mail, a powerful database and excellent line-of-business applications.

However, knowledge management, as a conscious practice, is still young (Hansen et al., 1999). Existing studies about knowledge management are often non-empirical and fail to provide practical guidelines to the development of knowledge management systems. How to support knowledge management is largely a research topic, and the roles of information technology in supporting knowledge management are not clearly recognized. As an MIT survey revealed, companies tend to overlook intangibles when they evaluate information technology (Brynjolfsson, 1994). Using information technology to support knowledge management is still in its infancy.

But with the web technologies are becoming sophisticated, this picture is quickly changing in the most recent years. Preliminary or lower level knowledge management systems have been developed and deployed. The emerging Internet and Web technologies are not only changing the landscape of competition and the ways of doing business, but also the ways of information organization, distribution and retrieval. Web-based technology is enabling the management of information at the document management level, in contrast to the record-level information management. For example, we solve everyday problems through communicating with each other by using documents and exchanging ideas or perspectives about an issue, rather than dealing with fields or records. We are transiting from record-level information management to document-level information management, with the latter is viewed as a lower level of knowledge management by the author in this paper.

In this chapter, web-based knowledge management is explored. Web-based technology is making effective knowledge management a reality, which can make a company gain an advantage over its competitors. Specifically, in this chapter, four representative types of the current web-based knowledge management models are studied. The study of these models will shed light on what should be contained in a knowledge management system, the levels of knowledge management support, and how knowledge management support systems can be technically implemented. The results of this study would also give some directions to the effective knowledge management. This chapter is organized as follows. In the next section, some theoretical issues about knowledge management are reviewed. Then, it is justified why web technology is an enabling technology to the effective knowledge management and why web-based knowledge management is desirable. Then, the four types of web-based knowledge management models are discussed and compared. Finally, there is a section to summarize the results of this chapter and to discuss the future directions about the web-based knowledge management.

SOME THEORETIC ISSUES ABOUT KNOWLEDGE MANAGEMENT

Traditional Information Systems vs. Knowledge Management Systems

By traditional information system, we mean those systems that were developed to capture data about daily business transactions (transaction processing systems), to access, process and analyze those internal or/and external data to generate meaningful information to support management (MIS, DSS, or EIS). These traditional systems make an organization up and running efficiently and effectively. However, they were developed at a time when the importance of knowledge management wasn't recognized. As a matter of fact, they all put a great emphasis on the quantitative data processing and analysis. But an effective organization does not just rely on quantitative analysis to deal with its problems. The non-quantitative side, such as knowledge creation and management, mental models, document sharing, human communications, information exchange, and meaning making, all play a great role in an organization's growth and development. Thus the non-quantitative area needs also to be supported. Knowledge management systems are supposed to fulfill this role. In other words, knowledge management systems should complement traditional systems in providing non-quantitative side support. A difficult task is to decide what is to be included in the knowledge management system. A lot of existing studies provide only theoretic suggestions. A study described and discussed 10 knowledge management frameworks (Holsapple and Joshi, 1999). These frameworks are generally concentrated conceptually on the knowledge creation and knowledge-building activities. They may be useful in deciding what functions a knowledge management system should eventually provide, but fall short in suggesting what should be contained in a knowledge management system and how such a system may be implemented. In this paper, the study of four types of web-based knowledge management models should provide some practical ideas about the content of a knowledge management support system.

Knowledge vs. Information vs. Data

A traditional view about the relationship between knowledge, information and data is knowledge is above data and information, data as a prerequisite for information, and information as a prerequisite for knowledge. This theory can be simply illustrated by the following diagram:

$$Data \oslash Information \oslash Knowledge$$

A study suggests a reversed knowledge hierarchy, which implies data emerge only after we have information, and that information emerges only after we already have knowledge (Tuomi, 1999). This view can be simply illustrated by the following diagram:

$$Knowledge \oslash Information \oslash Data$$

Another situation is also possible. We have a large amount of data collected but fail to make use of the data because of our lack of relevant knowledge. A historical example can illustrate this about the making of the everyday weather map. For a long time in history, weather data were collected and there were very rich data available. But the usefulness was limited when these data are not combined with map (Monmonier, 1999). Once we have the relevant knowledge about how to process data, how to visualize data, the boring data start making sense and generating meanings. Therefore, in this situation, the knowledge is the catalyst that transforms data into information. . This situation can be simply illustrated by the following diagram:

$$Data \oslash Knowledge \oslash Information$$

These different logic and understanding about the relationship, association, and the sequence between data, information and knowledge are all meaningful, depending on the context. They are very important when deciding the content of knowledge management systems, and in describing the difference between a conventional information system and a knowledge management system. Actually, these three theories may represent different levels of management. In this paper, the four models we are going to review actually follow the third path, which means that we are concerned about how (the "*how*" is the knowledge) data may be collected and organized, associated and retrieved so that meaningful information can be produced for a certain task. In other words, the following understanding about knowledge is followed in this paper: Knowledge is about the organization of information (how information can be meaningfully organized), the association of information to a task, the meaningful retrieval of information for a task, and the identification of expertise for a task.

THE ENABLING TECHNOLOGY

The content of a knowledge management system will not be originated from one individual. The content collection and the access of the content will be a collective behavior. Therefore, a technological infrastructure must be installed to facilitate the collective behavior of knowledge management. In a study, conducted by Davenport, De Long and Beers (1998), 31 knowledge management projects in 24 companies are examined. Eight factors are identified to characterize a successful project. One of these factors is the use of a technology infrastructure that includes common technologies for desktop computing and communications. The web technology is providing such a *common* technological infrastructure to support the collective nature of knowledge management, which is justified by the following observations (Zhang and Chen, 1997):

- Web-based technology uses standard TCP/IP protocol, which is quite mature and are supported by most vendors (Panko, 1997; Telleen, 1996; Strom, 1995).
- Information can be collected, retrieved and shared through popular browsers like Netscape Navigator and Internet Explorer.
- A homepage can be quickly developed, deployed and shared.
- There are languages specially developed for web-based applications, such as Java. Java applets can be embedded in web homepages. The applets are executed on the client PC and make it possible to develop interactive homepages with instant user responses and with multimedia features.
- With web technologies, an organization enjoys platform independence or cross-platform operation. World Wide Web client software (e.g., FTP and email) and JAVA applets do not have to be rewritten to work with PC browsers, Macintosh browsers, and UNIX browsers. (Panko, 1997).

In addition to the common technical infrastructure that is being enjoyed by the web technology, there are three major reasons why web-based knowledge management is desirable:

1) The basic unit of knowledge is at the document level, which is equivalent to the level we human beings normally communicate. Documents are usually created to deal with particular issues, and we live our everyday life by dealing with issues. Different from an expert system, a document-based knowledge management system can not automatically derive solutions. Instead, its usefulness lies in its large repository of classified documents, its multi-indexed powerful searching capabilities, the links between documents, the links within a document, and the potential of including other advanced features (e.g., animation). The interpretation of the documents provided by a knowledge system largely lies in the users. The function of a document-based knowledge management system is largely supporting.

2) The association between knowledge can be easily established by creating hypertext links. Hypertext links can be created between documents and within a document. By creating the links, the knowledge to make data meaningful has been embedded.

3) The collective behavior of knowledge management can be supported. With a web site properly constructed, any one at any time can access any documents

stored in a web site and make any modifications or any additions to the existing collection of documents. When taking about the knowledge management architecture, Morey (1999) suggests that successful knowledge management architecture must have the following characteristics: available, accurate, effective, and accessible. Web-based technology is enabling such architecture for knowledge management.

THE WEB-BASED KNOWLEDGE MANAGEMENT MODELS

The following web-based knowledge management models are identified, based on an ongoing research project sponsored by the College of Business at the University of Wisconsin-Eau Claire. These models are believed to represent the current level of knowledge management based on the existing web-technology. Nonetheless, it is not implied that these four types of models represent all of the knowledge management models available on the web. These four representative models are:
- Library Model
- Association/Attachment Model
- Directory Model
- Press Center Model

Library Model – towards the content level search

Under this model, a large collection of documents is established. The most salient characteristic is that both the attributes and the *content* of a document are indexed, in contrast to that traditionally only the attributes of a document are indexed. The attributes of documents include title, subject, author name(s), publication (creation) date, number of pages, and so on. Under this model, powerful search functions are provided, where not only these attributes (title, subject, etc.) are searched, but also the contents of documents are search.

An example of this model is the ITKnowledge.com web site. Its knowledge base is a repository of IT-related books. The contents of the books are fully available. The chapters in a book are hypertext-linked and a book is essentially a set of hypertext documents. Not only the attributes of the books are classified and indexed and can be searched easily, but also the chapter titles (the content) are indexed by keywords and can be searched. This makes it possible to find a document whose attributes (title, subject) does not meet a search criterion, but which may contain chapters that are relevant to the search criterion. In Figure 1, the ITKnowledge.com search screen is displayed. In Figure 2, a search result is returned. As can be seen in Figure 2, a chapter in the book "Handbook of Data

Figure 1: ITKnowledge.com Expert Search Screen

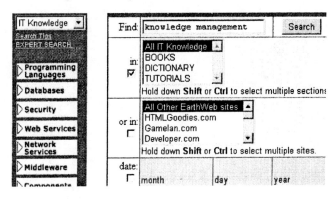

Figure 2: Search Results Returned

Your search matched **38** of **87511** documents.
10 are presented, ranked by relevance.

[Prev] 1 2 3 4 [Next]

Title/Information

Handbook of Data Management:Introduction
Date: 05-13-99 - Rank: 11 - Score: 0.82
Table of Contents . .Introduction. Data management is the process of
understanding the data needs of an enterprise and making that data opti...
http://www.itknowledge.com/reference/library/084939953x/index.html

Handbook of Data Management:Knowledge Management Architectur
Date: 05-13-99 - Rank: 12 - Score: 0.82
Previous .Table of Contents .Next . .Accurate in Retrieval .Accurate retrieval o
documents is critical to the success of any knowledge arch...
http://www.itknowledge.com/reference/library/084939953x/ch53/727-729.html

Handbook of Data Management:Content-Based Retrieval and Inde

Management" which is relevant to the search criterion "knowledge management"
has been returned. If the book is only indexed by its title, this search result should
not have been possible.

Attachment/Association Model

Under this model, information is organized around topics. If we search for a
particular topic, all information associated with the topic will be returned. New
information can be attached to a topic once it becomes available. In fact, anyone
at any time can attach new information to a topic. The new information attachment
process is an on-going process.

An example of this model is Amazon.com, which is trying to become an Internet
shopping hub. But book selling is still its major business. Amazon.com maintains a

Figure 3: A Matching Title with Relevant Titles

Working Knowledge : How Organizations Manage What ⅂
by <u>Thomas H. Davenport</u>, <u>Laurence Prusak</u>, <u>Lawrence Prusak</u>

List Price: $~~29.95~~
Our Price: $20.97
You Save: $8.98 (30%)

Availability: Usually ships within 24 hours.

Hardcover - 224 pages (December 1997)
Harvard Business School Pr; ISBN: 0875846556 ; Dimensions (in inches): 0.96 x 9.54 x 6.52
Amazon.com Sales Rank: 2,132
Avg. Customer Review: ☆☆☆☆☆
Number of Reviews: 13

<u>Write an online review</u> and share your thoughts with other readers!

Customers who bought this book also bought:
• <u>Harvard Business Review on Knowledge Management</u> (Harvard Bu
• If Only We Knew What We Know : The Transfer of Internal Know

Figure 4: Reviews Associated to the Book, Working Knowledge

Reviews
Working Knowledge examines how knowledge can be nurtured in organization
creating a knowledge-oriented corporate culture, a positive environment in whic
efficient, productive, and innovative. The book includes numerous examples of s
British Petroleum, 3M, Mobil Oil, and Hewlett-Packard. Concise and clearly w
managers who want to better harness the experience and wisdom within their or

Upside, Ron Hogan
At the corporate level, knowledge is a key component of what has become kno
company a sustainable advantage over less-savvy competitors. For an entire coɪ

Figure 5: Customers' Comments Attached to the Book, Working Knowledge

Customer Comments
Average Customer Review: ☆☆☆☆☆ Number of Reviews: 13

A reader from London, UK , September 9, 1999 ☆☆☆☆☆
Apt and concise introduction to knowledge management
Very readable. Real examples of experiences of todays' organisations (across industry) C
commonplace buzz words. Book is made even more interesting by quotes starting each cl

A reader from Atlanta , August 26, 1999 ☆☆☆☆☆
At 178 pages it packs a big punch
Short and to the point. This book can be read in one night and will make you think for ma

Figure 6: The Form One Can Use to Add New Review to a Book Title

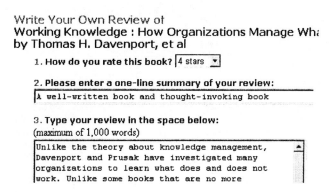

large database of book titles. To help sell a book faster and to maker users understand a book better, all information relevant to a book title is stored and organized around a book title. Therefore, essentially, the book database is more than just a collection of book attributes. Amazon.com provide users more than book titles. Suppose we want to find books that are relevant to "knowledge management." After a title that matches the search criterion is returned, other relevant titles, which customers often bought together with the current title, are also displayed (Figure 3). In addition, one can learn more about a book by reading the reviews associated to the book (see Figure 4) and other customers' comments attached to the book (see Figure 5). If one likes, one can write comments about a book and attach the comments to the existing pool of information about this book. Figure 6 shows the form used to attach new information to a title.

Directory Model

Under this model, the experts in different areas are identified and a directory of experts is created. The areas of expertise of these experts are classified and organized. That is, a directory of experts together with their areas of expertise is provided.

A representative example of this model is the Round Table Group (round.table.com). Round Table Group (RTG) was founded in 1994 with a vision of being a virtual consulting firm where business leaders, management consultants, and litigation attorneys could shop for answers to critical questions from world class thinkers, anywhere in the world – in Internet time (STVP, 1999). According to SVTP case study, RTG has formed a worldwide network of over 3,000 Round Table Scholars – professors, researchers in well-known think tanks, and other

Figure 7. The Area of Expertise by Topic

RTG Expertises (by Topic)

[Industry Groups] [Functional Groups] [Political & Soci
[Emerging Economies -- Countries & Related Topics] [T
[Biotechnology & Environmental Issues] [Law] [Employe

Industry Groups

Accounting, Aerospace, Agricultural Production/services, Amusement and Recreati
Policies, Astronomy, Auctions, Automotive, Auditing, Banking, Chemical, Chemica
Construction, Defense, Educational Services, Electronics, Energy, Engineering, Fina
Health Services, High Technology Industries, Housing and Mortgage Markets, Hot
Brokering, Insurance, Legal Services, Lumber, Manufacturing, Metal Mining, Motic
Products, Petroleum, Primary Metal Industries, Printing and Publishing, Radio and T
Business, Social Services, Sports, Telecommunications, Textile Mill Products, Toba

experts. Essentially, RTG's most valuable competitive asset is its directory of professors from around the world who were available to consult with clients on demand. RTG provide the *answers-on-demand services to its clients*. In Figure 7 below, the classified area of expertise by topic is displayed.

Press Center Model

Under this model, all information that can be possibly collected, including news, relevant articles, solution providers, publications, and discussions about knowledge management is collected. A representative model is Kmworld.com, where a rich collection of relevant information about knowledge management can be found. If one is interested in knowledge management, a good starting point will be to go to visit a site like Kmworld.com. One could be overwhelmed by the information available there, such as discussions, news, and solution providers. In Figure 8, a list of solution providers about knowledge management is displayed after a search was conducted.

Figure 8. A List of Solution Providers on Knowledge Management

50 results found for "**knowledge management**".
Showing matching items 1 - 25.

Buyer's Guide Results:

0.92 - Dataware Technologies - Dataware II Knowledge Management Suite
0.90 - Arthur Andersen - **Arthur Andersen??s Knowledge Management Solutions**
0.87 - Innodata - SPD
0.87 - Arthur Andersen - **Performing Knowledge Audits and Diagnostics**
0.87 - Delphi Group
0.84 - ZYGA Corporation - **ZYGA's Knowledge Management Program**
0.84 - Dataware Technologies - SPD
0.84 - ByteQuest Technologies - SPD
0.84 - Autonomy, Inc. - **Knowledge Management Suite**
0.84 - Arthur Andersen - **Collaborative Knowledge Management Research**

A Comparison of the Models

The 4 types of web-based knowledge management models as discussed above are believed to be able to reflect the current level of web-based knowledge management, which can be concisely described as: the content-based information retrieval and topic-oriented information organization.

These four models share the following common characteristics:

- Basically document-based and content-indexed
- Have powerful searching capabilities
- Focus on a specific application area (task-specific: IT knowledge, book selling)
- Anytime anywhere access
- Potential to have more advanced features (e.g., multimedia, animation)
- All have an external-orientation and are customer-focused.

On the other hand, the four models discussed above also have their own unique characteristics, which are indicated in the following table.

Model	Key Characteristic
Library Model	Content-based document retrieval
Association/ Attachment	Topic-oriented information association/ organization
Directory Model	A directory of classified human expertise
Press Center Model	A clearing house with rich organized information

DISCUSSIONS AND CONCLUSIONS

Current Web-based knowledge management is essentially at the document management level – a lower level of knowledge management, but indeed beyond the pure document management (pure classified collection of documents in a central file cabinet) to allow content-based retrieval, distributed access, and topic-oriented information organization and association. In this paper, four different web sites that represent four different models of web-based knowledge management are discussed. But it is believed that a web site could employ multiple models at the same time. For example, a web site can be constructed based on the library model while supporting the association & attachment model. As a matter of fact, the ITKnowledge.com is planning to include the association & attachment model in its site. It is expected that a sophisticated web site provide a menu of knowledge models for its users to choose from so that the potential of a web site can be fully utilized.

A study, conducted by Hansen, Nohria and Tierney (1999), discussed two strategies of knowledge management, based on the authors' studies on the practice of knowledge management in consulting firms, computer vendors, and health care providers. One strategy is called personalization strategy, where knowledge is closely tied to the person who developed it and is shared mainly through direct person-to-person contacts. The computer information systems are used mainly to help people communicate knowledge, not to store it. Other examples like the use of groupware products to support the knowledge management process also fall into this category. This may be called communication-based knowledge management level.

Another strategy, from the same study conducted by Hansen, Nohria and Tierney (1999), is called codification strategy, where knowledge (actually, *a variety of documents*) is codified and stored in databases to be used by anyone in the company. The knowledge is extracted from documents and may take the forms of interview guides, work schedules, benchmark data, market segmentation analysis. These knowledge forms are codified and stored into a database with search capabilities. This is may be called document-based knowledge management level.

The existing web-based knowledge management, as evidenced by the four types of models identified and discussed in this paper, basically corresponds to these knowledge management levels (especially the second one). However these levels are considered as lower levels of knowledge management, because they do not consider the support of meaning interpretation or sense making, they are generally text based, and they don't challenge whether the knowledge inherent in the document is accurately transmitted (knowledge transfer). But, after all, good steps on the right track have been made.

As future research directions about the web-based knowledge management, the higher levels of knowledge management may need to be addressed. Other functional areas should get involved, such as sales and marketing, customer support, and research and development. More models about web-based knowledge management may also need to be identified. Automatic and intelligent knowledge extraction and retrieval (knowledge agents) should also be studied for web-based knowledge management.

REFERENCES

Brynjolfsson, E. (1994). Technology's True Payoff – An MIT survey finds that business tends to overlook intangibles when evaluating information technology, *Information Week* 500, Issue 496, October.

Davenport, T. H., De Long, D., and Beers, M. (1998). Successful Knowledge management Projects, *Sloan Management Review*, 39(2), Winter.

Gates, B. Keynote Speech for the Microsoft's second annual CEO Summit meeting, Seattle, May 27-29.

Hansen, M. T., Nohria, N., and Tierney, T. (1999). What's Your Strategy for Managing Knowledge, *Harvard Business Review*, March – April.

Holsapple, C.W., and Joshi, K. D. (1999). Description and Analysis of Existing Knowledge management Frameworks, *Proceedings of the 32nd Hawaii International Conference on System Sciences*.

Monmonier, M. S. (1999). *Air Apparent : How Meteorologists Learned to Map, Predict, and Dramatize Weather*, Univ of Chicago Press.

Morey, D. (1999). Knowledge Management Architecture, in *Handbook of Data Management*, CRC Press LLC.

Panko, R. R. (1997). *Business Data Communications*, Prentice Hall.

Stewart, T. A. (1997). *Intellectual Capital: The New Wealth of Organizations*, Doubleday/Currency.

Strom, D. (1995). Creating Private Intranets: Challenges and Prospects for IS, http://www.attachmate.com/Intranet.

STVP (Stanford Technology Ventures Program) (1999). Round Table Group at a Crossroads: Market Maker or Market Driven? February 28.

Telleen, S. L. (1996). The IntraNet Architecture: Managing information in the new paradigm, Amdahl Corporation.

Tuomi, I. (1999). Data Is More Than Knowledge, *Proceedings of the 32nd Hawaii International Conference on System Sciences*.

Zhang, R. and Chen, J. An Intranet Architecture to Support Organizational Learning, *Proceedings of 1997 DSI Conference*.

Chapter 15

The Innovation Link Between Organisation Knowledge and Customer Knowledge

Helen J. Mitchell
UNITEC Institute of Technology, New Zealand

The knowledge economy is the future. Organisations need to harness their knowledge and put it to advantage if they are to survive in the new age. Innovative approaches to the market place through the products and services offered will become critical for survival. While some of the knowledge they need is held within the organisation's systems, it also resides in employees and customers. Linking that knowledge together will provide an innovative approach to the future.

Research was carried out to identify whether organisations recognise, and utilise the knowledge of their customers. It is important to identify whether they analyse the information gathered about their customers, and whether they value their customer relationships. The potential to be innovative is considerably enhanced when the accumulated knowledge of organisations, and their customers is brought together for the purpose of providing satisfaction and success in the future for all those involved. The way of the future is to link knowledge and become innovative.

INTRODUCTION

The knowledge economy is being heralded as the "new age" and for organisations wanting to move forward, and to survive in a highly competitive

Previously Published in *Challenges of Information Technology Management in the 21st Century* edited by Mehdi Khosrow-Pour, Copyright © 2000, Idea Group Publishing.

environment, embracing the knowledge economy will be critical. By their very nature organisations are repositories of knowledge. Employees have a great deal of knowledge about the organisation and its operations, and a large amount of knowledge is held by the organisation in document form by virtue of regulatory requirement and general operation. Customers too are a valuable source of knowledge about the organisation and its products and service, but it is a source that is not always recognised.

Innovation springs from the knowledge employees have and their interaction with others. Sharing knowledge involves everyone who has something to contribute to the organisation, and this includes customers. It is the collective knowledge of all those involved, internally and externally, which spawns innovation. Using that knowledge in an innovative way will enable organisations to grow and survive in the future.

KNOWLEDGE AND THE ORGANISATION

Traditionally, the focus of organisations has been based on land, labour and capital but over recent years, attention has been drawn to the value of knowledge as a very important economic resource. In their quest for a means of survival in an environment that is rapidly becoming more competitive, organisations will be looking to knowledge to provide the means of success (Nonaka, 1991; Drucker, 1994; Demarest, 1997; Teece, 1998).

Knowledge is a resource that organisations do not appear to fully recognise as providing the means through which they can meet future competitive challenges. While knowledge is accumulated in organisations it is not harnessed in a way that will provide benefit. Each employee has an individual knowledge bank acquired as a result of education, skills and competencies developed over time, along with life experiences. The longer they work in an organisation the greater the knowledge they acquire about the organisation, its products, and its customers. The organisation also has a repository of knowledge through its documents, processes and routines (Marshall, Prusak, and Shpilberg, 1996; Demarest, 1997; Jordan and Jones, 1997; Fahey and Prusak, 1998). Marshall et al. (1996) point to the volumes of information sitting in organisations, and Evans and Wurster (1997) identify every business as being an information business. Questions arise as to why this information is not put to use, and it may simply be there is a lack of knowledge to interpret it to provide possible opportunities.

According to Kanter (1996: 94) "Structures and practices that may work well for the perpetuation of the known tend to be at odds with innovation." The organisational environment is therefore important if innovation is to occur. It is known that there is knowledge within the organisation but it needs to be stimulated by new events and sparked to action (Fahey and Prusak, 1998). If the right information signals are received, and the culture is appropriate, ideas will emerge from anyone at whatever level, or age (Darling, 1997; Marshall, 1997).

Technology offers many benefits for the organisation particularly information gathering but knowledge must be applied to the interpreting of that information if it is to bring benefit to the organisation. For example organisations do not seem to pay as much attention to information on their databases as they should. While it is important that databases are set up in such a way that employees have ready access to information to respond to customers quickly and efficiently. It is also important that information in the database is regularly analysed, if for no other reason than looking for changing patterns in customer buying,

Nonaka (1991) talks about the spiral of knowledge in the organisation and says that knowledge begins with the individual. Matrix structures used by organisations for projects identify those people who through their expertise need to be involved in the project. Such teams frequently include customers with very beneficial results. Customers view the organisation and its product and services from a different perspective and are able to contribute value ideas, perspectives and information that will have value for the organisation.

Knowledge is important for developing new products or services, and for adding value. While much of that knowledge can be obtained primarily through employees, databases, and business documentation, it will also come from meetings with customers (Byrne, 1993; Kanter, 1996; Amidon, 1997; Evans and Wurster, 1997; Jordan and Jones, 1997; Fahey and Prusak, 1998; Teece, 1998). Customer knowledge is extremely valuable. However, Evans and Wurster (1997) and Teece (1998), give a warning that technology has provided customers with the means for accessing information from may sources to provide comparative assessment, and they are no longer so reliant on their traditional supplier organisations for information. This signals that it is critically important for organisations to recognise the value of customers and to work alongside them.

Too often organisations do not give credit, or belief, to information received from customers even though customer surveys may have been carried out (Fahey and Prusak, 1998). Customers have considerable knowledge not only about the products and how they are used, but also about the products of other suppliers. Observing how products are used also provides valuable feedback that may instigate modifications, new customer solutions, or the customising of products. It is important to know what customers are thinking, and their rationale for changing to another supplier (Fahey and Prusak, 1998). Kanter (1996) suggests focusing on demanding customers. Difficult as these customers may be, it is a sensible approach as it is those customers who are likely to produce the greatest and most valuable knowledge, which may well lead to new ideas.

Amidon (1997: 122) goes further than the immediate customer when she suggest there will also be a benefit from knowing what the customer's customer wants. It is also suggested by Amidon, that there should be a focus on customer success rather than looking only to customer satisfaction. This involves helping customers to achieve their goals and to bring greater wealth to their organisations. Success is what customers want.

All organisations want to be successful and when Drucker (1998: 149) talks about entrepreneurship, he says the size of the organisation, or its age, is not significant. What is important is the type of activity. He goes on to say that "At the heart of that activity is innovation: the effort to create purposeful, focused change in an enterprise's economic or social potential." However, there is also a reminder from Drucker that "Knowledge-based innovations differ from all others in the time they take" and indicates lead-time can be as much as 50 years. Although necessary knowledge was available by 1918 the digital computer did not appear until 1946. In today's environment, however, technology provides opportunities for access to information as it becomes available and the timeliness of this may well make it possible for that long lead time to be considerably reduced.

As competition intensifies, it will become very important for organisations to build closer relationships with their customers. Working together provides the insight and perspectives about the product that can enhance its use and provide the customer with greater satisfaction. Organisations working alongside customers on new products, or process innovation, or designing innovative solutions to meet specific needs of customers add value to both the organisation and its customers, (Grant, 1997).

Trust is very important when working alongside customers. Each side has knowledge, but is each side willing to give away what it knows? It is difficult to give away knowledge and there are dangers. Competitors in the market are always on the look out for useful information. Other customers may react unfavourably to the observed relationship and possibly cause them to change, wherever possible, to another supplier. Failure to maintain a trusting relationship could have immense problems. It is important, therefore, to develop a sound understanding of the goals of the customer organisation, and what it needs to be successful, will be critical to the working relationship (Amidon, 1997).

To ensure the maintenance of good relationships with customers, to benefit from the knowledge harnessed, and to develop an appropriate environment for innovation, it is essential to have in place a good management system. According to Drucker (1998: 156) "It may be difficult, but knowledge-based innovation can be managed. Success requires careful analysis of the various kinds of knowledge needed to make an innovation possible." Organisations need to consider setting in place a strategy for innovation. Many organisations have, according to Amidon

(1997: 127) started "to systemise the process with an established innovation office, staff, and initiatives." This indicates there are organisations recognising the importance of linking their knowledge with that of their customers, and moving towards an innovative approach to solving their requirements, and considering new ideas.

Spending time with customers to build good relationships is going to be critically important in the future. Organisations with a culture that is flexible and open to change, where staff and their knowledge is valued, and good relationships exist with customers, will be able to position themselves for survival in the future. According to Kanter (1996: 97), "Opportunity exists because need exists, so it is not surprising that closer customer or user contact is an important innovation activator."

AIM OF RESEARCH

Research was carried out to investigate how organisations in New Zealand gather information about their customers, whether there is a sharing of knowledge between organisations and customers, and whether the sharing of knowledge is likely to provide a link to innovation.

METHODOLOGY

Four hundred organisations, selected from a database of New Zealand's top companies located throughout the country, were surveyed. A further 26 organisations were randomly selected from the telephone directory. The purpose of the "26" selection was to capture within the survey public/government institutions, and professional organisations.

The questionnaire contained 25 questions. General information was requested about industry association and number of employees. Specific questions relating to customer relationships, use of customer knowledge, and whether organisations were working collaboratively with their customers, were asked. Other questions covered knowledge sharing by employees, use of technology, and identifying factors important to the organisation today and in five years. The focus of this paper is on customer relationships and the sharing of knowledge.

The response rate of completed questionnaires was 21 per cent. A further 3 percent acknowledged the questionnaire but indicated it was company policy not to take part in surveys. A few questionnaires were returned as a result of addressing problems. The accompanying letter explained the purpose of the research and assured confidentiality of responses. However, an opportunity was provided for organisations to give names if they wished to be contacted about the research. A number of those who gave names will be contacted for further information about how ideas are generated, and the effects on the organisation of working collaboratively with customers.

SPSS software was used to carry out the analysis.

RESULTS

Industry types were divided into five areas: Public, Primary, Service, Manufacturing, Sales and Retail. The largest response rate of 45 per cent came from the service area, followed by manufacturing, primary, sales and retail, and public/government institutions.

The number of employees was divided into four groups: 1-199, 200-499, 500-999, 1,000-10,000, and the largest response, 46.5 per cent, was received from the 1-199 employee number group. It is perhaps worth noting that New Zealand has a population of just over 3.7 million people, and that 90 per cent of business units fall predominantly into the small business category of less than 100 people.

Organisations were asked to indicate their method for gathering information about customers. Five choices, were offered and as many choices as appropriate could be ticked. The following indicates the way organisations gather information:

Client/Customer Database	70
Sales Analysis	40
Guarantee, Warranty cards	7
Sales, Service Invoices	27
Other – Not specified	17
Missing (no response)	7

It is clear that the Client/Customer database is the approach used by the majority of organisations. Combinations of choices indicate that organisations use several methods but the combinations of Client/customer database and Sales analysis was the most popular, with Client/customer database, Sales analysis and Sales/service invoices, the next most common method for gathering information about customers.

Organisations were then asked to identify which was of greater importance to them so far as relationship with customers was concerned. The results indicate that customer satisfaction is of greatest importance (55 per cent). Customer retention followed in second place (30 per cent), with perceived customer success showing at 15 per cent. In view of Amidon's (1997) comments regarding customer success, organisations may need to rethink how they regard their customers.

Asked whether the organisation had in place a process through which the organisation could systematically learn from its customers and 73 responded "Yes," with 10 saying "No." Three gave no response to this question indicating that it was not applicable to their circumstances.

The question following asked about the processes used by organisations to learn from customers. Several choices were offered, and again more than one choice could be identified.

Focus Groups	41
Surveys	58
Analysis of needs and wants	55
Information about competition	32
Data Warehouse	17
Analysis of Sales Trends	47
Customer Retention studies	11
Other	4
Missing (no response)	13

The most popular combination was Focus groups, Surveys, Analysis of Needs and Wants, and Analysis of Sales Trends indicating that organisations use a range of methods to gather information. This survey did not ask how the organisations used the information, and what benefits they gained from it.

In response to a question about using customer knowledge for new product development, 70 indicated they did, while 13 said "No." Three did not respond.

The processes taken to make use of customer knowledge were selected again from a choice and several choices could be identified. Results show:

Screening ideas	25
Analysis of Customer Complaints	46
Partnership to develop new ideas	46
Meetings Needs and Wants	42
Working Collaboratively to add value	43
Other	3
Missing (no response)	16

The most popular combination was Analysis of Customer Complaints, Partnership to develop new ideas, Meeting needs and wants, and Working Collaboratively to add value. Results indicate organisations recognise the importance of analysing customer complaints and to learn from them. It is also recognised by organisations there is value in working alongside their customers for the generating of new ideas, meeting their needs, and to work together to add value.

CONCLUSIONS

From the information provided through the survey, it is evident that organisations do gather information about their customers. Gathering the information is done using several methods but the most commonly used one is through the customer database. While the database provides good opportunities for analysis of the customer data, there is a tendency for organisations to use it as a repository for information rather than seeing it as an active and current resource that has the ability to provide a considerable amount of information about customers. If appropriate knowledge is applied to this information there is the potential to reap many benefits. There is perhaps a need for organisations to identify why they gather and hold information on the database and that the idea of analysing the information from a perspective of gaining knowledge about how and where the organisation will grow rather than simply storing the information will bring greater rewards.

Surveys of customers ranked high on the list of ways that organisations learn from their customers which is interesting as Fahey and Prusak (1998) indicate that although organisations may carry out surveys, they do not always seem to be prepared to give cognisance to what they say. What was not asked in the survey was how organisations make use of the data gathered, and those organisations giving contact names will be approached for information covering this area.

The acknowledgement by respondents that they have methods in place to learn from their customers shows clearly that organisations do recognise the value in learning from the customer. However, what is important is that they really do analyse the information and apply their knowledge to the findings. There may be criticism of the product or service, or procedures surrounding them, in which case they need to be addressed. Positive suggestions, triggering an innovative approach to the offerings of the organisation, may well yield unexpected opportunities and profits.

Amidon (1997) suggests that organisations should be looking to the customer's customer and it appears that 15 per cent of organisations responding are looking in that direction. This is interesting as it indicates that those organisations are looking beyond their immediate customers and that the satisfaction and success of those more distant customers does impact on their own success. However, for the majority of organisations, satisfying their immediate customer is the point at which they measure their success.

Organisations are also, of course, concerned about customer retention, yet from the question relating to learning from customers, only 11 respondents indicated that they carried out customer retention studies. This is surprising, as organisations should be concerned about why customers leave. It is a hard job, and an expensive one, to seek new customers. An analysis of the reasons for leaving is likely to elicit information that could provide a better product or service, and could well generate an innovative environment leading to new products and services which may well have the effect of turning around the defecting customer.

The literature indicates the value of working alongside customers. It is from good organisation/customer relationships and working collaboratively together that innovative approaches to problems, or the development of new products emerge. Responses indicate that working with their customers is indeed something that many organisations do. Further enquiry is, however, needed to identify how they do this and how each side benefits. They realise the value of developing good relationships and the benefits that are likely to accrue to both the customer and the organisation.

To move forward and grow in the knowledge environment, organisations should take greater cognisance of the knowledge to be gained from analysing their own accumulated knowledge and combine it with their customers' knowledge. This may well provide a perspective of the organisation and its potential not previously identified.

Bringing together organisational knowledge, the knowledge of employees, and the knowledge of customers is critical if the innovation link is to be developed to take the organisation, its employees and its customers forward successfully into the new age of the knowledge economy. Encouraging all parties to work together to develop a culture of sharing knowledge, will energise an innovative approach to the future.

There is no real evidence from the research that innovation takes place as a result of organisations working alongside their customers. It is encouraging that the survey appears to identify in general terms where organisations are positioned at the present time with regard to the knowledge economy, and whether in fact they work alongside their customers. However, the data gathered identifies a number of in depth studies can be carried out covering a range of issues not least of which will be a more specific study of the organisations, its customers, and innovation.

REFERENCES

Amidon, D. M. (1997). *The Ken Awakening*, Butterworth-Heinemann, Newton, USA.

Byrne, J. (1993, February 8). The Virtual Corporation, *Business Week*, pp 98-102.

Darling, M. S. (1997 February 8). The Virtual Corporation, *Business Week*, pp 98-102.

Demarest, M. (1997). Understanding Knowledge Management, *Long Range Planning*, 30(3), pp 374-384.

Drucker, P. F. (1994, November). The Age of Social Transformation, *The Atlantic Monthly*, pp 53-78.

Drucker, P. F. (1998, Novmber-December). The Discipline of Innovation, *Harvard Business Review*, pp 149-157.

Evans, P. B., and Wurster, T. S. (1997 September-October). Strategy and the New Economics of Information, *Harvard Business Review*, pp 71-82.

Fahey, L., and Prusak, L. (1998 Spring). The Eleven Deadliest Sins of Knowledge Management, *California Management Review*, 40(3), pp 265-276.

Grant, R. M. (1997). The Knowledge-based View of the Firm: Implications for Management Practice, *Long Range Planning*, 30(3), pp 450-454.

Jordan, J., and Jones, P. (1997). Assessing your Company's Knowledge Management Style, *Long Range Planning*, 30(3), pp 392-398.

Kanter, R. M. (1996). When a Thousand Flowers Bloom: Structural, Collective, and Social Conditions for Innovation in Organizations, *Knowledge Management and Organizational Design*, Ed Myers P, Butterworth-Heinemann, Newton, USA.

Marshall, C., Prusak, L., and Shpilberg, D. (1996 Spring). Financial Risk and the Need for Superior Knowledge Management, *California Management Review*, 38(3), pp 77-101.

Marshall, L. (1997). New Opportunities for Information Professionals, *Online*, pp 93-98.

Nonaka, I. (1991, November-December). The Knowledge Creating Company, *Harvard Business Review*, pp 96-104.

Teece, D. J. (1998). Capturing Value from Knowledge Assets: The New Economy, Markets for Know-how, and Intangible Assets, *California Management Review*, 40(3), pp 55-79.

Chapter 16

Implementing Knowledge Management: Issues for Managers

Charles A. Snyder
Auburn University, USA

Larry T. Wilson
LearnerFirst, Inc., USA

KNOWLEDGE MANAGEMENT

Knowledge Management (KM) has become a pervasive topic in management practice. The proliferation of KM is the result of concentrated and deliberate efforts on the part of many organizations. Scores of books, articles, and conferences tout KM. There is widespread belief that KM can lead to competitive advantage. Some authors have attempted to show that competitive advantage based on knowledge is highly valued by stock markets (see, e.g., Sveiby, 1997).

The purpose of this chapter is to present some definitions of KM and to raise issues that managers should consider. There is a discussion of categories of knowledge and their relevance for managers. We provide the elements that every organization should consider in assessing their readiness for KM. The components of knowledge harvesting are presented and organizational considerations are introduced. Reasons that KM efforts fail are provided as well.

KNOWLEDGE MANAGEMENT DEFINED

KM, a relatively new concept, has many definitions. Many authors define it through tenets or characteristics; however, some attempt to derive a basic understanding by defining its base words. According to Webster's Dictionary (1994),

Previously Published in *Challenges of Information Technology Management in the 21st Century* edited by Mehdi Khosrow-Pour, Copyright © 2000, Idea Group Publishing.

*Table 1: Some Definitions of Knowledge Management
(Source: The Knowledge Management Forum, 1997; Snyder & Templeton,
1997)*

KM Source	Definition of Knowledge Management
Thomas Bertels	The management of the organization towards the continuous renewal of the organization knowledge base – this means e.g. creation of supportive organizational structures, facilitation of organization members, putting IT – instruments with emphasis on teamwork and diffusion of knowledge (as e.g. groupware) into place.
Denham Grey	An audit of "intellectual assets" highlights unique sources, critical functions, and potential bottlenecks which hinder knowledge flows to the point of use. It protects intellectual assets from decay, seeks opportunities to enhance decisions, services and products through adding intelligence, increasing value and providing flexibility.
J. Hibbard	Knowledge Management is a process of locating, organizing, and using the collective information and expertise within an organization, whether it resides on paper, or in the minds of people, and distributing it wherever it benefits most.
Ray Hoving	The organization and use of a company's intellectual assets to create value.
Brain Newman	Knowledge Management is the collection of processes that govern the creation, dissemination, and utilization of knowledge.
Karl-Eric Sveiby	The art of creating value from an organization's intangible assets.
Karl Wiig	Focusing on determining, organizing, directing, facilitating, and monitoring knowledge-related practices and activities required to achieve the desired business strategies and objectives.

knowledge is all that is apprehended clearly and with certainty. The definition suggests that knowledge is a great deal more than facts or information. It suggests that the information must undergo a further process of experience or association to become knowledge. Additionally, Webster's (1994) defines management as the act of directing, planning, controlling, handling, and implementing. By putting the definitions together, we can infer that KM is the directing, planning, controlling, handling, and implementing of processed information. This approach results in an oversimplification and has limited usefulness. Several definitions lead to confusion as to the meaning of the term.

The Virtual Library on Knowledge Management (1998) states:
Knowledge Management caters to the critical issues of organizational adaptation, survival and competence in face of increasingly discontinuous environmental changes.... Essentially, it embodies organizational processes that seek synergistic combination of data and information processing capacity of information technologies, and the creative and innovative capacity of human beings.

Table 1 presents a few definitions of KM. This is not intended to be an exhaustive list, but merely to indicate the variety.

Most definitions with an organizational focus now include some idea of improving organizational performance and stakeholder value. Many KM pundits emphasize that managing knowledge has the potential to uniquely improve decision processes, increase effectiveness of key business processes, help foster and sustain innovation, support the learning organization, and to obtain and sustain long term competitive advantage. The organization's knowledge has been called its only true source of competitive advantage and as taking the place of capital as the driving force in organizations worldwide (Drucker, 1995).

Knowledge based solutions tend to fall into categories depending on the focus of the proponents: harvesting expert knowledge, collaborative work environments, best practices data bases, performance support, innovation support, publishing, continuous improvement, business (competitive) intelligence, and intellectual asset (capital) management.

The scope of this paper precludes detailed discussion of all solutions areas. Recent work by Holsapple and Joshi (1997,1998) is recommended to explore this area further.

It is useful to categorize the types of knowledge as this has significant impact on the implementation of KM. In the next section, we examine some of the categories.

TYPES OF KNOWLEDGE

While all companies create knowledge, not all of the knowledge is of high value. Our focus is primarily on the knowledge that is needed to perform key organizational processes. The logic is that these processes must be performed well in order for the organization to succeed (Snyder & Wilson, 1997). This emphasis was echoed by Alee (1997) who stated that the most valuable knowledge a company produces is knowledge related to the company's core competencies or tied to its core performance capabilities.

Knowledge may be manifest as raw information, applied information, comprehended information, or justified information (Norman & Wikstrom, 1994). Raw information is a collection of data or facts that represents simple answers to the questions of what, where, when, who, how big, or how many. Applied information equates to worker skill or know-how to perform value-added tasks and answers the question, "How do I do it?" Comprehended information relates information that is understood or retained and answers the questions: " What sort of pattern is there? How does this tie in? What is the underlying motive?" Finally, justified information is processed information that requires an explanation to be duplicated and answers the questions, "Why and how does it affect things?" Our research has led us to focus on the category of applied information, or in our terms: guidance information. We have emphasized the combination of what we refer to as support information and guidance information in software (Wilson & Snyder, 1999).

Among the most important knowledge classifications are the categories of explicit and tacit. Some researchers now differentiate additionally by adding the category of implicit separate from tacit, although most include implicit knowledge as a part of tacit. Polanyi (1966) defined the tacit knowledge category. Explicit knowledge is that which is rather precisely and formally articulated and often is readily available through books, manuals, software, etc. On the other hand, tacit knowledge is subconscious, not easily articulated, and usually believed to result from experience and deep understanding. Tacit knowledge is often the type of knowledge that makes an expert the expert (Snyder & Wilson, 1997). The tacit knowledge of experts is of prime interest in the knowledge harvesting process.

KNOWLEDGE PROCESS

According to Norman and Wikstrom (1994), KM involves three processes: generative, productive, and representative. When an organization produces new knowledge as a result of problem solving, the knowledge process is called the "generative" process. The generative process is how most businesses create knowledge; however, if the business fails to learn from this process, the organization must reprocess the same knowledge repeatedly, wasting resources that might be applied elsewhere. The "productive process" is usually that whereby businesses succeed or fail since this process is directly correlated to sales. The productive process is the knowledge process required to build a product and its future refinements. The "representative process" occurs when a product is sold to a customer and that customer perceives the product purchased as embodying the company's knowledge pertaining to that product.

It is important to note that there is a requirement to constantly refresh or renew the stock of knowledge. Thus, it is unlike other resources that can be put on a shelf until needed.

It is useful to examine the value system of the organization. We discuss the expanded value system next.

AN EXPANDED VALUE SYSTEM

In today's environment, most companies are aligning themselves with their customers, suppliers, and other partners to form interorganizational systems. In these systems, the partners are taking an active role in the value creating process. The classical value chain (Porter & Millar, 1985), mostly a closed system in which the company adds value through internal processes, must be expanded into a value system view and that is what the value star attempts. In the value star process (Norman & Wikstrom, 1994), all members of the enterprise are involved in the value creating process. By bringing the enterprise's knowledge together and sharing it among its partners, the company is learning and renewing its knowledge. Halal (1998) introduced five main tenets of value star partners for knowledge links to be successful. The knowledge links must have a unifying purpose, be voluntary, be independent members, have multiple leaders, and have integrated levels. The links must have a unified purpose to approach the knowledge process with the same underlying goals. It is important for the links to clearly identify the unifying purpose as early as possible since the complete knowledge process is based on that purpose. Each knowledge link may provide input as they see opportunities to increase value added; however, no link is forced participate. Each link remains independent and runs its own operations. By remaining independent, they are able to run day-to-day operations in the best interest of the company without interference. The value star is considered as having multiple leaders because each organization's own leader can provide leadership in the best interest of the organization. Multiple leaders are a key strength of the star in that it can have a functional leader when a problem requires a functional expert. The organization must be integrated at all levels to be able to share knowledge with the appropriate level in the other organizations without restrictions. Halal (1998) proposed that there were four main principles of knowledge links: equitability, equal distribution of power, distributed authority, and an infinitely malleable, yet durable, relationship. Equitability means that all the partners must benefit from the alliance. Distribution of power and distributed authority are both related to the concept that no single link has a disproportionate share of either power or authority.

KNOWLEDGE NAVIGATION

Some authors have introduced various metaphors to try to guide organizations in KM efforts. Allee (1997) introduced the analogy of navigation aids to direct organizations through KM. The aids introduced by Allee (1997) are the symbols: a North Star, a compass, the crew, maps & guides, sound vessels, and feedback and measurement. The North Star is seen as the unifying purpose or values. The organization's values must be communicated at all levels of the company. The compass symbolizes the organization's ability to know where it is in relationship to its objectives. The organization's knowledge strategy in relation to its core competencies provides the company direction. The crew symbolizes the sum of the organization's knowledge assets.

Knowledge assets must be encouraged to take chances and experiment in developing new knowledge if the organization is to attain a level of uncommon knowledge (Myers, 1996). Uncommon knowledge, according to Myers (1996), is knowledge that is so unique and rare that it can't be discovered through conventional means. Maps and guides are used to symbolize the organization's established knowledge processes that span all levels of the company. Knowledge of processes is sometimes overlooked. It is important to document the processes that foster knowledge creating so that they can be refined and repeated. The symbol of sound vessels is used to sum all of the organization's IT and learning assets used in the knowledge creation process. Allee (1997) referred to feedback as a gauge to see whether the company is "on course." Myers (1996) used feedback and measurement as a method of measuring the value of an organization's knowledge assets. There must be a feedback loop for knowledge workers to improve on the level of knowledge and an effective method to measure the result that knowledge has on both the bottom line and core values.

The organizational objectives are also important. Zack (1999) divided KM applications into two classes: integrative and interactive. The integrative applications involve sequential flow of explicit knowledge into and out of a repository that serves as the organization's medium of exchange. Interactive applications focus on supporting people with tacit knowledge. In our model, the software that contains codified tacit knowledge is directly employed to support people. In the pursuit of the KM implementation theme, it is first important to find out if the organization is ready. This assessment is discussed in the following section.

ASSESSING ORGANIZATIONAL READINESS FOR KNOWLEDGE MANAGEMENT

One of the first tasks is the process of determining if your organization is ready for implementing KM. Since this effort involves a significant strategic change in most firms, it is important to look at several factors that may be considered as the foundation for successful KM implementation. According to Wilson (1999), There are seven key elements. Each is described below:

Knowledge Orientation has to do with the extent that the firm gives priority to overt or deliberate efforts to manage knowledge as an asset in the fulfillment of its mission.

Climate refers to the extent to which the organization's people are receptive to change.

Culture is the extent to which the organization's vision, mission, business strategies, policies, and procedures support change.

Daily Operations refers to the extent to which the practical aspects of managing the daily operations of the organization actually support change.

Information Architecture is the extent to which the systems, policies, and procedures that affect the flow and availability of information throughout the organization support change.

Leadership is the extent to which the persons in leadership positions support change.

Magnitude of Proposed Change is the number of people in the organization who will be affected by the proposed change and the extent to which they will need to shift paradigms in order to accommodate the change.

Each of the above elements must be assessed and scored to determine readiness to proceed. If the areas are sufficiently advanced, the implementation efforts may proceed. If all are not, then it is appropriate to take action to improve the low scoring areas. The goal is to make obstacles to KM apparent so that action may be taken to eliminate or minimize the risks associated with the issues.

LOCATING KNOWLEDGEABLE PEOPLE

Unless an organization is fairly advanced in KM, it is unlikely that knowledge mapping has been done. This refers to a deliberate development and maintenance of an up-to-date inventory of the organization's most knowledgeable people. Wilson (1999) suggests using a work profiling process in order to build the inventory of the organization's human knowledge assets.

After the inventory of the organization's human knowledge assets is available, the task of identifying experts is facilitated. It is necessary to find experts in order to harvest their knowledge. The aim is to determine how the best performers accomplish their work. A successful methodology, such as LearnerFirst's Knowledge Harvesting" can be employed in order to assist in rating experts and in selecting the experts for eliciting their tacit knowledge.

CORPORATE MEMORY MANAGEMENT

Organizations need a systematic methodology for implementing knowledge management. Corporate memory management is about thinking better, learning faster, sharing what is known as needed throughout the organization (Snyder, Wilson, & McManus, 1999). There are several work processes that are performed in the corporate memory process. The subprocesses are:

Focus
Find
Elicit
Organize
Optimize knowledge
Share
Apply
Evaluate
Adapt

Each of the above processes should be viewed as an overall iterative process. The components are discussed on the next page:

Focus means that there must be a means to identify core processes that are the target for the corporate memory activities. This is the process followed in selecting a knowledge-based problem or task. *Find* is the process of indexing people, skills, expertise, or know-how that are needed to build the knowledge asset that will become decision support. Interviews conducted during the *Elicit* process are similar to knowledge engineering techniques. Know-how needs to be captured so that it may eventually be shared. *Organize* is required in order to structure the relationships between support information and the process guidance and to structure the relationships. *Optimize* is to refine the knowledge software to improve the ability to act and increase the understanding for action. *Share* is the process of addressing the cultural dynamics *Apply* is the support of each person in performance of their tasks. *Evaluate* is the calculation of the value of the knowledge assets and the effectiveness of the knowledge. *Adapt* is to provide continuous improvement and to incorporate newly discovered knowledge.

The tacit knowledge of experts is elicited, codified, and published in electronic form. This software may be considered as a type of Electronic Performance Support System (EPSS). Gery, G. (1991) discussed the role of EPSS and has expanded the concept to integrate it with KM. Essentially, the idea is to provide just in time expert support for a person performing a task through software.

The key to capturing the relevant knowledge is to select the right expert. Thereafter, the task of eliciting must follow. Here, observation and interviewing are use-

Source: Snyder, Wilson, & McManus, 1998

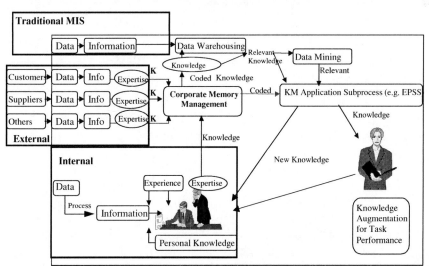

<u>Figure 1</u>-   The Corporate Knowledge Management Process Model

ful techniques. It is important that a comprehensive process be followed and that both guidance and support information are gathered. See Figure 1 for a model of the overall KM process.

CONFIGURATION IN THE ORGANIZATION

Klein (1998) developed a configuration for knowledge framework that places knowledge as the fulcrum with the fluidity of knowledge balanced against institutional requirements of an organization. Klein contends that for KM to exist and thrive, a delicate balance must be maintained. KM must balance the structured, disciplined side of knowledge against the creative processing side. By achieving the balance, the organization is able to turn the knowledge into business outputs while still developing new, innovative knowledge. Knowledge creation and KM practice must be a continuous process within the organization. Many organizations have created a Chief Knowledge Officer (CKO) to manage and integrate the knowledge assets of an organization (Davenport, 1996; Amidon, 1997; Halal, 1998). The CKO position reports directly to the CEO and provides vital information pertaining to the organization's learning productivity. CEO's must commit to implementing KM and emphasize its importance to all levels of the organization in order for KM to succeed. The organization must set the proper climate conducive to KM and reward individual performance that increases organizational knowledge. Setting up a knowledge environment can be conceived of as vision, planning, design, and implementation. Senior management must have the vision of what the organization should look like after KM and must focus on the KM objective. The KM vision must be shared and communicated throughout the organization. The vision should set a few priorities focusing on the role of knowledge within the organization. The organization must plan for the use of knowledge and use of KM tools to achieve their vision. Planning must include preparing the organization, managing knowledge assets, and leveraging knowledge to attain competitive advantage. It is important to set aggressive targets and demand rapid improvement in the initial phases of KM. During the initial phases, it is important to set the climate for learning. Additionally, the plan must include incentives to encourage the knowledge process. The organization must design the KM structure in which IT assets will be utilized. Last, the organization must implement KM according to its vision and design.

WHY KM FAILS

According to Klein's (1998) research, KM failures relate to four areas: business objective, program architecture, strategic priorities, and sponsorship. The KM business objectives must be clear and specific for the organization and allow the organization to measure itself against milestones and provide for self-correction. The program architecture spells out the tools and methods for KM. If the architecture is incomplete or not compatible with the organization, KM will likely fail. The first step in KM is to set the organization's strategic priorities. If the organization members believe top management is not concerned with KM, they will feel that KM is unimportant to the organization's survival. Sponsorship problems will affect the organization's ability to change and adapt to KM.

CONCLUSION

Implementing KM is no easy task and requires each organization to go through its own analytical process to see what role KM can and should play. The organization must assess its readiness for KM, inventory its knowledge assets, and determine which assets focus on its core capabilities and capacities. The core knowledge assets must be assigned a relative value and assessed as to their potential in the KM process. Next, the organization must establish its strategic priorities and vision for implementing KM. Additionally, the organization must set the environment and provide for the IT infrastructure to support KM. KM needs a facilitator to direct change management and to continually assess the value KM plays in the organization. After implementing KM, it is imperative to motivate knowledge workers and to provide active sponsorship in the KM process.

REFERENCES

Allee, V. (1997). *The knowledge evolution: Expanding organizational intelligence*. Boston: Butterworth-Heinemann.

Amidon, D. (1997). *The ken awakening: Management strategies for knowledge innovation*, Boston: Butterworth-Heineman.

Davenport, T. (April 1,1996). Knowledge roles: The CKO and beyond, *CIO*, 9:12, 24-26.

Drucker, P. (1995). The post-capitalist executive, in *Managing in a time of great change*. New York: Penguin.

Gery, G (1991). *Electronic performance support systems: how and why to remake the workplace through the strategic application of technology*, Boston: Weingarten Publications.

Halal, W.E. (1998). *The infinite resource*. San Francisco: Jossey-Bass.

Holsapple,C.W. and Joshi, K.D. (1997). Knowledge management: A threefold framework. *KIKM Research Paper* No. 104, 1-21.

Holsapple,C.W. and Joshi, K.D. (1998). In search for a descriptive framework for knowledge management: Preliminary delphi results. *KIKM Research Paper* No. 118, 1-29.

Hoving, R. (1998). Presentation at the SIM Interchange, Knowledge Management Working Group session, Seattle.

Klein, D. (1998). *The strategic management of intellectual capital*. Boston: Butterworth-Heinemann.

Mayo, A. & Lank, E. (1994). *The power of learning: A guide to gaining competitive advantage*. London: IPD.

Myers, P.S. (1996). *Knowledge management & organizational design*. Boston: Butterworth-Heinemann.

Normann, R. & Wikstrom, S. (1994). *Knowledge & value: A new perspective on corporate transformation*. New York: Routledge.

Polyani, M. (1996). *The tacit dimension*. Garden City, NJ: Doubleday.

Porter,M. & Millar, V. (1985). How information gives you a competitive advantage, *Harvard Business Review*, 151.

Snyder, C & Templeton, G. (1997). Toward a method of providing database structures derived from an ontological specification process: The example of knowledge management, *Proceedings, KI'97*, 1-11.

Snyder, C. & Wilson, L. (1997). Computer augmented learning: The basis of sustained knowledge management, *Proceedings, AIS Americas*, pp. 875-877.

Snyder, C. & Wilson, L. (1998). The process of knowledge harvesting: The key to knowledge management, Business information management: Adaptive futures, *8th Annual Bit Conference*, 43.

Snyder, C., Wilson, L. & McManus, D. (1998).Knowledge management: A proposed process model. *Proceedings, AIS Americas*, pp. 624-625.

Snyder, C., Wilson, L., & McManus, D. (1999). Corporate memory management: A knowledge management process model, *International Journal of Technology Management*, Forthcoming.

Sveiby, K. (1997). *The new organizational wealth: Managing & Measuring Knowledge-based assets*, San Francisco: Berrett-Koehler.

Templeton, G. & Snyder, C. (1999). A model of organizational learning based on control , *International Journal of Technology Management*, 18, 5/6/7/8, 705-720.

Virtual Library on Knowledge Management. Available: www.brint.com/km (November 5, 1998).

Webster's Encyclopedic Unabridged Dictionary. (1994). New York: Portland House.

Wiig, K. (1994). *Knowledge management: The central management focus for intelligent acting organizations*, Arlington, TX: Schema.

Wilson, L.T. (1999). Assessing readiness, Knowledge Harvesting Workshop, Version 2.0 , Birmingham, AL: LearnerFirst, Inc.

Wilson, L. T. & Snyder, C. A. (1999). Knowledge management and IT: How are they related? *IT Professional*, 1 (2), 73-75.

Zack, M. (Summer 1999). Managing codified knowledge, *Sloan Management Review*, 45-57.

Chapter 17

Knowledge Sharing Across Organizational Boundaries with Application to Distributed Engineering Processes

Gerd Frick, Eric Sax and Klaus D. Müller-Glaser
Forschungszentrum Informatik, Karlsruhe, Germany

Collaborative engineering processes with more than one company involved raise the need for knowledge sharing across organizational boundaries. The problem is analyzed in general, but on the background of this real-world application domain encountered, e.g., in automotive industry. A solution concept called virtual project database is presented; deficits in the status quo of information technology are hinted at as well as directions of future work for implementing the solution concept.

INTRODUCTION

Today, a complex and innovative technical product is rarely being developed as a whole by one single company alone. Demands for higher productivity and shorter times-to-market in global-scale competition and the high and continually increasing system complexities have lead to intensified "outsourcing" and strategic alliances. Components or subsystems of an entire system can be developed (and produced) by firms with specific know-how and supplied to a system integrator. E.g., over 50% of a motor car is produced by suppliers (Pfannmüller, 1999). As

Previously Published in *Challenges of Information Technology Management in the 21st Century* edited by Mehdi Khosrow-Pour, Copyright © 2000, Idea Group Publishing.

a result of this, interlaced development processes and shared knowledge about a product and its environment (such as product ideas, specification documents, system models, or simulation data) have to be managed across site and company boundaries (Distributed Concurrent Engineering).

Time-consuming manual processes such as printing and mailing of documents, shipping of diskettes, travelling to meetings etc. cause interrupts in information exchange leading to interrupts in the individual design processes or additional iterative changes due to intermediate work with old data. The delays resulting from inappropriate synchronization between development processes and partners accumulate during project lifetime and increase the total development time. Furthermore, unorganized redundancy in project data management is a permanent source of inconsistencies. Therefore, effective cross-organizational knowledge management in the context of development projects is required as a basis for improved distributed engineering processes. Expected effects are shorter times-to-market and – since there is a strong correlation between process and product quality – better products.

The authors' primary target within the application domain of distributed cooperative work across enterprises in the engineering field is electronic systems development. Electronic systems (embedded hardware/software systems) are of high economic importance since embedded software is one of the key innovation factors in many product areas, e.g., in the automotive industry (Müller-Glaser et al., 1999)[1]. Nevertheless, similar principles should apply to a more general context.

CROSS-ORGANIZATIONAL KNOWLEDGE SHARING

"Outsourcing" of engineering tasks will be implemented in form of development projects with external partners. Therefore the knowledge sharing problem can be attached to a *project* context. For simplicity, in this chapter we assume a bilateral relationship between two organizations.[2]

Project Knowledge Sharing and Reuse

Projects start with some initial knowledge taken from the companies' expertise and produce additional knowledge during project lifetime. As a whole, a *"project memory"* is built up. It can be represented by a *project database*, a repository set up for all data specific for a certain project. The basic idea presented in this paper is the integration of all project-relevant knowledge by a *virtual* repository which consists of physically distributed parts (section).

Reuse of knowledge, i.e. retrieval and repurposing/adaptation of existing information from other projects, ideally is facilitated by a general repository, called *"reuse database"* or (with respect to process knowledge) "experience factory"

Figure 1: Project Memory and Organizational Memories in a Bilateral Project

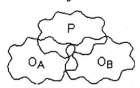

Figure 2: Reused and Generated Project Knowledge

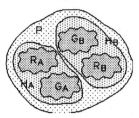

Figure 3: Shared Knowledge and Views

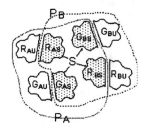

(Basili and Rombach 1988). It is the property of a company and resembles a part of its *"organizational memory"* (Stein and Zwass, 1995). Results of the current project that are valued of general importance shall be fed back to the reuse database, integrating it into a larger context (separately for every project partner).

This first distinction between project memory and organizational memory and their overlappings are illustrated in Figure 1.

Taking out the project memory only (Figure 2) we can distinguish between reused knowledge extracted from a company's organizational memory (R_x, $X \square$ {A,B}), e.g., existing products in case of add-on developments, and new knowledge generated by a company during project execution (G_x, initially empty). The reused knowledge sets of the organizations may overlap (cf. Figure 1), as there may be new knowledge generated in common. For uniqueness of responsibility it is possible to attribute a unique "home" organization to every information object (and create additional cross-links to every alternative provenience in case of reused knowledge). By this "homing" approach we can assume disjoint R_x and G_x; $H_x = R_x G_x$ be the knowledge homed by organization X.

Although the cooperation partners share some knowledge around the product under development the protection of intellectual property must not be compromised. Hiding of proprietary data is crucial not only towards third parties (competitors) but also towards business partners.

If we therefore have to distinguish between shared and unshared (private) project knowledge[3] we can split R_x the G_x and sets into disjoint subsets (denoted with S

Figure 4: Two Dimensions of the Product Data Space

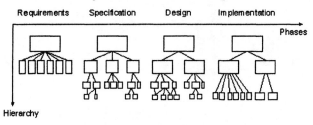

and U suffixes in Figure 3). Taking together the appropriate subsets we can define the **project views** P_x and the overall shared knowledge S (Figure 3).

Structural Characteristics of Engineering Data

The most important set of information objects in an engineering project are the product data. They are characterized by the sequence of development phases. Objects are derived from other objects preceding them in the design flow. These dependencies establish "horizontal" links between individual objects. Orthogonally, objects (products) are composed hierarchically. An object is decomposed into smaller parts which are developed independently and integrated to the object under development. This decomposition may be applied recursively. Thus we get "vertical" relationships between product data objects. A third dimension is the version history of each object that can be followed back. Together we can generally speak of multidimensional relationship structures spanning a navigable information space (see Figure 4). Distributed Engineering across multiple organizations causes links to logically cross company boundaries, leading to a "global" information space. The project views defined above can be considered as projections of the overall space onto restricted information spaces.

The inner structure of these views is built by micro-level views, defined in terms and structures of the application field:

Considering a hierarchically described product, the integrator needs not know the internal realization of a supplied subsystem, neither the supplier the details of the supersystem. So only the developer of a system has the detailed **white or clear box view** whereas the client gets a **black box view** which describes the interface with the external behaviour but abstracts from internal realization details. There may be several cases where a black box description of a component is not adequate as the client view and some parts of the realization are made visible to or prescribed by the client. The result is a white box-like structure with local black boxes, termed as a grey box (Tan et al., 1996; Büchi and Weck, 1997) resp. **grey box view**.

Figure 5: Replication

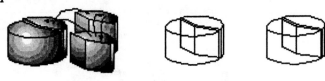

Figure 6: Fragmentation

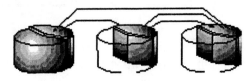

VIRTUAL PROJECT DATABASES

This section describes a solution concept, termed "virtual project database," that we propose as the central tool for the realization of the knowledge sharing scenario. A physically and organizationally distributed data basis is virtualized with respect to distribution and views.

Physical Project Database Architectures

Three main architectures come into consideration for establishing a project database in a distributed environment.

A **central repository** can be used to manage all (**P**) or at least the shared project data (**S**) at a central place, hosted by an external provider or one of the project partners. Thus sensitive data may be given out of physical control and put under foreign administration. Further disadvantages of a central solution are the large number of remote accesses (performance, network dependency, vulnerability) and "single point of failure" characteristics.

A decentralized architecture of **distributed, replicated repositories** can be used to compile a partner's complete project view (P_x) at a local project repository (Figure 5). The main drawback is the necessity of a consistent replication mechanism, which is difficult to accomplish in heterogeneous environments.

In an architecture with **distributed, fragmented repositories** every object is managed redundancy-free at its "home" site only. A project view can span multiple repositories (Figure 6).

Fragmentation is not limited to having one repository per site (managing H_x). There are reasons favoring an inner local fragmentation. Reused knowledge can remain in the reuse database(s) (separating G_x from R_x). Private data can be kept separate from shared data (e.g., behind an inner firewall). And last but not least, different data management tools can be used for different kinds of data (such as document and content management systems, software configuration management

Figure 7: Virtual Project Server

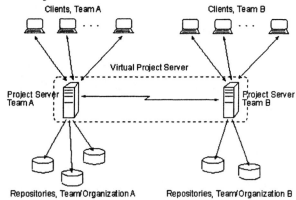

Repositories, Team/Organization A   Repositories, Team/Organization B

systems, engineering data management systems, specialized in-house solutions etc.). Of course, it is possible that the contents of a repository only partially belongs to the project view under consideration.

Even more complicated architectures are possible, such as fragmented user data combined with replicated metadata (cf., Abramovici et al., 1998).

Integration of a Fragmented Information Space

We now propose a 3-tier client/server approach that is able to hide the individual distribution strategy and the number of physical repositories and is especially suited to fragmentation (Figure 7). It provides a single access point to a company's complete project view by identifying it with a company-hosted *project server* communicating with one or more local repositories and other external project servers.[4]

The coupled group of distributed project servers collaboratively forms a virtual project server for the entire project. Clients only contact the local server that behaves like a "proxy" for the external servers. Based on an address space of global identifiers, the server group routes a client request to the repository where the original object or a replica is stored. Together they act as a virtual information management system, managing the *virtual project database*.

A possible client application is a *project browser* that allows navigation in the user's view of the project information space and up-/downloading of objects (documents, files) worked on with specialized tools.

Virtualization has not only to provide every project member with the illusion of a uniform repository but also to restrict the global information space to a view. Data objects that do not belong to a user's view have to be hidden while access has to be granted to the objects in the view. Access control thus is the basic mechanism for view implementations and has to be complemented by properly managed metadata (especially access right definitions). It is normally performed on the repository level already and can be backed by directory services for user management.

Technological Status Quo and Future Directions

Currently an increasing number of data management tool vendors offer own solutions for managing distributed (fragmented or replicated) repositories. Abramovici et al. (1998) and Vital et al. (1998) describe the state of the art for engineering data management (EDM) systems (used mainly in Mechanical Engineering). In these *one-tool-solutions* project server and repository merge into a single system. The drawbacks are the monolithic approach (it works only as long as all project data are stored by one tool) and the requirement that all partners use the same tool, altogether resulting in inflexibility and vendor dependency.

The general case is that different tools are best-suited for different kinds of data and different companies use different tools for the same type of data. So integrative solutions according to the virtual project server concept are needed. Currently a lot of work is done around World Wide Web technologies (including Web browser interfaces and XML[5] middleware technology). There are first products on the market, mainly targeting at e-commerce and transaction-oriented business-to-business integration, although they can potentially be extended towards knowledge management. But even these solutions still suffer from high customization efforts (adapters to the integration platform have to be written for every data management tool).

A major step forward towards fast and flexible integration of heterogeneous repositories into a virtual project database would be industry-wide harmonization of metadata, addressing, linking, navigation interfaces, import, export and synchronization of data.

In general the WWW seems to be the determining model of a universal information space, the Web browser being a universal software client.

CONCLUSION

Distributed engineering processes exemplify knowledge sharing across organizational boundaries in real-world situations. Beginning with a description of the application domain this paper focused on knowledge sharing between organizations in a project context.

Following a distinction between project-related knowledge and organizational knowledge and the idea of *project* and *organizational memories*, the knowledge sharing problem was broken down to *projections (views) of a global information space*. In a second step this was broken down to an solution concept called *virtual project database,* and for this an architecture of coupled information systems rendering a virtual project server was proposed.

The problem analysis was complemented by a survey of the technological status quo. While data hiding mechanisms for tailoring the virtual database to a specific view essentially are at hand, the integration of distributed and heterogeneous data repositories is not yet satisfactorily solved. Current solutions are inflexible and expensive in terms of customization effort. Topics of future work are harmonization of data management models and infrastructures, consistent with the Word Wide Web model, and standardized federation of heterogeneous repositories.

REFERENCES

Abramovici, M., Gerhard, D., and Langenberg, L. (1998). Unterstützung verteilter Entwicklungsprozesse durch EDM/PDM ["Support for distributed development processes through EDM/PDM", in German]. *Informationsverarbeitung in der Konstruktion '98.* VDI Berichte Nr. 1435, 69-86.

AIAG - Automotive Industry Action Group (1999). ANX, Automotive Network eXchange [WWW document]. URL http://www.anxo.com.

Basili, V.R. and Rombach, H.D. (1988). The TAME Project: Towards Improvement-Oriented Software Environments. *IEEE Transactions on Software Engineering,* 14, 758-773.

Bray, T., Paoli, J., and Sperberg-McQueen, C.M. (Eds.) (1998). Extensible Markup Language (XML) 1.0. W3C Recommendation [WWW document]. URL http://www.w3.org/TR/1998/REC-xml-19980210

Büchi, M., and Weck, W. (1997). A Plea for Grey-Box Components. Proceedings of the *Foundations of Component-Based Systems Workshop,* Zürich, Switzerland.

Frick, G., Jenne, F., Renner, D., and Sax, E. (1999). Verteiltes Engineering, Zwischenbericht ["Distributed Engineering, Interim Report", in German]. Forschungszentrum Informatik, Karlsruhe, Germany, Technical Note FZI-ESM-VVE-TN-1-1.0.

Müller-Glaser, K. D., Burst, A., Spitzer, B., and Schmerler, S. (1999). Rapid Prototyping of Automotive Information Systems. *it + ti – Informationstechnik und Technische Informatik* 41/5, 12-18.

Pfannmüller, M. (1999). Mehr Kompetenzen, aber auch höhere finanzielle Risiken – Neuorientierung der Zulieferer [„Higher competence but also higher financial risks – re-orientation of automotive suppliers", in German], *Frankfurter Allgemeine Zeitung,* 14.8.1999.

Stein, E.W. and Zwass, V. (1995). Actualizing Organizational Memory with Information Systems. *Information Systems Research,* 6(22).

Stroezel, M. and Strecker, K. (1999). EDI 21 – New co-operation concepts for global enterprising. Proceedings of the *6th European Concurrent Engineering Conference, From Product Design to Product Marketing*, 168-171.

Tan, K. C., Li, Y., Gawthrop, P. J., and Glidle, A. (1996). *Evolutionary Grey-Box Modelling for Nonlinear Systems*. Technical Report CSC-96019. University of Glasgow, U.K., Faculty of Engineering, Centre for Systems and Control.

Vital, E., Vilela, J. B., Baake, U., and Haussmann, D. (1998). Introduction of Virtual Product Development in practice. *Informationsverarbeitung in der Konstruktion '98*. VDI Berichte Nr. 1435, 41-56.

NOTES

[1] Our analysis has been stimulated and influenced by co-operations with German automotive industry companies (Frick et al., 1999).

[2] Additional categorizations of bilateral relationships depending on company sizes and project characteristics are possible. See, e.g., Stroezel and Strecker (1999) who identify five types of suppliers.

[3] Sharing can be refined by multiple degrees (from private to public, with different access rights for different operations and the like). We can summarise all these by the distinction between private (no access) and shared in the meaning of 'potentially shared' (controlled access).

[4] Remote communication can utilize Virtual Private Networks over the Internet or industry-specific subnets like ANX® (Automotive Network eXchange®, AIAG 1999) as well as dial-up connections.

[5] XML = Extensible Markup Language (Bray et al., 1998)

Chapter 18

Organizational Learning by 'Segmented Networks': Breeding Variations and Similarities Together - What is Optimum?

Bishwajit Choudhary

Bankenes BetalingsSentral A/S, Norway

Researchers have long argued that a "right" degree of closeness among team members is necessary for innovation. At unhealthy extremes, while closeness leads to cloning and copycat attitude, increased distance can result in incompatibility and dissonance. Hence, actually building teams that possess "creative-tension" is easier said than done. This chapter develops specific factors that conceptualize an "optimum" distance (vis-à-vis closeness) in teams and later extends the factors to argue for a novel organizational form, the "segmented network."

INTRODUCTION

Organizations have increasingly realized the need to build knowledge base through available and *potential* resources. The importance of maintaining a *right balance* between exploiting the existing and exploring new knowledge base for innovation has been well realized (Cox, 1993; Jackson et al., 1995). However, in practice, achieving right "variation" in teams is not so easy.

We begin by sharing our broad research concern: Which types of organizational forms would support greater innovation in future? Here, we have two specific objectives: One, to conceptualize the notion of "balanced variation" in man-

Previously Published in *Challenges of Information Technology Management in the 21st Century* edited by Mehdi Khosrow-Pour, Copyright © 2000, Idea Group Publishing.

agement teams. Two, to identify the important factors that define the *degree* of balance. Our objectives have been well captured through a humorous quote in sociology: "If two people always *agree*, then one is useless and if they always *disagree*, then both are useless!" Finally, in this chapter we shall focus on the potential sources for enhancing innovation and suggest new organizational forms.

REFLECTIONS FROM PAST RESEARCH

Concomitant to the globalization of industry over the past decade, there has been a proliferation of strategic linkages. Almost all empirical analyses of inter-organizational networks focus on inter-organizational groupings (Pfeffer & Salancik, 1974; Van De Ven & Walker, 1984). Here, we accept the definition due to Andersen et al. (1994), who define a business network as a set of two or more connected business relationships. The authors claim that the parties in networks (traditionally) come from the same industry. Another reason for and dimension of network is synergy (Ansoff, 1965), which is based on the economies of scale (especially true for the large MNCs). Please note that our concern here is to investigate the conditions in teams that enhance innovation (in learning). This essentially takes a view beyond scale-based synergies.

Research on networks has been primarily concerned with knowledge creation at organizational levels. For example, Kogut and Zander (1992) examine the transformation of personal knowledge into organizational knowledge and Nonaka et al. (1994) have studied the knowledge creation in firms. Organizational learning gained currency when collecting and interpreting market information ahead of competitors was found to be a potential source of competitive advantage (DeGeus, 1988; Dickson, 1992). The importance of market forces (and hence an "external" orientation) is stressed by several researchers (Shapiro, 1988; Deshpande & Webster, 1989; Day, 1990, 1992). Argyris (1977) stresses the need to practice "double loop learning," while Senge (1990) recommends "generative learning." Both these pioneers have attempted to enhance innovation in management teams. Since managers mostly work in teams, there is a need to transfer the individual knowledge at a company level (Hedlund, 1994). Most theorists also agree that organizations ultimately learn through individuals (Senge, 1990; Kim, 1993; Dodgson, 1993).

COMMENTS ON PAST RESEARCH

*I*n spite of pioneering attempts to conceptualize organizational learning, several researchers have expressed concerns lately. Ritcher (1998) remarks that the current literature does not adequately explore the micro dynamics of learning process. Although DeGues (1988), Stata (1989), Senge (1990a), Nonaka (1991), among others have underlined the need for "creative tension" in teams, they have, since then struggled to concretely theorize and experiment with the notion of "strategic balance." In fact, Nonaka et al. (1995) claim:

> "…There is very little research on how knowledge is actually created *and hence there is a need to understand the dynamics of knowledge creation*." (italics added).

Alter and Hage (1993) and Hamel et al (1988) have argued that new theories be developed that can encompass knowledge creation as a result of inter-firm collaboration. Such an ambition demands novelty in theorizing, that captures knowledge creation more broadly (than merely understanding it as the result of social discourse within an organization). Further, the contemporary theories on organizational learning have not considered the possibility of a firm influencing its environment (Hamel, Doz and Prahalad, 1988). Follett (1942) suggested the importance of variation among the decision-makers by stressing the need to look inside and outside the firm quite early. Echoing similar views, Macdonald (1995) claims that the current theories have neglected the external-to-firm factors. This is especially surprising after the importance of market forces have been well studied in the past (Shapiro, 1988; Deshpande & Webster, 1989; Day, 1990, 1992). Incorporating market forces in the current theories on organizational learning becomes even more important with D'Aveni's (1995) work on hypercompetition. The author argues that competition, if understood in traditional sense, can be grossly misleading because the industries are now marked by new sources of competitive (dis)advantages. Consequently, firms need breakthrough innovations through industry-directed learning to outsmart competition. Nonaka (1994) stresses that the underlying focus in all learning activities should be to actually enhance innovation and not merely learning (for the sake of it). To sum up the dis-satisfaction with the existing literature on organizational learning, we are challenged by three concerns:

1. Unclear conceptualization of "optimum distance" among the team members.
2. Weak research linking team dynamics (and team composition) with innovation.
3. Finally, a missing unified theory of organizational learning that simultaneously encompasses and links internal and external-to-firm factors.

Taking some of the key points from the above concerns, in this paper we shall limit ourselves to developing a theory that incorporates internal and external (to firm) factors and links "optimum distance" in teams with their ability to innovate.

HOW MUCH VARIATION IS "ENOUGH"?

With increasing market uncertainties, firms need to continually explore newer means of accessing, processing and applying knowledge. Several researchers argue that a "right" degree of variation in teams breeds conditions for innovation (Stata; 1989; Senge, 1990a etc.). While the notion of "optimum difference" among the members is well recognized, two issues deserve greater attention:

- How much variation among members can result in an "optimum distance"?
- What factors lead to "strategic dissonance"?

Lack of a comprehensive theory linking team-composition with managerial innovation makes the absence of the above-mentioned issues little less surprising.

Member Distance

Understanding "distance" that the team members experience from each other is key to defining "balanced variation." By "distance" we mean differences among the members, based on objective factors such as previous work experiences, education, professional training and more subjective issues as values-at-work and personality. Inkpen (1988) argues that in intra-industry and inter-firm teams, substantial mutual distrust among members of each firm (who perceive each other as potential competitors) inhibits an atmosphere of "openness," that is essential for learning. Extending the approach of Inkpen (1988) of classifying members based on the type of firm and industry, we conceptualize four types of teams:

1. Between managers of same industry and same type of firms (typically between the head-on competitors, discussed by Inkpen, 1988);
2. Between the managers of same industry, but different firms (typically the complementors or indirect competitors);
3. Between the managers of different industry, but same type of firm. Example includes retailers' associations in different industries (indirect complementors); and
4. Between managers of completely unrelated firms.

We now develop two generic constructs that help us investigate the above-mentioned teams for their ability to initiate, sustain and exploit "creative tension." In the following space we conceptualize the factors constituting "member distance."

Knowledge Distance (KD)

At a broad level, companies in different industries demand specific knowledge. While the managers in an investment bank need to know well volatility, risk evaluation, etc., those in consumer goods need the knowledge of consumer psychology. Similar companies within the same industry usually possess common knowledge (complementors are exception, as they may operate at different value-added "levels," even in the same industry). By "similar companies within an industry," we mean companies that focus within the same scope of value chain based on the primary activities (Porter, 1985). Hence, KD conceptualizes the degree of industry-relatedness in terms of primary activities. Based on these arguments, we propose:

P1: There exists a set of knowledge requirements in different industries, which leads to the presence of knowledge distance (or difference) across various industries (at a broad level).

Professional Distance (PD)

Goffee and Jones (1996) argue that various departments within the same firm can influence managers' personalities (and hence their "perceived distance"). The way in which a prolonged (and specialized) work experience influences the managers is similar to the way in which culture conditions people (many times, even without their consciousness). The process in which different (and changing) work responsibilities influence a manager's personality is elaborately documented by the noted Harvard social scientist, Shoshana Zuboff (1988), based on years of observations and interviews in firms that underwent change (notably with increasing automation). We refer to such a job-specific, personality difference as Professional Distance (PD). PD is affected by the intensity of workload and/ or prolonged work experience with specialized responsibilities. Based on these arguments, we propose:

P2: There exists a set of (intuitive) personality requirements (leading to personality differences) across different departments.

Note that the above proposition is especially true for the MNCs, which are marked by greater number of more highly specialized divisions.

Using KD and PD to conceptualize 'conditions' for innovative learning:

In this section, we delve deeper into KD and PD to investigate their joint effects. From the arguments presented earlier, we can conceptualize various divisions of an MNC as (micro) "personality domains" (based on PD) and the MNCs themselves, as macro "knowledge domains" (based on KD). It is a common observation in many firms that the sales managers work more closely with product managers than with the production managers. Why so? We believe that this is due to higher degree, directness and ease of the compatibility between the sales and product development (compared to sales and production department) based on their competencies. We now summarize some of the key arguments presented in the paper:

1. While KD captures (dis)similarities existing among managers due to external-to-firm knowledge-specific differences, PD conceptualizes the department-specific, internal-to-firm behavior-related (dis)similarities. This addresses the concerns of Follett (1942) and Hamel et al. (1988), as stated earlier.

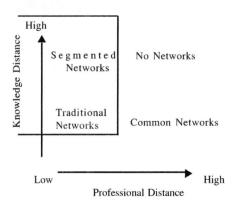

2. KD captures the "member-distance" based on objective and more formal knowledge-based competencies, at a macro (industry) level. PD, on the other hand, represents subjective and relatively more complex (personality-based) differences at a micro (department) level.

3. At the cost of repetition, it should be noted that based on past research, we inferred that managers' overall job-related knowledge is a function of company's line of business (or its "position" in the industry). Similarly, a manager's personality is argued to depend on the degree of specialization and length of job (while the effects of social discourse, family life cycle, etc. were ignored for simplicity).

4. Finally, the unit of analysis when using PD is a manager (or department) and in the case of KD, the unit of analysis is the firm.

We believe that KD and PD, taken together, hold the potential to define teams with "optimum distance." Based on various combinations of PD and KD, we have developed a simple 2 by 2 matrix that shows different teams based on varying levels of KD and PD.

It is evident that the traditional networks occur when both KD and PD are low. These are typically the intra-firm, intra-department teams. An example includes the periodic department meeting in a company (between the head and his/her employees). Since such meetings are found in all the firms, we refer to them as the traditional internal "networks" of managers. However, as the need for integrating knowledge across the departments, within a firm is realized, managers from different departments have started to work together. We refer to such teams as the common internal "networks" (more commonly known as "cross-functional" teams). As their name indicates, they are found in many companies. Note that if managers are poor in managing intra-department teams, it would be immature to develop cross-functional teams.

When both KD and PD are high, we believe that no teams can (and should) be formed. Hence, we do not investigate such teams further. A team with high KD and PD is not merely ineffective, but also difficult to manage. Ease of managing a team is an important practical consideration that must be borne in mind. The notion of "optimum distance," by its definition demands that least one of the factors (constituting "distance") should have an opposing effect, thereby resulting in a sort of "balance." This obviously rules out teams where both KD and PD are high (or low).

Perhaps, the most interesting case arises when the members experience low PD and high KD. We refer to such a team as a "segmented network." Varying (knowledge-based) competencies and similar personalities mark the conditions in such a team. Past research provides ample proof on how job specialization can influence manager's personality (Zuboff, 1988; Goffee and Jones, 1996). Consequently, the members can more easily 'empathize' with each other, while rooting their differences in knowledge based, more factual interpretations. A segmented network, by its definition (and composition) encourages managers to look at learning possibilities outside their firm.

Anatomy of "Segmented Networks"

Each division of an MNC, due to specialization usually has one or set of highly related activities. We illustrate this by stating the "key" activities in a Marketing division in different industries (managers from which can constitute a "segmented network"):

a) Selling image (brand management);
b) Hard selling (door-to-door sales for introductory products and services);
c) Selling care (customer support);
d) Selling ideas (creating demand, negotiating deals or price discounts with retailers, etc.);
e) Selling a character (building customers' confidence);
f) Selling an atmosphere (customer services);
g) Selling relationships (relationship marketing), etc.

It is evident that a common thread (of "selling") runs throughout these activities. Hence, the marketing executives in different industries have the potential to share this "primary knowledge around selling." They can complement each other's knowledge bases about the consumer behavior. Different firms in a given region serve the same client-base. This argument is violated in two cases: One, when the firms have different end-users (business clients versus private consumers). Two, at department level, when managers from different sides operate at different "levels" of value chains in different industries for, e.g., managers from accounting department in a bank and those from sales in a consumer good firm. Note carefully that a segmented network is team of two (or more) similar "departments" from two (or more companies, essentially in different) industries and builds on the notion of "strategic balance" among its members. Obviously, making such teams demands flexibility and delegation from the senior management, who should encourage the departments identify respective "key" activities and then develop "Strategic Learning Partnerships" (SLPs).

While a segmented network incorporates the idea of "co-optetition," it is still averse to making SLPs with head-on competitors (problems of which are well noted by Inkpen (1988)). We firmly believe that there is a need to "calculate well" before opening up to new learning possibilities from external players. Learning from external players has become critical, especially with the proliferation of network products (Arthur, 1994).

Our argument that the presence of high KD (as in a segmented network) can create conditions for better decisions (in terms of quality and innovativeness) draws support from past research. Schweiger et al. (1986) and Sandberg et al. (1989) show that the quality of decisions is proportional to the number of "task" oriented conflicts. Further, in line research on hypercompetition (D'Aveni, 1995), segmented networks can support conditions for "non-linear learning," since it is based on the assumption that the "fateful signals" can come up in any quarter of the industry. As most of the companies still exploit traditional and common networks, it is strategic to experiment with newer types of teams. In fact, Achrol (1991), Dickson (1992) and Kanter (1989) agree that the primary focus of market orientation is based on knowledge derived from customer and competitor analysis and a firm must be careful not to underestimate the contributions of "external" sources.

KEY MANAGERIAL IMPLICATIONS

The contemporary literature linking competitive strategy and knowledge creation stresses on learning faster than competitors (DeGeus, 1988; Dickson, 1992). We depart from this view and suggest that in future learning smarter would be more important. Segmented networks present not only the opportunities, but also the conditions for smarter learning. They can prove to be particularly useful in the following situations:

1. *When firms internationalize:* Here there is a need to understand the consumer "as completely as possible." Segmented networks would prove helpful, as they comprise managers from selected "departments" from various industries (serving a "common client base," discussed earlier.

2. *When markets change:* This happens when new competitors enter and/or the consumers' demands shift. A more "complete" understanding of consumer behavior would be helpful. Here we challenge the future researchers with a proposition:

P3: For a firm operating in competitive environment, knowledge of the "complete consumer" is more important than a "complete product."

3. *Placing the "right" person in the "right chair" :* This is a common policy guiding the human resources activities in the companies. We argue that such a practice falls in line with our theory as the underlying objective here (in our language) is matching KD and PD.

A FINAL NOTE

The chapter attempted to capture the potential link between team composition and managerial innovation. We argued that at professional levels, it is more difficult to manage teams with greater personality differences than those with greater knowledge differences. Segmented networks appeal well beyond their current theoretical domains and offer a practical solution for making innovative teams in the future. A working proposition throughout this research was to link grounded (and rather static) theoretical descriptions with practical and dynamic prescriptions. We now identify some of the key limitations and highlighting directions for future research.

While we attempted to conceptualize PD and KD, it remains challenge as how to theoretically measure and actually report them (in firms). Another challenge is to identify the "key value-adding" activity common to a department "across" the major industries (illustrated only for Marketing here). Further, thinking in terms of "discrete" activity has the limitation in network industries (for, e.g., Telecom and Banking), which are marked by overlaps in value-creating activities (Stabell et al., 1998). This implies the presence of (and need for) an overlap in managers' knowledge and even personalities. Accepting a dichotomized classification of managerial innovation (due to Schein et al (1970)) as "role innovation" (new definitions of roles, approaches, coordination etc.) and "content innovation" (new products and services), we admit that our study remained limited to "role innovation." Again, the influence of hierarchy in team dynamics and innovation was not considered for simplicity.

Will segmented networks be easy to manage? Honestly, we don't know. However, if the implications from past research are to be believed, we are optimistic. Finally, leading such a team would demand greater managerial competence at result-orientation, due to the existing knowledge distance among managers.

ACKNOWLEDGEMENT

Author appreciates the comments from two anonymous reviewers on the earlier draft of this chapter.

REFERENCES

Achrol, R. S. (1991). Evolution of the marketing organization: New Forms for Turbulent Environment. *Journal of Marketing, Vol. 55 (Oct.)*, pp. 77-93

Alter, C. and Hage, J. (1993). Organizations working together. *Newbury Park, CA: Sage Publications Inc.*

Anderson, J.C., Håkansson, H. & Johanson, J. (1994). Dyadic business relationships within a business network context. *Journal of Marketing, Vol. 58 (Oct.)*, pp. 1-15.

Ansoff, H. I. (1965). Corporate strategy. *New York: McGraw-Hill.*

Argyris C. (1977). Double loop learning in organizations. *Harvard Business Review, Vol. 55 (Sept.- Oct.)*, pp. 115 – 125

Arthur, B (1994). Positive feedbacks in economy. *The McKinsey Quarterly, No. 1*, pp. 81-95.

Cox, T.H. (1993). Cultural diversity in organizations: Theory, Research and Practice. *Barrett-Koehler*, San Francisco, CA.

Day, George S. (1990). Market driven strategy, processes for creating value. *New York: Free Press.*

Day, George S. (1992). Marketing contribution to the strategy dialogue. *Journal of Academy of Marketing Science, Vol. 20 (Fall)*, pp. 323-329.

D' Avneni, R.A. (1995). Coping with hypercompetition: Utilizing the new 7S's framework. *Academy of Management Executive, Vol. 9 (No. 3)*, pp. 45-60.

DeGeus, Arie, P. (1988). Planning as learning. *Harvard Business Review, Vol. 66 (March- April)*, pp. 70-74.

Deshpande, R. and Webster, F.E., Jr. (1989). Organizational culture and marketing: Defining the Research Agenda, *Journal of Marketing, 53 (Jan.)*, pp. 3-15.

Dickson, P.R. (1992). Towards a general theory of competitive rationality. *Journal of Marketing, 56 (Jan.)*, pp.69-83.

Dodgson, M (1993). Organizational learning. *Harvard Business Review. 75 March-April*, pp. 375-394.

Follett, M.P (1942). Constructive conflict in H. C. Metclaf and L. Urwrick (eds.), *Dynamics of administration: The Collective Papers of Mary Follett*. New York: Harper and Row.

Goffee, R. and Jones, G. (1996). What holds the modern company together? *Harvard Business Review*, 74(6), Nov.-Dec., pp. 133-148.

Hamel, G, Doz, Y.L. and Prahalad, C.K (1988). Collaborate with your competitors-and win. *Harvard Business Review,* 66, pp. 133-139.

Inkpen, A. (1998). Learning, knowledge acquisition, and strategic alliances. *European Management Journal*, 16(2), pp. 223-229.

Jackson, S, May, K.E. and Whitney, K (1995). Understanding the dynamics of diversity in decision-making teams. In (eds.) R.A Guzzo and E. Salas: *Team effectiveness and decision-making in organizations*. San Francisco, CA: Jossey-Bass, pp. 204-261.

Kanter, R.M. (1989). When giants learn to dance. *New York: Touch Stone*.

Kim,D.H. (1993). The link between individual and organizational learning. *Sloan Management Review. Fall*, pp. 37-50.

Kogut,B. and Zander, U. (1992). Knowledge of the firm, combinative capabilities and the replication of technology. *Organization Science, 3(3)*, pp. 383 – 397.

Macdonald, S (1995). Learning to change: An information perspective on learning in the organization. *Organization Science, 6(5)*, Sept.-Oct. pp. 557-568.

Nonaka, I (1991). The knowledge creating company. *Harvard Business Review 69, Nov.-Dec.*, pp. 96-104.

Nonaka, I., Byosiere, P., Borucki, C.C., and Konno, N. (1994). Organizational knowledge creation theory: A first comprehensive test. *International Business Review, 3(4)*, pp. 337-351.

Nonaka, I. and Takeuchi, H. (1995). *The knowledge creating company*. New York: Oxford University Press.

Pfeffer, J. Salancik & G.R. (1974). The bases and use of power in organizational decision-making: the Case of a University. *Administrative Science Quarterly, 19(4)*, pp. 453-473.

Porter, M.E. (1985). *Competitive Advantage: Creating and Sustaining Superior Performance*. New York: Free Press.

Richter, I. (1998). Individual and organizational learning at the executive level. *Management Learning, 29(3)*, pp. 299-316.

Schein (1970). The role innovator and his education. *Technology Review 72*, pp. 33- 37.

Schweiger, D.M, Sandberg and Ragan, J.W. (1986). Group approaches for improving strategic decision making: A comparative analysis of dialectical inquiry, devil's advocacy, and consensus. *Academy of management Journal, 29(1)*, pp. 51-71.

Schweiger, D.M., Sandberg, W.R. and Rechner, P (1989). Experimental effects of dialectical inquiry, devil's advocacy and consensus approaches to strategic decision-making. *Academy of Management Journal, 32*, pp. 745-772.

Senge,P.M. (1990). *The Fifth Discipline: The art and practice of the learning organizations*. New York: Doubleday.

Senge,P.M. (1990a). The leader's new work: Building learning organizations. *Sloan Management Review. Fall*, pp. 7-23.

Shapiro, B. P. (1988). What the hell is market oriented?, *Harvard Business Review, 66 (Nov-Dec)*, pp. 119-125

Stabell,C.B and Fjeldstad, Ø.F. (1998). Configuring value for competitive advantage: On Chains, Shops and Networks. *Strategic Management Journa,l 19* pp. 413-437

Stata,R (1989). Organizational learning: The key to managerial innovation. *Sloan Management Review. Spring*, pp. 63-74

Van de Ven, A.H. and Walker, G. (1984). The dynamics of inter-organizational coordination. *Administrative Science Quarterly, 29(4)*, pp. 598-621

Zuboff, S. (1988). *In the Age of Smart Machine-The Future of Work and Power.* Basic Books.

Chapter 19

Client/Server and the Knowledge Directory: A Natural Relationship

Stuart D. Galup and Ronald Dattero
Florida Atlantic University, USA

Developing and supporting knowledge management systems that seamlessly integrate with the existing information technology infrastructure is a major challenge. This development requires the functionality to locate and disseminate knowledge. An integral part of this requirement is the knowledge directory - a layered component accessible by any knowledge requester that can direct the knowledge requester to the location of the knowledge, in whichever format it may exist. This chapter discusses a client/server architecture that employs the knowledge directory to support the development and ongoing maintenance of knowledge management systems.

INTRODUCTION

The downsizings of the 1980's, the information technology driven productivity gains of the 1990's, and the pending retirement of baby boomers has and will result in a massive loss of enterprise and job specific knowledge. Business and government cannot afford the massive loss of intellectual capital resulting from these three events. Consequently, those enterprises that can retain and use the knowledge will have a significant competitive advantage.

Knowledge is an intellectual property that although paid for in part by the employer is a difficult asset to control as it is fragmented in documents, policies, procedures, and other data storage mediums. Another challenge for management is to retain this knowledge in a form that is easily retrievable. This is not an easy

Previously Published in *Challenges of Information Technology Management in the 21st Century* edited by Mehdi Khosrow-Pour, Copyright © 2000, Idea Group Publishing.

task, since the enterprise must first identify the location of all needed knowledge, and second, determine the easiest way to retrieve it.

We begin this paper with a general discussion about knowledge management (KM) and client/server technology. Next, we develop an architecture for a directory server which client/server knowledge management systems (KMS) use to search and retrieve knowledge. We end with a discussion of KMS cases in the context of this architecture.

KNOWLEDGE MANAGEMENT

Data, information, and knowledge are three related but not interchangeable concepts. Data is a set of discrete, objective facts about events. Information is organized data presented in context. Data becomes information when its creator adds meaning or value. Similarly, knowledge derives from information as information derives from data. Knowledge can be viewed as information in context, together with an understanding of how to use it. Knowledge can be either explicit (knowledge for which a person is able to make available for inspection) or tacit (knowledge for which a person is unable to make available for inspection). (Davenport and Prussak, 1998; Brooking, 1999)

There are many definitions of Knowledge Management but the Gartner Group (1999) description seems most appropriate for the perspective expressed in our paper. "Knowledge management promotes an integrated approach to identifying, capturing, retrieving, sharing, and evaluating an enterprise's information assets. These information assets may include databases, documents, policies and procedures, as well as the uncaptured tacit expertise and experience stored in individual workers' heads."

This definition implies that information assets are plentiful and are stored in numerous locations throughout the organization. Storage options include documents, documents in document management systems, groupware such as Lotus Notes, and expert or knowledge based systems (Brooking, 1999). Physically these information assets can be electronically stored on Compact Disk, Laser disk, mechanical hard drives, microfilm, microfiche, and embedded in computer programs. Further, information assets are also stored in books, documents, and other paper-based medium. Knowledge that is particularly critical include (Brooking, 1999):

1. Knowledge of a particular job;
2. Knowledge of who knows what in a company;
3. Knowledge of how to get things done in a company using the corporate culture;
4. Knowledge of who is best to perform a particular job or task;
5. Knowledge of corporate history (how and why);

6. Knowledge of business customs;
7. Knowledge of a particular customer account;
8. Knowledge of how to put together a team that can achieve a particular task; and
9. Knowledge of how to approach a particular problem which is difficult to solve.

CLIENT/SERVER TECHNOLOGY

Computing sources for the first thirty years of the information technology revolution were dominated by isolated hardware and network environments. Mainframes, mini-computers and local area networks were initially set up to support specific business functions. Each computing complex was installed with a separate physical data network. IBM mainframes used coaxial cable and 3270 terminal emulation and the IBM System 38 mini-computer used twin-axial cable and 5250 terminal emulation. Local area networks used their own respective cabling medium and data network architecture. As a result, these environments were isolated and data sharing was almost impossible. (Kern et al., 1998)

Information systems written for these monolithic computer complexes contain three basic components, a presentation layer, a processing layer, and a data storage layer (Boar, 1996; Borthick, 1994). All three layers execute on one hardware platform.

During the 1980's and 1990's, multiple protocol support between different platforms across inexpensive connections became more common. This connectivity enhancement helped the development of client/server technologies, which distributed these layers across hardware and operating systems platforms (Boar, 1996; Schulte, 1995; Duchessi, 1998). Although there are many variation of the client/server model, two-tier and three-tier are the two basic deployments (Edwards, 1999; Weston, 1998).

1. 2-tier splits the processing loading in two. The majority of the applications runs on the client (often referred to as "fat client"), which typically sends SQL requests to a server-resident database
2. 3-tier splits the logic between 1) clients that run the graphical user interface (GUI) logic, 2) the application server running the business logic, and 3) the database and/or legacy application. This configuration is often referred to as "fat server" or "thin client." The middle tier in most of these 3-tier applications is not implemented as a monolithic program. Instead, it is implemented as a collection of components that are used in a variety of client-initiated business transactions where each component automates a relatively small business function. This derivation of 3-tier is sometimes referred to as N-tier.

The 3-tier client/server architecture has many advantages over the 2-tier client/server architecture including less complexity, higher security, higher encapsulation of data, better performance efficiency, excellent scalability, excellent application reuse, a good server-to-server infrastructure (via server-side middleware), legacy application integration (via gateways), excellent internal support, support for heterogeneous databases, rich communication choices, excellent hardware architecture flexibility, and excellent availability. The main disadvantage is the difficulties in development but these difficulties are getting less and less over time (Orfali et al., 1999). One way around this development problem is to adopt a component-based architecture design. The benefits of a component-based architecture design include (Edwards, 1999):

1. Big applications can be developed in small steps.
2. Applications can reuse components.
3. Clients can access data and functions easily and safely.
4. Custom applications can incorporate off-the shelf components.
5. Component environments don't get older – they only get better.

CLIENT/SERVER AND KNOWLEDGE MANAGEMENT SYSTEMS

Information and knowledge are everywhere. In a world of multiple computer languages, database management systems, assorted collaborative and group support software, network technologies, and data storage methods, it can be a difficult and complex problem to locate and retrieve enterprise knowledge. If KM promotes an integrated approach to identifying, capturing, retrieving, sharing, and evaluating an enterprise's information assets, then the challenge is to get the right information to the right person at the right time.

"An integrated and integrative technology architecture is a key driver for Knowledge Management Systems (KMS) ... KMS seem to require a variety of technologies: database and database management, communication and messaging, and browsing and retrieval. The need for seamless integration of the various technologies may lead to the dominance of the Internet and Internet-based KMS architectures." (Alavi and Leidner, 1999)

Alavi and Leidner (1999) also note: "since access to internal organizational knowledge sources was also rated relatively highly and desirable by our sample, we predict that organizational intranets will also play a dominant role in support of internal knowledge management activities due to cost-effective technical capabilities including: access to the legacy systems, platform independence, access to multimedia data formats, a uniform and easy-to-use point-and-click interface, and capability for easy multi-media publication for knowledge sharing."

O'Dell, et al. (1998) state that the benefits of these "knowledge enabled Intranets" include:

1. Lower communication costs, driven by reducing expenses related to printing, mailing, and processing of documents;
2. Improved productivity by making information more widely and quickly accessible;
3. Higher team productivity, created through collaborative work environments;
4. Rapid implementation as a result of open protocol standards; and
5. Relatively low costs for hardware and software.

We agree in general with the above conclusions and benefits but "in no way does Internet computing replace client/server computing. That's because it already is client/server computing" (Herb Edelstein, quote given in Edwards, 1999). On the other hand, we believe that focusing only an Internet/Intranet architecture greatly limits the client/server architectural choices for KMS.

A CLIENT/SERVER ARCHITECTURE FOR KMS

Client/server and specifically three-tier client/server permits the process layer software (written in C, Java, Visual Basic, COBOL, etc.) to interact with multiple data sources simultaneously. Since knowledge is located in so many data sources and housed in many data storage mediums, integrated source data presentation is extremely complex. If the knowledge is located in a departmental procedure, geographic information system, video, and e-mail, the process layer must support the APIs (application program interface) to retrieve these four data sources and present them on a single workstation's display device.

Employing a three-tier client-server architecture would provide a good flexible architecture for KMS. The structure would be very similar to the three-tier client-server architecture detailed by (Orfali et al., 1999) except it would also have a Knowledge Directory (covered in the next section). The client layer would have at least the following: a nice GUI, a web browser, the client operating system, and any required client-side applications for KM (such as Lotus Notes). The middle layer would contain a network operating system, and transport stack (such as TCP/IP) and service specific middleware for:
1. databases (such as ODBC, JDBC, and SQLJ),
2. internet/intranets (such as HTTP and CGI),
3. e-mail (such as SMTP and POP3),
4. storing and accessing multimedia documents,
5. coordinating group conferencing,
6. linking individuals in group scheduling, and
7. work flow processes.

The server layer would contain the server operating system and specific server based applications such as database management systems, document management systems, server side groupware (such as the Lotus Domino server), etc.

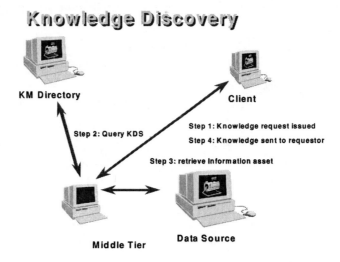

KNOWLEDGE DIRECTORY

Achieving the connection to numerous data and information sources is a serious challenge for the development of KMS. The demands placed on the information technology infrastructure to support an integrated approach to identifying, capturing, retrieving, sharing, and evaluating an enterprise's information assets is a major undertaking; especially since these information assets may include databases, documents, policies and procedures stored in electronic forms.

One of the major requirements of KM is the ability to locate the knowledge and present it to the knowledge requester. The need for a directory of information assets is imperative. A knowledge directory (some sort of list or picture) points to knowledge (in people, documents, or databases) but does not contain it (Davenport and Prusak, 1998). The Knowledge Directory resolves the client request to connect to an information asset by translating the keyword into a data source location. Thereby, permitting the customer to navigate the numerous information asset resources and locate the best match.

The knowledge directory process would retrieve data as follows.

Step 1: The knowledge requester issues an inquiry for knowledge.

Step 2: An inquiry is sent to the Knowledge Directory Service (KDS) Server and a summary listing similar to an Internet search is presented.

Step 3: A second request is sent to retrieve the information asset from the respective server.

Step 4: The knowledge is sent to the requester.

CASE EXAMPLES AND CONCLUSION

The relationship between client/server and the knowledge directory is quite visible in the case examples found in the KM literature. Davenport and Prussak (1998) discuss several cases that illustrate the variety and challenges of retrieving information assets.

"Ernst & Young, Andersen Consulting, Price Waterhouse, and Coopers & Lybrand all have very large repositories of knowledge from serving clients, several of which exceed a thousand different databases."

"Chrysler has used it to create an "Engineering Book of Knowledge," a set of lessons learned in the design and engineering process about particular car components." In general, "finding the knowledge one wants from so many different places to look is very challenging."

Andersen Consulting "has developed at least 3 levels of navigation tools for its enormous "Knowledge Xchange" system, but users still find it difficult to negotiate…"

The missing link in these cases is the broad-based knowledge directory in order to locate enterprise knowledge. The KDS is a critical component of KMS because the need for the knowledge is not always a planned event. For example, Texas Instruments' (TI) Best Practices Knowledge Base – a Lotus Notes application accessed through TI's global intranet – documents each practice using a title, a short narrative, and contact information. TI calls it ShareIt. TI has also launched an Internet application called "yellow pages" which lists TI employees' contact information, experience, knowledge, and interests" (O'Dell et al., 1998). The breath of TI's KDS permits employees to search on knowledge subjects outside of their domain. Once the KDS is in place and populated with location data, software (i.e., web browser) using an application program interface can search the KDS and make the location and retrieval of knowledge viable and efficient.

In conclusion, a 3-tier client/server architecture provides a seamless integration of the variety of technologies required for a KMS such as database management, document management, groupware, and e-mail. In order to locate specific knowledge when the total amount of knowledge stored is so varied and large, a knowledge directory that stores the specific locations of the knowledge is essential. Ensuring that this location data is correct is extremely important for the success of the KMS. Further, the identification of new knowledge should be an ongoing process as the Knowledge Directory must be up-to-date to have value in a rapidly changing world.

REFERENCES

Alavi, M. and Leidner, D. (1999). Knowledge Management Systems: Issues, Challenges,and Benefits, *Communications of the Association for Information Systems*, 1(7), February.

Boar, B. (1996). *Cost-Effective Strategies for Client/Server Systems*, John Wiley & Sons, Inc.

Borthick, A. F. and Roth, H. P. (1994). Understanding client/server computing, *Management Accounting* (76:2), August, pp.36-41.

Brooking, A. (1999). *Corporate Memory*, International Thomson Business Press.

Davenport, T. and Prussak, L. (1998). *Working Knowledge*, Harvard Business School Press.

Duchessi, P., and Chengalur-Smith, I. (1998). Client/server benefits, problems, best practices. *Communications of the ACM* (41:5), May, pp. 87-94.

Edwards, I. (1999). *3-Tier Client/Server At Work* (revised edition), Wiley.

Gartner Group (1999). White Papers on Knowledge Management.

Kern, H., Johnson, R., Galup, S., & Horgan, D. (1998). *Building the New Enterprise: People, Processes, and Technology*, Sun Microsystems Press – Prentice Hall, California.

O'Dell, C., Grayson, C.J. Jr., and Essaides, N. (1998). *If Only We Knew What We Know*, The Free Press.

Orfali, R., Harkey, D., and Edwards, J. (1999). *Client/Server Survival Guide* (3rd edition), Wiley.

Schulte, R. (1995). Middleware and Three-Tier Architectures *GartnerGroup Symposium/Itxpo 95: Managing the Revolution*, October 9-13, Day 5.

Weston, R. (1998). Client/server evolution: Thin clients, fat servers, *Computerworld*, Feb 9, 32(6), p20.

Chapter 20

An Informational Perspective Towards Knowledge Work: Implications for Knowledge Management Systems

Brian Detlor
McMaster University, Canada

This paper presents an informational orientation towards knowledge work and draws implications of such a perspective on the functionality offered by knowledge management technologies. Discussion ensues on the nature of organizational knowledge and its strong association with information. In light of this discussion, knowledge work is defined as the application of comprehended information and viewed as a set of knowledge creation, distribution, and use processes. Implications are drawn based on this perspective for knowledge management technologies to provide organizational participants with access to information content, the ability to communicate this information with others, and the means by which to utilize this information in work practice. It is argued that by doing so, these technologies can better support organizational knowledge work.

INTRODUCTION

The purpose of this chapter is to present an informational perspective towards knowledge work in organizations and to draw implications for the design of knowledge management technologies.

Previously Published in *Managing Information Technology in a Global Economy* edited by Mehdi Khosrow-Pour, Copyright © 2001, Idea Group Publishing.

To facilitate this objective, the paper is organized into three primary sections. The first two sections discuss the constructs of knowledge and knowledge work respectively. The goal is to provide the reader with a firm understanding of these core concepts highlighting the central role information plays in the creation, distribution, and use of knowledge in organizational contexts. The third section utilizes these insights to make recommendations on the functionality knowledge management technologies need to provide to promote the creation, distribution, and use of knowledge across the firm.

KNOWLEDGE

Knowledge is said to be a powerful organizational resource (Drucker, 1993; Quinn, 1992; Toffler, 1990), but what exactly is knowledge? Various interpretations exist. Some suggest knowledge is "justified true belief," the capacity for (social) action (Stehr, 1994; Sveiby, 1997), or professional intellect (Quinn et al., 1996). In terms of organizational know-how, Davenport & Prusak (1998) provide a holistic description of the knowledge construct. They state that knowledge is both fluid and formally structured, neither neat nor simple, and offer a working definition of knowledge as a

"fluid mix of framed experience, values, contextual information, and expert insight that provides a framework for evaluating and incorporating new experiences and information. It originates and is applied in the mind of knowers. In organizations, it often becomes embedded not only in documents or repositories but also in organizational routines, processes, and norms" (p. 5).

From this definition, knowledge in organizations is viewed as a dichotomous construct that exists both *tacitly* in the minds of people and *explicitly* in formal products and procedures. This distinction is recognized and discussed by Nonaka & Takeuchi (1995) in their classification of two types of knowledge: explicit knowledge, that which can be partly expressed in formal, systematic language and transmitted to individuals easily; and tacit knowledge, that which is personal, context-specific, and difficult to articulate formally (Polanyi, 1966).

These descriptions are enriched by Schultze's (1998) overview of functionalist and interpretive perspectives towards organizational knowledge. Utilizing Burrell & Morgan's (1979) paradigms of social and organizational inquiry as a guide, Schultze distinguishes the difference between objective and subjective perspectives.[1] A *functionalist* view adopts a realist ontology and assumes that facts about the world exist and are waiting to be discovered; hence knowledge is perceived as an object that exists in a variety of forms (e.g., tacit, explicit) and resides in a variety of locations (e.g., individuals, culture, work routines, roles, physical setting) (pp. 160-161). An *interpretive* perspective maintains that reality is socially constructed; hence knowledge is perceived as a process of knowing that is continually emerging, indeterminate and closely linked with practice.

Wikstrom & Normann (1994) recognize both functionalist and interpretive characteristics in their description of knowledge. They describe the major components of knowledge as consisting of: *skills and know-how* which are embedded in the individual; *explanation* which refers to "traditional positivist scientific knowledge concerned with causal relationships and regularities" (p. 12) and exists outside the individual; and *understanding* which is learning and occurs within the individual.

Similarly, Blackler (1995) acknowledges functionalist and interpretive perspectives. In his review of current approaches to knowledge found in the literature on organizational learning, he identifies five conventional (i.e., functionalist) images of knowledge as embrained, embodied, encultured, embedded and encoded. With *embrained*, knowledge resides in the conceptual skill and cognitive abilities of people. With *embodied*, knowledge is rooted in specific contexts and situations. With *encultured*, knowledge is achieved through shared understandings and dialogue. With *embedded*, knowledge resides in systemic routines. And with *encoded*, knowledge is conveyed by signs and symbols. Blackler cautions that there are problems with this traditional view of knowledge in that it is both static and compartmentalized and, in its place, offers an alternate (i.e., interpretive) approach to knowledge as an active process of knowing.[2] According to Blackler (p. 1023) "rather than regarding *knowledge* as something that people have, it is suggested that *knowing* is better regarded as something they do." Under this paradigm, knowledge is mediated, situated, provisional, pragmatic, and contested. It is *mediated* in the sense that it is manifest in systems of language, technology, collaboration and control. It is *situated* in that it is located in time and space and specific to particular contexts. It is *provisional* by being constructed and constantly redeveloped. It is *pragmatic* in that it has purpose. And, it is *contested* in the sense that it is challenged.

Though the functionalist and interpretive perspectives may be at opposite ends of the epistemological scale, an underlying common component is the recognition of the strong association between information and knowledge within these two paradigms. Throughout the literature, many references describe the close kinship between information and knowledge, where the two co-exist in a "dialectic, mutually constitutive relationship" (Schultze, 2000).

For instance, Dretske (1981) describes information as a commodity capable of yielding knowledge (p. 44) and knowledge as "information-produced (or sustained) belief" (p. 86). Machlup (1983) identifies that information affects knowledge by adding something to it or restructuring it. Nonaka & Takeuchi (1995, p. 58) state that "information is a necessary medium or material for eliciting and constructing knowledge" and that "information is a flow of messages, while knowledge is created by that very flow of information."

Wikstrom & Normann (1994) include information within the broader concept of knowledge. They state that information is "simple fragmented knowledge, which supplies answers to questions such as: What? Where? Who? How many? How big? When?" (p. 10) and gives details about an event, situation, or indisputable scientific fact. To these authors, information provides the stimuli to generate action requiring skill and forms the building blocks for the understanding of a connection between disparate pieces of facts and insights. As such, information can be viewed as a foundation for the generation of new knowledge.

This chapter recognizes the strong association between information and knowledge and the duality of knowledge as an object that exists in various forms and locations and as a process that is socially-constructed and linked with practice. As such, knowledge is defined as comprehended information that exists both tacitly in the minds of people and explicitly in formal products and procedures.

KNOWLEDGE WORK

One of the earliest definitions of knowledge work was proposed by Machlup (1962) in his investigation of the production and distribution of knowledge in the U.S. labour force. Machlup defines knowledge work broadly as the production and transmission of knowledge.[3] Stehr (1994) develops this definition further by suggesting knowledge work to be the *production and re-production of information*. Stehr views the transmission of information as an active process where a worker's knowledge is applied to the information being transferred, thus changing the information in some way before it is communicated. By doing so, knowledge work can be understood as action, namely the application of comprehended information.[4]

Several references describe knowledge work as a process or a set of activities involving knowledge creation, distribution, and use. For example, Davenport et al. (1996) describe knowledge work as a series of activities, namely the acquisition, creation, packaging, application and reuse of knowledge. These are characterized by variety and exception rather than routine and are performed by professional or technical workers with a high level of skill and expertise (p. 54).

In terms of knowledge creation, Nonaka & Takeuchi (1995, pp. 62-70) draw upon Polanyi's work on tacit knowing to describe four major modes of knowledge creation which involve the interaction between tacit and explicit knowledge and the individual and the organization. The first mode, *socialization*, is the process of sharing experiences and represents tacit-to-tacit knowledge exchange. The second mode, *externalization*, is the process of articulating this tacit knowledge into explicit concepts. The third mode, *combination*, is an explicit-to-explicit exchange of knowledge where concepts are systematized into a knowledge system. The fourth mode, *internalization*, is the process of converting this explicit knowledge back into tacit knowledge.

In a related discussion, Wikstrom & Normann (1994) identify three knowledge processes that exist within organizations: *generative processes*, where new knowledge is created by activities aimed at solving problems; *productive processes*, which take this new knowledge as a basis for the commitments and offerings the organization provides its customers; and *representative processes*, where an organization transmits its manifest knowledge to its customers for their use in their own value-creating processes. Though these processes are to some extent synchronous and reciprocal, Wikstrom & Normann recognize that these processes overlap and that at "different times or in different places at the same time one piece of knowledge can be part of generative, productive or representative processes" (p. 14).

Likewise, Leonard-Barton (1998) describes four key activities that create flows of knowledge and direct them into core capabilities: 1) *integrating problem solving* across different cognitive and functional barriers where employees with a diversity of backgrounds and skills are brought together to generate creative and innovative solutions; 2) *implementing new methodologies and process tools*, especially those that encourage user involvement as a means of fostering user acceptance and improved design; 3) *experimenting* through the development of prototypes and learning through experimental failures; and 4) *importing know-how* from outside technological and market sources by scanning broadly and continuously for technological opportunity and by identifying employees who can act as technological gatekeepers and boundary spanners.

Choo (1998, pp. 130-132) summarizes and identifies three broad similarities in the knowledge creation, distribution, and use processes described by Wikstrom & Normann (1994), Nonaka & Takeuchi (1995), and Leonard-Barton (1998). The first is that *organizations generate new knowledge* which extends their capabilities by sharing and converting the tacit knowledge of its members. This requires organizational participants to engage in face-to-face dialogue and work collectively together as a means of reflecting and solving the problems organizations face. The second is that *organizations operationalize new concepts* so that they can be applied to new or enhanced offerings and allow organizations to operate more efficiently. The third is that *organizations diffuse and transfer new knowledge* both within and outside the enterprise. This involves new knowledge spreading across organizational boundaries and peripheries, which in turn generates new cycles of learning.

Choo's description points to how organizations *create* (i.e., generate), *distribute* (i.e., diffuse and transfer), and *use* (i.e., operationalize) knowledge. It is argued that these are core processes involved in knowledge work. More importantly, given the close relationship between knowledge and information, this paper suggests that *information plays a central role in these core processes*. That is, due to its close association to knowledge, information is perceived to be a tangible conduit for knowledge creation, distribution, and use. For example, Sveiby (1997, p. 19) supports this orientation in his description of the work of knowledge workers as consisting "largely of converting information to knowledge," where people for the most part use their own competencies and sometimes the assistance of suppliers of information or specialized knowledge. Likewise, Alavi & Leidner (1999) in their description of knowledge management practices argue that information becomes knowledge when it is processed in the minds of individuals and knowledge becomes information when it is articulated or communicated to others in the form of text, computer output, spoken or written words, or other means. Similarly, Davis (1991) defines knowledge work as a set of activities that use individual and external knowledge to produce outputs characterized by information content. Here, "knowledge is actionable information" (Nonaka, 1994) and utilized in the knowledge work practices of organizational participants.

IMPLICATIONS FOR KNOWLEDGE MANAGEMENT SYSTEMS

The above review of the literature on knowledge and knowledge work identifies how information plays a central role in knowledge work activity. Knowledge work is defined as the application of comprehended information and is viewed as a set of knowledge creation, distribution, and use processes.

Adopting such a perspective has implications on the design of Knowledge Management Systems (KMS) if these systems are to support organizational knowledge work. Specifically, it is argued that KMS need to incorporate features and functions that facilitate knowledge creation, distribution, and use—a set of information-laden processes. To do this requires the provision of certain functionality: the ability to access information; share this information with others, and utilize this information in work practice.

Several note the need for KMS to support information access as well as the communication and coordination of activities. For instance, Schultze (1998, p. 162) acknowledges the ability of Web-based infrastructures to provide firms with not only repositories of knowledge, that offer "knowledge bases of best practices" and search tools "that make the retrieval of the stored knowledge objects possible," but also the ability to support narration, self-reflection, and multi-vocal dialogue (Boland et al., 1994) as a means of helping communities within the firm understand one another's practices of knowledge creation, transfer, and use.

Similarly, Cole (1998, p. 20) suggests knowledge management technologies support information access and flow, as well as facilitate network communications among organizational groups. Specifically he notes the increasing trend for companies to utilize tools such as Web information systems to support knowledge creation, distribution, and use:

"the use of the new information technologies in the service of knowledge has strongly tended toward increasing the flow of information and to a certain extent knowledge, most notably in creating and facilitating interactive networks and in extracting, making explicit, and spreading individual expertise... Enterprising companies are learning as they engage in novel uses of these technologies... new uses will emerge which do contribute... to improved knowledge creation and knowledge transmission." (p. 20)

Likewise, Snis (2000) finds empirical evidence in her field investigation on knowledge workers for the need for knowledge management system solutions to support access to information (namely through environmental scanning, information acquisition, and the codification of knowledge), as well as to facilitate collaboration and communication through the establishment of "knowledge networks" (like discussion forums and e-mail lists) which connect experts together and support interaction between people. By viewing information technology as a mechanism for augmenting and interconnecting both people and resources, Snis encourages the development of a computer supported collaborative work space where knowledge can be created, organized, secured, distributed, and used. This line of thinking falls in line with the ideas of Schmidt & Bannon (1992) who posit the need to create a common information space to enable cooperative work and knowledge sharing.

Kidd (1994), in her field investigation of knowledge workers, also calls on the need for computer tools in firms to provide an electronic workspace for organizational participants to use. Observing that knowledge workers do not rely heavily on information once its filed but rather use their desks and floor space extensively as spatial holding areas for paper-based inputs and ideas, Kidd suggests designers of knowledge management systems focus on "supporting the *act* of informing people, rather than storing or processing information on people's behalf" (p. 190). Specifically she encourages designers to avoid trying to help knowledge workers in ways which involve the system to understand or interpret information, but rather concentrate on providing work areas, such as electronic whiteboards, to help knowledge workers externalize their own thinking and extend the ability of the physical environment.

A view on the design of corporate portals and departmental intranets to serve as a shared information work space for the creation, distribution, and use of knowledge is given by Detlor (Choo et al., 2000; Detlor, 2000). Here, the shared information work space comprises three primary components: a content space to facilitate information access and retrieval; a communication space to negotiate collective interpretations and shared meanings; and a coordination space to support cooperative work action. By functioning in this way, Web information systems can help support organizational knowledge work. As a *content space*, they can give users the capability of browsing and searching for both structured and unstructured information to help formulate new understandings or stimulate innovation. As a *communication space*, they can provide a means for organizational participants to gather others' experiences and negotiate a shared consensus towards common goals and ideas. As a *coordination space*, they can allow users to browse information created by fellow employees more easily, helping them become aware of other employees in the organization and their availability for cooperative action.

In terms of predominant design and use, most organizations have tended to concentrate on utilizing knowledge management technologies to provide firms with information access only; little has been done to utilize these tools as communication and coordination spaces. Brown & Duguid (1998) note this trend in their call for organizations to move away from the management of knowledge as a resource that is accessed and retrieved by individuals and towards the support for *knowledge ecologies* that facilitate the creation and sharing of knowledge between *communities of practice* (Lave & Wenger, 1995). Specifically, they state that

> "a good deal of new technology attends primarily to individuals and the explicit information that passes between them. To support the flow of knowledge, within or between communities and organizations, this focus must expand to encompass communities and the full richness of communication. Successful devices such as the telephone and the fax, like the book and newspaper before them, spread rapidly not simply because they carried information to individuals, but because they were easily embedded in communities." (p. 105)

In response, Brown & Duguid argue the need for technology to encourage and guide the flow of knowledge between communities of practice within the organization. To do this, they suggest that technology be designed to provide both *reach* (i.e., access to information) and *reciprocity* (i.e., support relationships that facilitate complex, multi-directional, implicit negotiation) as a means of fostering organizational knowledge creation. Brown & Duguid note the success technologies such as e-mail and the World Wide Web have had in both exchanging information and supporting collaborators in a common project (p. 106). As a result, they encourage a duality in the design and use of technologies to provide access to both social and information networks if these technologies are truly to support organizational knowledge work activity.

CONCLUSION

This paper recognizes the strong association between information and knowledge, and the dual nature of knowledge as an object that exists in various forms and locations and as a process that is socially-constructed and linked with practice. As such, to foster knowledge work, this paper calls for the incorporation of certain functionalities in the design of KMS which promote knowledge creation, distribution, and use. Specifically, the paper suggests KMS provide organizational workers with three broad functionalities: 1) the means by which to access information content; 2) the ability to communicate this information across the firm; and 3) the means by which to utilize and incorporate this information in work tasks. It is argued that doing so can facilitate the use of these systems for knowledge work.

ENDNOTES

[1] She also discusses a critical perspective.

[2] Other references to knowledge as activity include Polanyi (1966) and Von Glaserfeld (1988).

[3] It is important to note that Machlup does not distinguish between the terms information and knowledge and uses the terms interchangeably.

[4] Saffady (1998, p. 4) observes the interrelationship between recorded information, knowledge, and action: knowledge is comprehended information that is capable of supporting action; action is the application of knowledge.

REFERENCES

Alavi, M., & Leidner, D. (1999). Knowledge management systems: Issues, challenges, benefits. *Communication of AIS, 1*(7), 2-41.

Blackler, F. (1995). Knowledge, knowledge work and organizations: An overview and interpretation. *Organizational Studies, 16*(6), 1021-1046.

Boland, R. J., Tenkasi, R. V., & Te'eni, D. (1994). Designing information technology to support distributed cognition. *Organization Science, 5*, 456-475.

Brown, J. S., & Duguid, P. (1998). Organizing knowledge. *California Management Review, 40*(3), 90-111.

Burrell, G., & Morgan, G. (1979). *Sociological paradigms and organizational analysis*. London: Heineman.

Choo, C. W. (1998). *The knowing organization*. New York: Oxford University Press.

Choo, C. W., Detlor, B., & Turnbull, D. (2000). *Web work: Information seeking and knowledge work on the World Wide Web*. Dordrecht, The Netherlands: Kluwer Academic Publishers.

Cole, R. E. (1998). Introduction. *California Management Review, 40*(3), 15-21.

Davenport, T. H., Jarvenpaa, S. L., & Beers, M. C. (1996). Improving knowledge work processes. *Sloan Management Review, Summer*, 53-65.

Davenport, T. H., & Prusak, L. (1998). *Working knowledge: How organizations manage what they know*. Boston, MA: Harvard Business School Press.

Davis, G. (1991). *Conceptual model for research on knowledge work* (MISRC working paper MISRC-WP-91-10). Minneapolis: University of Minnesota.

Detlor, B. (2000). The corporate portal as information infrastructure: Towards a framework for portal design. *International Journal of Information Management, 20*(2), 91-101.

Dretske, F. (1981). *Knowledge and the flow of information*. Cambridge, MA: MIT Press.

Drucker, P. F. (1993). *Post-capitalist society*. Oxford: Butterworth Heinemann.

Kidd, A. (1994). The marks are on the knowledge worker, *Proceedings of CHI '94, Human Factors in Computing Systems, Boston, Massachusetts* (pp. 186-191): ACM.

Lave, J., & Wenger, E. (1995). *Situated learning: Legitimate peripheral participation* (Vol. first published in 1991). New York: Cambridge University Press.

Leonard-Barton, D. (1998). *Wellsprings of knowledge: Building and sustaining the sources of innovation* (paperback ed.). Boston, MA: Harvard Business School Press.

Machlup, F. (1962). *The production and distribution of knowledge in the United States*. Princeton, NJ: Princeton University Press.

Machlup, F. (1983). Semantic quirks in studies of information. In F. Machlup & U. Mansfield (Eds.), *The study of information* (pp. 641-671). New York: John Wiley & Sons.

Nonaka, I. (1994). A dynamic theory of organizational knowledge creation. *Organization Science, 5*(1), 14-37.

Nonaka, I., & Takeuchi, H. (1995). *The knowledge-creating company: How japanese companies create the dynamics of innovation*. New York: Oxford University Press.

Polanyi, M. (1966). *The tacit dimension*. London: Routledge & Kegan Paul.

Quinn, J. B. (1992). *Intelligent enterprise: A knowledge and service based paradigm for industry*. New York: The Free Press.

Quinn, J. B., Anderson, P., & Finkelstein, S. (1996). Managing professional intellect: Making the most of the best. *Harvard Business Review, 74*(March-April), 71-80.

Saffady, W. (1998). *Knowledge management: A manager's briefing*. Prairie Village, KS: ARMA International.

Schmidt, K., & Bannon, L. (1992). Taking CSCW seriously: Supporting articulation work. *Computer Supported Cooperative Work, 1*, 7-40.

Schultze, U. (1998). Investigating the contradictions in knowledge management, *Proceedings of the IFIP WG8.2 & 8.6 Joint Working Conference on Information Systems: Current Issues and Future Changes, Helsinki, Finland, December 10-13* (pp. 155-174).

Schultze, U. (2000). A confessional account of an ethnography about knowledge work. *MIS Quarterly, 24*(1), 3-42.

Snis, U. (2000). Knowledge is acknowledged? A field study about people, processes, documents, and technologies, *Proceedings of the 33rd Annual Hawaii International Conference on System Sciences (HICSS), January 4th-7th*. Maui, HA: IEEE.

Stehr, N. (1994). *Knowledge Societies*. Thousand Oaks: CA: Sage Publications.

Sveiby, K. E. (1997). *The new organizational wealth: Managing and measuring knowledge-based assets*. San Fransico, CA: Berrett-Koehler.

Toffler, A. (1990). *Powershift: Knowledge, wealth and violence at the edge of the 21st century*. New York: Bantam Books.

Von Glaserfeld, E. (1988). *The construction of knowledge: Contributions to conceptual semantics*. Salinas, CA: Intersystems Publications.

Wikstrom, S., & Normann, R. (1994). *Knowledge and value: A new perspective on corporate transformation*. New York: Routledge.

Chapter 21

Argumentation and Knowledge-Sharing

Mike Metcalfe and Samantha Grant
University of South Australia, Adelaide, Australia

This paper discusses the conceptual basis for a social-technical system aimed at assisting geographically separate companies to use the Internet to achieve the economic benefits of clustering. The knowledge sharing literature, and the evolutionary economics literature, is used to focus on tacit knowledge sharing and learning through verbal interaction. The first section looks at the evidence for "structured talk," which includes the role of argumentation systems on research, problem solving, communication and decision-making. The chapter goes on to argue that rural regions have the core competencies needed to cluster but not the interaction. Ensuring appropriate arguments between appropriate people may provide a policy around which to design Internet conferencing infrastructure aimed at enabling the benefits of clustering.

INTRODUCTION

This paper discusses the conceptual basis for a social-technical system aimed at assisting geographically separate companies to use the Internet to achieve the economic benefits of clustering. In Komito's (1998) terms, it is about managing a disperse community's knowledge by building knowledge sharing systems for "wicked unstructured, ill-defined" problems. The knowledge sharing literature, and the evolutionary economics literature, is giving more attention to tacit knowledge sharing and learning through the verbal interaction of group members. This includes Argyris

Previously Published in *Managing Information Technology in a Global Economy* edited by Mehdi Khosrow-Pour, Copyright © 2001, Idea Group Publishing.

and Schon's [1996] concept of learning or inquiry systems and Lawson's (1999) comments that initiatives follow from dynamic verbal interaction between persons with core competencies.

A lack of verbal interaction between knowledgeable people suffering the tyranny of distance offers new communications technology a chance to overcome the market failure. However, as is now well documented, merely dumping communications technology on people in geographically-disperse areas is not sufficient. Having access to appropriate infrastructure is essential but it may not be sufficient. If an effective system is to be built, then some understanding of how to structure conversations needs to be thought through. Why would talk bring economic benefits? What types of groupings might benefit from more talk? How is the talking to be structured? The example that will be used for illustration purposes is farm and mining companies working in remote regions seeking to cluster to achieve further vertical integration up or down their supply chain. The paper provides a conceptual roadmap of why and how such industries might learn how to develop economically. More specifically this paper argues that:

A well-structured interactive community based discourse (argument/ debate) provides a mechanism for an appropriate virtual community to achieve economic development.

The evidence to support this claim will be presented in 5 sections. As the claim is that "structured talk" will bring outcomes, the first section looks at the evidence for this, which includes the role of argumentation systems on research, problem solving, communication and decision making. This is followed by discussion on how clustering works in the context of the paradox of some management writers calling for geographically-independent organisational structures, while others are calling for physical clustering by core competencies. Next the application of these systems will be considered by first identifying essential attributes for a group likely to be in a position to turn this talking into commercial outcomes. An example using remote rural communities is then given.

Talk for Knowledge Sharing

Nonaka and Takeuchi (1995) have suggested that knowledge can be created through four different modes:

1) Socialisation, which involves conversation from tacit knowledge to tacit knowledge,

2) Externalisation, which involves conversation from tacit knowledge to explicit knowledge,

3) Combination, which involves conversation from explicit knowledge to explicit knowledge, and

(4) Internalisation, which involves conversation from explicit knowledge to tacit knowledge.

As Argyris and Schon (1996) then point out, merely building databases of existing explicit knowledge may not be sufficient especially in wickedly un-knowledgable domains. Unstructured environments would appear to call for a variety and complexity of re-interpretations of that environment. Hegelian inquiry systems seem more appropriate based upon a synthesis of multiple, diverse and contradictory interpretations allowing continual re-examination of any core rigidities. These systems depend upon dialectical inquiry based on dialogue allowing a free flow of meaning between people. So, in Nonaka and Takeuchi's terms there is a need for all four of their modes, which in turn supports the need for dialectic or argumentative processes to create knowledge.

Speech, which allows complex dialectical inquiry, is a unique human attribute. It is unclear if we are more intelligent than other species, but we do have the advantage of being able to use language to solve our problems. While media richness theory may be an oversimplification, the massive telecommunications industry as a tool of business suggests speech has a dominant place in problem solving, thus knowledge sharing. Indeed, Lievrouw (1998) refers to this as a "communications ideology," that is, western culture appears to include a belief that if people can talk then problems can be resolved, even territorial ones. This needs a lot more consideration but suffice to say, not talking seems less likely to solve commercial or technical problems than talking.

Conversation per se may not be useful, a dialectic, and argumentative process is required. Horrocks et al. (1999) find that in order to be effective, human interaction needs to be managed and structured. Anyone with organisational experience will know that an interaction with a purpose, agenda, propositions, and delegated actions is more likely to achieve outcomes. Put in more conceptual terms, the management literature reports that having a formalised process of reasoned argument (or debate) has been found to be very effective for large "wicked" or unstructured, ill defined, problem solving and decision making.

What is a reasoned argument? Argument is the noun of arguing or argumentation, the directed construction of convincing evidence (see Perelman and Olbrechts-Tyteca, 1969; Eemeren, Grootendorst and Kruiger, 1987), the argument being the one line claim (conclusion) that is supported by various evidence. The courtroom analogy has been used. Court protocol has also been designed around the open public forum approach suggested by Aristotle. A court case is a research activity; the courts are searching for knowledge, indeed, the truth. Evidence is presented to a universal audience (jury) to convince. In a courtroom, the argument is typically about a person's guilt. In information systems development the argument is more likely to be something like; that system design X is preferable to design Y. It is not possible to say what will be sufficient to convince the audience. Hopefully it is sufficient just to say an argument will be accepted only if the reasons it provides seem plausible, relevant, oriented in favour of the conclusion, and sufficient to support it (Apotheloz, Brandt and Ouiroz, 1993).

Eemeren, Grootendorst and Kruiger (1987) also provide a definition of argument:

> *Argu[ing] is a social, intellectual, verbal [spoken or written] activity serving to justify or refute an opinion [idea, conception, and policy], consisting of a constellation of statements and directed towards obtaining the approbation of an audience.*

Eemeren et al go on to explain their definition. They start by pointing out that arguments are a social activity because there needs to be two people present, with two worldviews. This is very relevant here because the argument approach, the dialectic, is gaining consensus from differing views to the extent that Crosswhite (1996) sees reasoned and structured argument as a means to avoid hostile conflict. So argument is an intellectual activity, "an activity of reason" where emotion (aggressive or tearful) is "subordinate to that of reason." Eemeren et al contrasts this with hierarchical communication, so typical of commercial organisations. It addresses the power issues. The cornerstone of the courtroom system is that there should be little room for bullying to hide evidence. So, the act of professional arguing should align itself with the accepted ethos of scientific decision making.

Reasoned argument always refers to a particular subject upon which opinions can and do differ and so is particularly relevant to human inquiry or scientific research. It is a scholarly means of collecting and creating human knowledge. Eemeren, Grootendorst and Kruiger (1987) go so far as to say any topic, without any exception, may be the subject of argument. Yet, arguing requires the use of language.

They continue that arguing is offering, defending against, taking account of, and anticipating criticism. It consists of a constellation of one or more statements. The common feature to both pro arguments and contra arguments is that both forms are directed towards testing opinion.

Ziegelmueller and Dause (1975) agree that research and convincing are the cornerstones of good argument. They point out that logical articulation or intellectual cohesion that makes an argument tight comes from thought and not from the mere recitation of the facts or instances. They also put this the other way around:

> *Research skills stand at the very heart of the inquiry phase of argu[ing].*

Both in the sense of providing good information for making decisions, and for assisting with the act of actually making the decisions, setting up a well managed process of argumentation research appears to have a philosophical basis and is integrated with the best scientific methodology.

The Problem Solving Literature

There is also extensive management literature on the use of argument in both problem formulation and decision making. For example, Niederman and DeSanctis (1995) report that,

"the structured argument approach led to a greater combination of both coverage of critical issues and consensus... Use of the structured argument approach also resulted in higher satisfaction with the problem definition and commitment to implementing results..."

Meyers and Seibold (1989) provide an extensive review of the use of argument in decision-making literature.

" ...investigators have studied whether utilising structured argument formats (i.e. devils advocate or planned dialectic enquiry) contributes to higher quality decisions. Results have indicated that utilisation of both ... are useful for surfacing assumptions and evaluating crucial information in uncertain and ill-structured decision-making situations."

They go on to say, "arguments are both the medium and outcome of group interaction" (Myers & Seibold, 1989). Making arguments both systems (observed patterns of interaction) and structures (the unobservable generative rules and resources that enable argument). This links into the structuration perspective derived from Giddens' (1984) theory, with a culturally appropriate and sanctioned way of disputing. Meyers and Seibold (1989) go on to align argument with Giddens' Theory, saying that argument provides the interaction system (in Giddens' sense) to make a structure. In this paper, this is applied saying argument can also be used to consolidate a computer based organisational information system. The managerial task is to manage this argumentative process so that individual managers' private agendas, emotions and power needs are held in perspective, while allowing innovation and reflection (Schon, 1983).

Meyers and Seibold (1989) summarise the extensive empirical research on analysing argumentative processes aimed at reaching a consensus in decision making. To date, much of this research has been done using the positivist methods such as quantifying individual and group interactions and trying to predict the decision outcome. However, Fischer and Forrester (1993) report on more interpretive research on the role of argument in Government policy formulation. At one stage they equate the argumentative literature with story telling research methods.

Decisions need to be communicated, and preferably enacted by those involved in the communication. In order to effectively design and implement an Information System (IS), especially with respect to senior management, it is necessary for them to be committed (internalised). The argumentation approach offers this opportunity. Users are more likely to be committed to a new design if they have been involved in an argumentative process that was seen to be reasonable. If nothing else, the advantages, purpose and context of the new system will be better communicated. The management literature supporting the role of argument to assist communications is even more extensive than the decision-making literature

> *" From its beginnings in late nineteenth-century forensics pedagogy, the study of argument has been a rich intellectual tradition in the field of communication." (Meyers and Seibold, 1989)*

A further attraction of the argument approach is that it makes no pretence of impartiality. Pretending to be impartial about the alternatives does not work in scientific inquiry (Broad and Wane, 1982) and causes offence in the political hierarchies of modern organisational life. Much time and emotion is saved if each actor openly states their preference, or claim, up-front rather than pretending to present impartial questions. Crosswhite (1996) argues that this aligns with human development where claims are learnt before the skill to question.

ESSENTIAL ATTRIBUTES

Moving on now to consider a virtual application of structured talking. Jones (1995) argues that virtual groups usually fail to achieve solidarity. He attributes this to the ease, with which people can enter and leave a group, and the ease with which new groups can form. Lehman (1999) argues that a successful group needs to agree on their essential purpose, to care about the same things with the same priority. Problems in doing this is expected to lead to tensions within the group that unless minimised will destroy the community. Lehman (1999) continues that any group needs to determine what is significant, such as achieving the correct balance between working to increase their wealth and their needs for leisure time. It is important that any group that wishes to become dependent on each other economically settles these issues. This is particularly true of virtual groups, as membership has to be constantly reasserted by logging-on to the group. In contrast geographically located groups have to make considerable effort to leave that group.

Komito (1998) identifies different types of groups, and lists them as:
- Moral: with a common purpose of caring, e.g., a family.
- Normative: with a common purpose of agreed rules of practice, e.g., work.
- Practice: with a common purpose of sharing common experiences, e.g., scientists, miners or farmers.
- Proximate: with a common purpose of maintenance of a lifestyle based on a geographical location, it is assumed this includes defence, e.g., a nation or neighbourhood.

- Foraging: with a common purpose of independence, non-commitment, raising the question if all web users are foragers, not looking for solidarity.

These vary in terms of their focus on seeking outcomes. While not mentioned by Komito (1998) it is also possible to view this list as the requirements for any group of persons that wish to achieve some purpose such as clustering for economic gain.

- Moral: the companies involved in a clustering exercise will need to care, maybe only for each other in terms of being mutually dependent, but also would need to care about economic growth.
- Normative: once remote industries had made contact there would inevitably follow some need for rules of interaction, from ethical behaviour rules to rules of correspondence.
- Practice: this characteristic needs little reflection, "with a common purpose of sharing common experiences eg: scientists, miners or farmers." Later, the centrality of sharing to clustering will be further explored.
- Proximate: rather than be thought of merely needing geographical locality, it can be interpreted as the need for effective communication.
- Foraging: this could be interpreted in two ways, first, in order to be effective, a cluster of companies may most usefully not be too rigid in its organisation of who speaks to whom, about what, and in controlling what activity follows from those discussions. Second, in order to learn and grow clustered companies may need to spend some time and effort in individually undertaking market and product research and reporting back to the cluster. This can be thought of as foraging.

The question for this paper is do any of these appear impossible for virtual organisations?

An Example - Remote Rural Communities

Most of virtual organisation depend on communication so, provided the technology does deliver the most appropriate communication, then reflection of the list above does not appear to bar virtual communities from achieving outcomes.

For example can remote farming and mining companies form a virtual cluster? Cothrel and Williams (1999) list some preliminary criteria to help "set realistic expectations about what a particular on-line group can hope to achieve." While rather naive, the list does provide a forum for considering whether remote rural companies are likely to form an effective virtual cluster.

(1) Are members relatively isolated from one another? This can spur the need for on-line interaction.

This statement rather supports the argument that virtual communities exist and can be created by suggesting *members* can be isolated. However, the farm and mining companies in remote regions clearly passes this test by definition.

(2) Do members share information among themselves already?

Clearly farming co-operatives and explorer partnerships are common place. Both keep public records of prices and other market data and Governments insist that other information is shared such as explorers geological findings. Naturally, there are some things that are "commercial-in-confidence" so any communications system between members would need to recognise this.

(3) Do members need information to do their work?

It is assumed this means "from each other," which then seems like a very relevant issue. It helps if there is a reason why members **need** to talk to each other. However, a thesis that structured conversation can lead to innovation departs from the "needs" approach. The attraction of the idea that structured conversation leads to idea generation does not clash with the "need to talk" view, but rather is dealing with a different part of the idea creation and implementation cycle. This issue will be re-visited in the final section.

(4) Do [opinion leaders] support the idea of on-line collaboration?

The issue of opinion leaders seems important. However, in Australia the explorer and farming industry is made up of a large number of relatively small, owner-managed, companies. This has led to a very competitive, highly innovative industry, which is less influenced by one or two dominant opinion leaders than say the automobile industry. Yet, one aspect of providing a well-structured conversation is to include persons with respected reputations. This is not an appeal to authority but rather an acknowledgment of experience and expertise (Walton, 1998).

(5) Is the subject of their work or common interest something they can be passionate about?

Given the comments above about "common purpose" this question again raises some important issues. Given the economic decline in remote Australian regions, which separates family and destroys towns, coupled with a general desire for an improved lifestyle, it is being assumed that miners and farmers will be passionate about economic development (see Linn, 1999).

Core Competencies

The recent economic literature advises that an appropriate community for economic development is a cluster based on core competencies. Exactly what constitutes core competency is unclear. Lawson (1999) reviews the literature, trying to separate out various "knowledge levels." Immediate product knowledge is thought to be too specific, to be classed as a core competency, it involves knowledge at a more general level involving "technological spillovers, conventions, rules and languages for developing, communicating and interpreting knowledge, etc. plus common understanding which makes up the cultural, socio-economic industrial atmosphere" (Lawson, 1999). To this he adds the ability to innovate, or "collective learning," defined as "the creation and further development of a base of common or shared knowledge among the individuals within a productive system, allowing for the coordination of action and the resolution of problems" (Lawson, 1999). Lawson goes on to argue that this is learnt from social interaction and learning by doing in a group, which facilitates knowledge flows, allowing unplanned, synergistic, expertise-mixing.

So, do the rural regions have the core competencies to cluster? Given that they are relatively successful and experienced in "the farming industry" and "the mining industry," it would seem they are competent in something. However, few are in the innovation industry. Knowledge of crop alternatives and customer tastes may be missing. The traditional focus of farmers was on cost, quality and quantity of a standard product. As Lawson (1999) summarises, effective clustering requires a core competency concentrating upon solving problems for customers, in the case of farmers that is innovation in food on the plate. An example, often mentioned in farming groups, is that farmers know how to make a product but they have little contact with the distribution and retail customer's issues.

It would, therefore, seem that successful clustering is about getting people with a wide range of technical and commercial knowledge talking to each other, but particularly those who really do understand customers' most urgent concerns. Lawson (1999) feels that the electronic industry has been very good at this thus clustering of these firms have been very successful. This of course is the same advice as saying networking with customers is important. Modern commerce requires the skills of a range of people. One-person alone can rarely cover all the design, production, distribution, financial and customer knowledge required.

An alternative way of looking at "appropriateness" of organisations is from a critical theory perspective. Therborn (1996) summarises this as including asking how some human foible has turned into organisations, assumably because of their being a herd animal. There may be two inter-related foibles here. First, humans as problem solvers, and second, this being made so effective by language. The herding (community) and language part can also be approached from the communitarian perspective of the self derived from community interaction (see Taylor in Lehman, 1999), well critiqued by Lehman (1999), which is something Liberalism sometimes forgets. The language and problem solving aspects are typified by the observation that the most useful problem-solving piece of IT is the mobile phone. So, if a group of humans have a common problem, and can talk about it, an effective community is expected to follow. The last foible that suggests the development of the entire communications industry is that of the tyranny of distance. The very presence of the communications technologies of writing, printing, flag signalling, telegraph, telephone and the internet, suggest a problem being solved. The problem being distance. Suggesting that any communications technology that shortens the distance between people, while maintaining their privacy, will continue to solve this problem.

Argument would thus seem to be useful method for inquiry, problem solving and decisions making, all attributers of knowledge sharing. Above, it was said that clustering required appropriate conversation between persons with core competency. Ensuring appropriate arguments between appropriate people may then provide a policy around which to design Internet conferencing infrastructure. The problem then becomes how to manage these arguments

CONCLUSION

This chapter has argued that knowledge sharing requires a dialectic inquiry process that allows tacit knowledge to pass between people with core competencies. Typically this process involves setting in place infrastructure to allow the time-honoured method of well-structured argument (debate) to take place between people with core competencies. In this way clustering of remote rural industries may be effective. That rural communities can cluster was discussed, pointing out that they easily passed the criteria for successful on-line groups.

The extensive management literature that has found argument and debate so effective in innovation, problem solving and decision making provides a pragmatic justification for looking to talk for effective clustering. Clearly, out of sight debate does exist at present. The next stage is to package it so as to extend its impact. Managing the debates will be an important management-system development to provide real economic benefit.

REFERENCES

Argyris, C. and Schon, D. A. (1996). *Organizational Theory 2: Theory, method, and practice,* New York: Addison-Wesley.

Apotheloz, D., Brandt, P., and Ouiroz, G. (1993). The Function of Negation in Argumentation, *Journal of Pragmatics*, 19, pp. 23-39.

Broad, W. and Wane, N. (1982). *Betrayers of the Truth,* New York: Simon and Schuster.

Cothrel, J. and Williams, R. L. (1999). On line Communities: helping them grow, *Journal of Knowledge Management*, 3(1), pp. 54-60.

Crosswhite, J. (1996). *The Rhetoric of Reason,* Madison, WI: University of Wisconsin Press.

Eemeren, F. H., Grootendorst, R. and Kruiger, T. (1987). *Handbook of Argumentation Theory,* Dordrecht: Foris Publications.

Fischer, F. and Forrester, F. (1993). *The Argumentative Turn,* NC: Duke University Press.

Foo, S. and Hui, S. C. (1998). A Framework for Evaluating Internet Telephony Systems, *Internet Research,* 8(2), pp. 14-25.

Giddens, A. (1984). *The Constitution of Society,* University of California Press.

Horrocks, S., Rahmati, N. and Robbins-Jones, T. J. (1999). The development and Use of a Framework for Categorising Acts of Collaborative Work, *Proceedings of the 32nd Hawaii International Conference on System Sciences,* USA: IEEE Computer Society.

Jones, S. G. (1995). *Cybersociety,* California: Sage.

Komito, L. (1998). The Net as a Foraging Society: Flexible Communities, *Information Society,* 23, pp. 151-166.

Lawson, C. (1999). Towards a competency theory of a region, *Cambridge Journal of Economics,* 23, pp 151-166.

Lehman, G. (1999). Chapter 1: Communitarianism, *Liberalism versus Communitarianism,* Flinders University: PhD Thesis in Progress.

Lievrouw, L. A. (1998). Our Own Devices, *Information Society,* 14(2), pp. 83-96.

Linn, R. (1999). *Battling the Land: 200 Years of Rural Australia,* Sydney: Allen & Unwin.

Metcalfe, M. (1995). Decision Making in Small Groups, *International Journal of Computer and Engineering Management,* 3(1), pp. 40-54.

Myers, R. A. and Seibold, D. R. (1989). Perspectives on group argument, *Communications Yearbook,* 14, pp. 268-302.

Niederman, F. and Desantis, G. (1995). The Impact of the Structured Argument Approach on Group Problem Formulation, *Decision Sciences,* 26(4), pp. 83-96.

Nonaka, I. and Takeuchi, H. (1995). *The Knowledge Creating Company,* New York: Oxford University Press.

Perelman, C. H. and Olbrechts-Tyteca, L. (1969). *The New Rhetoric: A treatise on argumentation,* Notre Dame, Ind.: University of Notre Dame Press.

Schon, D. (1983). *The Reflective Practitioner,* New York: Basic Books.

Taylor cited in Lehman, G. (1999). Chapter 1: Communitarianism, *Liberalism versus Communitarianism,* Flinders University: PhD Thesis in Progress.

Therborn, G. (1996). Chapter 2: Critical Theory, In *Social Theory,* B. S. Turner (ed.), Mass: Blackwells.

Walton, D. (1998). *The New Dialectic,* Toronto: Toronto University Press.

Ziegelmueller, G. W. and Dause, C. A. (1975). *Argumentation: inquiry and advocacy,* New Jersey: Prentice Hall.

Chapter 22

Supporting Knowledge Creation: Combining Place, Community and Process

I.T. Hawryszkiewycz
University of Technology, Sydney, Australia

The chapter identifies the three major components of knowledge sharing and creation within enterprises as a combination of place, community and process. The way these are combined will depend on the particular goal and enterprise structure. The chapter then claims that computer support systems must provide user driven methods to easily integrate these components to fit in with organizational culture and knowledge goal. It then describes a way to provide this kind of environment.

INTRODUCTION

Knowledge management is now becoming almost a requirement in most enterprises, although in many cases its meaning to the enterprise in a clearly expressed paradigm is not obvious (McAdam and McCreedy, 1999). To many, knowledge management is based on the paradigm of collecting information and making it easily accessible using Intranet technologies and document management software. Many writers (Riggins, 1998) argue that knowledge creation within enterprises must go beyond this simple paradigm. It must include ways to combine the tacit knowledge within the enterprise with explicit knowledge using a process that eventually leads to an identified goal. It must also facilitate such combination towards a goal. Knowledge management must thus be a combination of place,

Previously Published in *Managing Information Technology in a Global Economy* edited by Mehdi Khosrow-Pour, Copyright © 2001, Idea Group Publishing.

community and process. The place provides the environment where tacit and explicit knowledge, which are combined within the organizational context. The community supports all people with the necessary tacit knowledge, whereas process ensures that their activities are coordinated and supported with necessary tools.

The chapter emphasizes business processes that are not predefined but require knowledge creation within the business process steps. The paper refers to such processes as knowledge intensive processes. The chapter proposes a way to create places that bring together explicit and tacit knowledge within steps of knowledge intensive processes and describes a system that includes functionality found increasingly necessary in knowledge creation environments. Such functionality calls for easy customization of work places to provide ways for teams to work together within enterprise contexts.

A PARADIGM FOR KNOWLEDGE SHARING

The paper sees knowledge intensive processes as going beyond workflows often found in enterprise processes and emphasizes the idea of place where all objects are brought together and various parts of the business process. This idea is illustrated in Figure 1.

Figure 1 illustrates two ways of modeling a supply chain. The traditional view is seen on the left with suppliers providing parts to producers and their partners and then produce goods going on to the client. This view requires the process as made up of a number of two-way relationships that make up the supply chain.

Figure 1: Towards knowledge sharing

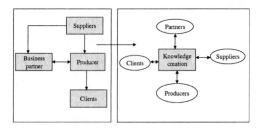

Figure 2: A place of work

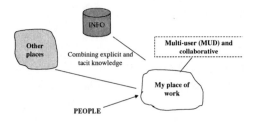

Figure 3: A network of places

Any changes will then have to pass through these relationships. The alternate is shown on the right where there is a place for all the participants to come together. Here a change can be raised at the one place with all participants together contributing their tacit knowledge to its solution.

The goal is to go beyond the simple paradigm of seeing computers as places to store and find information but to see them as "my place of work." One now departs from the traditional view to a view that contains people as well as documents and supports governance structures and flexible ways of interaction between the people.

The work environment in any enterprise will be made up of many such places connected together and working towards a common goal. Such a connection of places is shown in Figure 3 and makes up a knowledge intensive business process. Thus for example one activity in the process may be market evaluation, while another may be brainstorming for concepts and still a third may be planning of new products. Each such activity has its focus and produces an identified output. Each activity may bring together people with different expertise. People in the enterprise may also participate in more than one activity.

Such connected places require additional support for workflows to be specified between them as well as maintaining awareness of what is happening in each place.

Figure 4: A place for sharing knowledge

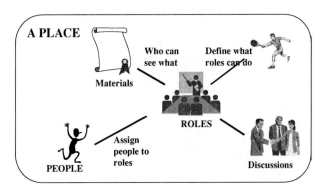

WHAT MAKES UP A PLACE

Figure 4 shows the most important concepts that make up a place. These center around roles that define responsibilities within the enterprise. Roles are given access to materials and authorized to carry out well-defined actions. People are assigned to the roles and can participate in various discussions to interpret materials and create new objects based on their deliberations. The assignment of responsibilities to the roles is flexible and can be dynamically changed as knowledge evolves.

There are a number of additional aspects to most places. These include:

- workflows that define sequences of actions needed to carry out a more complex activity,
- ways to maintain awareness through notification schemes and other features, and
- ability to create independent workgroups within the enterprise.

Furthermore places should be flexible in that responsible roles can restructure the places as work evolves.

Our implementation of such a place is shown in Figure 5. It uses the LiveNet system, which was developed at the University of Technology, Sydney. Figure 5 shows a place for delivering teaching materials but could equally apply to any training or consulting situation that requires the interaction of many people in different roles and with different and varying governance structures. The place shows the main objects shown in Figure 4 accessible through selections on the screen.

Figure 5 also illustrates a number of parameters used to maintain awareness. These include goals, milestones, surprises, new items and terminology.

Figure 5: A place for sharing and discussion

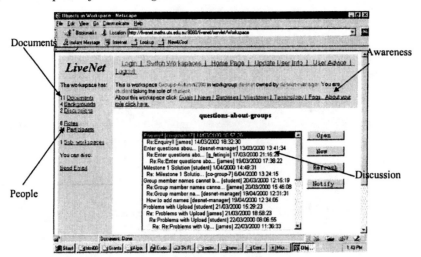

We have used LiveNet in a variety of learning environments, including:
- A place for distributing and clarifying materials,
- A place for developing ideas through facilitated discussions,
- A place for students to set up their own applications,
- A moderated distance place.

To do this we can use customization features that enable new roles and relationships to be easily created.

Customizing places

The advantage of a flexible system is adaption and customization. There are two levels of customization, namely:
- Restructuring the process through the creation of new places and relationships between the places including creation of new places, and
- Restructuring or creating new places

An example of such restructuring is in creating different learning and teaching environments (Hawryszkiewycz, 2000). Thus there can be standard places that are combined to form new environments through copying and adapting them into places within that environment. The idea is illustrated in Figure 6. Here there are standard places that are combined into an environment that includes tutorials and groupwork that is moderated through a master workspace.

Such environments can be created within a matter of minutes using wizards available in the system.

BUILDING COMMUNITIES

The semantics in our system are to create independent workgroups and organize their work into a number of activities. Each workgroup can pursue any number of activities, where each activity becomes a place with roles defined in ways that correspond to a community of knowing (Boland and Tenkasi, 1995) and can include experts, novices, facilitators and others. Thus the activities in Figure 3 may be the joint responsibility of one workgroup but each activity may be

Figure 6: Creating an Environment

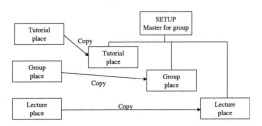

Figure 7: Nonaka's process

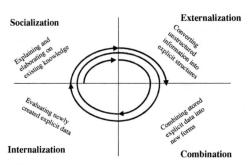

carried out by a subset of people in the workgroup in one place. All the people in the workgroup are continually kept aware of the status of each of the activities and the activities are coordinated to an agreed goal.

The semantics of each workgroup are such that there are designated roles that can create activities and assign people to these activities. Each activity itself may be moderated through the creation of roles with different responsibilities.

PROCESS

What is also needed in knowledge creation environments and ways to interpret information in community settings and form news perspectives (Boland and Tenkasi, 1995) based on such interpretations. These activities have to be integrated into process cycles that combine tacit and explicit knowledge (Nonaka, 1994). Typical business processes that emphasize knowledge creation include innovation, product planning, evaluation of proposals, responses to bids and so on. A typical empirical innovation process is that defined by Kuczmarski (1997), as a process for innovation that includes a number of groups such as market evaluation group, production group that are combined to evaluate and trial a new product or service. They differ from many place paradigms in that they must support exchange of knowledge from different domains but interpret it in ways needed to develop new products and services to give the enterprise competitive advantage.

Such processes require ways to capture and combine tacit and explicit knowledge from people, each in a different specialized area (Grant, 1996) often partici-

Figure 8: Agents in the knowledge sharing process

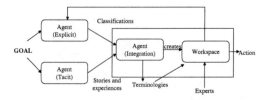

pating as workgroup communities in organizational settings. Increasingly they are carried out in global enterprises where such knowledge must be developed across distance. The knowledge creation processes are dynamic in the sense that they evolve and as new directions are identified or new opportunities arise. Often such processes link a number of workgroup communities. In this paper we call these processes knowledge intensive processes.

Process facilitation

Agents can provide ways to facilitate processes. The agents can select the people and artifacts needed at a process step, create a workspace for them and notify them of this workspace. Figure 8 for example shows the kinds of agents.

The agents include:

- Search agents for explicit knowledge as well as people with the needed tacit knowledge. These agents will need access to enterprise document repositories and people profiles,
- Agents to manage the tools needed to facilitate the process, such as managing terminologies, and
- Agents that create the workspaces and monitor their progress including notifications when needed.

Our goal here is to develop agents that are general in nature and can be adapted to a variety of places.

SUMMARY

The paper suggested that three components must be included in any system that supports knowledge creation. These are place, community and process. The paper then described a way of creating places that facilitate the creation of moderated communities and illustrated a system, LiveNet, used for this purpose. The paper then outlined ways of integrating processes into such places. The combination of these three is proposed as a way of supporting knowledge creation.

ACKNOWLEDGEMENTS

A number of people contributed to the work described in this paper especially Dr.L.Hu and Dongbai Xue for assistance in the development of the LiveNet system and Dr. T. Rura-Polley, and Dr. E. Baker for their contribution to planning its use for knowledge creation.

REFERENCES

Boland, R. J. and Tenkasi, R. V. (1995). Perspective Making and Perspective Taking in Communities of Knowing, in Fulk, J. and DeSanctis, G. (ed.) (1995),

Focused Issue on Electronic Communication and Changing Organizational Forms, *Organizational Science*, 6(4), July-August.

Grant, R. M. (1996). Prospering in Dynamically-competitive Environments: Organizational Capability as Knowledge Integration, *Organization Science*, 7(4), July, pp. 375-387.

Hawryszkiewycz (1999). Evolving Knowledge Intensive Community Networks, *Proceedings of Ausweb2000*, Cairns, June.

Kuczmarski, T. D. (1997). *Innovation: Leadership Strategies for the Competitive Edge*, Lincolnwood, IL: NTC Business Books.

LiveNet – http://linus.socs.uts.edu.au/~igorh/workspace/explore/cliks.htm.

McAdam, R. and McCreedy, S. (1999). A critical review of knowledge management models, *The Learning Organization*, 6(3), pp. 91-100.

Nonaka, I. (1994). A Dynamic Theory of Organizational Knowledge Creation, *Organization Science*, 5(1), February, pp. 14-37.

Riggins, F. J. and Rhee , H-K. (1998). Developing the Learning Network Using Extranets, *Proceedings of the Thirty-First Hawaiian Conference on Systems Sciences*, January.

Chapter 23

A Study of Knowledge Benefits Gained From Projects: The Electric Utility Industry Y2K Project Experience

Murray E. Jennex
San Diego State University and University of Phoenix, San Diego, USA

Joseph Weiss
Electric Power Research Institute, USA

Projects can cause organizations to perform in new ways resulting in the generation of knowledge. It is postulated that organizational learning occurs when new knowledge is captured and disseminated to the organization. It is expected that knowledge management facilitates organizational learning. Members of utility Y2K projects were surveyed with respect to knowledge benefits gained from their projects. Strong agreement for the existence of knowledge benefits was found and a listing of benefits generated. However, there was much less agreement on how to capture the benefits with many organizations taking little, if any, action. The conclusion is that while organizations recognize knowledge benefits, many do not have the tools or processes in place to take advantage of them.

INTRODUCTION

Organizational activities such as projects can result in knowledge generation. Organizational learning occurs from the acquisition, distribution, and interpretation

Previously Published in *Managing Information Technology in a Global Economy* edited by Mehdi Khosrow-Pour, Copyright © 2001, Idea Group Publishing.

of this knowledge by the organization. It was propositioned that organizations would use knowledge management to facilitate organizational learning by providing methods/tools for capturing and disseminating the generated knowledge. To test this proposition, members of utility Y2K projects were surveyed on knowledge generation, perceived knowledge benefits, and methods used to capture knowledge benefits. Utility Y2K projects were selected due to their large scope, high cost, high risk, and high stress suggesting that if any project would result in knowledge generation, then these would be it. However, the results of the survey were mixed. While project personnel were strong in their belief that there were knowledge benefits and could identify several, they were much less positive in their identification of methods for capturing knowledge benefits. This lends doubt as to the amount of organizational learning that actually occurred.

BACKGROUND

Organizational Learning

Organizational Learning has been defined as a quantifiable improvement in activities, increased available knowledge for decision making, or sustainable competitive advantage (Easterby-Smith, 1997; Miller, 1996; Cavaleri, 1994; Dodgson, 1993). Malhotra (1996) defines organizational learning as the process of "detection and correction of errors." In this view organizations learn through individuals acting as agents with individual learning activities facilitated or inhibited by an ecological system of factors that may be called an organizational learning system. Huber (1991) considers four constructs as integrally linked to organizational learning: knowledge acquisition, information distribution, information interpretation, and organizational memory.

Y2K Knowledge Benefits

The result of utility Y2K projects was a quiet rollover into 2000. What began as a high pressure, high visibility project ended suddenly and quietly. The aftermath saw many experts and critics questioning the validity and resources spent on Y2K. Several organizations published responses to these questions. All agreed that Y2K was a real issue and cited knowledge generated from the projects as one of the major gains from Y2K expenditures. Findings from these reports include:

- Success for those who did not spend heavily on Y2K was a result of knowledge sharing by those companies who took the lead in resolving Y2K issues, Cauley and Roth.
- The cost of contingency planning is worth it if organizations take the knowledge gained from Y2K and roll it into improved business continuity planning, Gartner Group.

- The benefits of Y2K need to be made permanent by changing government practices, Modernising Government in Action: Realising the Benefits of Y2K.
- Many benefits were gained from Y2K. These include contingency planning, risk assessment, understanding of systems, and IT management, The Many Silver Linings of the Year 2000 Challenges.
- The global Y2K experience created a unique opportunity to learn about how the world works and how international cooperation could be improved, Y2K: Starting the Century Right, Report of the International Y2K Cooperation Center.

METHODOLOGY

A survey was prepared to determine the extent of knowledge benefits gained from Y2K and the strategies used to capture them. The subject audience was selected using email lists of utility Y2K project personnel from the Nuclear Energy Institute (NEI) and the Electric Power Research Institute (EPRI) Y2K projects. To ensure similar projects were surveyed the list was edited to lead project personnel from Y2K member utilities in the United States and Canada. The revised list contained three types of individuals: those from corporate wide projects, those from technical site projects (generation or transmission and distribution), and those from IT projects.

The survey was generated from discussions with lead project personnel from utilities and EPRI and consisted of yes/no survey items that asked respondents to mark all the benefits and strategies that applied to them. Each item also allowed respondents to add benefits and/or strategies not listed. Items were also generated for:

- Establishing grouping by type of projects they supported;
- Determining how wide spread the search for secondary benefits was; and
- Determining how strongly respondents agreed that there were knowledge benefits.

The survey was distributed at the end of January, 2000, via email with responses collected, also via email, by February 15, 2000. To encourage openness and improve response rate, anonymity was promised to all respondents. A total of 88 responses were received:

- 7 from IT projects,
- 18 from Nuclear projects,
- 30 from Non-Nuclear Generation/T&D projects, and
- 33 from Company wide projects.

The 7 IT responses were received from 4 of the 98 companies (4.1%) surveyed and are not considered significant enough to be representative of the industry. This low response was expected as the EPRI and NEI programs targeted embedded systems which are normally designed and maintained by engineering departments so the survey distribution lists included few IT personnel. Results from the IT responses are presented for information. The 18 nuclear responses were received from 16 of the 47 companies (34%) operating nuclear plants and represented 34 of the 103 plants (33%). The 30 non-nuclear generation/T&D responses were received from 24 of the 98 companies (24.5%) surveyed. The 33 corporate wide responses were received from 28 of the 98 companies (28.6%) surveyed. Overall, 53 of the 98 companies (54.1%) provided at least one response. These are considered acceptable for analysis and representative of the industry since the aggregate representation of companies surveyed is over 50% and over 20% for each project.

FINDINGS

Requests to Find Benefits

This item was a yes/no response to: "I/we have been asked to identify ancillary benefits resulting from our Y2K project." 38 of 88 respondents were asked to justify cost and/or identify benefits. However, for corporate wide projects 19 of 33 had been asked to identify benefits. The implication is that corporations are asking about benefits but this request is not getting to the non-corporate projects. These smaller "line" organizations may not have a history of being asked to look for benefits or justify cost and do not feel it is necessary. This is likely a reflection on the regulated aspect of utilities as historically these organizations have had a monopolistic business. This implies utilities may not be used to learning from their projects but that their parent corporate organizations do learn and seek to find as many benefits as possible. Table 1 summarizes these responses.

Are There Knowledge Benefits

This item used a 5-point Likert scale item where 5 was strongly agree and 1 strongly disagree. 34 of 88 responses strongly agreed there were knowledge

Table 1: Response Summary to the Request to Find Benefits

GROUP	STRONGLY AGREE/ AGREE	ALL RESPONSES
Overall	4.45	4.20
Corporate Wide	4.68	4.58
IS	4.57	4.57
Nuclear	4.33	4.18
Non-Nuclear Generation/T&D	4.18	3.70

Table 2: Response Scores from Are There Knowledge Benefits

GROUP	NUMBER ASKED TO FIND BENEFITS	NUMBER NOT ASKED
Overall	38	50
Corporate Wide	19	14
IS	4	3
Nuclear	5	13
Non-Nuclear Generation/T&D	10	20

benefits, 42 agreed, 8 neither agreed or disagreed, 3 disagreed, and 1 strongly disagreed. This is very strong support in favor of there being knowledge benefits. Table 2 summarizes the responses. An overall score is provided for each group and for the survey as a whole. Also, two scores are provided; the first score is the average score for only agreed/strongly agreed responses. The second score is the average score of all respondents in the group. This was done to evaluate how strongly those who believed there were knowledge benefits supported that belief. The table shows that corporate wide respondents significantly agreed stronger than the other groups. The non-nuclear generation/T&D respondents agreed least strongly. Corporate wide respondents were privy to benefits and knowledge from all groups and succeeded with their projects by brokering this knowledge to all their groups. This group was the most likely to see knowledge benefits and their score supports that assumption.

Knowledge Benefits

This item asked for observed knowledge benefits. Table 3 summarizes the responses by indicating the percentage of respondents who indicated the item as a

Table 3: Percentage Indicating Items as Knowledge Benefits

Knowledge Benefit	% Respondents Indicating Item as a Benefit				
	All	Corporate	Nuclear	Non-Nuclear	IS
Contingency/Business Recovery Planning	86	88	75	91	86
Equipment/software inventories/databases	80	84	76	65	100
Collaborative Problem Solving	72	72	63	74	86
Relationship Management	68	69	56	68	100
Test Processes	68	59	69	74	86
Risk Identification/Management	58	63	44	48	86
System Interfaces	55	59	56	41	86
Configuration Management	55	52	56	55	86
Project Management	55	55	63	52	57
Data/Information Management	54	42	94	39	71
Public Relations	51	62	56	41	43
Software Management	33	39	31	27	43

Table 4: Added Knowledge Benefits

Knowledge Benefits	Group Adding Benefit
Improvements in broad based resources management and leveraging	IS, Nuclear, Non-Nuclear Generation/T&D, Corporate Wide
Cyber security visibility	Non-Nuclear Generation/T&D, Corporate Wide
Record retention plans for project information	Nuclear
Creation of corporate wide automated problem reporting systems	Nuclear
Learning to work with contractors and suppliers more cost effectively	Nuclear
Increased level of knowledge for systems and interfaces	Nuclear
Heightened awareness of Software Quality and tracking processes	Nuclear
Overall upgrades of systems to current versions or new systems	Non-Nuclear Generation/T&D

knowledge benefit. Table 4 lists additional knowledge benefits and the group that added it.

Contingency Planning/Business Recovery is indicated as the overall top knowledge benefit. This is not unexpected as 1999 was spent by most of the respondent generating contingency plans. Prior to Y2K contingency planning and business recovery were not routinely performed. As a result, organizations learned a great deal about the dependencies within their processes and organizations and how to work around postulated failures in these processes. Two unexpected findings were the strong showing of Public Relations, 51% overall but 62% corporate wide and 56% nuclear; and the relatively weak showing of Software Management, 33% overall and a low of 27% from non-nuclear generation/T&D. Public Relations were highly rated because Y2K was a media event. NEI and EPRI emphasized this. The intense press for the two years prior to the rollover forced companies to learn how to respond and work with the media with respect to tough issues. Software Management doing so poorly is harder to understand. Throughout the Y2K project utilities reported software problems such as version control, lack of configuration management, poor documentation, and lack of expertise on how the software worked. It must be assumed that the respondents felt they knew how to manage software and so did not learn anything from Y2K, they just did not practice it.

The most commonly added knowledge benefits were resource management across functional areas/organizations and added awareness of cyber security.

Actions Taken to Capture Knowledge Benefits

This item identified actions organizations were taking to capture knowledge benefits and make them permanent. Table 5 summarizes the responses and provides several surprises. The most surprising is the weakness of responses. All

Table 5: Percentage Indicating The Action As Being Taken

Knowledge Capture Action	%Respondents Using Knowledge Capture Action				
	All	Corporate	Nuclear	Non-Nuclear	IS
Modifying processes/procedures	58	48	50	61	86
Creating/Modifying support tools	51	42	50	52	86
Creating new processes or procedures	42	35	25	43	100
Re-assign Y2K personnel to more responsible assignments	38	35	38	30	71
Increasing use of Intranets/ Bulletin Boards	31	19	38	26	71
Creating/Modifying training	27	26	25	26	43
Post Y2K Lessons Learned Report	27	32	25	22	29
Encouraging Industry Participation	16	13	25	13	29
Leveraging Y2K Success	16	19	6	13	29
Changing Company Goals/Initiatives	12	6	19	13	29
Still Deciding how to make permanent	32	39	19	39	

Table 6: Added Actions

Other Knowledge Actions Taken	Group Taking the Action
Incorporating Y2K analyses into system files or documentation/ Building a Body of Knowledge	Nuclear, Non-Nuclear Generation/T&D
Change corporate culture to be more knowledge and team oriented	Non-Nuclear Generation/T&D
Change perception of Y2K to something that we learned from	Nuclear
Implementing more integrated systems such as SAP	IS

but one of the knowledge benefits had 50% or more agreement. For actions, only two had 50% or more agreement. The highest agreement was only 58%. Table 6 lists respondent added actions taken but only adds four actions. This indicates a consensus that there are knowledge benefits but little consensus as to what actions should be taken to capture and make these benefits permanent.

A somewhat surprising finding is that corporate respondents had the least consensus as to what actions to take with no action exceeding 50%. What makes this surprising is that corporate respondents had the strongest agreement to there being knowledge benefits. It implies that while corporate respondents could more easily see knowledge benefits, they were less able to implement actions to capture them, particularly if the action was in a functional area not "owned" by corporate respondents. It is anticipated that this is caused by these organizations not having well integrated processes making implementing corporate wide actions to capture knowledge benefits difficult.

A final surprising finding is that although several of the identified knowledge benefits included people skills such as cooperative problem solving and relationship management only about 1 in 3 respondents indicate that these Y2K personnel are being further utilized in important projects or positions. Comments made on the responses included:

- "I am the last surviving project member."
- "Management couldn't wait to disband the team."
- "We released people as soon as possible to cut costs."

Two causes are postulated. The first is that many of these projects used personnel from non-IT organizations while the project itself was an IT organization responsibility. Therefore, even though project personnel developed useful people skills, the IT organization did not feel they had the IT skills necessary for the IT organization. The second cause is that Y2K projects tended to use a large number of contract personnel including retirees and these personnel were simply not needed following completion of the project.

LIMITATIONS ON RESEARCH

The main limitation is from the use of a selected target audience. The audience was selected because they had participated in a knowledge sharing project and were expected to be aware of knowledge benefits. However, this audience is not necessarily reflective of the entire electric utility industry. There are several hundred electric utilities in the United State and only 98 were members of EPRI. These 98 utilities represent the bulk of electrical generation and transmission in the United States. The majority of the companies that did not participate with EPRI were distribution companies or rural electric associations. These companies were considered to have the least risk from Y2K. Additionally, the response rate of around 30% for each group allows that there were sufficient subjects who may have considered the knowledge benefits from Y2K to be too trivial to respond to the survey. This is not considered to be the case. Both authors discussed Y2K knowledge benefits in great detail with participants of the EPRI and NEI efforts and are confident the findings are reflective of electric utility Y2K knowledge benefits.

CONCLUSIONS

There are knowledge benefits from Y2K projects. The strongest agreement with this came from the Corporate, IS, and, Nuclear projects. However, utilities are having trouble capturing these benefits. It is concluded that while many organizations talk of capturing and using knowledge, putting that into practice is difficult and not well understood by the electric utility industry. This does not support the original proposition that organizations would use knowledge management techniques/tools to capture and disseminate knowledge benefits from projects.

Chapter 24

Designing Organizational Memory for Knowledge Management Support in Collaborative Learning

Kam Hou Vat
University of Macau

This chapter investigates the design of organizational memory (OM) which is targeted for knowledge management (KM) support tailored for collaboration among academic staff and students in a university environment. Specifically, we describe our KM initiatives to support organizational learning in terms of the knowledge processes evolving over selected knowledge domains for training and research purpose. The chapter also depicts our ideas on knowledge items regarding their meta-modeling, indexing, and ontological aspects. The overall design of our OM is then discussed in terms of its context for knowledge work. The paper concludes by re-iterating the challenges in knowledge sharing and depositing into the OM for its continuous growth and utilization.

INTRODUCTION

In the emerging knowledge economy, the recognition that knowledge is one of the organization's key assets, has fueled interest in researching into the various activities of knowledge management (KM): identification, collection, adaptation, preservation, application and sharing of the organization's knowledge (Dieng, 2000;

Previously Published in *Managing Information Technology in a Global Economy* edited by Mehdi Khosrow-Pour, Copyright © 2001, Idea Group Publishing.

Van der Spek and Spijkervet). A university can be considered as a knowledge organization whose valuable assets come from her teams of knowledge workers, who have a strong formal education, have learned how to learn, and have a habit of continuing to learn throughout their lifetime. Yet, intellectual assets belong inherently to people, and are the organization's assets only through their application and reuse (Conklin, 1996). These are good reasons to capturing the intellectual knowledge of people, however implicit it may be, and making it explicit within an organization whose competitive advantage comes from having and effectively using knowledge. We believe that an organizational memory (OM) is a facility that could extend and amplify this knowledge asset by capturing, organizing, disseminating and reusing the knowledge created by our knowledge workers. It can be shared among individuals working alone, by teams needing a project memory, and by the organization as a whole for long-term and short-term goals. This paper investigates the design of such an OM together with the KM support necessitated by organizational learning (collaboration) (Argyris and Schon, 1978; Dodgson, 1993; Kim; 1993) among knowledge workers in an electronic university environment we call VU, representing our Virtual University model.

THE CURRENT STATUS OF KNOWLEDGE MANAGEMENT

According to O'Leary (1998, 1998), KM entails managing knowledge resources in order to facilitate access and reuse of knowledge, typically by using advanced information technologies (IT). It attempts to address such issues as: capitalizing on individual know-how in a collective knowledge; improving newcomer learning and integration; disseminating best practices; improving organizational work processes and productivity (Dieng, 2000). Essentially, knowledge is often classified according to some pre-specified (but evolving) categories into structured and semi-structured data and knowledge bases. Typically, KM systems represent knowledge in both human-readable and machine-readable forms. The former is accessed using browsers, whereas the latter is often designed as an expert system's knowledge base to support decision-making. Meanwhile, ontology specifications are generally endemic to KM systems because they refer to taxonomies of the tasks that define the knowledge for the systems (Chandrasekaran, Josephson and Benjamins, 1999; Swartout and Tate, 1999). Specifically, ontologies define the shared vocabulary used in the KM system to facilitate communication, search, storage, and representation of knowledge. According to Conklin (1996), there are generally two types of organizational knowledge: formal and informal. Formal knowledge refers to the stuff of books, manuals, documents, and training courses. It is the primary work product of the knowledge worker, captured easily by the organization. And informal knowledge is the knowledge created and used in the process of creating the formal results. It includes ideas, facts, assumptions, meanings, questions, decisions, guesses, stories, and points of view. It is as important in the work of the knowledge worker as formal knowledge is, but is more ephemeral and transitory. Thus, it is hard to capture and to keep, especially in the artifact-oriented culture of our work environment, where we tend to value results – the output of the work process – far above the process itself. As knowledge employees turn over in today's job market, organizations are likely to lose access to large quantities of critical knowledge. The question is how we can create an OM-based system that will capture organization-wide knowledge (formal and informal) and make it widely available to all its members.

THE VISION OF ORGANIZATIONAL MEMORY

We envision that an OM's major function is to enhance the organization's competitiveness by improving the way it manages its knowledge. It is the core of a learning organization, supporting sharing and reuse of individual and organizational knowledge and lessons learned. It is supported by intelligent KM services actively providing any user working on a knowledge-intensive task with the information required for fulfilling the task. Such information is largely based on the organization's formal knowledge, captured through explication of informal knowledge within the organization, and is supported by such IT tools as expert systems, issue-based information systems (IBIS), best-practice databases, and lessons-learned archives. This perspective of the OM emphasizing the support of the human user by providing, maintaining, and distributing relevant information and knowledge, is not centered around the idea of a passive information system or an autonomous problem-solver, but an intelligent assistant to the user (Abecker, Bernardi, Hinkelmann et al., 1998; Baek, Liebowitz et al., 1999; Silverman, Bedewi and Morales, 1995). Actually, this intelligent assistant view of OM corresponds well with the shift of focus in AI. While an important AI goal has been to build knowledge-based systems that solve challenging problems on their own, an intelligent assistant system cooperates with a human user in contributing to a possible solution by performing what might be done, but letting the user decide, thus distinguishing workload versus decision competence. This combination of the assistant system and the user should improve both problem-solving capabilities and user acceptance. According to Brooks (Brooks, 1996), this vision of OM is often characterized as IA, denoting intelligence amplification, which carries the connotation that a machine and a mind is superior to a mind-imitating machine (conventional AI approach) working by itself in problem-solving.

THE OM SCENARIO FOR KM SUPPORT

One of our VU's learning experiences is to enable knowledge development and transfer among teachers and students in an interactive and collaborative atmosphere. Students actively participate in generating, accessing, and organizing the required information. They construct knowledge by formulating their ideas into words and then develop these ideas as they react to other students' or teachers' responses to their formulations. Knowledge construction can then be considered as the process of progressive problem solving, which encourages students to be innovative, create intellectual property, and develop and acquire expertise. To achieve these knowledge tasks, our academic staffs need considerable skill and knowledge to deal with the acquisition, creation, packaging, and application of emergent knowledge. An OM could help users perform these knowledge tasks through knowledge sharing across academic domains. It is about leveraging the expertise of people and making the most effective use of the intellectual capital of an organization (Stewart, 1997). Typically, when a knowledge worker (professor or student) recognizes an information need within the actual flow of work, a query to the OM must be derived. This query is generated as specifically as possible according to the actual work context. On the other hand, the OM can also store new information created within a given working scenario in a contextually enriched form such that subsequent retrieval processes might compare the query context with the creation context for relevance estimation. Thereby, knowledge sharing among organization members must be supported by the ability to search for information based on different contextual criteria, to find linkages between different types of information, and to relate information with people. These represent some of the key aspects of KM support to be addressed when building an OM system to realize context-sensitive knowledge supply.

THE OM REQUIREMENTS FOR ORGANIZATIONAL LEARNING

In the literature on knowledge management (Nonaka and Takeuchi; Van der Spek and Spijkervet; Van Heijst, Van der Spek and Kruizinga, 1996; Wiig, 1993), four basic knowledge processes are identified, with OM concerns: a) *Developing knowledge (development)*. Organizations survive by the continuous development of new knowledge based on creative ideas, the analysis of failures, daily experiences and work in research and development (R&D). OM can support these processes by tracking failures and successes; b) *Securing knowledge (storage)*. Individual knowledge must be made accessible to others in the organization at the right time and place. Knowledge stored in the OM is meant to be persistent and if indexed properly, can be retrieved easily; c) *Distributing knowledge (dis-*

tribution). Knowledge must be actively distributed to those who need it, with the shortest turn-around time to enhance organizational competitiveness. OM needs a facility to determine who should be informed about a particular piece of new knowledge; d) *Combining knowledge (combination)*. An organization can perform at its best if all available knowledge can be combined in its new products and services. OM may facilitate this combination by making it easier to access knowledge developed in different parts of the organization. To understand how these processes are inter-related, we consider a scenario of organizational learning among knowledge workers. They often test their learning by applying the new knowledge themselves. Then they will communicate the results to their fellow workers. If the lesson learned is truly effective, they will put it down in their manuals that become part of the knowledge records of the organization.

When implementing an OM for organizational learning, we consider the following modes of learning: 1) individual, 2) group, and 3) repository. Individual learning is characterized by knowledge being developed, and possibly the result of combining an insight with know-how from other sources in the organization, but it is often not distributed and is not secured for reuse. Group learning is centered about the concept of communication in two possible modes: supply-driven, or demand-driven. The former is characterized by an individual who has found a way to improve the work process and communicates this to one's co-workers. The latter refers to a worker who has recognized a problem in the current process and asks fellow workers whether they have a solution for this problem. In each case, knowledge is developed, distributed, and possibly combined with knowledge from other parts of the organization, but it is seldom secured. In repository learning, the communication element is replaced by collection, storage and retrieval of knowledge items. Namely, it is typified by storing lessons learned in some information repository so that they can be retrieved and used when needed. Overall, in repository learning, knowledge is developed, secured, distributed, and is possibly the result of knowledge combination.

It is convinced that the requirements of an OM implementation should be formulated in terms of the above KM processes. Namely, an OM should facilitate individual workers to access the knowledge required by combination, to submit a lesson learned, and to decide which of the co-workers would be interested in a lesson learned. Also, there should be criteria to determine if something is a lesson learned, how it should be formulated and where it should be stored, and how to distribute some newly asserted knowledge piece to the workers in need. The perceived technical issues, nevertheless, could include the following: How are we to organize and index the OM to enhance its diffusion? How to retrieve relevant elements of the OM to answer a user's request or proactively push relevant elements towards users? How to adapt the answer to users, in particular to their tasks, according to the knowledge contexts? These problems are largely related to information retrieval, and they are bound to the OM framework for knowledge distribution, whose goal is to improve organizational learning, with the aid of some organizational KM support.

DESCRIBING OM'S KNOWLEDGE ITEMS

In developing the mechanism to secure organizational knowledge, our experimental OM has chosen the CommonKADS organization model proposed by de Hoog et al (1994; 1996; Van der Spek and de Hoog, 1995), where knowledge items are modeled as objects with a number of attributes commonly classified into three groups as shown in the following table.

- *Activities.* This attribute refers to the organizational activities to which the knowledge item is related. Every organization should have an explicit model of the activities that are performed as part of the work processes. The names of these activities can then be used as values on this attribute.
- *Domains.* This attribute is related to the subject of the knowledge item. To use this attribute, organizations should have an inventory of relevant knowledge domains. This inventory is a meta-description of the types of knowledge that exist in the organization. And it is specifically developed according to the contexts of knowledge work in the individual organization.
- *Form.* This attribute concerns the physical representation of a particular piece of knowledge. De Hoog et al. identify four possible values for this attribute: paper, electronic, mind and collective, where the last one is actually referring to the availability issue instead of the physical form. Overall, the number of possibilities should be sufficient to allow an organization to specify the different forms in which knowledge is available physically.
- *Type.* This attribute specifies the type of document relating the knowledge item. Possible values include concepts such as protocol, procedure, guideline, handbook, manual, best/worst practice, progress report, white paper, evaluation report, and many others. Such values are assumed to be reusable across a wide range of organizations, even though individual organizations may choose to use only a limited subset.

Table 1: Knowledge items as used in the CommonKADS organization model

General	Name:	
	Role description:	The Role the knowledge is associated with
	Activity:	The related organizational task(s)
	Domain(s):	Reference to organizational areas/objects/processes
Content	Generic task type:	From the CommonKADS library tree
	Nature:	Heuristic, formal, uncertain...
	Products/services:	Marketable products of the organization
	Functions:	Organizational functions involved
Availability	Time:	When available
	Location:	Where available
	Form:	Paper, electronic, mind, collective

- *Products/Services.* These attributes relate the knowledge items to the products and services of an organization. These attributes enable the OM to improve communication with the knowledge workers and outside clients. The possible values are often organization-specific, and should be obtained with no particular difficulties.
- *Time and location.* These attributes are relevant for knowledge items, which have "mind" as value on the form attribute. Since certain knowledge is only available in a personal form, the OM should make it easy to find out how and where this particular person can be contacted. Actually, the OM should contain knowledge profiles of all the workers in the organization. These profiles should be formulated using the same attributes and attribute values as used for knowledge items. More specifically, such profiles, usually under the control of knowledge workers, should carry knowledge items that are about the activities, domains, and products/services, which are directly related to their current knowledge work.

INDEXING OM'S KNOWLEDGE ITEMS

In implementing the indexing mechanism for knowledge items in our OM, we have considered the installation of three basic types of navigation mechanisms for searching flexibility. They include hierarchical search, attribute search and content search. The first method organizes knowledge items in a fixed hierarchical structure. An example of this search is illustrated by following hyperlinks on the Web documents. The second method searches the OM by specifying values for attributes, and knowledge items are returned which have the specified values on the attributes. Database engines typically use this type of searching. The third method entails users entering arbitrary search terms related to the topic of interest. The search simply returns all the knowledge items in which the terms occur. An example is the crawler of most search engines on the World Wide Web. Basically, content search could be considered as the most flexible method; however, its ability to find the appropriate documents depends heavily on the capacity of the user to formulate suitable search terms. And it is confined to textual knowledge items, the amount of structure in the OM, and the number of possibly relevant knowledge items. And attribute search is the second most flexible method because indexing through hierarchical structure can be considered as a compiled form of attribute indexing where the order in which the attributes are specified is preset. But it still requires a pre-defined set of attributes.

CONCEIVING OM'S ONTOLOGIES

Two types of ontologies that have been useful to our OM development are domain ontologies and enterprise ontologies for describing an organizational model.

Examples of enterprise ontologies include the Enterprise Ontology proposed by the University of Edinburgh's Artificial Intelligence Applications Institute (AIAI), and the TOVE (Toronto Virtual Enterprise) ontologies, proposed by the University of Toronto. The former has five sections: activity, organization, strategy, time and marketing. The latter comprises five core ontologies: activity, organization, product, resource, and service. These ontologies characterize knowledge items on a global level for organizational modeling. And they have been used to standardize the allowed values for some of the attributes of knowledge items in our OM. As for the domain ontologies, since they could be largely different for different knowledge domains, they have to be derived separately. Our job is to identify the vocabulary and thus the underlying conceptualizations of the kinds of objects and relations that can exist in the domain. In most cases, the emerging ontologies (Devedzic, 1999) have the form of networks of categories of concepts, with an explicit representation of hierarchy among them. In developing our domain ontology, we have concentrated on representing the vocabulary of the problem domain, different kinds of relationships between its concepts, concept properties, constraints, and rules for extending the vocabulary. To help modeling the specific domain, we have also borrowed the following concepts from object-oriented analysis and design (Chandrasekaran et al., 1999): There are *objects* in the world. Objects have *properties* or *attributes* that can take *values*. Objects can exist in various *relations* with one another. Properties and relations can change over *time*. There are *events* that can occur at different *time instants*. There are *processes* in which objects participate and that occur over time. The world and its objects can be in different *states*. Events can cause other events or states as *effects*. And objects can have *parts*.

CHARACTERIZING OM-BASED KNOWLEDGE WORK

According to Spek and Spijkervet (Spek and Spijkervet, 1996), organizational knowledge can be characterized by knowing which information is needed (know what); knowing how information must be processed (know how); knowing why information is needed (know why); knowing where information can be found to achieve a specific result (know where); and knowing when which information is needed (know when). Individual knowledge workers construct and reconstruct organizational knowledge through sharing with their colleagues. These include (Dieng, 2000): human knowledge sources, whose knowledge must be made explicit so that others can access through the OM; knowledge engineers, who acquire and model knowledge; knowledge watchers, who gather, filter, analyze, and distribute knowledge elements from the external world; OM developers, who concretely build, organize, annotate, maintain, and evolve the OM; a team of validating experts, who validate the knowledge elements before their insertion in the OM; OM users, who can easily access and reuse memory elements; and OM managers, who supervise the OM project. Meanwhile, the OM context for our VU could further be refined for different faculties, departments, programs, courses, groups, or communities, gathered by a common interest of organizational learning.

CONCLUSION

This paper sketches our preliminary effort to design an OM to secure organizational knowledge that is shared among organizational members. Although organizational knowledge is created via individual knowledge, complete organizational knowledge is achieved only when individuals keep modifying their knowledge through interactions with other members (Argyris and Schon, 1978; Kim, 1993). This is the process through which organizations continually refresh and update their intellectual capital. Organization members act as learning agents, responding to changes in the internal and external environments of the organization. More importantly, the agents' discoveries, inventions, and evaluations are shared through the organizational shared memory. We are convinced that implementing the VU's OM is an important effort to realize our university's shared memory. And the recent popularity of the Web has provided a tremendous opportunity to expedite the dispersement of various creation/diffusion infrastructures (Corby and Dieng, 1999; Eriksson, 1996; Euzenat, 1996; Shum, 1998), particularly those of developing global collaborative KM platforms. It is believed that a well-devised OM with user-friendly KM services enhances the probability of seamless knowledge acquisition, sharing, and integration among organization members. The challenge that organizations now face is how to design KM services to turn the scattered, diverse knowledge of their knowledge workers into well-structured knowledge assets ready for deposit and reuse in their OMs.

REFERENCES

Abecker, A., Bernardi, A., Hinkelmann, K., et al. (1998). Toward a Technology for Organizational Memories, *IEEE Intelligent Systems*, 13(3), May/June, pp. 40-48.

Argyris, C., and Schon, D.A. (1978). *Organizational Learning: A Theory of Action Perspective*, Reading, MA: Addison Wesley.

Baek, S., Liebowitz, J., et al. (1999). Intelligent Agents for Knowledge Management – Toward Intelligent Web-Based Collaboration within Virtual Teams, In J. Liebowitz, (ed.), *Knowledge Management Handbook*, Springer-Verlag.

Brooks, F.P. (1996). The Computer Scientist as Toolsmith II, *Comm. ACM*, 39(3), Mar., pp. 61-68.

Chandrasekaran, B., Josephson, J.R., and Benjamins, V.R. (1999). What Are Ontologies, and Why Do We Need Them? *IEEE Intelligent Systems*, 14(1), Jan/Feb, pp. 20-26.

Conklin, E.J. (1996). Designing Organizational Memory: Preserving Intellectual Assets in a Knowledge Economy, white paper, Group Decision Support Systems, Washington, D.C.; http://www.gdss.com/DOM.htm.

Corby, O., and Dieng, R. (1999). The WebCokace Knowledge Server, *IEEE Internet Computing*, 3(6), Nov./Dec., pp. 38-43.

De Hoog, R., et al. (1994). Organization Model: Model Definition Document, Technical Report. Univ. Amsterdam and Cap Programmator. Deliverable DM6.2c of ESPRIT Project P5248 (KADS-II).

De Hoog, R., et al. (1996). The CommonKADS Organization Model: Content, Usage, and Computer Support, *Expert Systems with Applications*, 11(1), July, pp. 247-260.

Devedzic, V. (1999). Ontologies: Borrowing From Software Patterns, *ACM SIGART Intelligence*, 10(3), Fall, pp. 14-24.

Dieng, R. (2000). Knowledge Management and the Internet, *IEEE Intelligent Systems*, 15(3), May/June, pp. 14-17.

Dodgson, M. (1993). Organizational Learning: A Review of Some Literature, *Organization Studies*, 14(3), pp. 375-394.

Enterprise Ontology. http://www.aiai.ed.ac.uk/project/enterprise/enterprise/ontology.html.

Eriksson, H. (1996). Expert Systems as Knowledge Servers, *IEEE Expert*, 11(3), June, pp. 14-19.

Euzenat, J. (1996). Corporate Memory through Cooperative Creation of Knowledge Bases and Hyper-documents, In *Proc. 10th Banff Workshop on Knowledge Acquisition for Knowledge-Based Systems (KAW'96)*, B. Gaines and M. Musen (eds.), SRDG Publications, Calgary, Canada.

Kim, D.H. (1993). The Link between Individual and Organizational Learning, *Sloan Management Review*, Fall, pp. 37-50.

Nonaka, I., and Takeuchi, H. The Knowledge Creating Company: How Japanese Companies Create the Dynamics of Innovation, New York: Oxford Univ. Press.

O'Leary, D.E. (1998). Enterprise Knowledge Management, *IEEE Computer*, 31(3), Mar., pp. 54-61.

O'Leary, D.E. (1998). Using AI in Knowledge Management: Knowledge Bases and Ontologies, *IEEE Intelligent Systems*, 13(3), May/June, pp. 34-39.

Shum, S.B. (1998). Negotiating the Construction of Organizational Memories, In U.M. Borghoff, and R. Pareschi (eds.), *Information Technology for Knowledge Management*, Springer-Verlag, pp.55-78.

Silverman, B.G., Bedewi, N., and Morales, A. (1995). Intelligent Agents in Software Reuse Repositories, *ACM CIKM Workshop on Intelligent Information Agents*.

Spek, R, and Spijkervet, A.L. (1996). A Methodology for Knowledge Management, Tutorial Notes of The 3rd World Congress on Expert Systems, Seoul, Korea.

Stewart, T.A. (1997). *Intellectual Capital: The New Wealth of Organizations*, New York: Doubleday.

Swartout, W., and Tate, A. (1999). Ontologies, *IEEE Intelligent Systems*, 14(1), Jan/Feb, pp. 18-19.

TOVE (Toronto Virtual Enterprise). http://www.ie.utoronto.ca/EIL/tove/toveont.html

Van der Spek, R., and De Hoog, R. (1995). A Framework for a Knowledge Management Methodology, In Wiig, K.M. (ed.), *Knowledge Management Methods*. Arlington, TX, USA: Schema Press, pp. 379-393.

Van der Spek, R., and Spijkervet, A. Knowledge Management: Dealing Intelligently with Knowledge, Utrecht, The Netherlands: IBIT series No. 1, Kenniscentrum CIBIT.

Van Heijst, G., Van der Spek, R., and Kruizinga, E. (1996). Organizing Corporate Memories, In *Proc. KAW'96*, University of Calgary, Knowledge Science Institute., 1996; http://ksi.cpsc.ucalgary.ca/KAW/KAW96/KAW96proc.html.

Wiig, K.M. (1993). *Knowledge Management: The Central Management Focus for Intelligent-Acting Organizations*, Arlington, TX, USA: Schema Press.

Chapter 25

Getting over "Knowledge is Power": Incentive Systems for Knowledge Management in Business Consulting Companies

Dr. Harald F. O. VonKortzfleisch
University of Kassel and University of Cologne, Germany

Ines Mergel
University of St. Gallen, Switzerland

INTRODUCTION

One of the most relevant aspects as to knowledge management is the need to make knowledge workers to actively participate in the diverse processes which are the objects of knowledge management. Especially the motivation to jointly share knowledge and to use the available knowledge of, e. g., colleagues or other third-party experts becomes an important issue for knowledge management in general and above all for business consulting companies which belong to one of the most knowledge-intensive and knowledge management-experienced industries. Therefore, we take a closer look at the importance of incentive systems for knowledge management in the business consulting industry.

The findings of our empirical qualitative investigation in 10 leading German business consulting companies show a range of special qualities: First of all and in correspondence with the assumptions in the literature incentive systems do

Previously Published in *Managing Information Technology in a Global Economy* edited by Mehdi Khosrow-Pour, Copyright © 2001, Idea Group Publishing.

(!) play an important role in this knowledge driven industry. However secondly, there are almost no incentive systems with a special focus on the issue of knowledge. Rather, the existing incentive systems are somehow implicitly expected to guarantee respective behavior of the consultants. Thirdly and finally, in contrast to our expectations and most of the recommendations in the praxis-oriented and theoretical literature for knowledge management the dominant incentives were not immaterial but material.

We conclude that the existing long-standing experience with the exchange and use of (new) knowledge, and the special knowledge-oriented culture of business consulting companies do motivate the consultants to share their knowledge and to use the existing knowledge of colleagues. However, in order to implement a more efficient knowledge management which supports the overall strategic goals in dynamic markets the examined business consulting companies should be aware of a special need for additional incentives – even if they do not know yet which incentives this can be and how to implement them.

STARTING POINT AND FRAME OF REFERENCE

Regarding strategic management at the turn of the new millennium, one of the central challenges for companies is the management of the firm's knowledge bases and learning processes in order to gain competence-based competitive advantages (see, e. g., Davenport and Prusak, 1997; Kumar, 1995; Drucker, 1993, Hansen, Nohria and Tierney, 1999). In strategic management theory, this is reflected by the establishment of the "resource-based view" of the firm, and more recently of the "knowledge-based view" of the firm (see below).

Knowledge-Based View of the Firm and Knowledge Management

For some time now research in the field of strategic management turns away from the traditional "market-based view" or "structure-conduct-performance paradigm" respectively (see Bain, 1968; Porter, 1981, 1998a, 1998b) and devotes itself to the question which role specific resources play in order to build up long-term company success (for early contributions to this research question see Selznik, 1957; Penrose, 1959). As a result the so-called "resource-based view" of the firm describes the uniqueness of companies as bundles of specific, non-transferable ("sticky"), difficult to imitate and appropriate resources (see Barney, 1991; Wernerfelt, 1984; Grant, 1991; Collis and Montgomery, 1995, 1998), stressing the capture of rents through the protection and deployment of these resources. Within the recent "knowledge-based view" of the firm knowledge as a specific kind of resource in terms of an essential competitive asset is in the center of research interests (see Prahalat and Hamel, 1990; Kogut and Zander, 1993; Hamel and Heene, 1994; Nonaka and Takeuchi, 1995; Grant, 1996; Spender and Grant,

1996; Oliviera Jr., 1998). The main role of the company is therefore to manage knowledge in order to improve organizational performance.

Knowledge Management is understood as the managerial process of setting knowledge goals and identifying, acquiring, developing, transferring, applying, preserving, and assessing the strategically relevant knowledge of the firm, through processes within and across the companies' boundaries (see Davenport and Prusak, 1997; Probst and Romhard, 1997). However members of companies will not necessarily automatically provide their knowledge, because knowledge often is interpreted to be equivalent to power that nobody wants to give away. Moreover, intraorganizational communication deficits do often prevent employees to effectively interact in the sense of knowledge management. Other empirical findings come to the conclusion that also the lack of time is often playing an important role why knowledge management is not carried out in the whole company (see Bullinger, 1997). Another important reason not to share knowledge is the ignorance of one's own needs for knowledge and also of the needs of colleagues.

Against this background, appropriate incentive systems should be created for knowledge provision and exchange. In the special literature on knowledge management mainly Probst, Raub and Romhardt (1999) repeatedly insist on the necessity of incentive systems for knowledge management: "For the successful sharing and distribution of their knowledge the staff must be motivated by adequate incentive systems to make their relevant knowledge available for and exchange it with others voluntarily" (p. 134).

Incentive Systems and Motivation

Incentive systems can generally be described as the sum of all with each other coordinated incentives which on the one hand side produce or reinforce desired behaviors of employees and on the other hand side reduce the likelihood that undesirable behaviors occur (see Grant, 1999). The term *incentive* is understood as a situational condition which can motivate members of companies because of their individual structure of needs with regard to a certain performance level of behavior within the context of an organization (cf., von Rosenstiel, 1987, p. 320). Incentives activate *motives* (= readiness to behave in a particular way; see Hackman and Oldham, 1980) and have a "stimulative nature" as they influence employees to take certain actions as intended by the organization (see von Rosenstiel, 1999). The benefit of the work done by an employee must at least reach the niveau of the incentives, for instance in terms of wages/salaries, or even extend it (see Becker ,1990). The following Figure 1 shows the effects of an incentive on the motivation:

According to the sort and source of satisfaction of one's needs we differ between *extrinsic* and *intrinsic incentives* which aim at extrinsic or intrinsic *motives* (see Deci, 1971; Lepper and Greene, 1978). First and foremost, the

Figure 1: The effects of an incentive on the motivation (cf. Comellie/von Rosenstiel 1995, p. 8)

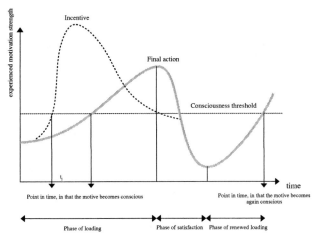

prospect of remuneration aims at *extrinsic motives*. Here the incentive for carrying out the performance is not inherent in the job but lies in the monetary effects. In addition, also status aims at the group of extrinsic incentives because it is visible to other colleagues, for example. In the case of *intrinsic incentives* the satisfaction of one's needs immediately evolves from carrying out the performance itself. This gives a particular feeling of challenge and satisfaction. Intrinsic incentives cannot be related to quantifiable rewards to the same degree as extrinsic incentives that can be expressed through a definite amount of money or status symbols and are thereby comparable.

We also differ between *material* and *immaterial incentives* according to the sort of the object of the incentives. The monetary remuneration (for the job) is deemed a *material incentive*. It constitutes a reward for the company members having performed her/his duties as she/he was asked to. The size of the reward indirectly contributes to the satisfaction of needs in view of status-power and determines the position of the staff member in the organization.

On the contrary, *immaterial incentives* express themselves in the conditions for carrying out the performance and have no immediate monetary effects. Examples for immaterial incentives are: satisfying contents of the job, participation in the decision-making process, open management style and career prospects. Since material incentives are usually limited through the salary-level and the likes the importance of immaterial elements is growing ever faster. For example in the business consulting industry, the immaterial incentives include the private use of mobile phones, lap tops, company cars for the office staff as well, private access to the Internet, possibilities for childcare or flexible working-hours, too.

Figure 2: Classification of incentives and motives

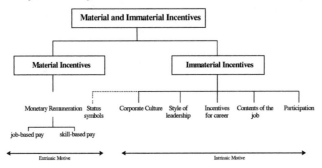

In correspondence with the differentiation between intrinsic and extrinsic motives as well as material and immaterial incentives it is possible to classify the sorts of incentives as follows (see Figure 2):

RESEARCH QUESTIONS

Generally, business consulting companies belong to the group of so-called "knowledge-intensive firms" (see Starbuck, 1992; Alvesson, 1995) and are therefore best suited for a study on knowledge management (see also Mentzas and Apostolou, 1998; Werr, 1998). Their main product is knowledge in form of methods and procedures and problem solutions, so that their customers finally shall become able to take action (see Senge, 1994) in a better way than they did before the consultation. Knowledge is the main production factor in business consulting companies (see Hansen et al., 1999). In addition to that, most consulting companies sell "knowledge management" as a consulting product, and finally, at least all leading consulting companies have already implemented knowledge management in their own businesses for a couple of years, i. e., they represent one of the industries with the longest experience with knowledge management.

Against this background the paper seeks to answer the following questions:
(1) First, do incentive systems play a dominant role for knowledge management to support above all the functions of knowledge sharing and use in the management consulting industry?

Since the success of management consulting companies more or less completely relies on knowledge, and the problems mentioned further above in terms of knowledge-transfer barriers can also occur in the business consulting industry, we expected that incentive systems do play an important role for knowledge management in the investigated management consulting companies.

(2) Second, is there a need for special incentive systems for knowledge management?

Due to the experience of the consulting industry with knowledge management we also expected that these companies will have such systems in place which are especially designed for the purposes of knowledge management (see also von Krogh 1998).

(3) Third, which kind of incentives are given for knowledge management to induce the consultants on the one hand to share their knowledge and experiences with their colleagues and on the other hand to use existing knowledge of other colleagues or third-parties to make their own work more efficient and effective?

Finally, since knowledge is tangible (see Stewart, 1997; Sveiby, 1997) we expected that the existing, mainly material oriented incentives will have been more or less replaced or at least complemented by non-classical, immaterial incentive systems especially designed for knowledge management (see also Grant, 1999).

DATA BASE AND METHODOLOGICAL APPROACH

The industry we investigated is the business consulting industry. In 1999, we interviewed 10 knowledge managers who had been consultants before out of the 20 leading consulting companies in Germany. Most of these companies are global players, that is, our findings are also representative for the consulting industry on the whole to a certain extent.

From a methodological point of view we chose a qualitative research design (see Rouse and Daellenbach, 1999; see also Venkatraman and Grant, 1986). In-depth interviews, on the basis of a semi-structured questionnaires with responsible knowledge managers of the consulting companies were carried out after the knowledge managers had already answered the questions in brief outlines in writing about four weeks before the personal interviews. The interviews had been transcribed and the most important findings were structured as synopses and visualized via mind maps following a qualitative content analysis. The use of more than one research instrument, also called "triangulation", allowed to open diverse perspectives on the object of investigation, provided more information supporting the elaborated findings, made cross controls possible, and altogether offered more empirical substance than an isolated use of only one single instrument (see Glaser/ Strauss, 1967).

FINDINGS

Against the background of the theoretical argumentation and methodological procedure as described before the most important findings of our study are as follows:

First of all and in correspondence with the assumptions in the literature *incentive systems do (!) play an important role* in this knowledge driven industry. This was confirmed by all interviewed knowledge managers. These systems are seen as an important instrument to bind the employees with the company and to motivate them for the desired outputs. Performance evaluation as the bases for the assessment of the consultants' careers is done once or twice a year, on average within the employee evaluations. The criterion is chargeability (in terms of hours which have been charged to customers) and also the fulfillment of the objectives agreed upon at the beginning of each year.

However secondly, there are *almost no incentive systems with a special focus on the issue of knowledge.* 40 percent of the interviewed knowledge managers even said that incentive systems do not play an important role for knowledge management. The remaining 60 percent said that they are aware of the importance of knowledge aspects against the background of incentive systems and that they will try to integrate them. They do see a need for special incentive systems for knowledge management, for example in order to intensify cooperative work with the objective to share existing knowledge resources more effectively and efficiently, but have not operationalized or implemented them, yet.

The use and sharing of knowledge slip in the performance evaluation of the consultants mentioned above. In most of the companies the performance evaluations are used to calculate the variable parts of the salary and – as already said – for career perspectives. Some interview partners made clear that the existing traditional incentive systems with their monetary effects (see below) somehow implicitly guarantee respective behavior of the consultants.

Thirdly and finally, in contrast to our expectations and most of the recommendations in the praxis-oriented and theoretical literature for knowledge management (see Nakra, 2000) *the dominant incentives were not immaterial but still based on material remuneration (including fix and variable parts of the salary, stock options, premiums;* see also Holmstrom and Milgrom, 1994*) and status symbols* for the employees, like cars, mobile phones, and special trips to interesting conference destinations for example. These status symbols, however and also the monetary incentives are normal in the business consulting industry and therefore loose in importance in view of incentives for additional outputs.

Only 30 percent of the consulting companies said that immaterial incentives do play an important role after explicitly asking them. One can assume that potential incentives in the areas of e. g. leadership style, corporate culture or education and training exist but that they are not recognized as additional incentives.

CONCLUSION AND FURTHER RESEARCH NEEDS

During our investigation a contradiction became obvious: the interviewed knowledge managers are aware of the need for specific knowledge management-oriented incentive systems, but they also are not able or do not see any need to develop and implement corresponding new incentive systems at the moment. The latter has to be understood against the background of the successful consulting services the interviewed companies are able to offer. The return conclusion of successful consulting services seems to be successful knowledge management on the basis of sufficient incentive systems. This leads to the hypothesis that companies which are in knowledge-intensive industries and are successful have developed a "culture of immaterial incentives and intrinsic motivation" (see Nakra, 2000) which supports the automatic sharing and use of knowledge. Normatively reformulated: The more a company is knowledge-intensive, the more it has to try to change the culture in a direction which supports intrinsic motivation to share knowledge against the background of immaterial incentives. The less a company is knowledge-intensive, the more it has to focus on material incentives and on status symbols in order to extrinsically motivate knowledge exchange and use. In the latter case remuneration not only should follow according to the features of personal performance of the company members but also with regard to their participation in processes relevant to knowledge management, for example. Furthermore, the incentives of remuneration could be linked to the extent of knowledge exchange, measured by the number and quality of contributions in terms of documents, lectures, or publications, for instance. Altogether, further research is necessary in order to place this hypotheses on a more profound empirical basis.

REFERENCES

Alvesson, M. (1995). *Management of Knowledge-Intensive Companies*. Berlin, New York 1995.

Bain, J. S. (1968). *Industrial Organization* (2nd Ed.), New York.

Barney, J. B. (1991). Firm Resources and Sustained Competitive Advantage. In *Journal of Management*, 17(1), pp. 99-120.

Bullinger, H. J., Wörner, K., and Prieto, J. (1997). Wissensmanagement heute: Daten, Fakten, Trends. Stuttgart.

Collis, D. J. and Montgomery, C. A. (1995). Competing on Resources: Strategy in the 90s. In *Harvard Business Review*, 73(4), pp. 118-128.

Collis, D. J. and Montgomery, C. A. (1998). *Corporate Strategy: A Resource Based Approach*. Boston, MA.

Comelli, G. and von Rosenstiehl, L. (1995). Führung durch Motivation: Mitarbeiter für Organisationsziele gewinnen. München.

Davenport, T. H. and Prusak, L. (1997). *Working Knowledge: How Organizations Manage What They Know*. Boston, MA.

Deci, E. L. (1971). The Effect of Externally Medicated Rewards on Intrinsic Motivation. In *Journal of Personality and Social Psychology*, 18(2), pp. 105-115.

Drucker, P. F. (1993). *Post-Capitalist Society*. Oxford.

Glaser, B. G. and Strauss, A. L. (1967). *The Discovery of Grounded Theory*. Chicago.

Grant, P. C. (1991). The Resource-Based Theory of Competitive Advantage: Implications for Strategy Formulation. In *California Management Review*, 33(1), pp. 114-135.

Grant, P. C. (1999). New Perspectives on Incentive System Design: Integrating the Theory of the Firm and the Theory of Individual Behavior. In *The Journal of Psychology*, 133(4), pp. 456-464.

Grant, R. M. (1996). Toward a Knowledge Based Theory of the Firm. In *Strategic Management Journal*, 17, Special Issue Winter, pp. 109-122.

Hackman, J. R. and Oldham, G. R. (1980). *Work Redesign*. Reading, MA.

Hamel, G. and Heene, A. (1994) (Eds.). *Competence-based Competition*. Chichester.

Hansen, M. T., Nohria, N., and Tierney, T. (1999). What's your Strategy for Managing Knowledge? In *Harvard Business Review*, 77(2), pp. 106-116.

Holmstrom, B. and Milgrom, P. (1994). The Firm As an Incentive System. In *American Economic Review*, 84(4), pp. 972-991.

Kogut, B. and Zander, U. (1993). Knowledge of the Firm and the Evolutionary Theory of the Multinational Corporation. In *Journal of International Business Studies*. Fourth Quarter, pp. 625-645.

Kumar, K. (1995). *From Post-Industrial to Post-Modern Society: New Theories of the Contemporary World*. Oxford.

Lepper, M. R. and Greene, Ch. N. (1978). *The Hidden Costs of Rewards*. Hillside/NJ.

Mentzas, G. and Apostolou, D. (1998). Managing Corporate Knowledge: A Comparative Analysis of Experiences in Consulting Firms. In Reimer, U. (Ed.), *PAKM 98, Practical Aspects of Knowledge Management, Proceedings of the Second International Conference*, October 29-30, 1998, Basel.

Nakra, P. (2000). Knowledge Management: The Magic Is in the Culture. In *Competitive Intelligence Review – Journal of Knowledge Management and Insight*, 11(2), pp. 53-60.

Nonaka, I. and Takeuchi, H. (1995). *The Knowledge-Creating Company: How Japanese Companies Create the Dynamics of Innovation*. New York: Oxford.

Oliveira Jr., M. (1998). Core Competencies and the Knowledge of the Firm. Paper presented at the *1998 Strategic Management Society International Annual Conference*, Orlando-Florida, November.

Penrose, E. T. (1959). *The Theory of the Growth of the Firm*. New York.

Porter, M. E. (1981). Contributions of Industrial Organization to Strategic Management. In *Academy of Management Review*, 6(4), pp. 609-620.

Porter, M. E. (1998a). *Competitive Advantage: Creating and Sustaining Superior Advantage* (2nd Ed.), New York.

Porter, M. E. (1998b). *Competitive Strategy: Techniques for Analyzing Industries and Competitors* (2nd Ed.), New York.

Prahalat, C. K. and Hamel, G. (1990). The Core Competence of the Corporation. In *Harvard Business Review*, 68(3), pp. 79-93.

Probst, G. and Romhardt, J. (1997). Building Blocks of Knowledge Management: A Practical Approach. Research Paper, HEC, Université de Genève, Genève.

Probst, G., Romhardt, K., and Raub, S. (1999). *Managing Knowledge.* Chichester, UK.

Rouse, M. J. and Daellenbach, U. S. (1999). Rethinking Research Methods for the Resource-Based Perspective: Isolating Sources of Sustainable Competitive Advantage. In *Strategic Management Journal*, 20(5), pp. 487-494.

Selznik, P (1957). *Leadership in Administration*. New York, Tokyo.

Senge, P. (1994). *The Fifth Discipline : The Art and Practice of the Learning Organization*, New York.

Spender, J. C. and Grant, R. M. (1996). Knowledge and the Firm: Overview. In *Strategic Management Journal*, 17, Special Winter Issue, pp. 5-9.

Starbuck, W. H. (1992). Learning by Knowledge-Intensive Firms. In *Journal of Management Studies*, 29(6), pp. 713-740.

Stewart, T. A. (1997). *Intellectual Capital: The New Wealth of Organizations*. Doubleday Books.

Sveiby, K. E. (1997). *The New Organizations Wealth: Managing Knowledge-Based Assets*, San Francisco, CA.

Venkatraman, N. and Grant, J. (1986). Construct Measurement in Organizational Strategy Research: A Critique and Proposal. In *Academy of Management Review*, 11(1), pp. 71-87.

Von Krogh, G. (1998). Care in Knowledge Creation. In *California Management Review*, 40(3), pp. 133-153.

Von Rosenstiehl, L. (1987). Grundlagen der Organisationspsychologie. Stuttgart.

Von Rosenstiehl, L. (1999). Motivationale Grundlagen von Anreizsystemen. In Bühler, W. and Siegert, T. (eds.), Unternehmenssteuerung und Anreizsysteme, Stuttgart, pp. 25-55.

Wernerfelt, B. (1984). A Resource-Based View of the Firm. In *Strategic Management Journal*, 5(2), pp. 171-180.

Werr, A. (1998). Managing Knowledge in Management Consulting. Working Paper, Ref. No.: 105403, Stockholm School of Economics, submitted to the 1998 Academy of Management Meeting, Best Paper, Stockholm.

Chapter 26

The Information Laws

Andrew S. Targowski
Western Michigan University, USA

INTRODUCTION

Mankind progresses in proportion to its wisdom which has roots in practice, acquired skills, available data & information, concepts and knowledge. To be wise, humankind needs to be informed and knowledgeable, otherwise will not survive own failures. Progress in knowledge was painfully slow as long as the racial memory was transmitted only by oral tradition. With the invention of writing and books the process of knowledge discovery and dissemination has been accelerated. Today, computers and their networks speed up that process far beyond our imagination. In 2000's the Information Wave significantly controls the Agricultural and Industrial Waves through millions of computers. IT supports decision-making based on knowledge-oriented systems such as "data mining" that, for example, discovers knowledge about customers, organizational dynamics, and so forth to achieve competitive advantage.

Information and knowledge become the strategic resource as engineering science was in the Industrial Wave. However, the discovery of human cognition potential must be guided by knowledge *s c i e n c e*, which just emerges. One of signs of any science is its set of scientific data, universal rules, laws, and systems of rules and laws. Hence, this paper offers the first attempt to develop main laws of information that should increase our awareness about the Information Wave which is a new stage of civilization's dynamics that is taking place at the beginning of the 3rd Millennium. The chapter also provides the framework for the analysis of the human capital from the information perspective. This set of considerations reflects a new emerging approach which I call macro-information ecology.

Previously Published in *Managing Information Technology in a Global Economy* edited by Mehdi Khosrow-Pour, Copyright © 2001, Idea Group Publishing.

MACRO-INFORMATION ECOLOGY

Macro-information ecology is based on the premise that the growth rate in the new information (knowledge) discovery is the key determinant of macroeconomic activities in the service-industrial-global economy (so called the new economy). This new emerging school of macroeconomics can be called knowledgism.

Macro-information ecology is the study of information (cognition) as a whole and it is concerned with *aggregates* across nations and markets. Macro-information ecology studies the behaviour of society and economy (nationally and globally) — wide measures, such as:

- the value of human capital,
- the potential efficiency of human capital,
- knowledge output,
- economy output driven by knowledge in a given period, and so forth.
- It also studies measures derived from many individual nations:
    - markets such as the price of human capital or
    - the total structure of employed workers by such categories as production workers, in-person service workers, and information workers.

Another interesting facet of this new emerging discipline is the qualitative analysis of civilisation paradigm shifts and the application of civilization tools as a result of increased cognition about us.

To control national output with the development of a global economy, knowledgists stress the need to control the growth of new knowledge discovery. Given the "long and variable lags" of knowledge and information policies and the difficulty in forecasting future economic events (such as recession), knowledgists question the ability of industrial or service-oriented macroeconomics to implement the "correct" economic policy.

The knowledge approach suggests that direct government intervention within the economic system should be guided by the "predicted history of the futures." The knowledge policy is the key to this intervention; in this sense, the knowledge policy is closer to Keynesian interventionists than to "conservative" monetarists.

The supply and demand of information (knowledge) is the most basic model of information ecology (IE). However, prior to this model, we have to examine the stages of the information reservoir development. Figure 1 illustrates this process.

Based on the information reservoir's (IR) dynamics the general information laws will be defined in the following section.

Figure 1: Stage III New Chaos and Complexity

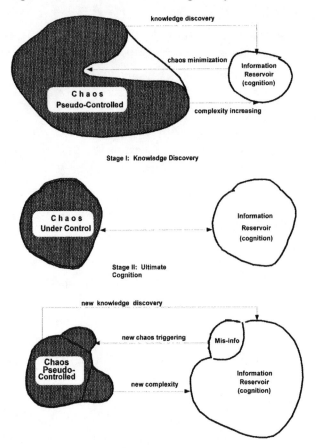

GENERAL INFORMATION LAWS

At the stage of knowledge discovery, the information reservoir (IR) minimizes or tries to "control" the chaos. Every increase in new information also increases a level of complexity of understanding. Based on the analysis of knowledge dynamics provided by Wojciechowski (1989), one can define the following laws of information:

Law I: The complexity of the ecosystem (man, material, information, and nature) is proportional to the level of the existing information reservoir. The complexity is the state of a system whose components and relationships co-evolve through an enormous number of interconnections, creating dynamic structures either chaotic or orderly. The more information we have at our disposal, the more complex the ecosystem is perceived to be. The more we know, the less we understand. The founders of the Santa Fe Institute, which explores the new science of complexity, investigates such questions as why ancient ecosystems often remained stable for millions of years, only to vanish in a geological instant—

and what such events have to do with the sudden collapse of Soviet Communism in the late 1980s.

Law II: Information generates consequences, which it cannot foresee. One of the forms of information is knowledge, e.g., such as atomic physics. Atomic physics produced rules and techniques that allowed man to build the atomic bomb. The consequence was the tragedy that befell thousands of Japanese who lost their lives or, at the very least, their health in 1945. On the other hand, the Cold War, sustained by the balance of atomic weaponry, was practically bloodless. Should science stop research on atomic physics or gene engineering because consequences can get out of control? Or, being under control, can said research produce positive results, such as the Cold War, which eliminated another Bloody War?

Law III: The precision and certitude of information is proportional to the simplicity of the object of information or inversely proportional to the complexity of the object. Relatively simple material objects can be described by relatively simple information in natural science. On the other hand, complex social phenomenon requires complex description; this is sometimes contradictory if description is provided by more than one observer. For example, in the 1991 Persian Gulf War, there was a question among the Allied forces about whether to go to Baghdad and seek the surrender of the Iraqi military regime. Almost every observer of this war had his or her own answer (information) to this question.

Law IV: The progress of the Information Wave generates relative ignorance and interdependence among people and globalizes humanity. The advancement of mediated information requires information skills to access information infrastructure, systems, and services. People without this access are becoming more ignorant than those who can retrieve and apply required information anytime and anywhere in the synchronism of events. The information poor are becoming more dependent on the information rich; the latter are motivated to globally seek more useful information to become even richer. A college professor or a graduate who know end-user computing have more chances to increase their material well-being than those who do know how to apply computers to gather and process important information and are ignorant about possible opportunities for them. Even a well-being business person who is ignorant about information technology may loose its resources or at least not to increase them if he/she does not know how to transform his/her business from *brick 'n mortar* to *brick 'n click* format.

At Stage II — Ultimate cognition, the amount of information is equal to the amount of chaos. From mankind's point of view, the equilibrium in macroecology never happens since the amount of time in which such equilibrium can be attained is infinite; in such disciplines as business management, perhaps, one can achieve short-term equilibrium. Therefore, the next law can be defined:

Law V: The information reservoir has no saturation point. Since the ecosystem is imperfect and still developing, the information about it has not become definite. What was right in the 19th century is revised in the 20th century, and what is right in the 20th century, perhaps, will be redefined in the 21st century, and so forth. Examples of Newtonian physics critique or post-modernism's challenge of "scientific truth" provide data, which prove this law in the 20th century. Each new discovery not only decreases the chaos; it also increases the confusion about the new directions and, *eo ipso*, requires more information to improve understanding.

Stage III — When the capacity of the information reservoir should exceed the capacity of chaos, new chaos and complexity is created by misinformation, which begins to penetrate the IR. It is only an assumption since, according to Law V, such a situation should not happen.

MACRO-INFORMATION ECOLOGY MODEL

The macro-ecology of the information equilibrium model (Figure 2) indicates that civilization, most of the time, operates in darkness. The mathematical model of the information reservoir is as follows:

Stage I: $I < E$

where: I = Information Reservoir capacity
E = Entropy, a measure of chaos
D = Darkness (or net entropy E-I)

The macroecology goal is D_t 0 and the task is to determine the elasticity of the increased entropy or information and how a user or organization responds to changes (+, -) caused either by the increase of information reservoir or by its "enemy"—entropy.

$$D(E_t) = f(I_{Mt}, C_t) \quad \text{or} \quad D(I_t) = f(E_t, C_t)$$

where: $I_{M = \text{Misinformation}}$
C = Complexity

Figure 2: Macroecology of Information

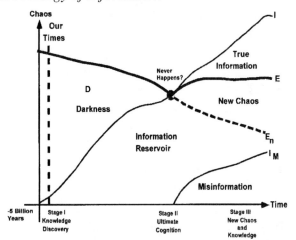

The elasticity of information is a measure of the sensitivity or responsiveness of the information value demanded to create changes in price, revenue, unemployment, and in other factors of the Information Wave. Information elasticity will be one of the major indexes of the emerging Information Wave.

Macro-information ecology is also interested in the creation of **human capital** as a medium of knowledge generation and application. Particularly, a relation between human capital and economic development is a strategic inquiry of IE.

The mechanism of the material civilization in modern capitalistic theory was built on the rule that market growth triggers the specialization of human capital and the growth of its income as well as its level of living. In the Information Wave, the situation is different. The new motoric forces of economy can express the following law of the human capital.

INFORMATION LAW OF HUMAN CAPITAL

Law VI: The human capital's growth in knowledge generates specialization and productivity and sustains the growth of income.

As Kevin Murphy[1] noticed that the old sequence in economic development in the Industrial Wave:

- (old) material sequence: **market growth - specialization - more income** transforms in the Information Wave into a new sequence in economic development:
- (new) early information sequence: **knowledge growth - specialization - more income**

The new sequence is true as long as the specialization of human capital sustains the increase of productivity in the material sector or in the information sector.

The necessary co-ordination of specialists, particularly those in the information sector, may consume the new "speed" of knowledge and not only contribute to the economic growth, but misguide it.

The most important question, however, is whether or not we should apply new knowledge to promote economic development by growth or whether we should just apply that knowledge's message, which says that zero growth is wiser and the only appropriate policy to achieve a sustainable society and economy.

There is a ruthless trend that is occurring in the American human capitalist system in the 1990s. It is implemented in the name of restructuring and trimming corporate "fat" as a "surplus" of human capital. American human capital is being downsized and atomized; as the Scottish farmers were torn away from their soil, millions of Americans are being evicted from the working worlds that have sustained them, the jobs that gave them not only wages, health care, and pensions, but also a context, a sense of self-worth, a kind of identity. Work was the tribe: there were IBM reps, Sera's men, GM workers, and Anheuser-Busch people. There are still, of course, but their world has changed.

The early Information Wave, controlled only by corporate profit, deconstructed the work force of America and other developed countries. In a time of surreal transition, America is working without a social contract or with one, which has been deeply violated.

In the industrial civilization, Americans practised long-term marriages, careers through apprenticeship, promotions, success, and retirement; getting fired was a disgrace. That epoch has passed. America has now entered the age of the contingent or temporary worker, of the consultant or subcontractor, of just-in-time human capital — fluid, flexible, and, worst of all, disposable. Is this really the future?

If the Information Wave is to work without knowledge and information policies, the work force of the future will constantly have to sell its skills and invent new relationships with employers, who must themselves change and adapt constantly in order to survive in a ruthless global market.

This is the new metaphysics of work. Companies are portable, workers are throwaway. The rise of the Information Wave means a shift, in less than 20 years, from the overbuilt systems of large, slow-moving economic units to an array of small, widely-dispersed networked economic centers. In the early stages of the Information Wave, highways are becoming electronic: even Wall Street has no reason to be in Manhattan anymore. Companies become virtual, based on a networked concept and their dematerialization, and strangely conscienceless. In 1988, contingent workers were about a quarter of the labor force; by 2000, they are expected to make up half of it.

The Industrial Revolution was inevitable, even as the Luddites howled and broke the machines. There are some solid economic reasons for a current restructuring of the American work force (for example low productivity due to over staffed companies), but the human capital costs are enormous. Profound betrayal of the American dynamic itself (work hard, obey the rules, succeed) runs through this process like a computer virus.

There may be an analogy that applies to this betrayal in the way that the U.S. fought the war in Vietnam. Robert McNamara's Pentagon became intoxicated by computer efficiency and pseudo-precision and began sending soldiers off to war alone instead of in cohesive units — the confused young soldiers, like temporary workers, were dispatched to a 365-day jungle job and then sent home alone. Thus vanished *esprit de corps*, team spirit, and the intangibles that are indispensable to winning. An economy that becomes addicted to treating its workers like interchangeable, disposable grunts may find itself with as little success as America found in Vietnam (McWhirter 1993).

The uncontrolled development of the Information Wave may lead to another economic sequence:

* further information sequence: **knowledge growth - specialization - collapse of economy (?)**

This sequence produces an economy that is too specialized and productive, requiring a small work force without the means to create a demand for economic output. In current practice, robots and computers do not pay taxes.

Information ecology has to include a human dimension of the Information Wave in its inquiry. Better knowledge should provide a better level of living, not inspire self-destruction and limit progress to technology alone. Technology is not neutral; the new knowledge should define telematic technology as a tool of honorable and sustainable living. This is possible if we consider the Electronic Global Village as a tool of information and knowledge creation and distribution (bottom-up and top-down), and as a globally interconnected aware tribe.

The steered Information Wave should offer the following sequence of events:

* expected information sequence: **knowledge growth - solutions - sustainable economy**

If "human capital" becomes wise enough, this sequence should probably be implemented in the 21st century. Otherwise, population and ecological bombs (about 2050) will return us to the beginning stages of the history of mankind.

HUMAN CAPITAL DEVELOPMENT

Human capital in the 21st century will become the most important economic resource. This is a medium, which generates and applies knowledge. Its architecture of "organs" is depicted on Figure 3.

Figure 3: Human Capital in Developmental Stages

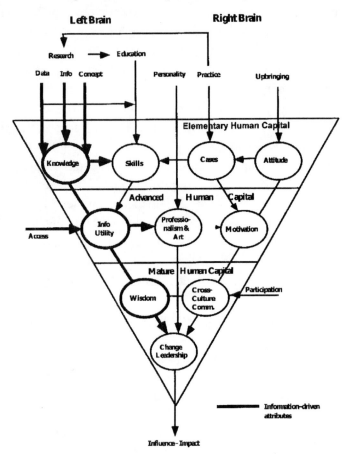

In post-modern notation, the architecture contains the left brain and right brain attributes, which determine the value of human capital. Human capital develops in three stages:

Stage I:Elementary Human Capital:
Knowledge, Skills, Cases, Attitude

Stage II: Advanced Human Capital:
Info Utility Access, Professionalism
and Artistry, Motivation

Stage III: Mature Human Capital:
Wisdom, Cross-culture communication,
Change, Leadership

Figure 4: The Value Space of Human Capital

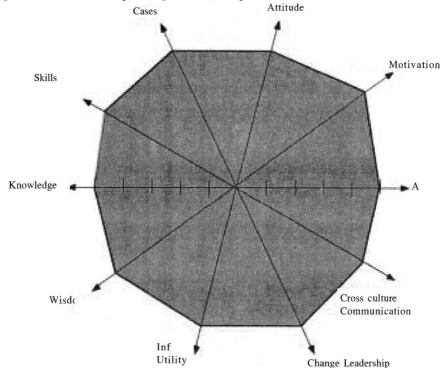

Only four attributes are information-driven: knowledge, skills, information utility access, and wisdom. This means that the development of human capital cannot be limited only to issues of information. The process of socialization plays a very important role in the estimation of human capital values; this process is culture-driven.

The measurement of human capital value can be done through the estimation of the value space of work force (macroecology) or through a given person (microecology). Figure 4 illustrates the value space of human capital.

Each attribute (A) can be measured on the five-point scale. A sum total of all attribute points provides a value of given human capital (V). This is a comparative unit of human capital value. It can be applied in comparisons of economies, organizations, or persons. It can also be applied in the analysis of human capital efficiency potential.

CONCLUSION

Macro-information ecology is just emerging, along with the development of Information Wave practice, and research should turn their attention into the application of the information laws and their further discovery and corrections in the analysis and design of values and tools of the Information Wave and civilization in general.

NOTE
[1] During his public lecture at Western Michigan University, (13-12-1992).

REFERENCES

Badaracco, Jr., J. L. (1991). *The Knowledge Link*. Boston: Harvard Business School Press.

Beach, L. R., Mitchell, T. R., Daeton, M. D., and Prothero (1997). Information Relevance, Content, and Source Credibility in the Revision of Opinions. *Organizational Behavior and Human Performance*, 21, pp. 1-16.

Behm, D., and Peat, F. D. (1978). *Science, Order and Creativity*. New York: Bantam Books.

Bell, D. (1973). *The Coming of the Post-Information Society: A Venture in Social Forecasting*. New York: Basic Books.

Blumenthal, A. L. (1977). *The Process of Cognition*. Englewood Cliffs, NJ: Prentice-Hall, Inc.

Drucker, P. F. M. (1988). The Coming of the New Organization. *Harvard Business Review*, 88(1), January-February, pp. 45-53.

Drucker, P. F. M. (1993). *Post-Capitalist Society*, New York: HarperBusiness.

Ekecrantz, J. (1987). The Sociological Order of the New Information Society. In *The Ideology of the Information Age*. (Eds.) J. D.Slack and F. Fejes. Norwood, NJ: Ablex Publishing Corp.

Gore, A. (1991). Information Superhighways: The Next Information Revolution. *The Futurist*, January-February, pp. 21-23.

Karraker, R. (1988). Highways of Minds. *Whole Earth Review*, Spring, pp. 4-15.

Laszlo, E. (1972). *Introduction to Systems Philosophy*. New York: Harper and Row.

McWhirter, B. (1993). Disposable Workers of America. *Time*, March 29, pp. 41-43.

Nowell, A., Perils, A. and Simon, H. (1987). What is Computer Science? *Science,* (157), pp. 1373-1374.

Parker, E. (1976). Social Implications of Computer/Telecoms Systems." *Telecommunications Policy*, 1, December, pp.3-20.

Porat, M. (1977). *The Information Economy*. Washington, DC: US Office of Telecommunications.

Poster, M. (1990). *The Mode of Information*. Chicago: The University of Chicago Press.

Pricher, W. (1987). Tours Through the Back-Country of Imperfectly Informed

Society. In *The Ideology of the Information Age* (Eds.) J. D. Slack and F. Fejes. Norwood,NJ: Ablex Publishing Corp.

Sakaiya, T. (1991). *The Knowledge-value Revolution*. New York: Kodansha International.

Shannon, C. E. (1948). A Mathematical Theory of Communication. *Bell Systems Tech Journal*, (3-4).

Targowski, A. (1999). *Enterprise Information Infrastructure*, Hershey, PA.: Idea Publishing Group

Toffler, A. (1980). *The Third Wave*. New York: Bantam Books.

Wojciechowski, J. (1989). Progress of Knowledge and Right-Left Dichotomy: Are Existing Ideologies Adequate? *Man & Development*, XI, (1), March.

Van Doren, C. (1991). *A History Of Knowledge*. New York: Ballantine Books.

Chapter 27

Supporting Organizational Knowledge Management with Agents

Prashant Pai, L.L. Miller, Vasant Honavar and Johnny Wong
Iowa State University, Ames, USA

Sree Nilakanta
Iowa State University, Ames, USA

Organizations are looking at ways to manage their information resources. Both the capture and the use of data created by the organization have come under scrutiny. Part of the concern comes from their desire to enhance the business process and part comes from the explosion of data available to any organization. In this context, the role of committees is being examined both as consumers and producers of information. The present work is focused on making the vast amount of unstructured text more useful to committees. An agent environment has been designed and implemented.

INTRODUCTION

Knowledge is rapidly becoming a key organizational resource and determinant of organizational performance and competitiveness. Consequently, knowledge management is a process that organizations employ to improve performance. Knowledge management, however, is best described as a concept that explains how information is transformed into actionable knowledge and made available to users. Knowledge management enables businesses to avoid repeating past mistakes, to assure the reuse of best practices, and draw on the collective wisdom of its employees past and present. Knowledge management thus relies on gathering,

Previously Published in *Challenges of Information Technology Management in the 21st Century* edited by Mehdi Khosrow-Pour, Copyright © 2000, Idea Group Publishing.

organizing, refining, and disseminating information and knowledge. Knowledge is often embedded in an organization in the form of experiences or memory.

Recent developments in information processing technologies have enhanced our abilities in building knowledge management systems. Knowledge is organized through searching, filtering, cataloging, and linking of information collected from a variety of sources and media. Information is refined in multiple ways and disseminated to recipients as reports, analyses, etc. While many vendors sell products meeting one or more features ascribed above, the lack of ability to apply many of these and other related technologies to complex knowledge such as that contained in prior decisions (including the decision making process) and other forms of organizational knowledge is a problem. In this paper we present a model for organizational knowledge management and discuss through the example of committee memory the integration of different technologies. We also present the design and development of the knowledge management system.

Organizational Memory

Organizational memory has been described to refer to corporate knowledge that is representing prior experiences and are saved and shared by users. It may be used to support decision making in multiple task and multiple user environments. The concept encompasses technical, functional, and social aspects of the work, the worker, and the workplace (Durstewitz, 1994). Organizational memory includes stored records (e.g., corporate manuals, databases, filing systems, etc.) (Ackerman, 1996) and tacit knowledge (e.g., experience, intuition, beliefs) (Nonaka and Takeuchi, 1995a, 1995b). Walsh and Ungson (1991) refer to organizational memory as stored information from an organization's history that can be brought to bear on present decisions. By their definition, organizational memory provides information that reduces transaction costs, contributes to effective and efficient decision-making, and is a basis for power within organizations. Researchers and practitioners recognize organizational memory as an important factor in the success of an organization's operations and its responsiveness to the changes and challenges of its environment (e.g., Stein, 1995; Chen et. al., 1994; Huber, 1991, Angus, Patel and Harty, 1998).

Information technologies (IT) contribute to the possibility of automated organizational knowledge management systems in two ways, either by making recorded knowledge retrievable or by making individuals with knowledge accessible (Ackerman, 1996). An organization's knowledge, explicitly dispersed through a variety of retention facilities (e.g., network servers, distributed databases, Intranets, etc.) can make the knowledge more accessible to its members. Stein and Zwass (1995) suggest that an extensive record of processes ("through what sequence of events?"), rationale ("why?"), context ("under what circumstances?"), and outcomes ("how well did it work?") can be maintained with the help of IT. The availability of advanced information technologies increases the communicating and decision making options for potential users.

An organizational memory supported by information technology provides several advantages The contents that are stored in information systems are explicit, can be modified promptly, shared as necessary, and changes can be propagated quickly and easily. Information systems should be however be designed to augment the interaction between knowledge seekers and information providers as it would lead to higher levels of organizational effectiveness and learning (Huber et al, 1998). Technological changes and shifting demands make rapid learning essential in organizations. The advent and increasingly wide utilization of wide area network tools such as the Internet and World Wide Web provide access to greater and richer sources of information. Local area networks and Intranets give organizations a way to store and access organization specific memory and knowledge. Used effectively, these tools support the notion of organizational memory.

Sandoe et. al.(1998) uses Giddens' (1984) definition of organizational memory to distinguish among three types of memory, namely discursive, practical and reflexive. Discursive memory is a collection of stories, anecdotes, reports, and other public accounts. Practical memory is the unarticulated know-how—the skills and practices that comprise the bulk of routine interactivity. Memory that is automatically invoked in organizations without any requirements for conscious thought or discussion such as organizational norms is considered reflexive. Sandoe et al (1998) argues that there is a continuum of characteristics that stretches between discursive memory on one end and reflexive memory on the other. Discursive memories are oriented to be flexible while reflexive memories are focused on yielding efficient memory use. Organizations have to balance the need for flexibility against the need for efficiency.

Sandoe et al (1998) treats IT based organizational memory as discursive. They argue that although IT-based memory operates at a discursive level, IT makes the discursive process of remembering more efficient by reducing the costs and effort associated with storage of and access to an organization's memory. IT changes the balancing point in the trade-off between efficiency and flexibility, permitting organizations to be relatively more efficient for a given level of flexibility. Another advantage of IT-based memory is the opportunity to provide a historical narrative (or rationale) for significant organizational events that would otherwise be remembered in non-discursive form. Reliance on IT-based memory, on the other hand, allows an organization to act in a rational manner through the discursive access to its major historical events and transformations.

Organizational Memory Systems (OMS)

Mandiwalla et al (1998) defines an organizational memory system (OMS) to include_a DBMS, a database that can represent more than transactional data, and an application than runs on top of the DBMS. They further describe the generic requirements of an OMS to include different types of memory, including how to represent, capture, and use organizational memory. The table shown below lists these requirements.

Types of memory	Meta data Structured data (records) Semistructured data (documents) Unstructured data (audio/video) Temporal data
Types of representation	Structure and internal organization of data the representation of data in the user interface
Capture schemes	Transparent versus assisted Hidden versus open
Use	Time and Space considerations Activity driven Coordination needs Boundaries including security

OMS Design Issues

Designing the ideal OMS is a difficult task, especially as definitions, technologies, and usage contexts continue to shift and evolve. Mandiwalla et al (1998) identified some of the barriers and issues facing designers. Agent based technologies have gained currency in many recent development (see web based search engines like AltaVista and Inktomi). We present an agent based approach to knowledge management in this paper.

MOBILE AGENT BASED COMPUTING PARADIGM

A mobile agent is a named program, which can migrate from one machine to another in a heterogeneous network for remote execution (Gray, 1996). The main features of a mobile agent are autonomy and mobility. Mobile agents are autonomous as they decide when they want to migrate and where. Perhaps, scripts dispatched to a remote language interpreter provide the simplest form of mobile agents. A remote execution mechanism permits an application to dispatch and sequentially execute a script to a remote interpreter. Such scripted agents were popularized by Telescript (GM, 1997), a language to script network agents. Development of mobile agent infrastructures has been an active area of research (GM, 1997; Gray, 1996; Harrison et al., 1997; Li, 1996; OSI, 1997; Rothemel and White, 1997; IBM TRL, 1997).

The mobile agent model has significant advantages over the traditional client/server model in some applications. For example, in the traditional Client/Server paradigm, functionality is associated with servers rigidly at their design time. A client can only invoke a fixed set of predefined services exported by each rigid server. These services remain constant until interfaces are redesigned, and the server is compiled, installed and instantiated anew.

The client and the server communicate with each other with a predefined communication protocol. The client sends a request to the server and a response will be sent back from the server to the client. In order to finish one task, the client and server may have to make many interactions. This may have poor performance and low efficiency in some situations, especially if the network has low bandwidth, long latency, or limited availability

Emerging networked systems often require servers that may be dynamically extended to remote applications. Consider for example, the booking of a vacation over a future network connecting reservation databases of airlines, car-rentals and other companies. These heterogeneous databases are not designed to provide the type of access required to perform arbitrary vacation arrangements. The search process, for example, may require scanning through large database subsets, contacting competing providers and so forth. Executing the search at the end user workstation will require massive transfers of data. Such transfers may be inhibited by the bandwidth constraints, storage limitations, transfer time costs, and data ownership considerations. Compared to this, if the database services could be programmed to perform specific search and transaction services as needed, end users could dispatch mobile agents to the various database sites involved in arranging a vacation. These agents would search, transact locally with service providers and report to the user the results of their computations, thereby improving the performance and saving a lot of server side configurations.

We can also view the mobile agent as an extension of traditional client/server model. Since the mobile agent model is bi-directional, the traditional client/server model can be replaced by this new peer to peer model. Hence, on one hand, a client can send a mobile agent to the server and enhance the server functionality. On the other hand, the server can send a mobile agent to client to provide some services. It has much more flexibility than the two-tier client/server model. Another advantage of mobile agent based computing is that two mobile agents can communicate with each other and gain knowledge from their past computations.

In certain situations, the traditional client/server model may be better. If the interaction between the client and server for a particular service is very minimal and the code for the service is very huge, it does not make sense to transfer the whole computation to the remote site every time the client wants this service. Ideally, we would want these two paradigms to co-exist.

ObjectSpace's Voyager (1997) has been designed to help developers produce high impact distributed systems quickly. Voyager is 100% Java [1997] and designed to use the Java language object model. Voyager allows us to use regular message syntax to construct remote objects, send them messages and move them between programs. The Voyager Object Request Broker (ORB) provides services for mobile objects and autonomous agents. It also provides services for persistence, scaleable group communication, and basic directory services.

Object Request Brokers like CORBA (1997), DCOM (1997) and RMI (1997) support fundamental distributed computing. They allow developers to create remote objects and send them messages as if they were local. They often include features such as distributed garbage collection, different messaging modes, and a naming service. However, none of them support object mobility or mobile, autonomous agents.

Agent platforms like Odyssey (GM, 1997) and Aglets (IBM TRL, 1997) allow developers to create an agent, program it with a set of tasks, and launch it into a network to fulfill its mission. However, they have minimal support for basic distributed computing and treat agents differently than simple objects. Aglets use sockets and Odyssey uses RMI to move agents between machines. But, none of these platforms allow sending a regular Java message to a stationary or moving agent. As a result, it is very difficult for objects to communicate with an agent after the agent has been launched and for agents to communicate directly with other agents.

The unique feature about Voyager is that it is the first platform to seamlessly integrate fundamental distributed computing with agent technology. Voyager supports both mobile objects and autonomous agents. In Voyager's point of view an agent is a special kind of object that can move independently, can continue to execute as it moves, and otherwise behaves like any other object. Voyager enables objects and other agents to send standard Java messages to an agent even as the agent is moving. In addition, Voyager allows us to remotely enable any Java class, even a third party library class, without modifying the class source in any way.

INFORMATION RETRIEVAL AGENT FUNCTIONALITY

We use the vector space model (Korfhage, 1997; Salton, 1989) for representing documents. Documents, queries (and profiles) all are represented by term vectors at retrieval time. The information retrieval (IR) aspects of the IR agents consist of three parts: indexing the documents, weight assignment and retrieval or filtering.

A profile is a list of possibly weighted terms provided by the user that reflects the user's long-term interests and can be used to filter out unwanted documents. Initially, a user profile can be created manually or based on a set of relevant documents. Fitting a profile to a user's interests is a non-trivial task, and may be based on optimization of many parameters. Finding the optimal parameter set for a particular user may require traversal of a large search space (Sorensen, 1992). However, experience with profiles has been shown useful (Korfhage, 1997).

The IR agents use the typical approach to automatic indexing. The agents carry a stop word list to remove low value index terms. The current implementation assumes that the stop lists are topic specific and that the launching software would assure the correct stop list for an agent to successfully complete its task. Porter's stemming algorithm (Porter, 1980) has been incorporated into the agent software to allow us to look at root words. The resulting set of terms is used to represent the documents as bags of weighted terms. During the retrieval phase each document is represented by a list of weighted terms and stored in an inverted file. Based on this inverted file, we will find the similarity between a document and a user's profile or query. The user profile is initially predefined to indicate the user's interest. For agents launched by the user interface, the response to the relevance of the documents will automatically influence the profile for future information requests. Based on the feedback, term weights in the user's profile are changed to reflect the user's actual interests.

We use the Term Frequency Index Document Frequency (TFIDF) approach where each term is weighted $wt(i,j) = tf(i,j) * log(N/df(j))$, where N is the total number of documents in a collection and $tf(i,j)$ and $df(j)$ are term and document frequencies, respectively. To determine the relevance, the IR agents use the standard cosine matching function:

$$cosine(AngleOf(DD, QQ)) = \frac{DD \cdot QQ}{\|DD\| * \|QQ\|}$$

where

$DD \cdot QQ = \Sigma DD[i] * QQ[i];$
$\|DD\| = sqrt(\Sigma DD[i] * DD[i])$ and
$\|QQ\| = sqrt(\Sigma QQ[i] * QQ[i])$ are the norms of document vectors DD and query vector QQ, respectively.

Similarity coefficients are computed between a query or profile and documents and the documents are ranked by these similarity coefficients. The agents use a threshold. Documents whose similarity coefficients exceed the threshold are added to the set of retrieved documents maintained by the agent.

Figure 1: Knowledge Management Model

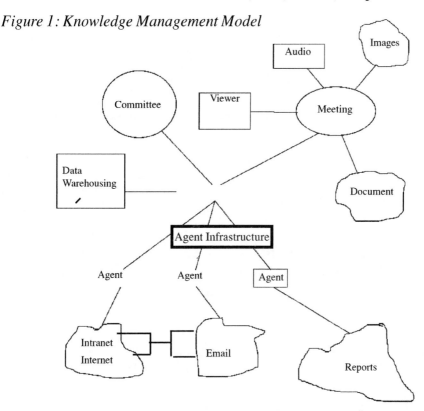

SYSTEM DESIGNS AND IMPLEMENTATION

We have developed two somewhat different systems to make use of the IR agents. In both environments the mobile IR agents are used to visit document collection sites and return with relevant documents. They differ primarily in the level of user interaction.

User Interface Based System

The first system (Figure 1) makes use of a user interface. The user interacts submits queries using this interface. The system then contacts the *Registry* object to find out the locations of various *document sources*. Then *mobile agents* are spawned to go to these document sources, with information about the user query and the profile. The mobile agents process information at the remote sites and receive the names and couple of lines of documents, which match the user profile and query. The interface displays the results. The user then makes his/her selection as to which documents he or she would like to view. Mobile agents are sent to the document sources to fetch these files and displayed to the user through the interface. The user then submits feedback to the system regarding each document viewed. If the user becomes aware of a new document source, he or she can update the Registry using the user interface.

We briefly look at the main components of the system.

User Interface

The user logs into the user interface. The login information is used by the system to locate the user's profile. After the login procedure is successful, the user is provided with the screen to enter query parameters.

The User Query Screen allows the user to submit a query as a set of terms, modify the registry of document sources, or work with his/her profile. The user can use the profile as part of the query, discontinue the use of the profile for upcoming requests or modify his/her profile. In our current prototype we assume that a user has one profile.

A result screen displays the results of the user's current search as choice boxes. The host address, the document name and the couple of lines from each of the documents matched are displayed. At a given time, 10 or less results are displayed. A document viewer is used to display the document the user has selected using the submit button and provides the user with the opportunity of indicating whether or not the document is relevant to the query.

The User Interface for our personalized document retrieval system has been implemented in Java (JDK 1.1.2) and uses the new Event model. The Java programs are standalone applications rather than an applet because it needs to do read and write to files, user's profiles and other system dependent default values. The various user-interface screens are implemented as public classes which extend the Java AWT class Frame.

Registry

This is an object, which maintains the database of the document sources. It provides interface to add a new document source, remove a document source and return the list of document sources. Whenever the system needs to spawn agents, it first contacts the Registry for the list of document sources and then spawn agents.

The Registry is implemented as a Voyager enabled Java class. It is created when the system is brought up. The life span of this object is unlimited. The registry item is made up of the document source host name, port number of the voyager server and the directory where the files are stored.

Mobile Agents

There are two kinds of mobile agents, they are described in the following sections.

Information Retrieval Agents

These are mobile agents spawned by the system, when the user submits a query. These mobile agents provide the functionality described in Section 3. The agents are provided with an itinerary, i.e. list of document sources to visit, the user query and the profile of the user. These agents then go to each of the document sources and process every document in the document source. The documents are assumed to be in text format. The processing involves passing the document, through a stemmer, stopper, an inverter and finally creation of a weighted vector of terms. These documents are then matched with the user's query and the matched list is stored in the internal structure along with their term vector. If the document source is unavailable, the same is reported to the user. After visiting all the document sources, the agent returns to the system that spawned it with the "name" of the relevant documents from the document sources.

File Retrieval agents

The information retrieval agent presents to the user the name of the document that matched the user's query and a couple of lines from the document. The whole document is not presented. When the user makes a selection, as to which document he or she is interested in, those documents are fetched by file retrieval agents. These agents get the whole document and present to user on a document viewer.

Document Sources

Document sources are the locations where the text documents are stored. They are represented by the address of the machine and the directory where these documents are available on the machine. Voyager servers are running at these sites to allow mobile agents from other sites to do computations. In the current system the documents are in text format.

Tests

Three document collections were used for testing. The document collections used were abstracts from following journals
- IEEE Expert
- Journal of Artificial Intelligence Research
- Neural Computation.

Voyager servers were executed on three different machines and the Registry contained the following entries

Host Name	Port	Directory
sunfire.cs.iastate.edu	9000	/home/aigroup/InfoRetrieval/Abstracts/ NeuralComp
dazzler.cs.iastate.edu	8000	/home/aigroup/InfoRetrieval/Abstracts/ IEEE.Expert
storm.cs.iastate.edu	8800	/home/aigroup/InfoRetrieval/Abstracts/ JAIR

Tests were conducted at two levels. First, the information retrieval software was tested on the individual document collections using the standard recall and precision measures (Hu, 1998). The second level of testing was based on the use of IR agents and the results were compared with the tests conducted for the stationary retrieval system. As expected the recall/precision results were the same.

Warehouse Collection

In the second approach, we used the IR agents to populate a data warehouse. A data warehouse is a strategy of placing the data and the tools required to analyze the data in the same software system environment. Our approach is to collect documents that the agents deem relevant for further analysis. The system launches an IR agent and uses the resulting set of documents to populate a class in our object oriented data warehouse (Miller, 1997). The system makes use of the view system that serves as the basis of the data warehouse to define a class either consisting of the "names" of the retrieved documents or of the full documents. The resulting "materialized view" is then populated by appending the retrieved documents to the class defined by the view. The system is illustrated in Figure 2.

A mobile agent class called *queryAgent* is the main class in this system. The *queryAgent* receives the query from the user. It goes to each machine listed in the registry, accesses the documents from that particular collection and finally returns to the machine where it started. The class *launch*, which started the queryAgent, receives the information from the *queryAgent* and displays the results on the screen.

There are two main parts to the system. One is the main class called *launch* and the other is the mobile agent called *queryAgent*.

- launch: the launch class initializes the itinerary of the mobile agent. It loads all the database locations into the itinerary of the mobile agent. Once the initializing is done, the mobile agent is sent to the first location using the function *moveTo(destination,function_name())}*. This function moves the mobile agent to the destination and executes the function *function_name* when it reaches the *destination*. Then the program *launch* waits for the mobile agent to finish its work and return to the starting machine. This is done periodically by checking whether the mobile agent is parked in the initial machine.
- queryAgent: the IR agent goes to a machine in its itinerary. Each of the results is added to a global Vector. Once all the sites have been visited this vector contains all the results. The agents go back to the initial machine and parks. The *launch* program will get the results from the agent and displays on the screen.

CONCLUSIONS

The personalized information retrieval system uses the TFIDF method with relevance feedback. It has been developed using Java 1.1 and Voyager platform is used for mobility. It provides a user-friendly interface and mobile agents are used to perform processing on remote sites and get back the documents, which match the user's interests. This system has been tested on HP-Unix machines of Computer Science department at our University.

The system has been designed with reusability and extensibility in mind. So each of these components could be used by any other system with ease. Since the classes are moved from one machine to another, they have to be implemented as serializable.

The warehouse population system is capable of building large sets of documents that can be further analyzed either using relevance tests or data mining tools.

ACKNOWLEDGEMENT

The authors would like to thank Ji Hoon Yang for his help with the Voyager software and Darren Manning for installing **Voyager** on the department machines.

REFERENCES

Ackerman, M.S. (1996). *Organizational Memory*, http://www.ics.uci.edu/~ackerman/om.html.

Angus, J., Patel, J. and Harty, J. (1998). Knowledge Management: great concept … But What Is It? *InformationWeek*, March 16, pp. 58-70.

Armstrong, R., Freitag, D., Joachimes, T., and Mitchel, T. (1995). WebWatcher : A Learning Apprentice for the World Wide Web; *1995 AAAI Symposium on Information gathering from Heterogenous, Distributed Environments*. March.

Balbanovic, M. and Shoham, Y. Learning Information Retrieval Agents: Experiments with Automated Web Browsing; Department of Computer Science, Stanford University.

Chen, H., McHenry, W.K., Lynch, K.J., and Goodman, S.E. (1994). A Textual Database/Knowledge-Base Coupling Approach to Creating Computer-Supported Organizational Memory, *International Journal of Man-Machine Studies*, July.

Common Object Request Broker Architecture Organization, CORBA homepage (1997). March 23. http://www.corba.org/.

Distributed Component Object Model home, Microsoft Inc. home page (1997). September 21, http://www.microsoft.com/com/dcom.htm.

Durstewitz, M. (1994). Newsletter on Corporate Memory, *Report from the Toulouse Workshop*, November 3-4, Eurisco.

Etzioni, O. and Weld D. (1994). A Softbot-based Interface to the Internet. *Communications of ACM*, 37(7).

General Magic Inc. (1997). Telescript Technology Whitepapers, April 5, http://www.genmagic.com/Telescript/Whitepapers/index.html.

General Magic Inc., Odyssey homepage (1997). May 26, http://www.genmagic.com/agents/index.html.

Giddens, A (1984). *The Constitution of Society: An Introduction to the Theory of Structuration. Berkeley*, CA: University of California Press

Gray R.S. (1996). Agent Tcl : A flexible and secure mobile-agent system, Fourth Annual TCL/TK workshop (TCL 96), January 8, http://www.cs.dartmouth.edu/agent/papers/index.html

Harrison, C. G., Chess, D. M. and Kershenbaum, A. (1995). Mobile Agents: Are They a Good Idea?, *Research Report*. T.J. Watson Research Center, IBM.

Huber, G. (1991). Organizational learning: The contributing processes and literature, *Organization Science*, 2, 88-115.

Huber, G., Davenport, T. H. and King, D. R. (1998). Perspectives on Organizational Memory, presentation at the *Thirty-First Annual Hawaii International Conference on System Sciences Task Force on Organizational Memory*, Jan.

Javasoft Inc., Javasoft homepage (1997). October 12, http://www.javasoft.com.

Knoblock, C.A. and Ambite, J.-L. (1997). *Agents for Information Gathering*. In Bradshaw, J.M. (ed). Software Agents, Cambridge, MA: MIT Press.

Korfhage, R.R. (1997). *Information Storage and Retrieval*, NY: Wiley

Leiberman, H. (1995). Letizia: An Agent That Assists Web Browsing. In *Proceedings of the International Joint Conference on Artificial Intelligence*.

Li, W. and Messerschmitt, D. G. (1996). Java-to-Go Project, http://ptolemy.eecs.berkeley.edu /dgm/javatools/java-to-go/.

Maes, P. (1997). Agents That Reduce Work and Information Overload. In Bradshaw, J.M. (ed). *Software Agents*, Cambridge, MA: MIT Press.

Mandviwalla, M., Eulgem, S., Mould, C., and Rao, S. V. (1998). Organizational Memory System Design, presentation at the *Thirty-First Annual Hawaii International Conference on System Sciences Task Force on Organizational Memory*, Jan.

Miller, L.L., Honavar, V., and Barta, T. (1997). Warehousing Structured and Unstructured Data for Data Mining. *ASIS'97*. Pages 215-224.

Miller, L.L., and Nilakanta, S. (1997). Tools for Organizational Decision Support: The Design and Development of an Organizational Memory System, *Proceedings of the Thirtieth Annual Hawaii International Conference on System Sciences*, pp. 360-368.

Nehmer H. et al., Thye Ara Project. http:www.uni-kl.de/AG-Nehmer/Ara/.

Nolan, R.L. (1993). Note on Information Technology and Strategy, Harvard Business School, Publishing Division, 9-193-137.

Nonaka, I. and Takeuchi, H., (1995a). *The Knowledge-Creating Company*, Oxford University Press.

Nonaka, I., & Takeuchi, H. (1995b). *The Knowledge-Creating Company: How Japanese Companies Create the Dynamics of Innovation*. New York: Oxford University Press.

Object Space Inc., Voyager Project homepage (1997). June 1, http://www.objectspace.com/Voyager/.

Pazzani, M., Muramatsu, J. and Billsus, D. (1996). Syskill & Webert: Identifying Interesting Websites. *Proceedings of AAAI*, Portland, Oregon.

Porter, M.F. (1980). An Algorithm For Suffix Stripping, Program 14 (3), pp. 130-137.

Remote Method Invocation product specification, Javasoft homepage (1997). October 12, http://www.javasoft.com/products/jdk/1.1/docs/guide/rmi/spec.

Rothermel, et al. The MOLE Project. http://www.informatik.uni-stuttgart.de/ipvr/vs/projekte/mole.html.

Salton, G. (1989). *Automatic Text Processing - the transformation, analysis, and retrieval of information by computer*. Reading, MA: Addison-Wesley Publishing Company, Inc..

Sandoe, K., Croasdell, D. T., Courtney, J., Paradice, D., Brooks, J. and Olfman, L. (1998). Additional Perspectives on Organizational Memory, presentation at the *Thirty-First Annual Hawaii International Conference on System Sciences Task Force on Organizational Memory*, Jan.

Simon, H.A. (1960). *The New Science of Management*, New York: Harper & Row.

Sorensen, H., and McElligott, M. (1992). Representation, Adaptation and Optimization in an Electronic Information Filter, Computer Science Department, University College, Cork, Ireland

Stein, E. W. (1995). Organizational memory: Review of concepts and recommendations for management. *International Journal of Information Management*, 15(2), 17-32.

Stein, E.W., and Zwass, V., (1995). Actualizing Organizational Memory with Information Systems, *Information Systems Research*, 6(2), 185-217.

Tokyo Research Lab, IBM, Aglet Workbench homepage (1997). January 16, http://www.trl.ibm.co.jp/index.html.

Walsh, J.P. and Ungson, G.R., (1991). Organizational Memory, *Academy of Management Review*, 16(1), 57-91.

Wen, H., Miller, L. L. and Nilakanta, S. (1998). PROMIS: A Profiler of Organizational Memory and Institutional systems. *The Ninth International Conference of the Information Resources Management Association*.

White, J.E. (1997). Mobile Agents. In Bradshaw, J.M. (ed). *Software Agents*, Cambridge, MA: MIT Press.

Yang, J., Honavar, V., Pai, P., and Miller, L. (1998). Automated Term Subset Selection for Document Classification. *European Symposium on Cybernetics and Systems Research.*

Chapter 28

Knowledge Management and Virtual Communities

W. Jansen
Royal Netherlands Military Academy, The Netherlands

G.C.A. Steenbakkers
Ordina Management Consulting, The Netherlands

H.P.M. Jägers
Royal Netherlands Military Academy, The Netherlands

A community of people is the best way to handle complex and fast-changing dynamics in any field of the knowledge business. And once you are in the knowledge business, you find you need knowledge communities to run them. (Botkin,1999, p.85)

The objective of this article is to illuminate the relation between knowledge management and virtual communities. A model which comprises four types of knowledge management is presented. A central theme in this article is the suggestion that knowledge management is not an unequivocal concept. Generalized knowledge management strategies do not enable managers and consultants to form an opinion on the effectiveness of virtual communities for their organization or network. Depending on the environment of the organization, the knowledge management will differ in focus and content. In this collaboration there will (and should) be more attention for virtual communities and the most effective type of these communities in the given situation.

Previously Published in *Challenges of Information Technology Management in the 21st Century* edited by Mehdi Khosrow-Pour, Copyright © 2000, Idea Group Publishing.

INTRODUCTION

In the literature there is frequent discussion on both virtual communities (VC) and knowledge management (KM). In this article we will indicate that these concepts are also mutually related. This relation, however, is not valid for all kinds of organizations and their KM. We postulate that generalized knowledge management strategies are not effective. More than ever before in the management of knowledge, the environment in which an organization functions will have to be taken into consideration. Thus, for example, in situations of high degrees of complexity and variability, the content of knowledge management will necessarily be fundamentally different from situations with a low complexity and variability.

This article suggests that in a highly dynamic environment new collaboration forms such as the virtual organization, and especially virtual communities, will play a significant role in knowledge management.

This article is structured as follows. In the next section, we will go into knowledge management. In this chapter the importance of the environment of organizations in terms of complexity and dynamics will be demonstrated. The section following is devoted to the concept of virtual communities. Its first subsection describes three models, which show the development of virtual communities. In the second subsection, three types of virtual communities are distinguished. In the section after that, we will state that virtual communities are not a phase in (or rather after) knowledge management but a possible form of knowledge management. This article concludes in the final section with a survey of types of virtual communities and the accompanying management functions, emphases and objectives.

KNOWLEDGE MANAGEMENT

The organization is often viewed as a knowledge-processing system.[1] Much attention is paid to the ever-increasing role of knowledge in the functioning of individuals and their affiliated organizations (refer to Davenport en Prusak, 1998). Measures are proposed, in order to better utilize the knowledge present in organizations and in addition, to promote its development. We define knowledge management as "the way in which organizations organize necessary knowledge." In this article, we focus on knowledge management as a design issue. We suggest that organizations implicitly adopt a certain manner of dealing with knowledge by choosing a certain organization form.

Complexity and variability

In the professional literature, managers as well as employees acknowledge that the majority of organizations have to function in an increasingly variable and complex environment. Thus, each organization-design model that aims to keep up with current developments, will have to give priority to finding solutions for this variability and complexity. Many organizations can no longer afford to be passive in their attempt to reduce the uncertainty stemming from these developments. However, this is not an effective strategy when seen from the point of view of the organization as a knowledge creation system. Uncertainty and complexity are conducive to the creation of knowledge. Organizations have to be able to deal with them and even, in some cases, increase the level of complexity in order to optimally create knowledge. On the other hand, organizations with a low uncertainty factor will continue to exist, due to the fact that, for example, they are mainly focused on the continued production of the same type of product or service, in which case, the issue is one of utilizing existent knowledge rather than the creation of knowledge. Here, reducing the uncertainty that stems from complexity can be an effective strategy. The following model indicates the options in the area of knowledge management as dictated by the nature of the organization's environment.

The aspects of complexity and variability are positioned on the axis in Figure 1.

Complexity regards the degree to which an organization is confronted with complicated issues and the number of factors which it needs to take into consideration. These can stem from the environment as well as from the work itself. Our understanding of variability regards the pace and unpredictability of developments in the environment, e.g., the pace of change in market demand. These situational factors determine the design. Organizations which insufficiently adapt to the degree of complexity and variability will, ultimately, not be able to meet up to the demands of the environment (Mintzberg, 1979; Jansen & Jägers, 1991).

It is obvious that an organization (-unit) will never make a perfect "fit" with one of the model quadrants, and that the model must therefore not be viewed as a precise tool of measurement, but as a conceptual framework.

Figure 1: Organization design and knowledge management[2]

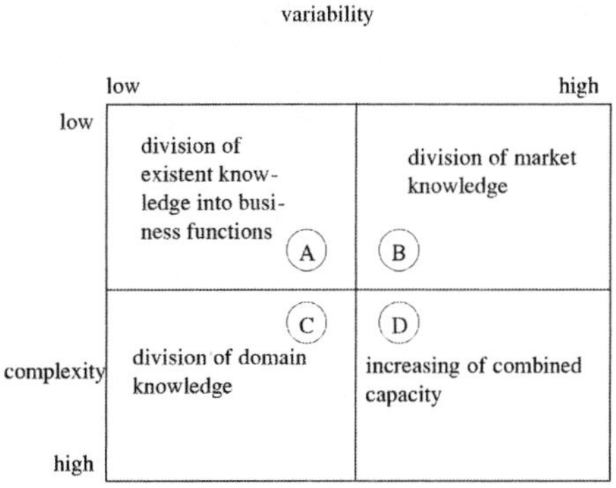

A. *The division of existent knowledge into business functions*

In a situation that is neither complex nor variable, an organization will have been structured in such a way as to optimally utilize knowledge. It does not, or barely, create knowledge itself. The knowledge used for the primary process is attained externally, or was developed in the initial phase of the organization and subsequently "frozen" (Hedlund, 1994). The staff organs are highly occupied with the continued refinement of this "frozen" knowledge, in the form of rules and procedures. The knowledge management choice in this type of organization form is to split up the knowledge into business functions (such as marketing, personnel, finance, etc.) and hence, in the organization design, to relegate this knowledge to departments that become responsible for these business functions.

The organizations in this quadrant are targeted towards the efficient utilization and recycling of knowledge. The measures for knowledge management serve primarily to make the existent knowledge explicit (codification), thus enabling additional parts of the organization and individuals to make use of it, as well as those who are outside the involved business functions.

B. *The division of knowledge into markets*

In situations with a high degree of variability and a low degree of complexity, organizations are structured in such a way that the presence of knowledge is concentrated within a single business unit (refer to Hedlund, 1994). This knowledge is specifically market-focused. By concentrating the increment and compilation of knowledge within one business unit, rather than spreading it out over the remaining business units, the organization attains a special manoeuvrability and flexibility, in that the changes required by the market are easily dealt with by the business unit due to this low complexity. Market knowledge is often quite subjective and has a low predictive value. As a result of this, the role of implicit knowledge becomes larger and can be supplemented with general knowledge (demographic developments, available income) and specific-explicit knowledge (business-unit sales figures, competition results).

Naturally, the strongest point of the organization form in this quadrant (focusing the knowledge on one unit) simultaneously forms its weakest point. The division of knowledge leads to a lack of innovation within the entire organization. As business units are largely driven in practice by financial results, in most cases little or no thought will be spared for innovation within the business units. A results-focused policy always leads to short-term efficiency. In this quadrant, the knowledge management will be largely decentralized and it takes place within the business units, having to focus on the exploitation and codification of the (hitherto implicit) knowledge within the units. This process is organized per business unit, when possible by knowledge-managers.

C. The division of knowledge into domains or areas of expertise

In a situation that is complex but not variable, the organization needs to manage this complexity. An important measure for the realization of this, is the division of activities into different areas of expertise or domains. By hiring professionals who are specialized in a limited area and who have the pertinent knowledge at their command, it becomes possible to adequately manage the complicated problems that arise in the environment. Examples of this are teachers, medical specialists and lawyers. The increment of knowledge *within* the organization does not, or barely, occur, as the professionals within the organization work autonomously and have little shared communication and co-ordination. The knowledge remains implicit, possessed by the individual organization members. Knowledge increase in the areas of expertise occurs outside of the organization in specific institutes or groups, which focus on the development of these areas of expertise, such as training institutes and professional groups. At the same time, the increase of knowledge occurs during the activities of individual professionals within their specific domain of knowledge. Professional groups often share this knowledge, for instance, by way of modern communication technologies (news groups, bulletin boards or listservers).The Internet makes countless other sites (often university-supplemented) available, which try to dam the overflow of information and publications by offering summaries. These sites are generally organized per expertise.

D. The creation of knowledge through the increase of the combined capacity

In situations that are highly variable and complex, the knowledge of each independent participant or employee is no longer sufficient for the management of this knowledge. The organizations have to be structured in such a way to ensure the sharing of knowledge. This is called the enhancing of the combining capacity or fusion (Davenport and Prusak, 1998). For example, organizing activities in projects enables the explication of implicit knowledge, as well as the transformation of "old" knowledge into new knowledge (projects result in learning and new knowledge). Organizations must take care to build in sufficient mechanisms to anchor this compiled knowledge (in knowledge banks, for example) and to make it transferable (via intranet and symposia, for example) and recyclable.

The increment of combined capacity, is the only way in which new knowledge can be created out of existent knowledge. This requires the highest possible degree of freedom to be built into the organization form and the minimization of rules and procedures.

The first three organization types discussed, are mainly focused on knowledge utilization. Up to now, the organization forms that have been chosen by organizations for knowledge utilization, have always led to the division of knowledge rather to the fusion of knowledge. As a result of the division of knowledge, those employees and organization-units not directly involved do not have this knowledge at their disposal. The knowledge utilizing organizations will have to do their utmost to anchor their knowledge at a central level and must develop measures and procedures that promote the easy accessibility of knowledge, as well as ensure that it is offered in a highly standardized form. This strategy is of importance in stable, uncomplicated organizations.

However, there are increasingly situations in which the variability as well as the complexity is high. In these cases, the organization focus is on creating as much knowledge as possible by collaborating with customers, suppliers and other relevant organizations and persons.

Collaboration between various organizations leads to an increment of combined capacities. The creation of added value for the client is an increasingly complicated process, in which divergent types of knowledge need to be fused. Independently, organizations do not have the necessary scale for this at their disposal, hence collaboration becomes a must. Virtual communities are a particular form of this collaboration.

VIRTUAL COMMUNITIES
The development of virtual communities

Virtual communities are seen as a stage in the organization of cooperation forms. They offer the possibility to give a fitting answer to the demands of innovation of products and services.

One of the earliest descriptions of functions of virtual communities can be found with Venkatraman en Henderson. Their model consists of two axes, the vertical of which contains three stages of virtuality, the horizontal three vectors. The vectors are independent in so far as the attainment of a stage within a vector produces the

Figure 2: Evolutionary Pyramid of collaboration (ontleend aan Coleman, 1997)

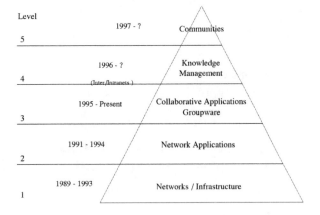

Table 1: The three stages of cooperation (following Venkatraman and Henderson, 1996)

Vectors / Stages of Virtuality	Market Interaction (Virtual Encounter)	Competency Leverage (Virtual Sourcing)	Work Configuration (Virtual Work)
Stage 1	Remote product or service experience	Efficient sourcing of standard components	Maximizing individual expertise
Stage 2	Product or service customization	Effective asset leverage	Harnessing organizational expertise
Stage 3	Shaping custom solutions	Create new competencies through alliances	Leveraging community expertise

Table 2: Stages towards knowledge communities (Botkin, 1999, pp.88-90)

Stages	(1) Stovepipe	(2) Sharing	(3) Cooperation	(4) Community
Technology	Desktop PCs	Internal e-mail	One-to-one customer connections	Interconnected to customers and suppliers
Connectivity	Unconnected	Departmentally connected	Cross-functionally connected	Enterprise-wide connected
Culture	Every man for himself	Get more of the pie	Sell the pie externally	Grow a bigger pie for all
Business purpose	Provide traditional products/services	Short term improvements to traditional products	Customer Solutions	Creation of new market and enterprises; Co-creation of future business
Organization	Individual	Task force	Team	Knowledge Community

expected benefit only if the other vectors are also considered properly. Stage three focuses on the interorganizational network to design and leverage interdependent communities for innovation and growth. Table 1 shows their three stages of development in which virtual communities represent the last stage. (Venkatraman and Henderson, 1996).

Coleman (1997) describes five levels of cooperation, making use of a pyramid (see Figure 2). At the lowest three levels there are not any real virtual communities, although all sorts of cooperation forms are taking place, supported by electronic connections (groupware, email). At the highest level virtual communities serving a certain objective can be found. The cooperation is directed towards the creation and maintenance of relations on the one hand, and at the content of the communication on the other. The exchange of knowledge and the creation of new knowledge in the relations with the partners of the virtual community makes up an important part of the cooperation. The Internet and intranet are important aids in this.

It is also possible to consider this pyramid as depicting the creation of a knowledge community, in which the several levels, as it were, form the foundation each time for reaching a higher level of knowledge.

Botkin (1999) heads in the same direction when he postulates that organizations have to go through four stages (stovepipe, sharing, cooperation, community) in order to reach the level of knowledge community. Table 2 shows his model, which describes four stages organizations go through to attain the level of knowledge communities.

Most older organizations are plagued by "stovepipes" or lack of vision beyond one's own function. At the second stage organizations form task forces with a mandate to work together and share ideas on what needs to be done to share information better. The culture does not change much. Teams with directives for cooperation are formed by organizations in stage three. At stage four, organizations start experimenting with knowledge communities. They often start by identifying communities of practice within the organization and supporting the growth of these kinds of communities. The aim at this stage is to organize radical innovation and create completely new enterprises.

What is striking in this model is that the knowledge communities stay within the organization boundaries. This is in sharp contrast with the other two models and the bulk of the literature, in which the boundary crossing character of virtual organizations is emphasized.

This survey of models offers only a limited selection of ideas in this field. It is intended to indicate the general direction of present-day thinking on virtual communities. In spite of some minor differences between these models, the common denominator clearly emerges. Virtual communities form a last phase in a development process and they are directed towards (radical) innovation and growth.

Characteristics and types of virtual communities

A virtual community is a group of people who, with the help of technology, engage in collective activities that also take place in real-life communities. The term activities should be seen in rather a broad sense. In a virtual community nice stories can be exchanged or people just chat. Sharing emotions, too, playing games, brainstorming or knowledge sharing are activities that can take place in virtual communities. The main difference with a real community is that, in principle, people cannot meet or see each other (Rheingold, 1993; Fernback and Thompson, 1995; Ratcliffe, 1996). Often, however, contacts in a virtual community do result in real meetings, or people can see each other because of the increasing possibilities of ICT, as is, for instance, the case in video conferencing.

For the division of communities into categories two aspects are of decisive importance, irrespective of whether the community is virtual or not. These aspects are content and (social) relations (Coleman, 1997; Otten, 1999). On the one hand, people exchange information or knowledge in communities. The content of this information exchange matters rather than the social character. On the other hand, relations form an important part of communities. The exchange of emotions, informal and personal information exchange and such like activities are good examples of the relational aspect of communities.

In no virtual community the sole objective is content or social relations. The emphasis on either of them, however, differs per type of community. Depending on whether the emphasis lies on content or on relations, three different types of virtual community can be distinguished, viz. the chat type, the expert type and the innovative type.

The chat virtual community

In the chat community social relations are more important than content. It is not so much the exchange of knowledge or information that matters, but more the talking to each other about this, that and the other. These communities are usually organized around certain themes, but they will be so general that they will offer starting points for everyone to start chatting happily away.

Communication and the organizing of social relations is inextricably bound to (virtual) communities (Fernback and Thompson, 1995). The content of the messages is not so important, which means that anyone can take part in this type of virtual community. The chat community has no direct link to knowledge management and therefore it will not be dealt with further in this article. There is, however, the possibility that the community will shift in due course towards one of the other types, for instance, when the content gains more weight or even begins to dominate the possibility to chat.

SmulWeb (Tuck-in Web). SmulWeb is a meeting place on the Internet for anyone who loves healthy and tasty food and drink. SmulWeb differs from what has been customary up to now on the Internet. It provides much information on anything that has to do with culinary enjoyment, like food and health, drink and health, eating in, eating out and 'slimming to last'. The success of Tuck-in Web lies not so much in information exchange, but in the possibilities that the site offers for chatting. Thus, a tea-chat has been created, because many people (women in particular) were present in Tuck-in Web at certain times and they felt the need to chat with each other. Apart from that it is possible to send in recipes, put together a menu, mix creative cocktails and rate restaurants.

The expert virtual community

In this type of virtual community the exchange of information and knowledge comes first. In general, the majority of this community consists of experts in a certain expertise. The exchange of information and knowledge holds pride of place in this type of virtual community. Having a common background (expertise) ensures that the meaning of the information/knowledge exchanged is unambiguous.

For several years now a number of scholars in the field of Information technology and Organizational Science have collectively carried out a research project, called PrimaVera (http://domino.fee.uva.nl/PrimaVera). In order to enhance the discussion in their field of expertise a discussion forum has been established. In this so-called Delphi-forum (http://www.delphi.com) they draw each other's attention to conferences and articles on the Internet or in periodicals. Apart from that there are discussions on topics of interest for the target group. The sole object is content. No (personal) information is exchanged that has no bearing on the field of research of PrimaVera.

The innovative virtual community

In this type of virtual community content as well as relations are important. The community has to ensure an integration of communication and content (Hagel III and Armstrong, 1997). Social relations can increase the trust between the parties that share knowledge (Nottingham, 1997). In general it is taken for granted that true knowledge encompasses more than just information. In the case of knowledge it all comes down to the meaning or content of the information (Davis en Botkin, 1994; Ratcliffe, 1995). Nohria and Eccles (1992), too, state that when personnel members want to strengthen weak ties, they have to exchange social as well as meaningful information. For this reason it is especially important in the case of new product development not only to pass on information, but also the meaning of information. A requirement for a potential knowledge information mechanism for innovations is therefore the possibility to express the meaning the holder of the information attaches to it (Otten, 1999).

The partners in a virtual community have different fields of knowledge, so that they can complement each other through knowledge sharing. Different roles can be fulfilled by different partners. This type of community will be characterized by a great variety of roles, such as experts, project-facilitators, discussion facilitators, technical development and support and nurturers/communicators. Because knowledge is shared, new products can be developed, which in knowledge management terms is called increasing the combining capacity.

Suppose your company wants to bid on a large project to build a dam in Africa on the Congo river. Initially a team would be organized from all over the U.S., some locals in Africa, and some people in Europe with expertise in building this type of dam. An e-mail goes out to all the prospective members of the team inviting them to be part of the project.

All reply affirmatively. They are given a password and asked to look at a discussion forum. This forum is located on a web page where everyone involved can look at the RFP and discuss the various parts their expertise impacts. The RFP is explicit knowledge, and the discussion is tacit knowledge which will lead to a proposal (explicit knowledge again).

If the company loses the bid, those on the team can go back and look at what decisions were made preparing the proposal to uncover how to avoid making those mistakes in the future (organizational learning). Finally, the team makes recommendations for itself (or any other group doing a similar project) on best practices, or what they think will win the bid. Afterward, this whole project is indexed and put on the corporate intranet so other teams can sidestep re-inventing the wheel (they can even modify the proposal the first team made), as well as see the decision processes and pertinent data that culminated in the initial proposal. The Congo Dam Project, although a short-lived community, has added value to the organization even if it has not contributed directly to the bottom line.

Taken from Coleman, 1997 (http://www.collaborate.com/hot_tip/tip1097.html)

THE RELATION BETWEEN THE KNOWLEDGE MANAGEMENT MODEL AND VIRTUAL COMMUNITIES

The three models/pyramid described in the previous section all give the impression of a linear and evolutionary development. An underlying supposition is that organizations pass on from one phase to the other, knowledge management (merely) being one of them. Another premise is that technological progress forms the basis for this phasing (see, amongst others, Coleman, 1997). We do not deny that a development can be noticed, in technology as well as in the emergence of organization forms and the alternative ways of organizing knowledge. We also recognize the relation between technology and these alternative ways, as technology greatly expands the number of choices for possibilities of cooperation.

Figure 3. Positions of Expert and Innovative Communities[3]

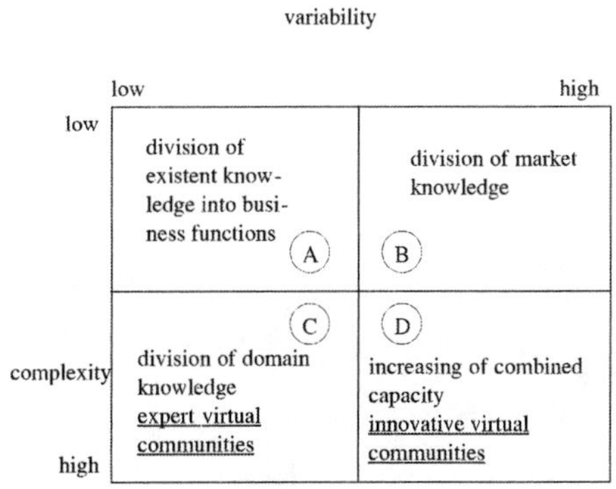

Nevertheless, we want to postulate that the emergence of virtual communities is not only a phase in an evolutionary development form of organizing. We are of the opinion that the formation of such communities - as a conscious or unconscious (but increasingly conscious, because organizations see the need for them) choice - is an effective answer to the demands the environment makes. Increasing complexity and variability ask for cooperation between experts within and across fields of expertise, business functions and even organization boundaries. Both suppliers and customers may become important participants in the collaboration and the sharing of knowledge (see the description of the Dell virtual community, by Venkatraman and Henderson, 1996). As more and more organizations find themselves in a highly complex and dynamic environment, they increasingly tend to form virtual communities. It may seem that this is a next phase in knowledge management. However, we state that the development of virtual communities, like the optimizing of knowledge in business functions or the chopping up of knowledge in business units, is a realization of knowledge management that is the most effective one with a view to the environment of that organization.

In practice we see forms of virtual communities in two quadrants of our model.

In quadrant C we see the emergence of virtual communities within the fields of expertise, usually on the initiative of the experts themselves. In these communities the emphasis lies on the content of the knowledge and not on the social relations, although they may develop over time. Because the exchange of knowledge between specialists in the same field is central here, it is understandable that the content of the knowledge is most important. The social component is not as relevant here as in other types, because the meaning of the knowledge does not have to be explicated anymore for the experts (Otten, 1999). The function of these virtual communities is also different from those in quadrant D, in that they do not strive for innovation for its own sake, but continuous improvement in the relevant field of expertise. It is also possible to say that virtual communities in quadrant C are not an absolute requirement, but a useful addition to forms of cooperation, supported by Groupware and other Collaborative Applications (phase 3 of Coleman's pyramid). Because specialists are geographically dispersed the forming of virtual communities (based on electronic connections) is an effective way of cooperating.

Table 3: Survey of types of virtual community and knowledge management functions

Virtual community	Environment	Knowledge Management	Emphasis	Objective
Expert community	high complexity, low variability	division of knowledge in domains	content	(quality) improvement
Innovative community	high complexity, high variability	increasing of combined capacity	content and relations	innovation

In contrast to this, the emergence of virtual communities is quadrant D is, in many cases, necessary and not so much a result of geographical distance. The fact that such communities also emerge on one and the same location is an indication for this. In this kind of knowledge communities the emphasis is on content as well as relations. This great attention for relations is necessary, amongst other things, because apart from the knowledge itself, there is also the meaning of that knowledge which has to be exchanged between people with often different expertise and background. The emphasis here will come to lie much more on the combination of implicit and explicit knowledge. The function of such communities is not so much continuous improvement as innovation, the development of new products and services.

IMPLICATIONS FOR RESEARCH

Our emphasis on the relations between knowledge management and the environment serves to complement more generalized knowledge management strategies.

In this article we have described the relations between knowledge management and the environment the organization finds itself in. Depending on the degree of dynamism and complexity organizations will (have to) make different choices in order to cope effectively. As they are increasingly confronted with variable and complex situations, we see new solutions for organizations to acquire and create the necessary knowledge. An important new development in knowledge management is the virtual community. In this article three types have been distinguished, two of which play a part in the knowledge management of organizations. The table below shows the two types of virtual community, which are relevant for knowledge management strategies, and the accompanying management functions, emphases and objectives.

We believe that our dimensions of the environment of the organization, our types of virtual communities, as well as the framework we have laid out, make a contribution to the understanding of the role virtual communities can play in knowledge management strategies and advance both theory and practice concerning knowledge management and virtual communities.

Future research is needed regarding our typology of knowledge management strategies in different situations, as well as elements of our framework and propositions concerning the types of virtual communities and their role in knowledge management.

Research questions are for instance:

- What are distinctive characteristics of the expert virtual community and the innovative virtual community?

- Is the innovative type of virtual community more effective in highly dynamic and complex situations than the expert virtual community?
- Which role plays informal communication in the functioning of virtual communities?
- What is the impact of Information and Communication Technology on knowledge management in general and virtual communities in specific?

Research is also needed on other contextual factors - besides variability and complexity - that may influence effective knowledge management strategies and virtual communities. For example cultural aspects (Hofstede, 1991), and/or the degree of interdependency and trust, may play an important role.

CONCLUSIONS

For the management of the organizations it is of the utmost importance to become aware of the most effective way of knowledge management. The combination of knowledge and competences in the form of virtual communities, with the objective of deepening of the expertise and/or innovation is an useful and (enabled by ICT) feasible choice. Managers will have to occupy themselves with identifying and stimulating virtual communities. We believe that virtual communities will become an increasingly important part of knowledge management strategies of organizations.

REFERENCES

Botkin, J. (1999). *Smart Business: How Knowledge Communities can revolutionize your company.*

Coleman, D. (1997). The Evolution of Sustainable Value-Added Communities, October, *http://www.collaborate.com/hot_tip/tip1097.html*

Davenport, T., and Prusak, L. (1998). *Working Knowledge: How organizations manage what they know*, Harvard Business School Press.

Davis, S., and Botkin, J. (1994). The coming of Knowledge-Based Business, in: *Harvard Business Review*, September-October, pp. 165-171

Fernback, J., and Thompson, B. (1995). Virtual Communities: Abort, Retry, Failure? *http://www.usyd.edu.au/su/social/papers/fernb.htm*

Hagel III, J., and Armstrong, G. (1997). *Net Gain: Expanding Markets Through Virtual Communities*, Harvard Business School Press.

Hedlund, G. (1994). Knowledge management and the N-form corporation, in: *Strategic Management Journal*, vol. 15, pp. 73-90

Hofstede, G. (1991). *Cultures and Organizations. The software of the mind.* London: McGraw Hill.

Jansen, W., and Jägers, H.P.M. (1991). *The Design of Effective Organizations*, Stenfert Kroese, Leiden.

Jansen, W., Steenbakkers, G.C.A., and Jägers, H.P.M. Knowledge Management and Organization Design; dealing with complexity and variability, Submitted to: *Knowledge Management and Virtual Organizations: Theories, Practices, Technologies and Methods*, Y. Malhotra (ed.), Hershey, PA: Idea Group.

Jones, Q. (1997). Virtual-Communities, Virtual Settlements & Cyber-Archaeology: A Theoretical Outline, in: *Journal of Computer Mediated Communication*, 3 (3), December.

Mintzberg, H. (1979). *The Structuring of Organizations*, Englewood Cliffs, NJ: Prentice Hall Inc.

Nohria, N., and Eccles, R.G. (1992). Face-to-Face, Making Network Organizations work, in: Nohria, N., Eccles, R.G. (eds.) *Networks, and Organizations, Structure, Form and Action*, Boston, MA: Harvard Business School Press.

Nottingham, A. (1997). The Virtual Organisation as a Community built on trust, *http://www.lmu.ac.uk/ies/conferences/nottingham.html*.

Otten, V.L.M. (1999). Kennismanagement als basis voor productinnovaties [Knowledge management as a basis for product innovation], in *M&O*, 4, July/August, pp. 55-69.

Ratcliffe, J. Virtual Communities, Or Get a Life? *http://wattlab.coms.uconn.edu/courses/coms239/spring97/ratcliff.htm*.

Rheingold, H. (1992). *A slice of Life in My Virtual Community*. CA: Whole Earth Review.

Rheingold, H. (1993). *The Virtual Community: Homesteading on the Electronic Frontier*, New York: Addison-Wesley.

Venkatraman, N., and Henderson, J.C. (1996). The architecture of Virtual Organizations: Leveraging Three Interdependent Vectors, Discussion Paper, *Systems Research Center*, Boston University School of Management, Boston, MA.

NOTES

[1] In knowledge management, distinctions are often made between the phases that need to be passed through in order to utilize knowledge in organizations. The following phases are distinguished:
- Knowledge creation and acquisition
- Knowledge compilation and organization
- Knowledge dissemination
- Knowledge application

For definitions and for the distinction between explicit and implicit (tacit) knowledge, we refer the reader to Nonaka (1995), Den Hertog and Huizinga (1997), Jacobs (1996), Chun Wei Choo (1997), Weggeman (1997). They all devote thoughts to this subject.

[1] In connection with this it is worth considering a comparable model of Blackler, in which different types of knowledge encountered in different organization forms are described.

[2] This model was presented in an article by the present authors: Jansen, W., Steenbakkers, G.C.A., Jägers, H.P.M., Knowledge Management and Organization Design; dealing with complexity and variability, Submitted to: Knowledge Management and Virtual Organizations: Theories, Practices, Technologies and Methods, Y. Malhotra (ed.), Idea Group. See also the typology of M. E. McGill and J. W. Slocum, Unlearning the organization, in IEEE Engineering Management Review, no. 2, 1994, pp. 36-43.

[3] See also for a distinction in Knowledge Management Strategies, which stresses the difference between standardized, developed concepts and the innovative, personalized approach, M. T. Hansen , N. Nohria, T. Tierney: What is Your Strategy for Managing Knowledge? In Harvard Business Review, March-April 1999, pp10

Chapter 29

A Research Model for Knowledge Management

Pamila Dembla
University of Memphis, Tennessee, USA

En Mao
University of Wisconsin-Milwaukee, USA

Knowledge has been identified as the key issue to gaining competitive advantage in any business. A successful company is one that can create new knowledge, disseminate it through its organization, and embody it in its products and services. All this is possible by careful planning and building a culture for creating and sharing knowledge. In this chapter, a research model for KM is suggested. The various components of KM are described in detail so as to explain the process of KM. Then, using the research model as a reference, two case studies, one of Buckman's laboratories and the other of the Nippon Steel- British Steel alliance, are analyzed to study the process of KM.

INTRODUCTION

In today's volatile global business environment, characterized by fierce competition, increasing interorganizational cooperation, and alliances, knowledge management is not only challenging but also necessary. Knowledge management can be viewed as a proactive approach that help organizations gain and sustain competitive advantages (Porter, 1998; Havens & Knapp, 1999). Increasingly, companies view knowledge management as critical to the success of businesses. The

Previously Published in *Managing Information Technology in a Global Economy* edited by Mehdi Khosrow-Pour, Copyright © 2001, Idea Group Publishing.

reality is that lack of knowledge management could result in slow product development and poor customer services and can be detrimental to companies in the near future (Havens & Knapp, 1999).

The practice of knowledge management has been around just as long as businesses have been around. However, the "conscious" realization of it has been a recent event. In today's market economy knowledge is becoming more and more "fragmented" and "redundant" (Zack, 1999) as more and more knowledge is created. On the other hand, organizations are becoming more and more distributed and dynamic. Consequently, comparing KM in any traditional business environment, knowledge management today has become more complex and requires greater effort.

Then, what is new in knowledge management? Apart from large volumes of knowledge, the use of information technology (IT) in managing knowledge has given KM a new dimension. It is important that the use of technology and the "social process of technology use" are harmonized (DeSanctis & Poole, 1994). Implemented properly with appropriate strategies, IT can help to carry out and maximize the benefit of many of the management initiatives, including knowledge management.

Therefore, it can be fairly said that knowledge management is not a technology; however, technology is fundamental to the knowledge management process. Knowledge Management (KM) is defined as "a process that drives innovation by capitalizing on organizational intellect and experience" (Daffy, 1999). KM is intended to promote and support the creation of new knowledge, thus contributing to innovation, an essential ingredient in business success. KM also:

- Capitalizes on both explicit and tacit knowledge;
- Supports business objectives and revenue generation;
- Stresses human interaction as the focal point;
- Capitalizes on lessons learned.

In addition to adhering to these principles, it is important to emphasize the relationship between sources of knowledge and knowledge and to ensure that participants (knowledge managers, consumers and contributors) are able to contribute and take advantage of the KM process.

There are a number of technical and business issues that need to be considered before initiating the KM process. Some of the technical issues important for the success of the KM process are providing assistance in setting up electronic delivery strategies for information, identifying information sources and services, re-architecting decision support tools, supplying data and/or document mining tools, and dealing with the whole information life cycle (i.e., avoid having irrelevant knowledge). Some of the business issues revolve around promoting a knowledge-centered environment in organizations, understanding information flows, and understanding the overall infrastructure that needs to be in place to improve collaboration and sharing (Emery, 1999).

One of the important factors that can influence the success of the KM process is having a champion, a leader who can influence organizational knowledge sharing efforts in a positive way. However, lack of an effective leadership, limited vision and general resistance to change can have a negative impact on an organization's willingness and ability to capitalize on its knowledge assets.

We divide the chapter into three sections. First, we review the literature relevant to the KM process. Then, we propose a knowledge management research model to explain the key components of the KM process in organizations. Some of the key components were the environmental factors, the strategy, the people and technology factors, the knowledge and the knowledge process factors. The knowledge process factors included creation, retention and sharing of knowledge. Finally, we map two case studies, one of the Buckman's laboratories and the other of Nippon Steel-British Steel technical alliance to the research model and propose our findings.

LITERATURE REVIEW

In this section, we will review the literature on knowledge management and organizational memory. Pemberton (1997) in their article talk of the importance of knowledge management and Chief Knowledge officers in organizations. According to Drucker (1989), we have entered a new era in which the centerpiece of an enterprise is the know-how (knowledge) of an organization's workers rather than the tools of production. The main sources of knowledge in organizations include: training (formal and informal), academic degree programs, workshops/ seminars, intelligence gathered about ones industry and competition, information sources-such as the internet and the WWW- which can be constantly scoured for ideas on better ways to do things, in-house databases (or data warehouses) of past activities and accomplishments made widely available to employees, and forms of intra-organizational electronic communication and groupware (e.g., Lotus Notes) for effective sharing of information gathered and lessons learned. Some of the other sources of knowledge are libraries, record centers and archival collections.

Pan and Scarborough (1999) analyze the KM system with the help of a case study of Buckman's laboratories and suggests that the socio-technical structure of KM can be broadly summarized into three layers: they are the Infrastructure, the Info-structure and the Info-Culture. Cisco and Strong (1999) explain that the KM system is an Information System Value Chain and includes the five components of capturing, transforming, storing, transferring and applying knowledge.

Pack (1999) in his article says that avoiding wheel invention is a big part of KM and that some companies are placing high value on knowledge sharing when it comes to things like job evaluations and promotions. Duffy (2000) explained the processes involved in KM and described the various opportunities that are available to businesses that employ KM. Some of the opportunities were business planning and operational excellence, employee management and excellence, product design and product/service leadership and customer management and customer intimacy. McDermott (1999), Mullin (1996) and Inkpen (1996) all stress on the fact that for a KM program to succeed in any organization, we need a community that possesses the knowledge and people who use it, and not the knowledge itself. Knowledge, if not utilized is just information.

Most of the literature reviewed discussed the knowledge management process in general and stressed on the knowledge acquisition aspect of KM. Very few provided a practicable and applicable research model for understanding the KM process. Furthermore, there is a lack of body of research that encompasses all the critical factors that affect the KM process in organizations. Our discussion intends to provide a bridge to this effect.

RESEARCH MODEL

Based on the literature review, we have come up with a model to describe the KM process. The model is as shown in Figure 1. The environment forces such as the importance for an organization to maintain its competitive advantage by managing their knowledge well or the requirement of the organization to distribute its knowledge among its geographically dispersed human resources may compel the organization to initiate a KM program. Through a combination of strategy, people and technology, information and energy are transformed into knowledge processes and structures that produce goods and services. There are mainly three processes in the Knowledge Processes. They are knowledge creation, retention and sharing. Each of these components is discussed below.

Figure 1

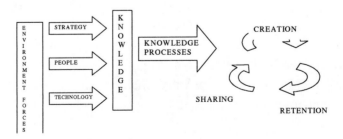

Environment Forces

In any work environments most jobs are imprecise: best decisions depend on circumstances and available knowledge, which drive the need to rethink current approaches to problem solving and decision-making. Time pressures demand that organizations capitalize on lessons learned; consequently there is a need for a sophisticated level of " know-how," "know what," know who," " know where" and "know why." Organizations need to have high performance to respond to market demands such as

- The right product at the right time,
- Customer focused service and marketing strategies,
- High performance organizational practices, and
- Access to high value information and knowledge.

A high performance organization pursues its goals in a changing environment by adapting and enhancing its behavior according to what it knows about itself and the world in which it needs to succeed. It is therefore a learning organization that is skilled at creating, acquiring, organizing and sharing knowledge that can gain competitive advantage.

Strategy

There are two knowledge management strategies that firms can adopt: codification and personalization (Tierney, 1999). Personalization strategy requires direct contact among people in order to share knowledge. Knowledge is shared mainly through direct face-to-face, phone, voicemail, or other types of contacts. Technology serves as a facilitator for knowledge communication (Tierney, 1999). On the other hand, codification strategy focuses on extracting and codifying knowledge for the purpose of mass sharing. Knowledge is stored in databases or knowledge bases, which can be accessed by anyone in an organization. Codification means extracting knowledge from people, codifying it and storing it in databases for reuse. Technology is the central point of knowledge repository.

In addition to business needs and strategy, the selection of strategy should be based on the type of knowledge shared. A recent notion, introduced by Tierney (1999), claims that companies should adopted an "80-20" strategy. According to him, companies that focus on mastering both strategies would fail; instead they should focus on one and not the other.

People

A challenge for KM is managing and training people to embrace a KM-oriented culture. According to Zack (1999), sharing knowledge especially proprietary or individual knowledge could result in power redistribution and face cultural resistance. Many studies emphasized the importance of corporate culture in successful knowledge management (Earl and Scott, 1999; Wah, 1999; Havens & Knapp, 1999).

Some even claim that knowledge management can be successful only with a change in culture. Furthermore, the new culture must be integrated with existing business processes and practices. Communication, reward systems, and leadership are important cultural factors identified in literature.

Communication

A knowledge-sharing environment is interactive. Organizational culture must embrace free-flow communication (Wah, 1999), which encourages sharing of knowledge and ideas. The first step is to make people aware of existing knowledge in the organization. Knowledge at both individual and organizational levels should be made accessible (Havens & Knapp, 1999). Everyone must participate in knowledge sharing and be able to access company knowledge base. More importantly, knowledge must be put within direct access to employees. More intermediaries there are while transmitting knowledge, the more likely will distortions occur (Buckman, 1998).

Reward System and Performance Metrics

Employee performance evaluation should be different in knowledge organizations. Knowledge sharing attitudes and behaviors should be rewarded. Lack of contribution to KM activities should be penalized (Buckman, 1998).

Leadership

Even though the types of activities involved in KM are to be accomplished by employees, such activities are supported by resources and top-level management. Leadership will not only reinforce knowledge management initiatives by providing resources and granting investment, but also direct them so that they align with organizational strategies (Wah, 1999).

Because of the strategic importance of knowledge and KM, a new management position is needed. Many knowledge-based organizations adopted a new management role: Chief Knowledge Officer (CKO). A CKO is knowledgeable in technology, organization, and strategy (Earl & Scott, 1999). He/she is the central point of a KM effort.

Technology

Knowledge, in today's organizations, can be characterized as "fragmented" (Zack, 1999). There are extremely large volumes of knowledge dispersed in organizations with ever-increasing size. Accompanied with mergers, acquisition, and alliances, companies are becoming more and more diversified in the type of businesses they operate. Information technology is only effective if used properly in data management. Now the question is whether IT can do the same for KM: to enhance knowledge management initiatives.

Buckman states that knowledge repositories need to be available to all employees at all time (1998). It is discovered that in Buckman Laboratories, employees spend 86% of their time outside their offices (Buckman, 1998). This is increasingly true to many companies. Without IT, overcoming time and space constraints and barriers can hardly be accomplished.

To allow knowledge sharing anytime anywhere, several types of technological tools are available. Mobile technology, portable hardware and software, and networks, email, teleconferencing, and intranets are some of the commonly used technologies for knowledge creation and sharing. Knowledge-bases/repositories, data warehouse, WAN are some of the technologies used for data retention.

Knowledge

The core of KM is knowledge. It is the source of innovation and competitive advantage (Porter, 1998). Moreover, it is the most important and valuable capital of a firm and it is vital to organizational growth. However, it is complex and there are various dimensions of knowledge under which knowledge is classified. Organizations need to understand the type of knowledge that flows among their employees so that they can be in a good position to determine the type(s) of knowledge management strategies to adopt.

Explicit knowledge can be easily articulated and shared. Zack (1999) proposed the use of "knowledge unit" in defining knowledge. Knowledge units are content components of knowledge. Explicit knowledge is further classified into declarative, procedural, and causal knowledge (Zack, 1999). Declarative knowledge is "about describing something." Declarative knowledge is believed to be the foundation of effective communication and knowledge sharing. Procedural knowledge is "about how something occurs or is performed." Causal knowledge is "about why something occurs." However, a large portion of organizational knowledge is not easily articulated. Such knowledge is called tacit knowledge and is "the implicit, non-codified accumulation of expertise and skills accumulated largely through experience" (Reed & DeFillippi, 1990)." Tacit knowledge often are embedded in organizational social systems and therefore, hard to extract and transfer. Sharing tacit knowledge, such as the best practice or know-how, is the main cause for knowledge management initiatives (Emery, 1999). The problem is that tacit knowledge is not easily transferred. However, tacit knowledge can be transformed into explicit knowledge. The process of transforming tacit knowledge into explicit knowledge is called articulation (Hedlund, 1994). Researchers asserted that some tacit knowledge should be left tacit in order to sustain competitive performance (Zack, 1999).

Knowledge Processes

Inkpen (1996) characterizes KM processes as "a set of organizational actions that establish the basis for accessing and exploiting" knowledge. Knowledge related work, categorized by Davenport and Prusak (1997), are accessing, generating, imbedding/reproducing, and transferring. Three major activities are involved in knowledge management: knowledge creation, retention, and sharing. The essence of KM is to manage those activities for organizational effectiveness.

Knowledge Creation

This is the process in which knowledge is captured and defined. Explicit knowledge can be easily captured and put in the form of a manual, booklet, or document. On the other hand, tacit knowledge is imbedded in social structures, and therefore, it needs to be extracted, codified, and made explicit. Through this codification process, tacit knowledge is transformed into explicit knowledge.

Knowledge Retention/Protection

Another important knowledge management activity is the retention and protection of knowledge. The main purpose of retention is to allow reuse of knowledge. Knowledge retained can be readily shared. Protection of knowledge is equally important. Without security measure, the integrity of the knowledge could be at stake. Erroneous knowledge is just as damaging as inaccessible knowledge if not more.

Knowledge Sharing

When we communicate knowledge, it is the process of sharing. Both explicit and tacit knowledge can be shared. However, explicit knowledge can be shared more easily and will have little risk of creating error in the process. Tacit knowledge, which is hard to articulate, is the challenging part of knowledge sharing. In any case, sharing should be as direct as possible with few intermediaries (Buckman, 1998).

CASE STUDIES

In this section, we attempt to compile the experiences of two companies that have succeeded in knowledge management. Using the case study approach, we analyze the knowledge management processes of Buckman Laboratories and Nippon Steel-British Steel.

Buckman laboratories (Pan and Scarbrough, 1999)

Buckman laboratories is a $300 million chemical company that serves industries in 102 different countries selling 1000 different specialty chemicals. The processes adopted by Buckman's laboratories were examined and the findings are grouped to fit the knowledge management research model.

Environmental Factors

Some of the environmental factors that compelled the company to go in for KM were the need to maintain customer knowledge, competitive intelligence, process knowledge and product knowledge. The knowledge management process was important to maintain the company's competitive edge as well as the proprietary knowledge, which is protected by patents and trade secrecy and is codified.

Strategy

The strategy adopted by Buckman's laboratories for KM was largely the codified way of distributing knowledge. The knowledge creating and sharing systems known as K' Netrix are divided into two basic categories: seven organizational forums and various codified databases.

People

The company's culture consists of its knowledge enterprising characteristics that promote knowledge sharing. Part of the unique culture puts the world's most knowledgeable experts at all levels of the Buckman organization to stay in touch, thus encouraging group problem solving and sharing of new ideas and knowledge. Top management is proactive in changing culture within the organization.

Technology

K'Netix is an interconnected system of knowledge bases used as a worldwide resource by Buckman laboratories associates. It is the network through which the Buckman associates share knowledge electronically and then passes it on to the customer. It is represented by an inter-related collection of databases that support rapid exchange of knowledge between associates who are separated by both time and space. Integrating bulletin boards, electronic forums, virtual conference rooms, libraries, and e-mail, K'Netix gives Buckman employees, partners, and customers' unlimited access to expertise, experience and resources in around 102 countries.

Knowledge

The knowledge bases come in many forms ranging from loosely organized expertise possessed by knowledge workers to highly organized and strictly represented knowledge bases that support knowledge based system applications. Buckman laboratories conveniently divided their knowledge into factual knowledge and behavioral knowledge. Factual corporate knowledge consists of technological and product know-how. The behavioral corporate knowledge included the cultures and working styles of the individuals in organizations.

Knowledge Management Process

A feedback loop was set up, so that after listening to customers, any queries relating to a particular area that could not be answered by the technical sales/field based associates were posted on the forum. Usually the request for help was picked up by anyone who had expertise in the related field. If the request was unattended for a few hours, two scenarios emerged. First, the forum specialist would pick up the request, identify the potential experts and try to get their attention in order to answer the questions. Second, there was also a team of experts with related industrial experience who volunteered to be listed as section leaders who would help answer any requests and weekly summaries. The knowledge was then organized, validated, and stored into the knowledge base and was ready for distribution and use/reuse if a similar query was requested in the future.

Nippon Steel – British Steel Alliance

Nippon Steel Corporation is the world's leading steel producer over a long period. It is a leading exponent amongst Japanese firms for quality assurance and it has developed long-term relationships with its customers, including Toyota, a Japanese leading car manufacturer. British Steel is a major supplier of steel to Toyota's UK manufacturing plants and it approached Nippon Steel to improve its quality control mechanisms. Nippon Steel and British Steel established a technical alliance that formed part of a broader program of change at British Steel focusing on improving the quality of its products and its Japanese customer relationships.

Environment Forces

For Nippon Steel and British Steel, it was important to improve human resources and management of human resource. That is, competitive advantage can only be sustained by continuously improving the knowledge and expertise of employees, motivating and empowering employees at different levels to use their knowledge to pursue the main strategic objectives of the firm, re-organizing and restructuring human resources, rearranging specialist divisions of knowledge and expertise, improving the interfaces (communication, knowledge integration etc), and maintaining close links with customers.

Strategy

Nippon Steel and British Steel depended on the personalized strategy for knowledge sharing. Most of their knowledge sharing was through seminars and training sessions. Task groups were sent by British Steel to Nippon Steel to observe the processes and management practices and share the knowledge with their fellow workers in British Steel. The processes were then codified and made into libraries that all levels of mill workers could access to gain knowledge.

People

The traditional differences between blue and white collar workers and the lack of skills and training, plus the cultural differences between the British and Japanese counterparts in terms of accepting ownership and responsibility were major challenges for technical information exchange between the workers.

Technology

Nippon Steel and British Steel developed libraries in the form of distributed databases that could be accessed by everyone. The libraries were developed and maintained by the mill employees, giving them an understanding of what the libraries represent, how they should be developed and the benefits that they could bring within the overall drive to improve quality.

Knowledge

Task teams from British Steel spent a week at the Nippon plant observing the firms systems for managing technology. The task teams were established to focus on particular plant level problems and transfer best practice solutions to the other plants.

Knowledge Process

Nippon steel had full time employees logging the defect samples into the libraries and maintaining them, which had an extensive range of examples and samples about the various faults and conditions and in some cases solutions that were used to overcome the problems. The libraries were used as a reference tool and store of knowledge and experience on process defects that contributed significantly to final product.

DISCUSSION

This section discusses the findings on KM that were observed in both the case studies. The main reasons that companies undergo KM are to improve the knowledge and expertise of their employees, to motivate and empower employees at different levels to use their knowledge, to reorganize and restructure human resources, and to improve the interfaces for knowledge sharing. Both companies examined depend on one type of strategy for KM, although the other is also used. Buckman's laboratories greatly depended on the codified method of KM while Nippon Steel-British Steel used the personalized method although they codified their processes into libraries and databases for all the personnel to use. The culture of the organization has to be made suitable for KM. As Buckman (1998) suggested KM is 90% of a cultural change. The top management has to take deep interest in the process of KM. A CKO (Chief Knowledge Officer) is usually appointed in most organizations to initiate and manage knowledge sharing. In both the organizations, the top management created awareness and a need for the KM process. Various technologies were used for KM. Databases and on-line forums were the most common types of technologies used for KM. Other forms of technology used were video-conferencing and e-mail. Knowledge, both explicit and tacit, can be created and retained in databases and shared among the employees.

CONCLUSION

In this paper, we highlighted the importance of KM for companies to maintain their competitive advantage. A research model is developed to explain the process of KM. The environmental forces compel the companies to take KM initiatives. Distributing knowledge among the employees so as to empower them to take timely decisions is one of the main reasons for KM in organizations. Through strategy, people and technology, knowledge is created in organizations. The knowledge that is created in organizations has to be retained and shared among the employees to complete the entire process of KM. Using the research model as a framework, we examined the two case studies, one of the Buckman's Laboratories and the other of Nippon Steel-British Steel Alliance, to study the KM process. Companies focus on one of the two strategies for KM either the personalized or the codified method of KM.

The contribution of this paper is two folded: One, the research model serves as a guideline for practitioners who wish to implement the knowledge management processes in their organizations. The feasibility of the model is demonstrated by the two case studies. Second, the model serves as a framework for future knowledge management research. For example, the various components of the KM framework and their relationships can be studied in detail.

REFERENCES

Blair, J. (1999). *Knowledge Management Is About Cooperation And Context*, Gartner Advisory Services Research Note, 14 May.

Buckman, R. H. (1998). Knowledge Sharing at Buckman Labs. *Journal of Business Strategy*, (19:1), pg.11-28.

Cisco, S. L. and Strong, K. V. (1999). The Value Added Information Chain, The *Information Management Journal*, Jan, pg. 4-15.

Collinson, S. (1999). Knowledge Management Capabilities for Steel Makers: A British –Japanese Corporate Alliance for Organizational Learning, *Technology Analysis & Strategic Management*, (11:3), pg. 337- 358.

DeSanctis, G. & Poole, M. S. (1994). Capturing the Complexity in Advanced Technology Use: Adaptive Structuration Theory, *Organizational Science*, (5:2), pg.121-147.

Duffy, J. (1999). *Harvesting Experience: Reaping the Benefits of Knowledge*, Prairie Village, KS: ARMA International.

Duffy, J. (2000). Knowledge Management: To Be or Not To Be, *The Information Management Journal*, Jan, pg. 64-67.

Earl, M. J., & Scott, I. A. (1999). What Is A Chief Knowledge Officer? *Sloan Management Review*, (40:2), pg. 29-38.

Emery, P. (1999). Understand Knowledge Management, *e-Business Advisor*, April, 14.

Greco, J. (1999). Knowledge is Power, *Journal of Business Strategy*, (20:2), pg.19-22.

Havens, C., & Knapp, E. (1999). Easing Into Knowledge Management, *Strategy & Leadership*, (27:2), pg. 4-9.

Inkpen, A. C. (1996). Creating Knowledge Through collaboration, *California Management Review*, Fall, (39:1), pg. 123- 140.

Kim, W. C., & Mauborgne, R. (1999). Strategy, Value Innovation, And The Knowledge Economy, *Sloan Management Review*, (40:3), pg.41-54.

McDermott, R. (1999). Why Information Technology Inspired But Cannot Deliver Knowledge Management, *California Management Review*, (41:4),pg. 103-117.

Mullin, R. (1996). Knowledge Management: A Cultural Evolution, *Journal of Business Strategy*, September-October, pg. 56-59.

Pan, S.L and Scarbrough (1999). Knowledge Management in Practice: An Exploratory Case Study, *Technology Analysis and Strategic Management*, (11:3), pg. 359-371.

Pemberton, M. J. (1997). Chief Knowledge Officer: The Climax to Your Career, *Records Management Quarterly*, April, pg.66-69.

Porter, M. E. (1998). Clusters and the New Economics of Competition, *Harvard Business Review*, November/December, (77).

Saffady, W. (1999). *Knowledge Management: A Managers Briefing*, Prairie Village, KS: ARMA International.

Tan, J. (2000). Knowledge Management-Just More Buzzwords? *The British Journal of Administrative Management*, March-April.

Tierney, T. (1999). What's Your Strategy for Managing Knowledge? *Harvard Business Review*, March/April, (106).

Werr, A.(1999). Managing Knowledge In Management Consulting, *Academy of Management Proceedings '98*, MC: A1-A7.

Zollo, M. (1998). The Impact Of Knowledge Codification, Experience Trajectories And Integration Strategies On The Performance Of Corporate Acquisitions, *Academy of Management Proceedings '98*, BPS: L1-L10.

Chapter 30

'Knowledge Management': A Telling Oxymoron?

Dr. D. A. White and Dr. Y. M. Sutton
University of Lincolnshire and Humberside, United Kingdom

INTRODUCTION

As organisations continue to seek optimal levels of competitive advantage and innovation, the search continues for more powerful and successful ways of achieving these goals. One such is the emerging discipline of Knowledge Management (KM). This is an approach, which is becoming firmly embedded in the panoply of management methods, as noted by Scarborough et al. (1999), "Knowledge Management (and the learning organisation) represent important new approaches to the problems of competitiveness and innovation confronting organisations." These are not insignificant claims and, typically, pursuing them requires organisational investment, which is also substantial. This paper seeks to develop a critique of KM, with a view to supporting more informed theory and practice in this area. This critique is based upon recent empirical research (Sutton, 2000; Sutton and White, 2000; White and Sutton, 2000). The nature, methods, and key findings of that research are, therefore, briefly described here.

NATURE OF THE RESEARCH PROJECT

The research explored the nature of, and relationships between, knowledge, data and information in the context of clinical practice in the United Kingdom National Health Service (NHS). It focused on the nature of clinical knowledge and the large-scale statistical datasets, which are generated from healthcare ac-

Previously Published in *Managing Information Technology in a Global Economy* edited by Mehdi Khosrow-Pour, Copyright © 2001, Idea Group Publishing.

tivities and decisions. These datasets are used for significant and far-reaching decisions about NHS policy.

The genesis of this research was a growing interest into what appeared to be a paradox pertaining to clinical data in the NHS. The paradox involved the fact that, while to the lay eye medicine appeared to be a discipline imbued with all the rigour and certainty of science, key elements of clinical knowledge and data seemed often to be characterised by uncertainty and vagueness, and to be opinion-laden. In short, these elements seemed to be characterised by subjectivity at least as often as they were by objectivity. Yet both objective and subjective types of data were all somehow regularly transformed into a homogeneous body of objective, statistical "facts," used by Government and various healthcare managers as the basis of significant decisions about healthcare in the NHS. Thus, this piece of research was developed and undertaken, in order to gain a better understanding of the nature of knowledge and data, and the underpinning social processes inherent in clinical care. This study sought to achieve its aim specifically by developing a better understanding of knowledge in the clinical context of the NHS and to achieve this by exploring the impact of social and organisational context, and transformation processes, on knowledge transferred between individuals and groups.

THE RESEARCH APPROACH

The research problem demanded an exploratory approach, which led, therefore, to the use of inductive methods. The key objective of the research approach was: "to describe, decode, translate or otherwise come to terms with the meaning, not the frequency, of certain more or less naturally occurring phenomena in the social world." Data collection was, therefore, undertaken partly by using ethnographic methods which involved the practitioner "participating covertly or overtly in people's daily lives for a period of time, watching what happens, listening to what is said, asking questions – in fact, collecting whatever data are available to throw light on the issues that are the focus of the research" (Hammersley and Atkinson, 1983). This extensive qualitative, field-based investigation included a long period of participant observation in clinical and coding settings, and thirty semi-structured interviews with senior clinicians, healthcare data statisticians and epidemiologists, administrative workers, healthcare managers and coders. This overall approach, of complex, discovery-based research yielding rich, qualitative data, produced a deep understanding of the processes and contexts involved in the domain of clinical decision-making. Data was analysed using Grounded Theory, as described by Glaser and Strauss (1973).

FINDINGS FROM THE RESEARCH

Conclusions from the research suggested that clinicians' use of information and subsequent recording of data represents a highly personalised area of professional activity. This does not subsequently translate easily into coded schemes, including data sets and the statistical classifications that are in common usage in healthcare management. Thus the research challenged the validity of the relationship between this knowledge and its coded counterparts, arguing that the fidelity of the statistical data to the original clinical knowledge is apparent and not real. Consequently, the rationality of decisions made on this basis is equally dubious.

Turning now to the implications of this for KM, the research resulted in the following views of KM, which suggest that a range of factors militate against the current KM notion of "knowledge" and how it might be "managed." These are explored below.

WHAT IS KNOWLEDGE MANAGEMENT AND HOW DOES IT WORK?

KM is a concept that achieved increasing prominence throughout the 1990s. It essentially seeks to create a type of organisational 'neural network', wherein key knowledge possessed by individual workers is made more generally accessible. As noted by Blake (1998), "KM is the process of capturing a company's collective expertise wherever it resides and distributing it to wherever it can help produce the biggest payoffs" (Blake, 1998 : 2). Such expertise, or "knowledge resources" are defined as "core competencies" (Prahalad and Hamell, 1990) or "routines" (Nelson and Winter, 1982) "capabilities" (Collis, 1991) and "core skills" (Klein et al, 1991). These are seen as ".... the well-spring of future product development .... the roots of competitiveness, and individual products and services are the fruit" (Prahalad and Hamell, 1990: 202). This is not restricted to those within an organisation: "(KM) is an approach to adding or creating value by more actively leveraging the know-how, experience and judgement residing within and, in many cases, outside an organisation." (Ruggles, 1998: 82).

In terms of how KM harnesses these resources, "KM is equated to data mining, digging and drilling .... its aim is to 'mine' the tacit knowledge, skills and expertise of people" (Gardner, 1998: 24). Furthermore, the idea behind KM is to collect and make accessible workers' knowledge ".... via a searchable application" (Cole-Gromolski, 1997: 6). Information technology is, therefore, a key enabler to KM: "KM is primarily IS/IT driven" (Scarborough et al, 1999: 27).

Typically in the KM literature the dimensions of knowledge types, which are addressed are tacit and explicit, subjective and objective. As evidenced by the objective of "mining" and making accessible through searchable applications, all knowledge types are assumed ultimately to be accessible and codifiable.

In summary, therefore, KM classifies knowledge along two axes: subjective/ objective and tacit/explicit. Furthermore it assumes no differences in the nature of these knowledge types, which would preclude its faithful representation via computers. It also assumes that knowledge can be fully and accurately articulated and transferred among different cultural groups: "(KM) depends on tapping the *tacit* and often highly *subjective* insights, intuitions, and hunches of individual employees and making those insights available for testing and use by the company as a whole" (Nonaka, 1998: 24).

KNOWLEDGE MANAGEMENT : A CRITIQUE

Methods of capturing and representing reality are operational manifestations of particular ontological and epistemological beliefs, and characteristic of a particular paradigm. This critique will, therefore, begin by exploring KM's underlying paradigm, and will then consider the validity of its relationship to the kind of knowledge underpinning human expertise.

As indicated in the above description of the processes involved in KM, it is characterised by a scientific approach to knowledge and knowledge transfer, reminiscent of that found in Artificial Intelligence and Computer Science. As noted by Scarborough et al. (1999:33) ".... the systematic use of knowledge for economic objectives .... is clearly a feature of Taylorism and related methods." Scientific methods are reductionist. Reality is perceived to be an immutable phenomenon; areas may, therefore, be fragmented without loss of emergent properties. This paradigm asserts that the world can be exhaustively analysed in terms of determinate data or atomic facts. The assumption that all knowledge can be faithfully represented in codes, and shared amongst individuals is a natural consequence of these beliefs. Thus, this "technocratic intervention" (Scarborough et al., 1999: 50) can successfully divorce knowledge from its organisational context, and *all* that is relevant to intelligent behaviour can be formalised in a structured description (Sowa, 1994; Fiegenbaum and McCorduck, 1983). In this scenario coding schemes and computers are neutral knowledge transfer media. In other words, emergent properties (Checkland, 1981, von Bertalanffy, 1968) or properties that emerge at certain levels of complexity and cannot be reduced in explanation to lower levels (because they do not exist there) are not perceived to exist. Computer representation, therefore, requires only adequate identification and understanding of the various entities and relationships between them. Finally, there is an implicit belief, again reflecting this mechanistic paradigm, in a rational, unproblematic and predictable relationship between knowledge, data, information and decision-making.

That being the case, one might expect data about such a world to be, ' ... discrete, explicit, determinate..." (Dreyfus et al, 1986: 188). This is precisely the kind of data required by digital computers: ".... otherwise it will not be the sort of information which can be given to a computer so as to be processed by a rule" (Dreyfus et al, 1986: 118). This is echoed by Weizenbaum (1985) in reviewing the work of von Neumann (1958) who asserts that, if he were to be presented with a *precise* description of what the computer was required to do, someone could program the computer to behave in the required manner. The following sections investigate this possibility in the context of the above-mentioned research.

KNOWLEDGE AND THE INDIVIDUAL

In the NHS consultations occur between clinicians and patients, and some clinical data about those encounters is coded, using clinical classifications. It is also computerised. The resulting data sets form the basis of Department of Health data about these clinical events. As described above, the research explored the nature of the relationship between the original clinical knowledge and the representation of that knowledge found in the data sets. The underlying premise was that, if all clinical work conformed to scientific principles, and clinical knowledge represented hard, immutable "fact," coding, classifying and computerising would be relevant activities. If, however, clinical work and knowledge did not conform to these characteristics, data produced as a result of these activities, and decisions that followed from that data, must be considered unsafe.

The research confirmed that clinical knowledge is not overwhelmingly characterised by hard immutable facts. As noted by Szolovits (1994:1), "Uncertainty is the central critical fact about medical reasoning. Patients cannot describe exactly what has happened to them or how they feel, doctors and nurses cannot tell exactly what they observe, laboratories report results only with some degree of error ...." A number of clinical participants to the research confirmed this further, a typical comment being: "Most (diseases) are pathognomically very difficult to diagnose definitively. There are some; for instance blood sugar above a certain level is pathognomic of diabetes mellitus, but these (instances) are rare."

As noted by Fox (1979) and De Dombal (1996) medical teaching reflects this. It is based on the recognition that an irreducible amount of uncertainty is inherent in medicine. Fox (1979) asserts that three basic types of uncertainty may be recognised. The first results from incomplete or imperfect command of knowledge available about the discipline of medicine. The second stems from limitations in current knowledge. The third can derive from the first two, and rests upon the difficulty in distinguishing between personal ignorance or incompetence and the limitations of present knowledge. Generally, the literature in this area makes clear that it is assumed that medical knowledge gained thus far must be regarded as tentative and subject to constant further enquiry, and that few absolutes exist. It reveals medicine as something less than an exact science. Indeed, it reveals it as being as much an art as a science, a matter of judgement as well as skill. Notably, judgement, in the same way as art, is about subjectivity and interpretation, not empiricism. This immediately raises questions about the knowledge types recognised within KM, which can now be seen as insufficient. To subjective/objective and tacit/explicit must be added uncertain/certain.

In addition, knowledge that is uncertain may also turn out to be incomplete. As noted by a clinical participant: "Conclusions, including written ones, are usually tentative .... i.e., 'found lying on the floor- ?,' 'fracture leg of femur ?,' 'cerebral haemorrhage?" The question mark here was routinely used in clinicians' handwritten medical records to denote these were options the clinician was considering, one, many, or none of which might turn out to be relevant. As another clinical participant remarked: "Often the clinician never has a clue why the patient is on the floor and often they never find out" Even so, as noted by Szolovits (1994:1) "…. we must make important decisions about testing and treatments and, despite our uncertainties about the bases of those decisions, the decisions themselves must be definitive." Thus, the clinician is trained to act independently and confidently on the basis of the information available or acquirable, even where certainty or completeness are not possible, and where clinical findings and the totality of those findings remain tentative, subjective and heterogeneous to an unquantified degree. The KM classification of knowledge types must, therefore, be further extended to include complete/incomplete. Individuals have been shown still to make sense with, and act upon, vague, uncertain and incomplete knowledge.

The literature further indicates that a wide range of factors can then affect this basic uncertainty, extending the heterogeneity of clinical knowledge. Levels of acquired competence and skill affect uncertainty, as do levels of "experience" generally. Experienced clinicians tend to elicit less information than their more junior colleagues, but they also tend to elicit more relevant information. They are also able to combine these items of information more appropriately than their juniors. Clinical experience generally operates as a weighting function that gives preference to these more effective types of connections. As discussed by Kluge (1996: 88) "…. these weighting functions are integral to the conceptual framework of the clinician as the clinician gains experience." This was further explained by a clinical participant to the research: "The clinician starts with two main groups of knowledge, prefaced by locational knowledge .... the setting confers some knowledge, i.e., if I know the patient will be in Outpatients I immediately assume they cannot be too sick. If I am scheduled to see them at home I assume they may be quite ill, or they would have been scheduled to attend Outpatients." That type of knowledge can then be seen to nest within the two main groups which he went on to describe as: "…. general knowledge and experience, which can apply to all patients, and consisting of formal knowledge: that which has been taught to me, and informal knowledge: that which has been gained through experience, (and) specific knowledge about each individual patient, gained from personal consultation and communications …." This was confirmed by another clinical participant, who remarked: "…. the basis of clinical medicine is an amalgam of others' knowledge and personal experience." Thus the knowledge clinicians bring to each consultation was seen to be variable in quantity, quality and nature, and its application, within the broad, standard framework of clinical examination and history taking etc., was seen to be equally variable.

The next stage in the process of knowledge generation and application was described, again by a clinical participant, as follows: "Following the initial discussion with the patient I take the data collected and put it to my personal knowledge base and conclude a number of things about the present state of the individual …. But what I conclude may be very different from what another clinician, faced with the same data might conclude …." Thus "weighting functions" or each clinician's unique psychobiological characteristics, are also influential in determining the reality perceived and represented. As noted by a clinical participant to the research: "The other day a colleague of mine reported feeling a hard liver edge in a patient. My own examination indicated this was not so." A second participant echoed this. Discussing a recent consultation he advised that his colleagues: "…. would be quite likely to go about the consultation differently and may even come to different conclusions, depending upon a number of factors, including the patient's personal characteristics, the relationship established, the Consultant's interests, experience, demeanour, etc."

The practical consequences of this conceptual framework are further enlarged upon by De Dombal (1996) particularly if, as discussed above, uncertainty is taken to mean not holding objective characteristics, i.e., not being hard, immutable "fact." In discussing the need to abandon simplistic models of clinical perception and information when designing computerised clinical information systems, De Dombal comments on factors affecting the objective value of a piece of clinical information. He presents an equation composed of a number of elements, which he asserts are not, so far, taken account of in either current determinist theory, current probabilist teaching or decision support systems. The equation includes the evidential value observed in previous surveys; the degree to which the local circumstances reflect the findings in various surveys; the confidence with which the clinical feature was elicited; the overall reproducibility of the process of elicitation of that feature; the clinical acumen of the individual eliciting the information; the relevance of the information to the role of the individual in the overall healthcare delivery system; and the timeliness of the information to the situation. De Dombal presents these factors as a list, indicating that, whilst he believes they influence the objective value of a piece of information, there is at present no knowledge of how they influence the value or how to combine them. What De Dombal is saying is that there is an acceptance, or belief in, simplistic representations of knowledge, "such as clinicians' expressed opinions" (De Dombal, 1996:1) but reality is much more complex than this. It is argued here that the characteristics of KM described above indicate an assumption of such simplicity. As De Dombal argues, reality is more complex. It is not only more complex for the reasons he states, but also because, as discussed below, expressed opinions rarely constitute firm ground for accurate representation of knowledge.

"MINING" CAPTURING AND TRANSFERRING KNOWLEDGE

The notion of "mining" knowledge assumes certain abilities on the part of the holder of knowledge and the person extracting it, which it is argued here are without substantial foundation. Assertions here draw on work by Dreyfus et al. (1986) who studied the learning process in humans to ascertain how far digital computers can safely go towards apparent "intelligence." Five stages are identified: novice, advanced beginner, competence, proficiency and expert. The novice is usually working on context-free information, i.e., not referring back to experience but learning by rote. The expert knows what to do on the basis of mature and practised understanding, with skill that is so much a part of them they are almost unaware of it. Dreyfus argues that this shows a progression from the analytic behaviour of a detached subject, consciously decomposing his environment into recognisable elements and following abstract rules, to involved skill-based behaviour involving holistic pairing of new situations. Thus a progression is seen, going from exercising no judgement to exercising judgement. Within this context, KM assumes that the user "domain expert" is someone who possesses and, more importantly, can articulate "know-that" knowledge and also "know-how" with respect to how those beliefs became accepted within that domain, hence all that is necessary to capturing and sharing key knowledge can be gleaned from them. Work by both Dreyfus (1986) and Giddens (1976, 1984) refutes this. When discussing the consciousness of the acting subject they assert that much of human knowledge is, in fact, held by some to exist on a tacit basis. Dreyfus argues that the level of articulation required by the domain expert would require an unproven ability to regress from the state of tacit knowledge to that of the novice, who is conscious of the relationship between decisions, knowledge and data. Work in the field of KM by Scarborough et al. (1999) and Nonaka (1994) which further supports the existence and importance of tacit knowledge, also asserts that it forms part of the background of shared assumptions on which culture is founded and as such *cannot* be articulated. This is not necessarily perceived to be a problem to KM practitioners.

The perception of clinical work described here led to a conclusion that it is a domain in which the universe of discourse is imperfectly understood. Perception, knowledge and information, methods of describing observations and views of elements of it remain, even after clinical training, subjective and heterogeneous to an unspecified degree. This is not to say that there are no definitives, simply that no work was found which analyses types of clinical knowledge in such a way as to define which phenomena fall into which category and what the relative percentages are.

Despite this, the Department of Health believes it holds objective, factual data about key clinical events within the NHS, and bases decisions on it. Thus KM notions that such knowledge can be comprehensively captured and is codifiable and transferable are clearly suspect. When IT applications are applied to areas of human expertise, they go beyond the kind of context-independent, rule-driven, objective features of the real world relevant to their design principles. Ensuing data then provides only a flawed representation of the area of reality addressed.

SUMMARY AND IMPLICATIONS FOR KNOWLEDGE MANAGEMENT

The research underpinning and discussed in this paper demonstrated that, as noted by Blackler (1995), "…. knowledge is multifaceted and complex, being both situated and abstract, implicit and explicit, distributed and individual, physical and mental, developing and static, verbal and encoded." It has also shown, using the domain of medical practice, that there are areas of knowledge where formalisation is inherently problematic, due t6o a range of social factors. As noted by Clancey(1995: 8) "…. medical practice is inherently unformalizable and truth-constructing, and that doesn't fit with the objectivist view of classic science." As discussed by Kay and Purves (1996) and Kluge (1996) the personal consultation is: "….. not an interpretationally neutral fact gathering exercise, because it involves something other than a neutral information transfer ….. this entire process carries its own phenomenological burden …the physician … records … information with an ineluctable phenomenological bias" (Kluge, 1996: 88). Clinical knowledge results, therefore, from enactment by clinical and non-clinical groups of their respective social contexts. These can be defined as knowledge-creating contexts, which determine how data might be both produced and also how it might be validly used in decision-making, both within and outside the domain of clinical work. Ability to translate such data in such a way as to transfer such knowledge across social boundaries, without disturbing meaning is questionable. Clinical data can, *technically,* be readily translated into data, and that data can be shared. However, accurate technical performance does not necessarily equate to transfer of knowledge. Rather this process gives a partly illusory and misleading representation.

In summary, the kinds of rationalist assumptions about knowledge creation and use, which characterise KM, are inadequate. Knowledge and meaning cannot be transferred as easily as data. The current approach adopted by KM is, therefore, simplistic, limited in scope and somewhat naïve. It is suggested that a broader approach to, and definition of, "knowledge" is not only possible in this context, but an essential pre-requisite to attempts to harness and exploit it. It is also suggested that KM must have a social dimension if it is to realise its potential. If it is to avoid being consigned to the ranks of yet another "management fads," it must recognise and address the issues raised by the fact that knowledge is socially-located and constructed and cannot successfully be detached from the social context within which it is created and operates.

REFERENCES

Bertalanffy, L. von (1968). *General system theory,* New York: Braziller.

Blackler, F. (1995). Knowledge, knowledge work and organisations: an overview and interpretation, *Organisation studies, 16,* (6) 16-36.

Blake, P. (1998). The knowledge management expansion, *Information today 15* (1) 12-13.

Checkland, P. (1981). *Systems thinking, systems practice,* Chichester: John Wiley & Sons.

Clancey, W.J. (1995). The learning process in the epistemology of medical information, *Methods of information in medicine Special Issue* 1-16.

Cole-Gromolski, B. (1997). Users loathe to share their know-how, *Computerworld 31* (46) 6.

Collis, D. (1991). A resource-based analysis of global competition; the case of the bearings industry, *Strategic management journal, Summer Special Issue 12* 49-68.

De Dombal, F.T. (1996). Assigning value to clinical information - A major limiting factor in the implementation of decision-support systems, *Methods of information in medicine 35* 1-4.

Dreyfus, H.L. and Dreyfus, S.E. (1986). *Mind over machine, the power of human intuition and expertise in the era of the computer,* New York: The Free Press.

Feigenbaum, E. and McCorduck, P. (1983). *The fifth generation: artificial intelligence and Japan's computer challenge to the world,* Reading, MA: Addison-Wesley.

Fox, R.C. (1979). *Essays in medical sociology, journeys into the field,* New York: John Wiley & Sons Inc.

Gardner, D. (1998). Knowledge that won't fit the database -people, *Infor world 20* (14).

Giddens, A (1976). *The interpretation of cultures,* New York: Basic Books.

Giddens A. (1984). *The constitution of society, outline of the theory of structuration,* Cambridge: Polity Press.

Glaser, B. G. and Strauss, A.L. (1973). *The discovery of grounded theory. Strategies for qualitative research,* Chicago: Aldine.

Hammersley, M. and Atkinson, P. (1983). *Ethnography principles in practice,* London: Routledge.

Kay, S. and Purves, I.N. (1996). Medical records and other stories - a narratological framework, *Methods of information in medicine 35* 72-87.

Klein J.A., Edge, G.M., and Kass, T. (1991). Skill-based competition, *Journal of general management, 16,* (4) Summer, 1-15.

Kluge, E.H.W. (1996). The medical record: narration and story as a path through patient data, editorial commentary, *Methods of information in medicine, 35* 88-92.

Nelson, R. and Winter S. (1982). *An evolutionary theory of organisational change,* Cambridge, MA: Harvard University Press.

Neumann, J. Von,(1958). *The computer and the brain,* USA: Yale University Press.

Nonaka, I. (1994). A dynamic theory of organisational knowledge creation' *Organisation science, 5* 14-37.

Nonaka, I. (1998). The knowledge-creating company, in *Harvard business review on knowledge management,* Boston: Harvard Business School Press.

Prahalad, C.K., and Hamel, G. (1990). The core competencies of the corporation, *Harvard business review May - June,* 79-91.

Ruggles, R. (1998). The state of the notion: knowledge management in practice, *California management review 40* (3) 80- 89.

Scarborough, H., Swan, J., and Preston, J. (1999). *Knowledge management: a literature review,* London: The Institute of Personnel and Development.

Sowa, J. (1994). *Knowledge representation,* USA, book in draft.

Sutton, Y.M. (2000). Knowledge transformation and representation: towards more informed provision and use of information, PhD thesis, Sheffield Hallam University United Kingdom.

Sutton, Y.M. and White, D.A. (2000). The representation and use of clinical knowledge through healthcare information systems in the UK National Health Service, *Proceedings, 33rd Hawaii International Conference of Systems Sciences* Jan.

Szolovits, P. (1994). Uncertainty and decision-making in medical informatics, *Proceedings, Conference of the American medical informatics association 1994* 1-30.

White, D.A. and Sutton, Y.M. (2000). Achieving data quality: beyond rules and standards, *Proceedings of the BCS Healthcare Computing Conference*, Weybridge; BJHC Limited (2000) 236-242.

Wiezenbaum, J. (1985). The myths of artificial intelligence, in Forester, T. (ed.), *The information technology revolution*, Oxford: Blackwell.

About the Editor

Dr. D.A. White

Don White graduated with a BA (hons) in History from the University of Birmingham in 1975. After a period in industry, he moved into information work. He took an MA in Information Studies at Sheffield University in 1982 and stayed at the University as a research student and then senior research worker. He holds a doctorate from the University of Sheffield based on research into organizational conflict.

From 1984 to 1986 he ran a funded research programme investigating information use and needs in manufacturing companies.

He joined Sheffield Business School in January 1988 where he was Course Leader for the MSc Information Systems in Management before taking responsibility for a number of developments with major corporate clients.

In May 2000, he was appointed to the post of Associate Dean at the faculty of Business and Management, University of Lincoln, with responsibility for business development and off campus programmes.

His main teaching and research interests are information and decision making in organizations and information behaviour. He has published several reports and articles on information and systems in management and acted as consultant to local authorities, private companies and the National Health Service.

Index

NEW from Idea Group Publishing